Bring Me Men and Women

Bring Me Men

and Women

Mandated Change at the U.S. Air Force Academy

Judith Hicks Stiehm

University of California Press

Berkeley · Los Angeles · London

University of California Press
Berkeley and Los Angeles, California
University of California Press, Ltd.
London, England
© 1981 by
The Regents of the University of California
Printed in the United States of America

1   2   3   4   5   6   7   8   9

Library of Congress Cataloging in Publication Data

Stiehm, Judith Hicks
   Bring me men and women. Mandated change at the U.S. Air Force Academy
   Bibliography: p.
   Includes index.
   1. United States. Air Force Academy—Students.
2. Women college students—Colorado. 3. United States.
Air Force—Women. I. Title.
UG638.5.Q1S74   358.4'007'1178856   80–18907
ISBN 0–520–04045–7

We survived it, Richard!

NOTE: *Funding for this project came
from the Russell Sage and Ford Foundations.
Military and civilian personnel were always helpful;
indeed, they were generous.
Special thanks go to John Lovell, Nadia Youssef,
Mariam Chamberlain, and Catherine Tame.*

Contents

Tables

Introduction

The kind of women we want in the Air Force are the kind who will get married and leave. —*A major at the U.S. Air Force Academy*

I disagree with the admittance of women to the academies. This is just another step taken for political reasons that will tend to weaken our combat capability. —*An Air Force general stationed in the Midwest*

Maybe you could find one woman in 10,000 who could lead in combat, but she would be a freak, and the Military Academy is not being run for freaks. —*Gen. William Westmoreland*
in Family Weekly, *September 25, 1976*

Thus spake the brass—in private and sometimes in public. The 1975 federal legislation mandating women's entrance into the service academies displeased them; in fact, among senior officers the decision was widely deplored. For once again (the obvious analogy is school integration) important governmental institutions were told by the federal government to change themselves in a fundamental (some said revolutionary) way. Moreover, they were told to do so at a specific time and they were under close public scrutiny. There was little hope that their change or failure to change could go unnoticed, nor was there much about the change that would be voluntary. It was required, and most of those charged with implementing it were opposed.

The Revolutionary Potential

The military is an hierarchical organization in which individuals are trained to accept assignments they might prefer to forego. Personnel are disciplined; they follow orders. Thus the atmosphere is conducive to top-down or mandated change. The military is also a pervasively male institution, one that may even depend on the exclusion

1

of females as part of its definition. If so, this exclusivity would make women's integration impossible—or revolutionary.

The use of weapons has traditionally been as uniquely male as child-rearing has been female. While women may have used weapons occasionally and individually, they have generally been forbidden to participate in the planned, publicly financed, collective, legal use of violence. Although women use force on children, they do not use it on adults. In fact, they are *de facto* pacifists in a world that defines government as that institution that holds a monopoly on the legitimate use of force. If U.S. women assume their share of the country's defense, if they come to command the weaponry of the state, if they come to participate directly in decisions concerning war and peace and the enforcement of law, a real change will have been made. Indeed, it will be a change so radical that one must turn to fiction rather than history to find a parallel.

The admission of women to the military academies was not thought of as revolutionary, however. In fact, the necessary legislation probably passed because it was *not* thought of in that way. That is, women were not said to be entitled to a full citizenship that would give them the right and duty to participate in their own defense. Nor did proponents of the legislation argue that women were the victims of an international protection racket that restricted them to the roles of either (1) the helpless victim, or (2) the legitimator (because protectee) of war. No, the legislation passed because it was considered a simple matter of extending educational opportunity. Economic opportunity in the form of a possible career as a military officer was already available to women. To most legislators P.L. 94–106 meant only that women could obtain the best education available for an already approved career.

Moreover, the revolutionary potential of the decision was explicitly curtailed by Congress's failure (refusal) to declare that women should be assigned to combat on the same terms as men. Indeed, the Department of Defense (DOD) and the various services were left to decide for themselves just how many women they could use. The first year the academies decided that between 90 and 95 percent of their openings should go to men. Their rationale was that, because certain jobs as well as rotation slots for persons in those jobs had to be held by men, only a limited number of women could be absorbed.

Yet even if women can compete for most *kinds* of jobs in the contemporary military, the impression that they can compete for *most* jobs is simply wrong. For example, in 1978 women entering the Air Force knew that they were eligible for all job classifications except pilot and navigator, although they also knew women were being trained for both those jobs on an experimental basis. It was widely assumed that the experiment would be proclaimed a success and that new opportunities would soon be available. Women also knew that they could be missile crew members. What many may not have known was that women were being assigned only to the Titan II missiles, which number fifty-four. Women were *not* being assigned to the one thousand Minuteman missiles. This practice meant that (in the first year) thirty-five women would be trained for the twenty-three-hundred missile crew slots, and this meant that only 1.5 percent of the positions would go to women while 98.5 percent would go to men. The reason was that the Minuteman crews were composed of two persons, and the military was just not ready to assign two women or one woman and one man to those crews. Even though women could be trained as missile operators, they were considered ineligible for most of the missile assignments! In short, women *could* become crew members, but the chances were that they would not. Apparently they would not because of a deep-seated suspicion of women and a deep distrust of their influence on men.

In thinking about the first year of women's integration, then, it is important to remember two points. First, the prejudice against women in the military and especially in combat is so profound as to amount almost to a taboo. Second, women's participation in the military has increased dramatically. Nevertheless, this participation is still severely curtailed, and the decisions that affect it continue to be made by male officers, officials, Congressmen, and Presidents.

The Writing of This Book

Women's integration into the military academies afforded an almost unique opportunity to study social change. It was a tidy, well-defined natural experiment. Furthermore, the Air Force Academy was willing to permit the kind of external scrutiny that afforded an objective account of the facts of the first year of integration.

For sixteen months the academy allowed me to interview freely and repeatedly all persons concerned with planning and implementing women's admission. Working as an historian (with individuals and documents rather than with questionnaires), I have attempted to report the first year fully and accurately. I have attempted to tell what was done and why. The point of view recorded is that of the (mostly) male staff; it is *not* that of the women cadets. Men cadets were interviewed because they, in fact, implement many of the academy's policies. Women cadets, therefore, are described only as the institution perceived them. This is *not* a study of "first" women. It is a study of an institution undergoing mandated change and, at least at the top, committed to making that change a success.

The text is intended first, and most importantly, to provide a record to which others can add their own data or alternative interpretations and, second, to provide one interpretation of events. That interpretation, my own, is provided by one who is an academic, a student of nonviolence, a feminist, and a mother of daughters—one of them old enough to apply to the academy (but not inclined to do so). On the one hand, the academy proved an environment so foreign to me that I found the process almost entirely one of inquiry; rarely was I tempted to judge or offer advice. On the other hand, the individuals with whom I worked shared enough of my values and experiences that I felt some confidence that we understood each other—that they understood what I was asking and that I understood their answers.

Every effort has been made to be clear about what is fact and what is interpretation. I have tried to confine my headiest speculation to this introduction and to the postscript. The most serious issues are frequently the most difficult to grasp, and even if one feels some personal enlightenment, conveying it to others often comes hard. Thus I have separated the issues of violence–nonviolence and the meaning of citizenship from the main text. The Air Force is certainly not responsible for that speculation—not even for triggering it.

A Preview

The book will first take up the mandate itself, P.L. 94–106. One chapter will detail the debate that preceded passage, the context in which the legislation was passed, and its precise content. I shall argue that this remarkable bill passed partly because the terms of debate centered on equal career opportunity rather than on whether women should be assigned to combat. Shaping the issue along these lines represented a victory for the bill's proponents. In addition the bill benefited from the recruitment pressure generated by the abolition of the draft two years earlier.

✻ Next an attempt will be made to describe the academy primeval—the academy before women. This section is important for two reasons: first, to show how much and in what way women's entrance changed the institution and, second, to show what it did not change. A military academy is both a federally funded national vocational school and a part of a military installation and chain of command. Its students, whose education is free (they do undertake a five-year service commitment upon graduation), take a heavily technical curriculum, which at the Air Force Academy is designed to train all of the students for careers as military officers and to prepare many of them to be pilots or navigators. Academy students wear uniforms, salute, and are subject to rigorous discipline. Their freedom is curtailed; their hair is cut frequently; their acquisition of stereos, autos, and spouses is controlled. Class attendance is required, decor is geometric, and color is subdued. The crucial questions are what is style and what is substance? What is male and what is military? What ✻ should change when women enter; what must endure?

To understand the academy's preparations for women, one must also know that an important aspect of academy life is being under continuous observation. Academy officials again and again describe themselves, if not as goldfish, at least as bowl occupants. The observers are numerous and their concerns are varied. Just before women's entrance, for instance, Congress requested a General Accounting Office (GAO) study of the academies, and the Air Force Academy was under special scrutiny because of its cadets' high rate of attrition. Congress men and women nominate most of the cadets, and Congressional committees and members of Congress on the Board of Visitors formally monitor academy policy and programs. The mandator, then, was watching, but, unlike a court mandator, this one had direct budgetary control. The Department of Defense was watching too. Watching officially from within the DOD were the Office of Education in the Manpower and Reserve Affairs Secretariat, and the Defense Advisory Committee on Women in the Services (DACOWITS). Watching unofficially were alumni, Air Force officers generally, and reserve officers involved in recruiting. Educators, tourists, women's groups, and the national media made their interest known too. The principal effect of so much observation seems to have been self-consciousness and conscientiousness. Officials were not controlled by these third parties; their circumspection was based more on anticipating (or perhaps overanticipating) the third parties' judgments. I shall argue that the result was careful planning.

Planning is routine in large organizations, particularly when risky
ventures are being undertaken by conservative people, institutions,
or both. Particular questions that this work will explore are: What
was planned and why? How does early and detailed planning affect
results? Why did the Air Force Academy staff make several decisions that were different from those made at Annapolis and West
Point? (The Air Force decided that women would be billeted
[housed] separately and that a group of young women officers would
be given a special assignment as Air Training Officers [ATOs] for
the women cadets.)

Colorado Springs, West Point, and Annapolis were under the
same legal mandate, but their different approaches to the admission
of women shows once again that a single stimulus can yield a variety of responses. A sketch of the decisions made by the Army and
Navy will lend perspective to the more thorough discussion of the
Air Force response. What was done at Colorado Springs can then
be seen more as a matter of choice than of inevitability. Different
actors, different missions, different traditions, and different distrac-
tions did yield different results. At the Air Force Academy, enthusiastic (or, at least, determined) support was given to making integration work. At West Point sober attention was given to maintaining standards, and minimal regard was given to changes "required
because of physiological differences," even though such changes
were legally permitted. At Annapolis, the official line was that this
was "a nonevent," and women were slipped as unobtrusively as possible into the academy. These women gained whatever advantages
were inherent in being overlooked. Those at the Air Force enjoyed
the advantages associated with high visibility. Those at West Point
may have benefited by "measuring up."

The work of the three Air Force Academy administrative units
will be discussed separately. (These three are the Department of
Physical Education and Athletics; the commandant and his staff,
which represents the military side of the academy; and the academic
dean and his faculty.) The Department of Physical Education and
Athletics (P.E.) was charged with deciding what physiological differences existed and with determining what program changes would
be required because of them. Beginning with deep pessimism and
assuming a regular need for such items as breast protectors, P.E.
found itself consistently—and pleasantly—surprised by women cadets' performance. However, the phrase "lack of upper body
strength" (which describes a physiological difference) became almost a code for women's inferiority, because of the implicit assump-

tion that upper body strength is related to performance as a cadet and as an officer. For P.E. the basic problem was measuring women's and men's capabilities without dramatizing invidious but invalid comparisons. Mostly P.E. thought of its task as determining to what extent women could and should measure up to the physical test standards required of men. The tests themselves were ones on which males perform well, females less well; yet P.E. did not add physical tests on which women characteristically perform better than men, nor did it examine just how its tests related to job performance. As it became comfortable with women in its programs, the Physical Education Department gradually shifted its concern to fatness and femininity. It deplored the first and approved the second. Ironically, while both concepts have a physiological component, the meaning of each is deeply embedded in culture, and authorities found themselves enmeshed in a debate that went far beyond the determination of strength requirements and capacities.

The U.S. Air Force Academy (USAFA) Commandant of Cadets and his staff are responsible for cadet activities and for military training. The prospect of women cadets was probably more unsettling for this unit than for any other. There was no precedent for training women for combat and certainly no precedent for training them for combat *with* men. True, the academy's "war-story" and role-model method of training obliquely suggested that women were crucial to the training of warriors, but it suggested that they were essential because they were complementary to, not the same as, warriors. In particular, women were a justification (as family) and sometimes they were a reward.

For the commandant the issues of inappropriately chivalrous behavior by men, reverse discrimination, and women's capacity to command were of great concern. Abstract questions are rare in the Com's Shop (the services routinely call an organizational unit a "shop"), but they became important in 1975. What is the difference between competition and fighting, and how does each relate to combat? Is a physical requirement such as running three miles in twenty-four minutes related to any service duty or activity? Or does it stand only for effort, for commitment, for devotion? Do scantily dressed "Spacemates" in cadet magazines bolster male morale? If so, how should that effect be measured against the effect "Spacemates" have on female morale? In the chapter focusing on the development of policy papers and programs designed to provide role models for the entering female cadets, it will be seen that the vice-commandant strove always to ensure the acceptance of women cadets by their male cadet-peers. Indeed, in some ways the wing (the cadet student body) was more on his mind than were the women.

The third unit reporting to the Air Force Academy Superintendent is the faculty. The reaction in this unit was especially complex. Many faculty believed that they were immune, that their programs were "sex neutral" and required no adjustment whatever. In addition the faculty had more permanence than had other units (its dean had been at the academy since its founding), and their allegiance to tradition was augmented because many faculty were alumni. Conversely, the Department of Behavioral Science and Leadership played an active role in women's integration. It sponsored research, developed a bibliography and briefings, and assumed primary responsibility for the Human Relations Education Committee. Thus some believed the faculty immune because it was not sexist, and some believed it immune because of its sensitivity and appropriate response. A few found it insensitive and immune to learning.

In the implementation-feedback-modification process, all proceeded naturally on one level. Minor adjustments were made (sometimes unconsciously) as an institution struck with disbelief in 1975 energized itself to preparation in early 1976, and although filled with anxiety when the women arrived in July of that year, it soon learned that coping was possible. Male officers learned to say the word "menstruation" in public; cadet officers who heard a noise in the night opened their doors and (stark naked) encountered a female cadet on a "spirit mission" (prank) learned to face the world (clad) the next day. Indeed, as relief followed anxiety in late 1976, so confidence followed relief by the end of the school year. But on another level, several major policy changes were made during the first year. For example, billeting arrangements were changed at the end of the first semester. Such administrative flexibility also led to confidence. But one must ask just what officials were feeling confident about. Did women become routine? Were they integrated? Or were they marginal? In short, did the institution's confidence stem more from its own unchanged survival than from successful change?

The first year was a transition year. The academy knew that and it looked forward to increased success in years to come. Success was defined simply: recruit as many women as desired and retain as many women proportionally as men. However, academy staffers did not heed the lessons of World War II that described a second-year backlash against the WAC that depressed morale and affected recruitment. If the staff had considered this potential for backlash, the academy might have anticipated that once women had proved they *could* do what only men had done before, they would feel free to say "but we choose not to." Or it might have realized that if a woman's original motivation had been to conquer a negative environment she would need a new kind of motivation if she were to be sustained through an era of neutrality. Another possibility was that after a year the women would decide that the environment was implacable, that there was no way they ever could prove themselves, and thus there was no reason to continue their training. In sum, confidence was predicated upon successful survival, not upon anticipation of the next year and preparation for it.

Long-term motivation will ultimately determine the success of academy integration. Possible differences between women, wives, and warriors will be discussed, and I will argue that the role of warrior partly depends on women and particularly depends on their not participating. I will also note that as women fill more and more noncombat military slots, the profession will become increasingly risky for men because their chances of being assigned to combat slots will necessarily increase. At some point men may feel that their risk has become *too* great and that women should be required to fully share that risk; then Amelia Earhart may be proved correct in her prediction that, when women join men in "the trenches, combat service in the air, transport jobs in advanced positions, and even the other less brilliant arenas of activity in the theater of war," men will decide that they would "rather vacate the arena altogether than share it with women."[1]

CHAPTER

1

The Mandate

On May 20, 1975, the House of Representatives approved (by a vote of 303 to 96) what was to become P.L. 94–106. The Senate assented by voice vote on June 6. President Gerald Ford signed on the evening of October 7, 1975. And so it was mandated that women would enter the Department of Defense (DOD) service academies by the summer of 1976.

The law provided that

> the Secretary of the military department concerned shall take such action as may be necessary and appropriate to insure that (1) female individuals shall be eligible for appointment and admission to the service academy concerned, beginning the appointments to such academy for the class beginning in calendar year 1976, and (2) the academic and other relevant standards required for appointment, admission, training, graduation, and commissioning of female individuals shall be the same as those required for male individuals, except for those minimum essential adjustments in such standards required because of physiological differences between male and female individuals. . . .
>
> It is the sense of Congress that, subject to the provisions of subsection (a), the Secretaries of the military departments shall . . . continue to exercise the authority

granted them . . . but such authority must be exercised within a program providing for the orderly and expeditious admission of women to the academies, consistent with the needs of the services with the implementation of such program upon enactment of this Act.[1]

The Background

This legislation culminated efforts that had begun when Rep. Robert B. Duncan of Oregon nominated a woman to West Point in the early 1960s. This first step was followed by New York Sen. Jacob Javits's 1972 nomination of Barbara J. Brimmer to the U.S. Naval Academy.[a] That same year he and Michigan Rep. Jack H. McDonald introduced a concurrent resolution, the import of which was that "a woman duly nominated to a military service academy should not be denied admission solely on the ground of sex."[2] This phrasing is similar to that of the Equal Rights Amendment, which had passed Congress only one week before. Thus Javits could argue that this resolution was merely a particular application of a general policy (already passed) against sex discrimination. He could also point out that the Navy recruited women officers and had women faculty at the Naval Academy, even though it refused to teach women there. He noted, too, that the Navy was the only service without a female "flag grade" officer (admiral/general), and that because women officers remained on active duty beyond their initial, obligated service at a 35 percent rate (as contrasted to 24 percent for male nonacademy graduates), they seemed to represent an excellent training investment.[b] The Senate passed this resolution with little debate. In the House, the resolution was referred to Louisiana Rep. F. Edward

[a]Because of the academies' Congressional nomination system, it was difficult for women to test admissions policies directly; they needed the cooperation of a representative or senator. Annapolis rejected Javits's 1972 nomination, but for the first time it did open the Naval Reserve Officers' Training Corps (NROTC) to women that year. Giving those who seek social change something related to but different from what they have asked for is one way of attempting to quash their drive. The responder then can claim concern and reasonableness and can hope that the public will perceive conciliation and lose interest. If those seeking change are unwilling to accept this "half a loaf," they must assume the burden of showing the respondent's unreasonableness and of distinguishing between what was asked for and what was received.

[b]Most of the Navy's admirals are Naval Academy graduates. Academy graduation also enhances an Army or an Air Force career, but it is not a traditional requirement for obtaining flag grade.

Table I. Chronology of Pre-entrance Events

March 1969	President's Commission on an All-Volunteer Force (the Gates Commission) appointed. Recommends the termination of peacetime conscription one year later.
June 1970	Anna Hays and Elizabeth Hoisington become generals in the U.S. Army.
March 1972	Equal Rights Amendment passed.
	Sen. Jacob Javits of New York nominates Barbara J. Brimmer to the U.S. Naval Academy.
	The U.S. Senate passes a concurrent resolution stating that a woman should not be denied admission to a military academy solely on the ground of sex.
May through September 1972	U.S. Air Force Academy completes first plan for admission of women.
May 1973	Frontiero v. Richardson, 411 U.S. 677 (1973) gives military women the same dependency benefits afforded military men.
July 1973	Draft ends. All-volunteer force comes into being.
September 1973	Representatives Don Edwards and Jerome Waldie of California initiate a suit against the Secretary of Defense with and on behalf of women nominated to the Naval and Air Force Academies.
October 1973	Rep. Pierre du Pont introduces the first House Bill to admit women to the service academies.
December 1973	The U.S. Senate passes a bill providing for women's admission to the service academies. The relevant provision is deleted by the conference committee.
May 1974	The House Military Personnel Subcommittee, chaired by Rep. O. C. Fisher, Texas, begins hearings on the admission of women to the military academies.

June 1974	The U.S. District Court in Washington, D.C., rules women applicants to the academies are not being denied equal protection.
November 1974	The U.S. Appeals Court reverses the district court and remands the case for full trial.
January 1975	The House Armed Services Committee refuses to act on women's admission to the military academies.
May 1975	House passes legislation mandating women's entrance into the academies, 303–96.
June 1975	U.S. Senate passes similar legislation.
September 1975	Inter-service conference on the admission of women held at the Air Force Academy. House-Senate conference report accepted.
October 1975	Pres. Gerald Ford signs P.L. 94–106, making women eligible for academy admission in June 1976.
June 1976	Women enter U.S. Air Force Academy.
July 1976	WAF (Women in the Air Force) abolished.

Hébert's Armed Services Committee. It did not emerge from that committee.

In 1973 the first House bill on the admission of women to the service academies was introduced by Rep. Pierre du Pont of Delaware. Two other important developments also occurred. First, California Representatives Don Edwards and Jerome Waldie not only made nominations to the Naval and Air Force Academies, they also sued the Secretary of Defense, James Schlesinger, with and on behalf of their nominees. Thus the judiciary became an alternate arena for pursuing this change. Second, in mid-1973 the Volunteer Army went into effect. The abolition of the draft placed continuing pressure on military recruiters; one of their responses to that pressure was to begin tapping the one-half of the population that had not previously been thought of as a part of the military pool. Even the Air Force (which had fewer problems in recruitment than the other services) developed a plan to more than double the number of its women line officers between 1972 and 1977. That one officer associated with development of the plan was Gen. Jeanne Holm may have had some bearing on its content, too.

On December 20, 1973, the first positive legislative action was taken when the U.S. Senate accepted by voice vote an amendment to the Armed Forces Enlisted Personnel Bonus Revision Act (S-27710). This amendment provided that "a female candidate for admission who is qualified to be trained in a skill or profession in which individuals of her sex are permitted to serve as commissioned officers . . . shall not be ineligible for admission on account of sex. . . ." Instead of simply barring discrimination on account of sex, this legislation limited its effect to those individuals potentially qualified for positions in which women were permitted by law or policy to serve. The amendment was sponsored by Sen. William Hathaway of Maine and co-sponsored by Senators Javits, Mike Mansfield of Montana, Strom Thurmond of South Carolina, and John Stennis, a Democrat from Mississippi and Chairman of the Senate Armed Services Committee. Support seemed broad and strong.

In the House, however, Representative Hébert, Chairman of the Armed Services Committee, was adamantly opposed to admitting women to the academies. In contrast, Rep. Samuel Stratton of New York, Chairman of the Subcommittee on Military Compensation to which the bill was sent, approved of women's admission. Nevertheless, Stratton ruled that the Senate's amendment was not germane to bonus pay and that it would have to be considered separately.[c]

Nevertheless, support was strong. In fact, the full Armed Services Committee upheld Stratton's decision to drop the amendment by a vote of only 18 to 16 and that solely because three members of the committee were prevented from voting by their tardiness. Rep. Pat Schroeder of Colorado, who was one of the latecomers, argued (to no avail) that this disfranchisement was against House rules. Proponents were further frustrated when the bonus pay bill finally reached the House floor with a ruling that forbade any amendment. After a Senate-House conference in April, the Senate agreed to drop its amendment, noting that House hearings would follow—and they did, in May.

[c]This was Stratton's stated reason. But he may also have assumed that Hébert's full committee would overrule the subcommittee and therefore agreed to this disposition in exchange for a promise that public hearings would be held by a more appropriate subcommittee—Personnel.

The House Hearings

The House hearings were held on May 20, June 4, 5, 12, 18, and 19, July 16 and 18, and August 8, 1974. The record of the hearings contains the distinctive positions of representatives and senators, military officials, and women's rights groups. Representative Stratton's testimony was clearly in favor of women's admission, even though he had killed the relevant legislation in his subcommittee. Although it would appear that the legislation could have passed without these hearings, they may have: (1) gained votes from reluctant supporters who might otherwise have voted in opposition because of a lack of information or an absence of full discussion, (2) maintained Stratton's leverage and reputation for fair play among his colleagues, and (3) modified the bill in such a way that the military found it easier to live with.

The hearings were conducted by the Military Personnel Subcommittee, chaired by Rep. O.C. Fisher of Texas, and assisted by Counsel William H. Hogan, Jr. As chairman, Fisher had the first opportunity to question each witness, and his first question invariably concerned women and combat. He began by asking whether all academy students ought to have the same combat obligation. As the hearings progressed, Fisher's query broadened to include all women in the military and, finally, all women. He asked witnesses their

Table II. Members of the Military Personnel
Subcommittee of the House Armed Services
Committee, May 1974

O. C. Fisher, Texas, Chairman

Lucien N. Nedzi, Michigan
Dan Daniel, Virginia
G. V. (Sonny) Montgomery, Mississippi
William J. Randall, Missouri
Charles H. Wilson, California
William L. Dickinson, Alabama
Walter E. Powell, Ohio
David C. Treen, Louisiana
Marjorie S. Holt, Maryland
Elwood H. Hillis, Indiana

William H. Hogan, Jr., Counsel

views on committing women to combat with or without their consent and also their views on requiring women to register with Selective Service. Each witness saw a different relationship between women, the military, the academies, and combat. Still, Fisher tried to get precise answers from each. Some preferred to hedge; with regard to military service and combat, only a few were prepared to make no sex distinction whatsoever; none wished to put an end to military service for women. For most, the central issues were whether women should be in combat and whether academy training was or should be for combat officers only.[d]

Members of the personnel subcommittee are shown in Table II. Two of the ten committee members, William J. Randall of Missouri and Walter E. Powell of Ohio, played no recorded role in the hearings. Only one, Charles Wilson of California, was a clear advocate of women in the military.[e] Indeed, he was prepared to go even further in his arguments than were supporters like Rep. Pat Schroeder of Colorado. Wilson's style was incisive and abrupt: he characterized most official arguments in opposition to women as simply silly. When the question of cost was raised, he pointed to the quarter of a million dollars that was being recommended to cover the costs of a temporary headquarters for the Chief of Naval Operations. When a double standard for admission was mentioned, Wilson referred to waivers granted to athletes. To arguments based on law, he responded that laws were no obstacle, because Congress had the job of changing laws: "Let's just change the law, and even the combat law . . . Congress is in the business of changing laws, and making laws, all the time." He also pressed academy superintendents to demonstrate that an academy was not "a very exclusive little country club type of thing," and doubted that this "pushup-pullup thing" was very important to military education.

Two subcommittee members, Representatives "Sonny" Montgomery of Mississippi and David C. Treen of Louisiana, were dubious about women's admission but declared their minds "open." Sometimes these two were inclined to view the issue humorously. Treen pursued the difference between sex distinction and discrimination and worried about co-ed dorms and pregnancies at sea. Mont-

---

[d]After World War II women's participation in the military was very much debated, and women's role was greatly restricted by Congress until 1967.

[e]Two separate suits that sought admission for women were initiated by California Congressmen (Waldie, Edwards, and Fortney Stark), and two of twelve Congressional statements came to the committee from Californians Ronald Dellums and Yvonne Burke.

gomery thought the bill would pass and that the academies should be getting ready. He also commented (several times) that *he* did not know much about women and combat since he had never been married.

Rep. Dan Daniel of Virginia regularly asked for definitions of combat and the mission of each academy; Rep. William Dickinson of Alabama worried about a two-track system and understood that one danger would be men's suing for their "equal right" to be on the women's or noncombatant track. Apparently Dickinson felt that the more similar the male and female roles became, the more it became likely that men would sue to be given the choice of a "female" role. Conversely, as long as women's roles were very different (i.e., no regular military service), there was only a slight possibility that men would sue to receive the treatment given women.

Rep. Elwood Hillis of Indiana found it hard to accept that all military educational institutions *except* the academies were already open to women. Rep. Lucien Nedzi of Michigan pushed witnesses on the issues of legal restrictions concerning combat assignments and the rotation of assignments further than did his colleagues.

The most ambivalent committee member may have been Marjorie Holt of Maryland. (Annapolis, site of the Naval Academy, is located in her district.) She granted that her own grave concern for families might not be relevant; nevertheless, she believed "the privilege of child bearing" *did* pertain: "We are different; would it be insurmountable to have a dual system? You do have a dual system now, in that you have unrestricted and restricted men." She found the Israeli model, in which women are trained and used quite differently from men, a possible alternative. No one else on the committee did. Representative Holt was virtually the only individual prepared to contemplate a dual track, although the idea of an exclusively women's academy did surface after World War II and in informal discussion during these hearings.

Those who testified in favor of women's admission included seven members of the House, representatives of women's groups, the American Civil Liberties Union (A.C.L.U.), an academy applicant, and Grace King, a woman lieutenant colonel in the Army Reserve, who appeared as an individual and not as an Army witness.

Lieutenant Colonel King's testimony was rooted in experience. The issue, she said, was not "'injecting' women; it was permitting women the same freedom of choice as men," as well as permitting the Army to tap a "pool of talent and intelligence more critically needed than ever." And since women are admitted to other entry-level training, she went on, what the three services are essentially arguing is that "ROTC [Reserve Officers' Training Corps] and OCS [Officer Candidate School] are good enough for women but not good enough for men." King raised the issue of promotions and advantageous assignments by noting that 39 percent of the new brigadier generals were West Point graduates, although only 9 percent of the Army's commissioned officers were academy graduates. She also noted that being a woman was without question a disadvantage in promotion, if only because women were eligible to compete for a restricted number of assignments. For instance, having field experience in armor would have increased her opportunity to become a full colonel, but she was not eligible for an assignment to armor *even though* she had completed both basic and advanced armor courses. Finally, King objected that no survey had ever been made that cited "the will of the American people" as the reason for limiting women's military role. In fact, King offered some survey results of her own: in 54 questionnaires filled out by Armed Service Committee members and their staffs, 88.8 percent favored admitting women to the academies and 87.4 percent favored allowing women to volunteer for combat. She cited yet another survey of 540 civilian men and women that showed 80 percent favored women's admission and 73 percent supported their voluntary participation in combat.

Opponents of the legislation included the Department of Defense, represented by its General Counsel, Martin Hoffman, and the Deputy Assistant Secretary of Defense for Military Personnel, Lt. Gen. Leo Benade. Each of the academy superintendents testified: Vice Adm. William Mack of the Navy, Lt. Gen. A. P. Clark of the Air Force, and Lt. Gen. William A. Knowlton of the Army. And each service provided other witnesses as well. The Navy sent its Secretary, J. William Middendorf II, and the Vice Chief of Naval Operations, Adm. Worth H. Bagley. As its additional representatives, the Air Force summoned Secretary John L. McLucas and Chief of Staff, Gen. George Brown. Army Secretary Howard Callaway testified at length. He was supported by Gen. Fred Weyand, Vice Chief of Staff; a recent West Point graduate; and a West Point cadet. The military was clearly serious about presenting its case.

The final witness was Jacqueline Cochran. Miss Cochran, an experienced pilot who logged more than 15,000 hours in flight and who also flew numerous experimental planes for test purposes, had consulted on the legislation first admitting women to the Air Force. She also directed the training of the Women Airforce Service Pilots

(WASP) during World War II and took twenty-five other women pilots to England, where they assumed ferrying duties then assigned to military men. She would seem to be a perfect example of what women can do and what they should be given the right to do. Miss Cochran, however, vigorously opposed women's admission to the academies and also their use in combat. Her colorful, unwavering testimony contrasts with that of the DOD witnesses, who were keenly aware that the members of the House Military Personnel Subcommittee were their lawful superiors and responded formally and with some caution. Nevertheless, her convictions were surely held by at least some of the military officials and by many other Americans as well.

Miss Cochran averred that "a woman's primary function in life is to get married, maintain a home and raise a family." Her own WASPs, she said, were always managed according to the principle that they were "women first and pilots second." A woman's leaving service for marriage was always appropriate; thus, Miss Cochran argued, women should not be given expensive training. Although the policy was her own, Cochran sounded as though she were reproving the women for their 36 percent post-training attrition in World War II when she commented, "They all got married just as fast as they could find a good-looking man who would marry them." Cochran added that the low number of women lawyers and physicians in the U.S. today resulted from women's failure to persevere. As doctors, she noted, women could be excellent pediatricians. Moreover, she said women are unable to render continuity of service; they do not perform with "regularity" (apparently because of pregnancy and menstruation). Also, she feared the disruption that would occur "if 100 normal women were entered with 4,000 normal men in the Air Force Academy." Miss Cochran was not enthusiastic about co-educational schools in general. "As future mothers," she went on, "there are certain areas where women should not be. . . . Even if they want to, they should be restrained." For instance, she found combat for women just plain abnormal: "Are we going to break up the whole pattern that the Lord intended that we follow? I think it is ridiculous. I don't see it." Even volunteers were unacceptable: "You don't let crazy people run around the streets. You put them in a home. I think women are nuts if they want to go into combat."

When asked whether she thought *men* wanted to go into combat, she answered that "they have to do it, you see."

"Why?"

"Because they are men and we don't have to do it because we are women."[f]

The feelings of the men testifying for the military were surely no less emphatic. Their style, however, was far more restrained. Secretary Callaway, a 1949 West Point graduate who served in the Army from 1949 to 1952, dominated the Army's presentation. He insisted that no institution had done more to advance the rights of women than the Army. To illustrate, he cited items like the support for women's dependents (recently won by women who had taken the Army to court), women's eligibility for ROTC scholarships (initiated only in 1972), and their access to the Army War College— also of recent vintage. Next he argued that the West Point mission was the training of combat leaders, that the introduction of women would not only irreparably alter the West Point product, but it would "in effect lead to the lowering of standards for men." The change "could only be for the worse":

> The Spartan atmosphere—which is so important to producing the final product—would surely be diluted, and would in all probability disappear before long. To modify the curriculum and alter the training so as to permit women to attend would weaken or destroy that intangible but indelible spirit which is the unmistakable hallmark of West Point graduates. Each future second lieutenant must have the same sturdy qualities—mental toughness and physical capacity—that have marked West Point's graduates for nearly two centuries. He must have the strength to endure and the will to persevere.[3]

Why would women necessarily dilute the Spartan spirit? Callaway thought that women's lesser physical capacity would lead to "two West Points," or at least to

> a very different West Point, one like ROTC with high academic standards, but not with the rigorousness, the Spartanness, the training of duty-honor-country, the spirit of being the hardcore that has made up the kind of

---

[f]Miss Cochran may have valued motherhood so highly, in part, because she did not have children who lived. Still, she did not acknowledge a need to provide opportunities for the one-in-ten women unable to bear children. Nor was she prepared to respect the views of women who choose not to have children.

those circumstances, would they follow women? We just don't really know. We doubt it.

We know we have had Joan of Arc; we've had the Troung sisters; and I'm sure throughout history many other wonderful women leaders, tacticians, strategists. But Joan of Arc was a saint. She got her directions from on High, and we don't have too many of those.[10]

The last two points (that training requires total immersion and that leadership depends on followers) are important because they suggest that even if women attended the academies they would not have the same experience men have there, and they would not emerge with the skills the men would have.

The Air Force testimony is interesting because it was similar to that of its "parent" force, yet it also was more modern and expressed some openness to change.[g] The Air Force opened its ROTC to women in 1969. From 1971 to 1974 it doubled the number of women on active duty, and from 1975 to 1978 it planned to double that number again. Also, the Air Force has a larger proportion of women officers and more uses for them. The principal Air Force testimony was presented by the Academy Superintendent, Gen. A. P. Clark, who was himself a West Point alumnus.

Clark began by supporting women in service but not in combat. It would be perilous, he observed, to ignore social roles that have evolved over time and that come from the physiological and biological differences between the sexes. He also argued that military history taught that fighting is a man's job and that to open combat to women would be to "offend the dignity of womanhood and ignore the harsh realities of war." He continued:

> Sherman was right: "War is hell and you cannot refine it." To seek to do so to accommodate the pressures of social activism is to invite disaster in battle. Our potential enemies would rejoice to see us make the tragic error of exposing American women to capture in combat. I firmly believe that this situation would inevitably weaken our national resolve in war.[11]

Clark also opposed women at the Air Force Academy on grounds similar to those of the Army—that an academy trained combat and

---

[g]After twenty-seven years as the Army Air Corps, the Air Force became a distinct service in 1947 and opened its academy in 1955. Nevertheless, the Army and West Point have always had more influence in Colorado Springs than have the Navy and Annapolis.

leadership that inspires the ROTC and OCS graduates to all become equal officers in the Army as you go forward. Then West Point has been changed and, in my judgment, changed for the worse.[4]

Moreover, those who advocate that (only) the fully qualified women enter combat

> have not really thought out what it means in a combat environment to young men who are scared to death and look up and see that new officer coming in, not as a combat associate, but as a combat leader, responsible for everything that happens to their lives.
>
> And, if not fully thought out, the implications of a woman in combat, then West Point could still be Spartan. But the effect is in the combat area, where again, I will repeat, we need every ounce of energy we can get for our combat leaders in this very difficult situation.[5]

Finally, Callaway invoked the long-time success, the enduring service of the institution, and inserted in the record Gen. Douglas MacArthur's 1962 farewell address to the Corps of Cadets. And it must be said that MacArthur's call to Duty-Honor-Country, to "the code of conduct and chivalry" that urges one "to be an officer and a gentleman," and to the mission "fixed, determined, inviolable," is stirring—even in the minitype of a five-year-old Congressional hearing transcript.

General Weyand (an ROTC-trained officer) added the need for a touchstone institution that not only sets standards but lives them:

> . . . unfortunately, we don't very often reach those standards and those heights, but that institution is precious to us beyond description because it is there setting those standards for all the rest of us. It's almost like it was the core of one of these circular high-rise buildings that gives strength to everything that hangs from it. The graduates of that institution and the institution itself have given me, at times, inspiration. They and it have set an example that as I move along in my own way I try to emulate and respond to.[6]

Following Callaway's prepared testimony, two other crucial themes emerged from the committee dialogue. The first is central to understanding the academies *per se*. It is not relevant to sex, but it concerns the total immersion that characterizes life in a military academy. There is probably no isolated aspect of the academy program that is beyond civilian understanding—the uniforms, the inspections, the study, the intramurals, the physical challenges. But in the living areas—in the dining hall and dormitories—one begins to understand that what is truly different is the "allness" of cadet life. When one sees fourth classmen march from their room to the bathroom, when one sees the control of the cadets' time, and their ever-alert, unfailingly correct responsiveness, one begins to understand that statements like the following do describe a nearly unique experience, one that few women ever have:

> The unique experience of West Point is the compiling of that fine academic atmosphere together with an immersion for 24 hours a day, 1 year-long after another, summer, winter, fall, spring, which ties in with the combat training and military effectiveness which . . . is all day long. When you finish classes you go to intramurals; when you finish intramurals you go to study. You do these things in an atmosphere. When the weekend comes, you don't go home, you stay there at West Point doing things which all tie together to make an experience.[7]

The second important, though subtle, theme concerned women's capacity to lead—or, rather, men's willingness to follow them. Because leadership is such an intangible phenomenon, few are willing to predict how and why it will emerge, but grave doubts were expressed about the possibility of its emerging from women. General Weyand said:

> I'm an infantryman and, as those of you who have been in the infantry know—and I know most of you have been in or around it—our motto is "Follow me." It's difficult to articulate what that is all about. . . .
>
> Part of the "Follow me" motto, though, has to do with the followers. The leader must be someone who—and again it's very difficult to grasp—must have those qualities that will cause men to follow him or her on belief and faith, to go into situations where they will follow him unto death. He has to have a quality, or the qualities, that cause men to want to follow his example, that enables him to, in a sense, transfer his own power,

his own qualities, into lesser men at a time of crisis. He has to be a man who is prepared to do everything that he asks of his men, and more.[8]

Secretary Callaway added:

> . . . in the confusion of the ground combat environment, the need for having the physical and mental qualities under stress and the need for the belief by everyone there in the leadership that's there is total. Without belief in the lieutenants and captains and colonels who are there, it all falls apart, and we've seen that in every war.
>
> Now at the present time it's my personal judgment that the attitude of the American soldier is not such that he sees the female role as one of a platoon leader in combat, of a company commander in combat, or doing the kinds of things, with the kinds of leadership skills, that platoon leaders and company commanders in combat do. I personally don't think that many soldiers see a woman in that role. I think that the attitude of most soldiers in combat would be that they would be very uncomfortable in that role. They would see the woman as someone who needs to be protected rather than their leader whose judgment they must have enormous respect for.
>
> That's my personal opinion, that a great many soldiers would feel that way, and, to the extent that one soldier feels that way, he's being deprived of the leadership that is absolutely vital to him.[9]

Weyand confirmed Callaway:

> . . . This relationship between the leader and the men. It's very important. We don't understand it as well as we would like to, but we've all experienced it.
>
> We do have grave reservations and doubts that women—and if they would go, under one proposal, to the Academy, that means they would be officers; that means in combat they would be leaders—and we do have grave doubts as to whether men of the type that we have would in these circumstances of crisis, when men are confused and beset on all sides by doubts and excruciating pressures, when, in fact, you might say they are susceptible to any reason to find calmer ground, under

combat-oriented officers and that women's entrance would "inevitably erode this vital atmosphere." Since he could hardly evoke the younger academy's "tradition," he evoked future history:

> To impair the fighting edge of the Air Force's future combat leadership in the face of the implacable, well-trained, ruthless, all-male military forces which characterize our most likely future enemies, in my judgment, would not look well in the history books. I urge that we not experiment in this direction with the future defense of the Nation.[12]

But it was hard for the Air Force to make the same argument the Army had made about combat, first, because only three combat-related career fields were then denied to women—pilot, navigator, and missile crewmember—and, second, because every year a large number of academy graduates entered other fields.[h] Indeed, as many as 20 percent of each class were ineligible for navigator or pilot training when they were admitted to the academy. The ratio between cadets who are eligible to fly (rated) and those who are ineligible (nonrated) varies with Air Force needs. When the academy opened, all cadets were expected to fly; in 1977 only 70 percent were. Further, because Air Force support personnel can be based far from the battle area (unlike most Army personnel), support jobs are not classified as combat jobs. As General Clark pointed out, however, in certain locations (such as Danang) officers in noncombatant specialties were exposed to ground fire. Usually women are not assigned to such locations, but (as General Clark did not point out) some 700 Air Force women *did* serve in Vietnam, and they received combat pay for doing so.[13]

Several new points were raised in the Air Force testimony. The first involved relative cost. The 1974 cost of educating an Air Force cadet was cited as $79,000; an ROTC scholarship officer, $13,200; and a nonscholarship graduate, $8,500. The Air Force (and the other services) found themselves arguing that (1) the academy price was justified, (2) nonacademy males could expect full opportunities in their career advancement, and (3) women could do just as well

---

[h]After lengthy discussion Air Force officials made women eligible for missile operations in 1978. The technology of this weaponry now separates attacking from being attacked by one's opponent as effectively as the pill has separated sex from procreation. However, these senior officers felt resistance to putting women into missile operations, because of worry about men and women being in silos together for long periods of time and because of doubt that women would launch a nuclear attack if so ordered.

through ROTC. Some subtlety is required to fit these arguments together. First, the value of academy training was said to be proved by officer retention (a 28 percent loss of academy trained officers vs. 59 percent of ROTC graduates). Second, it was argued that academy graduates held leadership and command positions "in a far higher ratio than their ROTC counterparts." (Of course, their academy graduation guaranteed all those who were eligible the opportunity to attend flight school, an opportunity that would lead to command. By contrast, only a limited number of ROTC graduates are selected for Undergraduate Pilot Training [UPT].) Third, early and high promotion rates demonstrated the quality of academy officers. (The contrary argument would hold that their loyalty and performance derived not from superior training but from privilege and "[class]ring-knocking," a camaraderie shared only by academy graduates.)

Nonacademy males were constantly advised that there was no proacademy bias—that the alumni did well because of rigorous screening and extensive training, but that all officers are promoted on the basis of their record. The reconciling argument was offered by Clark: "it takes some years for an ROTC graduate, who is a probationary Reserve officer with only a smattering of professional training, to achieve the point of effectiveness that our graduates have upon graduation as Regular officers."[i]

How could outsiders, as all women were, know whether they were receiving the training they needed to advance their careers? If they were to receive academy training, how would it affect their rate of retention and promotion? There was almost no way to answer such questions. After all, until 1967 no woman could be permanently promoted past lieutenant colonel, and there were also restrictions on the number of women who could be officers (10 percent of female enlisted strength, which could not exceed 2 percent of total enlisted strength). By 1977 active duty women were being promoted at the same or at a higher rate than men in all occupations open to women.[14] This represented an improvement. However, men and women officers in jobs open to women did less well than officers in men-only fields and were more likely to leave the military. Thus women overall continued to do less well than men overall.

The question of quality also complicates comparative promotion and retention data. Since only a limited number of women were

---

[i] The difference between being a probationary and a regular officer is real; there has been some debate over the policy of automatically granting all Air Force Academy graduates regular status.

recruited into the military and since none faced the alternative of being drafted, their quality and motivation were probably higher than that of their male peers; if so only equal promotions and retention could represent a more serious loss of talent than is at first apparent.

Still another concern arose during the discussion of the superintendent's testimony. During the Vietnam War, good aircraft escape mechanisms inadvertently created many Air Force officer Prisoners of War (POWs). The very idea of women as POWs was unacceptable to most Air Force officials. There was great concern about what would happen to such women, and there was equally great concern about how the public would react to women as POWs. The unspoken assumption was that the public would falter, would withdraw its support. Yet the World War II nurse POWs in the Philippines were said to have come out well. If those nurses had been combatants, would they have earned even more respect from their captors? Or would vengeance have been wreaked upon them? The POW support organizations that had been active in the U.S. were often led by women. Would those groups have been differently constituted or reacted differently if the prisoners were women? Would their response have been to acquiesce in order to get the women out, or would it have been to react even more strongly to rescue or avenge them? These concerns were grave, but thoroughly speculative. They were to assume a concrete form only when the Air Force Academy's survival training program began in the second summer of integration, for this training included a mock POW compound.

The last question raised by General Clark during the hearings was of even more moment for the Navy than the Air Force: rotation. Clark explained that

> all of the graduates of the Academy are fully trained for combat service, which is a flexibility that the Air Force needs to protect at great cost. We all know that at any one given time only a small fraction of our people are actually involved in combat, even in war, but you have to recognize losses and rotations, which means you have to protect a rotation base of fully-qualified and ready people to enter combat on short notice.[15]

For the Air Force, rotation involves enormous training expense and also a long lead time. Pilot training, for instance, lasts a year. To have a large number of pilots available when needed demands that many be trained and then held in readiness in other jobs—jobs that could be taken by noncombat officers (perhaps even civilians) if all pilots were suddenly called to fly.

Rotation is somewhat different for the Navy. While Air Force officers love their aircraft, Navy officers are more likely to have a love-hate relationship with the sea and ships. Being at sea entails living in a limited, isolated, male environment. For the sake of morale, it is imperative that shore (noncombat) billets be periodically available. But if all shore duties were turned over to women officers, the men would always—and literally—be at sea. This could have a grave effect on morale. Similarly, if women actually entered the services in large enough numbers so that they occupied *all* the noncombat jobs, where would the men be? Exposed to perpetual combat. But most men, like most women, prefer not to be in combat or to risk death. Men's acceptance of whatever military service is required of them must be eased by their knowing that the risk to any particular individual is small. That acceptance might languish if the risk were greatly increased. Military service that is *all* combat and that offers no rotation of assignments could threaten the kind of sacrifice Japan asked of some 2,000 Kamikaze pilots during World War II. Under those circumstances, only the highest morale, the greatest coercion, or a combination of both could maintain discipline.

Even in World War II, the "release a man for the front" theme was soon removed from recruiting posters for women. This theme did not make men enthusiastic, and women felt guilty about releasing men to a place many of the men did not wish to go. Indeed, one must assume that if the number of women in the Navy dramatically increases, men will demand that the Navy assign women to sea duty. Even those most opposed to having women on ships now may come to insist that as professionals women must assume all the risks and burdens that are a part of the profession.[j]

Because men hold nearly all the sea billets and also need to be able to rotate to shore duty, there are few women line officers. Thus the Navy's plans for women's admission to Annapolis would be based on considerations like the following. Of the 7,105 accessions planned for 1975, 4,080 were to be unrestricted (as to assignment) line officers (URL). However, because the interpretation of federal law then current prohibited Navy women on ships (other than hos-

---

[j] In Owens v. Brown, 17 FEP 1292 (1978), Judge John Sirica ruled that Navy women could not be barred from "all duty assignments aboard all Navy ships" even though section 6015 Title 10 of the U.S. code limited Navy women to hospital and transport ships—neither of which is now in use.

pital and transport ships), the Navy estimated that 3,895 of the 4,080 new jobs would have to go to men. (During their first ten years of service, lieutenants and below are rotated between sea duty and shore duty to ensure six or seven years at sea.) If the entire Navy were to admit only 185 women as officers and if they were to be distributed through the academy, NROTC, and OTS programs in the same way male accessions are distributed, Annapolis should supply only 20 percent of 185, or 37 (plus an overage to cover attrition). Such a small number, argued Admiral Bagley, Vice Chief of Naval Operations, "would represent noncompliance with the principle of equal opportunity and be neither a practical nor desirable course to follow." He concluded that women should be excluded entirely.

The chief Navy spokesman was Annapolis Superintendent William Mack. The precision and subtlety of his testimony seemed persuasive. For instance, instead of saying that women's entrance would dilute the standards (suggesting women's inferiority), he said it would dilute the mission to train unrestricted line officers. In discussing the academy as a "fixed resource," he did not say women would be taking away "men's slots" but that restricted and staff officers would be replacing line officers, and not ordinary line officers at that, but line officers who received four times the training received by line officers trained elsewhere. This displacement would mean that the nucleus of the best-trained, career line officers would be reduced in size.

Mack is said to have prepared two different statements opposing women's admission. The second presentation was probably required (or suggested) by his superiors because Mack had been "too soft" in his original discussion. Still, at one point in his testimony before the subcommittee, Mack expressed no reservations whatsoever about women's inherent capacity:

> In my estimation, women could serve in any role in the U.S. Navy at any time if this law were changed. They could come to the Naval Academy; they could pass the courses in large numbers, and do all that's required of them physically, mentally, professionally, and in any other way, and there would be little requirements for change in any course curriculum, physical facilities, or anything of that sort. If the law were changed, in my mind, women could do anything that men could do, and in some cases, perhaps even better.
> . . . Having seen summer Olympics on television,

having seen Billie Jean King on television, there are
many women who can do all sorts of things that they are
prepared for, and it would be a question, sir, of taking
the training, passing it successfully, and demonstrating
that that particular person, man or woman, could do the
job.[16]

Mack also noted that while the other services could train women
without changing federal law, the Navy could not provide even its
regular summer training cruises for women without legislative action.

The law restricting women was not changed at that time, and in
1977 (after their first year at the academy) women midshipmen had
their "cruise" on YPs—yard patrol ships. To fend off reports of a
double standard, the Navy also assigned forty men (around 3 percent of the class) to YP cruises. The methods for selecting the forty
men varied from company to company. Some selectees were said to
be volunteers, some to be the lowest ranked in their company, and
rumor even had it that one cadet collected $50 each from his fellow
midshipmen to volunteer for the position. However fine the training
and no matter what their motivation, men assigned to YP cruises
had to take a ribbing.

Cost became an issue in the Navy's testimony because ship space
is always small and expensive to maintain (or create). As a result
the Navy was asked to provide further data on the difficulty and
expenses involved in ship conversion. A rather full response was
provided, along with "An Appraisal of the Impact of Integrating
Women into the U.S. Naval Academy and Aboard Ship." This document stated in part:

Going to sea and organized combat are two of the
oldest endeavors of civilized man. Traditionally, either
by social custom or by the demand for physical
strength, these fields have been open only to men. In the
16th century, when armed combat and the sea-going
profession were welded into the first standing Navy, the
product was predictably male dominated. . . .
. . . Only recently has there been pressure for
change. The naval profession—specifically the business
of going to sea—has been advertised as, and accepted
as, a closed club for men. . . .
. . . Men join the Navy for many different reasons;
however, a certain portion join and remain in the Navy

because they enjoy being in a job which has been historically associated with fellowship among men in a difficult and dangerous endeavor. Changing the fabric of
the Navy by integration [*sic*] women into all combat
roles might well reduce the attractions of the Navy to
this segment of mankind, as well as to some of those
men who might, in the future, join the Navy and make
it a career. . . .

. . . In addition to the reactions and perceptions of
Navy men and women, it is important to consider the
reactions and perceptions of their families. The prospect
of long deployments with mixed crews could be viewed
with some degree of uneasiness by spouses of crew
members. If this occurred, morale and readiness would
certainly be affected. Even single members might find
that families and friends do not support this new role for
Navy women. Traditional elements of the population are
certain to find problems understanding and dealing with
this concept. . . .

. . . The present wave of breaking down the barrier
between the sexes is good and is long overdue in sports,
education, government and the white collar professions.
However, the waging of war is by its nature different
and requires professional attributes and characteristics
which are the antithesis of what we in this society consider essentially feminine qualities. To make a precipi-
tous change in this area ignores both biological and psychological differences and may by its very novelty
threaten national security at a time when our country
may already be only marginally defended.[17]

In prepared statements one can say what one wishes. But answering
questions can be frustrating when the questions one desires to answer are not asked. In this follow-up document on the costs of ship
conversion, fears and anxieties surface that did not appear in the
hearing room. Even if such arguments were not voiced in the formal
hearings, they appear authentic. If so, they are clearly relevant to
the implementation and impact of any policies concerning the integration of women, relevant because an order would not change these
beliefs, even if they ceased to be articulated.

In their testimony Navy officials made what would seem to be
contradictory arguments that claimed, on the one hand, that the

American people did not want women in the combat arms and that young women, at least "the typical normal, healthy American young women whom we are looking for," would not want to enter the academies; and on the other, that so many women might apply that an academy might suddenly end up with 1,000 women in a 1,400 "man" class. Officials with the latter concern believed that some kind of limitation on women would have to be established. For some reason the Navy especially feared being swamped with women. By contrast West Point (according to several Congressmen) was even having trouble getting men, while the Air Force was getting men but having difficulty keeping them. College ROTC units for all services were said to be surviving only because of women's admission. Again, the pressure to admit women to the academies coincided with a military need for personnel.

The advocates of women's admission focused on an entirely different set of issues. Generally, they described the military as an opportunity, a career, a profession—all the things recruiting materials say it is. But when they spoke in terms of education and employment, they were told, in effect, that the essence of the military is combat (killing and dying, flying and fighting) and that women are not allowed to take part. The views of women's proponents are exemplified by the testimony of Rep. Pat Schroeder:

> I don't think women are asking for any special favoritism. As I say, no one is making them go, and I think if they elect to take that option, they are wanting to do what the others do. They are not asking for a special curriculum at all.
>
> . . . It has nothing to do with the equal rights amendment. Congress is the one who writes the draft laws and we could call up women if we needed them anyway. I think so much of this is really moot. If there were an all-out war situation, we wouldn't be sitting around deciding whether or not we would be calling up women. If we really needed them, women wouldn't be saying, "I am really sorry." At least I hope we are not raising that kind of generation.
>
> . . . I don't think women want to be treated differently. They don't want to be carried on a sedan chair.[18]

When pressed, Schroeder was willing to go on record for complete equality. Her strategy, however, was to ask for the minimum change—admission—and to leave the debate on combat and the draft to another day. This strategy sometimes resulted in verbal "tap-dancing" (evasion). Other women who supported women's admission did the same thing. Apparently they feared that taking too radical a position would hurt the bill's prospects. Ironically, male proponents seemed ready to go further than the women in endorsing full equality. Perhaps they had the advantage of greater credibility in making such arguments.

Rep. Samuel S. Stratton of New York was just such an advocate.[k] He began:

> I have long favored the admission of women to the service academies, long before it became so fashionable in the House and the Senate, and as a member of the Naval Academy's Board of Visitors over a period of years I urged some 3 years ago the admission of women and warned academy officials at that time they were opposing the inevitable; and instead of thinking up reasons to keep women out, they ought to be making plans to make their admission a simpler and less traumatic experience.
>
> Mr. Chairman, let me say in all candor that I do not regard the official Department of Defense report on our bill—the letter from Secretary Clements, which he signed, which was referred to earlier in the hearings— as a serious document or even as worthy of what should regularly and predictably be the intellectual level of the Department of Defense. They have no official arguments, only excuses. In fact their official response makes it clearer than ever that the overwhelming bulk of the opposition to women in the service academies—as the gentlewoman from Colorado has just said—is based on nothing more than inertia and resistance to change.[19]

He went on to say that the expense of needed facilities argument was "utter nonsense" and that the combat careers and training argument was specious because

> service academy training gives almost no military or combat training to its graduates whatsoever. These are primarily engineering schools, and I think most experts would regard them as second-rate engineering schools.

[k]His testimony followed that of Schroeder. In introducing him the Chair said, "Now we want to get it from the horse's mouth."

There is some exposure to military life during the summer vacations. The naval midshipmen sail abroad, sometimes in combat vessels and sometimes in transports. There is some exposure at West Point during the summer vacations up in the hills of Camp Buckner and they get to see what a rifle looks like and they fire one once or twice; but basically they are not combat schools, and you are no better trained to be a platoon commander when you get out of West Point or out of Annapolis than you are to be a lawyer when you graduate from Harvard University before going to law school.

Stratton also discussed what he called the discipline question:

. . . this is something that has not been mentioned in the Department's letter, but it is the kind of thing that is breezed around the corridors—the matter of Academy "discipline," or what is really involved, Academy "Mickey Mouse." These are the sophomoric, neanderthal traditional practices that still apply at West Point and Colorado Springs, and to a somewhat lesser degree at Annapolis, designed to inflict physical and psychological punishment on new plebe cadets and midshipmen to "condition" them to the rigid disciplinary procedures of service Academy life as contrasted with civilian life on the outside. Actually, there is no excuse for these practices in the military academies anyway. The Navy has wisely taken some steps to modify them. They ought to be abolished altogether, and if the admission of women is needed to do it we ought to admit women to the Academies for that purpose alone.

. . . It is time for us to pass this bill, Mr. Chairman, and it is time for us to tell the service academies to grow up, get rid of their Mickey Mouse, and catch up with the rest of America and the rest of the world.[20]

Another strong proponent was Rep. Pierre du Pont of Delaware, but while standing strong on "the basic elements of fairness" and on selecting "the best qualified people we can get," he was not sanguine about the number of available qualified women. To Air Force Academy Superintendent Clark's argument that a minimum number of women should be established, he responded, "I would not lower the standards to get up to 100. And I wonder if General Clark isn't proposing that in order to make it more difficult to have women there at all."[21] (Apparently du Pont was thinking in terms of 1 percent women instead of the minimum of 10 percent urged by Clark.) And while du Pont argued for absolutely no discrimination and sameness in all regards, he came down heavily on the side of separate quarters for women.

Rep. Bill Frenzel of Minnesota also made a positive statement, but his assumptions were quite different. He expected that during his lifetime military service for men and women "would be approximately equal." He also believed that women should meet the same standards as men, but was not at all sure that he agreed with the current standards:

> . . . I would say that I don't think the public or the Congress would react very well if we set a lot of silly physical barriers such as pole vaulting 14 feet or crawling through the mud, when you are preparing people for jobs where most of the people who hold those jobs don't have to crawl through the mud.
> . . . if we say we're going to admit women on an equal basis and then have got a lot of silly rules which keep women from getting in, I don't think Congress will accept that.[22]

Proponents did not refrain from making debater's points. Schroeder noted that if men were so eager to spare women from combat, the military should use only male nurses. She also observed that having women on submarines might reduce homosexuality and would also guarantee the race's survival in the event of nuclear holocaust (if the sub survived). There were several references to Marlboro country and to frontier women who helped win the west, as well as references to foreign students who were allowed to attend the academies. In particular, Representative Wilson of California asked if Admiral Bagley was not concerned about foreigners' occupying a future U.S. combat officer's slot. Bagley responded:

> . . . with the size of the Navy we have, with the decreases over the past years, one of the most important things that we can do is keep very close to our allies. This has been traditional in the Navy, and we have relationships, particularly in South America, but it's now expanding to other parts of the globe, where very lasting and close relationships are established in the Naval Academy. . . .

Wilson countered:

> . . . We've trained some of the South Americans at
> our Naval Academy, and they've gone out and partici-
> pated in the raiding of American tuna boats in Chile,
> and Peru, and Ecuador. This is a two-edged sword, I
> think, in some cases. I think sometimes we overdo this
> business of involving our allies. I think it does not alto-
> gether work out the way it should work out.

The Admiral could only reply:

> . . . I don't believe that [capturing U.S. tuna boats]
> is in the curriculum though, I'll say that.[23]

Even the pregnancy issue was debated. One witness noted that
when the current Secretary of the Army (Callaway) was a lieutenant, he got leave from Korea to be with his pregnant wife; he then
stayed in the U.S. and did not return to his overseas duty station.[24]

The Legislation

No report was issued following the hearings. (Some members of
Congress may have hoped that a judicial decision would render
moot the need for legislated change.) Nevertheless, a year and a
half later, in January 1975, women's admission to the military academies was brought before the House Armed Services Committee.
By this time, Representative Hébert had been forced out of his
chairmanship by the Democratic caucus. He was replaced by Rep.
Melvin Price of Illinois. The new chair of the Military Personnel
Subcommittee, Representative Nedzi of Michigan, successfully objected to committee consideration, arguing that the services should
have a further opportunity to comment. But military officials did not
take advantage of that opportunity, perhaps because they considered
the measure safely pigeon-holed. It was not. Four months later Representative Stratton bypassed the committee and subcommittee by
bringing the issue of women's admission to the academies before
the full House. He did so by amending a military appropriations bill
to grant women access to the service academies. To Stratton's surprise and satisfaction, Representative Nedzi withdrew his opposition. Other members of the House did not.

The principal opponents on the floor were subcommittee members Representatives Montgomery and Treen, who proposed considering a separate academy for women. Rep. Lawrence P. McDonald of Georgia gave the most impassioned speech. Arguing "as a practicing physician," he asked:

> . . . how will the female officer serve this obligation of 5 years if she also has three—9-month—full-term pregnancies? Further, how will this obligation of 5 years be fulfilled if this same female officer also elects to breast feed her infant over a 1-year period before her next pregnancy? It is truly difficult to visualize an effective defense force that included a portion of officers serving while 7, 8, or 9 months pregnant. Going on, can anyone seriously imagine an officer giving a lecture or leading a tank column but requiring a pause to breast feed her infant?[25]

After an amendment to exempt West Point failed, the measure passed, 303 to 96, indicating that the House was far more disposed toward this issue than its Armed Forces Committee and Military Personnel Subcommittee had been.

In the other chamber, eighteen senators co-sponsored the amendment; most were liberal Democrats. Sen. William Hathaway of Maine led the debate. Because Sen. Barry S. Goldwater was absent, there was no roll call vote, but later he took care to register his opinion that "allowing women into our military academies will be to irrevocably change the academies, weaken them, and impair the combat credibility of the military service in the face of the ruthless, all-male units of our enemies."

The Senate, which had passed similar measures in 1972 and 1973, passed the bill on June 6; the House-Senate conference report was handed back and forth and finally accepted on September 26. The mandate became law October 7, 1975, following its signature by the President.

Despite the rigorous opposition of the military, the bill succeeded. It did so because Congress did not agree with the DOD representatives that the mission of the military academies was to train *combat* officers. Instead, it determined that mission was to train *career* officers. As a result, the official mission statements of each service academy dropped all reference to combat:

> *Military Academy (West Point)* To instruct and train
> the Corps of Cadets so that each graduate will have the

qualities and attributes essential to his progress and continuing development throughout a career as an officer of the Regular Army.

Air Force Academy To provide instruction and experience to each cadet so that he graduates with the knowledge and character essential to leadership and the motivation to become a career officer in the United States Air Force.

Naval Academy To prepare midshipmen morally, mentally, and physically to be professional officers in the naval service.

By making this distinction between combat and career training, Congress sidestepped having to decide whether women should enter combat; that, it reasoned, was not the central issue.[1] Rather, the admission of women was a matter of granting them equal access to career education. Put into this context, the bill could not be defeated.

The legislation required that women be eligible for appointment, but it left two complex issues to the individual academies and services to work out. First, the academies were told that standards "shall be the same" except for "minimum essential adjustments required because of physiological differences." The only existing standards that large numbers of women were likely to fail were those involving physical strength and endurance. Little was known about purely physiological differences in strength, for social pressure and training affect women's and men's physical development quite differently. (Physical education programs for men often emphasize "building up"; those meant for women work on "slimming down.") Nevertheless, Congress clearly expected that enough "minimum essential" adjustment would occur so that *some* women would qualify. Second, even after these adjustments were made, admission was not to be granted by competition alone. It was not a matter of setting standards and permitting the best qualified to win. The legislation contained a hooker: the admission of women was to be "consistent with the needs of the services," and the needs were to be determined *by the services.* Moreover, these needs were not for certain kinds of

---

[1]All services have combat and noncombat officers, and career differences already exist between rated and nonrated Air Force officers, restricted and unrestricted Navy officers, and officers in the combat arms and in other units in the Army. With women only in noncombat, nonrated, and restricted branches, these distinctions become harder to overlook.

excellence but for women as contrasted to men. Sex, therefore, remained a category (not at all suspect) for admission.[m]

Perhaps because the military *was* an unusual career for a woman, and because more and more opportunities were being made available to women, there were few complaints from women that needs were actually quotas.[n] Probably the strongest (because the most continuing) pressure favoring women's increased participation in the military was the Volunteer Army. Women were being admitted (in small numbers and with great fanfare) into something that not enough men wanted to be in. Two ironies should be noted. First, the Air Force, which had the least difficulty recruiting, made the most room for women. Second, everyone agreed that in a national emergency everyone would do whatever was required. Women *would* fight if needed. This meant, of course, that what women were most excluded from, and what men were most closely guarding, was the *peacetime* military. In a sense it was the role, the posture, the career, the profit—not the actual activity—that was being protected. Indeed, there is almost a correlation between barring females and a *non*fighting military, and including females and a *fighting* military. Yet women's exclusion had been justified on the grounds of something not then existing—fighting!

The Courts

Congress decided women could enter the service academies. As is so often the case, it could have been the Supreme Court, for the issue of women's admission was also being tested in the federal court system. Indeed, the U.S. District Court in Washington, D.C., ruled on the Waldie and Edwards cases on June 19, 1974, the very day that Army personnel testified before the Fisher subcommittee.[26] Ordinarily changes in the military are not accomplished through court order. Judges prefer not to second-guess the nation's defense establishment, and members of the military are not litigation-oriented. Also, most people find it is easier to get out of the military than to change it. Of course, in the case of women, the issue was one of getting into a military school, not out.

[m]A discussion of sex as a "suspect category" may be found in *Frontiero vs. Richardson*, 411 U.S. 677 (1973).

[n]In contrast, when women were first admitted to previously all-male civilian colleges, such as Princeton and Yale, women immediately decried the fact that they were restricted to a certain percentage of the entering class.

In its ruling, the court held that women applicants were not being denied equal protection and that discrimination against them "was reasonably related to furthering a legitimate governmental interest"—preparing young men to assume leadership roles in combat. The question of standing—of certifying the class of plaintiffs—was also at issue and also decided against the plaintiffs. The plaintiffs had sought to include "all past, present, and future female applicants" to the U.S. Air Force and Naval Academies. The briefs had been filed the preceding September (1973), and, because of expected delays, an agreement had been reached to hold open five slots both at the Naval and Air Force Academies until June 18 or until the suit was settled. The plaintiffs held that the test should not be a "reasonable relation to governmental interest" but a "compelling state interest," since sex (like race) was a "suspect classification."

On May 15 the plaintiffs had amended their motion. Hoping for a decision by the academies' June admission date, they narrowed the grounds, asking simply that women not be totally barred from the academies. The plaintiffs left open the question of reserving positions for male applicants by making only one claim: that it was illegal to train only men for careers that were open to both men and women. As noted above, the district court held for the DOD, which had argued that, even though women were not expressly excluded, the "plain language" of the legislation, its history, and the general historical background made it evident that the exclusion of women was "an unexpressed Congressional assumption." The DOD also argued that Congressional debate on the Equal Rights Amendment (1971) and on Title IX (1972) showed an acceptance of the fact that current law excluded women.

The attorneys for the plaintiffs were Virginia M. Dondy, Margaret Gates, and Thomas Martin from the Center for Women Policy Studies. They based their argument on the Fourteenth Amendment's equal protection clause and the Fifth Amendment's due process clause. They pointed out that similar language and history governed ROTC programs but that the Defense Department had opened those programs to women without asking for a statutory change. They also argued that, while the Navy was constrained from having women *serve* on combat ships, women could *train* on them; the U.S.S. *Sanctuary*, a hospital ship, was also noted as available for both service and training. In particular, the plaintiffs noted that each year the Air Force Academy graduated hundreds of officers who entered specialties open to women. (West Point was not a defendant in this case.)

After losing at the district court level, the congressmen and their nominees appealed to the U.S. Court of Appeals, District of Columbia circuit, on October 30, 1974. Judges David L. Bazelon, J. Skelly Wright, and Carl McGowan heard the case. They reversed the lower court and remanded the case for a full trial on its merits (November 20, 1974). The Court held, first, that a summary judgment was proper where there was "no genuine issue as to any material fact," that in this case disputed facts did exist, and that the district court had relied on affidavits of "the very persons charged with unconstitutional discrimination." Second, it found that constitutional law is still evolving and is often highly dependent on the facts of each case "in the area of sex-based equal protection claims" and that "the rationality standard has not been settled upon."

Thus the courts were not only following the integration issue; their positions appeared similar to those of Congress: they were unwilling to advocate full equality for the sexes, yet they were equally unwilling to uphold tradition and the facts as some men described them. In this instance, the courts worked the issue until it became moot; it was finally resolved by Congress through the October 1975 legislation.

The closest the Supreme Court came to declaring women's equality was in *Frontiero vs. Richardson*, 411 U.S. 677 (1973). The issue was whether women members of the armed forces had to prove that their husbands were dependent on them for more than one-half their support before they could receive dependency benefits. (Wives of male members of the armed forces received them automatically.) The decision held, 7 to 1, that this practice involved unconstitutional discrimination. Four judges concluded that sex was an "inherently suspect" classification, just as race, alienage, and national origin were, and that it required "strict judicial scrutiny." To make this a binding precedent, a fifth judge would have had to agree. Two judges said specifically that it was not necessary to characterize sex as a suspect classification in order to decide *Frontiero* and declined to address that issue.

The Mandate in Context

Women's admission was mandated to a reluctant military. Because the directive came from Congress and from the President, who is also the Commander-in-Chief, the military accepted it as legitimate. In addition to their legal authority over the military, the Congress and President exercise budgetary leverage. A Supreme Court decision might also have been accepted, especially if the grounds were constitutional, but the Court's legitimacy is always less certain, partly because the Court is removed from the electoral process and partly because the Court possesses no coercive power. Its legitimacy literally derives from its legitimacy. Its power is only that of persuasion.

Acceptance was also enhanced because all other military training facilities were already integrated, because no distinctions were to be made in the training of combat as opposed to noncombat officers, and because many males then being trained would not, in fact, ever enter combat.

The mandate was palatable for other reasons too. It would cost little, it would hurt no one in particular, and, most important, it did not personally touch any of the institutional managers. All that was required of them was that they allow different kinds of consumers to partake of their training. The situation was like that of lunch counter integration: it involved the consuming of a product, not the sharing of power. And because the military does not recruit except at an entry level (except in time of emergency), there would be no new competition for the current managers.

Mandated change usually requires altered behavior by active opponents of the change. But because the regular, short-term rotation of military officers permits opponents to move on and "innocents" to move in, a change is sometimes easier to effect in military institutions than in institutions in which moves are made only for cause. The superintendents of all three academies testified against the admission of women in 1974. By the time women entered the academies in 1976, all three had been replaced.

Unfortunately, the new West Point superintendent did not read the writing on the wall. He publicly opposed women's admission, threatened to resign if women came, but did not when they did. He was later reassigned because of another issue—cadet cheating. The superintendent at Annapolis had expressed confidence both in women and in the Navy's capacity to train them if told to do so by Congress. He was replaced by a superintendent whose behavior was correct, but who was generally perceived as being unsympathetic to women as line officers. In both cases, rotation may not have eased change. However, at the Air Force Academy, the new superintendent, Gen. James Allen, conveyed emphatic official and unofficial support for the program. Whether his personal views differed from those he expressed publicly was not known. It is likely that General

Allen's testimony would have closely resembled former Superintendent Clark's, had Allen been in the position earlier. Nevertheless, at the Air Force Academy, acceptance was almost certainly made easier by the rotation of its most senior officer.

That women's roles in the military had been continually increasing and expanding also eased the integration of women at the academies. The 1948 Armed Services Integration Act made it possible for women outside the medical corp to make the military a career. That career was limited in certain ways, however: first, the highest regular rank for women was lieutenant colonel; second, women were retired earlier than men; and third, 98 percent of the regular slots were reserved for men. In 1967 new legislation removed all three of these restrictions, although, in fact, women's participation was far below even their 2 percent quota.° In 1969 the Air Force opened ROTC to women. The Army and the Navy followed in 1972. The first women to become generals (Army) won their stars in 1970. New job classifications were constantly opening to women. Thus, room was being made for them both vertically and horizontally.[27]

Similar changes were being made elsewhere in American society. More women were applying to and being accepted by institutions of higher education. Between 1964 and 1974, the percentage of bachelor's degrees awarded to women rose from 42 to 45 percent; M.A.s increased from 34 to 45 percent; Ph.D.s climbed from 11 to 21 percent; and first professional degrees from 4 to 21 percent.[28] Yale, Princeton, and a number of other single-sex colleges went co-ed, and women became presidents of Hunter College and the University of Texas. Women faculty increased in number but actually decreased (both relatively and in absolute numbers) at the higher (usually tenured) ranks. Senior women who had entered the profession in the 1940s were retiring and junior women were not being promoted to replace them.

In government there was little actual but much perceived change. Women lost their only (elected) seat in the U.S. Senate and made a few gains in the House of Representatives (they peaked at 19 of 475

°At their peak in World War II, women made up 3 percent of the armed forces. By the end of fiscal year 1978, the Air Force expected its active duty force to be 8 percent female. This is a relatively high percentage, although in absolute numbers there are less than half as many women in the military today as there were in 1945. The ratio of officer and enlisted personnel is also different. In 1945, almost one-third of the military women were officers; today the ratio is closer to one out of eight. The higher ratio evidences the number of military women who were nurses in World War II and thus officers.

in 1975). Still, they increased their representation at the state and local government levels, won two governorships (Connecticut and Washington), a state chief justiceship (North Carolina), and several mayoralities (e.g., San Jose, California). Perhaps more important than the change in numbers was the change in women's attitudes (they caucused) and in their visibility. In the 1950s and early 1960s, the few women in public life were often marginal and overlooked. In the late 1960s and early 1970s the same numbers were called "tokens," could command a good deal of visibility, and were assumed to be part of the wave of the future.

The handful of congresswomen was particularly important to passage of the Equal Pay Act (1963), Title VII of the Civil Rights Act (1964), the Equal Employment Opportunity Act (1972), Title IX of the Education Amendment (1972), and the Equal Rights Amendment (1972). In 1974 domestic workers were brought under coverage of the Fair Labor Standards Act, Public Law 93–647 provided federal assistance in collection of alimony and child support, August 26 became "Women's Equality Day," and legislation was passed giving women equal opportunities to purchase homes and obtain credit. In 1975 the U.S. celebrated International Women's Year, and legislation was passed to admit women to the military academies.

At precisely this time, women began to feel a political backlash. Supreme Court cases began to go against them, anti-abortion forces began to gather strength, and for the first time doubts surfaced about the ratification of the Equal Rights Amendment. Congress had passed it overwhelmingly, polls showed a majority of the voters approved, a majority of the states had passed it, but three short of the three-fourths majority had not. One of the potent arguments against passage held that the amendment would require the drafting of women into the military and their assignment to combat—exactly those issues that had been raised by opponents of Public Law 94–106.

CHAPTER

2

The Academy Primeval

A *caveat*: being in the military is unique. Because theirs is the profession of arms, military personnel accept contracts with a tacit "unlimited liability clause" that binds them to give their lives for their country if so required. Military professionals may never fight, but they are prepared for war and for the possibility of sacrifice. Even though much of military life is routine, and risk is unusual in the typical career, the possibility of having to give one's life remains at the core of the profession. This possibility is unchanging; Congress and the President can evoke the unlimited liability clause regardless of women's presence or absence and regardless of the validity or invalidity of arguments or fears about women's integration.

The U.S. Air Force Academy graduated its first class in 1959.[a] When women entered in 1976, no alumnus had become a general and no children of alumni had entered the academy. By any measure it was a new institution. Even so, women's entrance was thought to violate a rich and long tradition. Three separate conditions contributed to this belief: first, many Air Force officers are West Point graduates, and in their minds West Point tradition has been added as a sort of pre-history to the Air Force Academy's history; second, tradition is so important to the justification of the military profession that there is a tendency to create it; and third, academy upperclass-

---

[a] In 1976, 128 of the 207 1959 graduates were still on active duty and 14 were dead.

45

men chronically complain that "the new class has it easy" and that "the wing [student body] has gone to hell" as a part of their initiation-like indoctrination of the doolies (the entering cadets). In 1976–77 women were often cited as the reason for the wing's deterioration, but at least one academy "brown shoe" (tough disciplinarian) believed that, while it was true that the wing had gone to hell, the true cause was a failure of leadership. Senior officers, he said, were tolerating unprofessional behavior, double standards for athletes, and the wearing of civilian clothes downtown; and cadet officers were trying to lead by administering instead of by example, by telling and ordering instead of by demonstrating.

The academy primeval, then, has a somewhat mythic character. In fact, the academy has probably changed more by expanding in size than it has by adjusting to changing times or by admitting women.[b] Its culture has always been heavily male and military. In theory, women's entrance ought to have had no effect on qualities military; qualities male, however, ought to have given way without a whimper. But male culture did *not* give way, perhaps because in many instances it was hard to separate male from military.

This chapter will describe academy life, emphasizing the elements that make it different from life at co-educational civilian colleges and universities. The question the reader must constantly ask is: Is this practice different because the Air Force Academy was all-male or because it is military? In addition, one might ask: Even if the received doctrine or procedure *is* military, is it critical to the mission of today's Air Force? For example, surplus M-1 rifles were used in basic training, for marching punishment tours, and in drill and ceremonies at the Air Force Academy. Even though few Air Force officers would ever use a rifle again, the M-1 was considered an important symbol of the profession; it was considered "military." Yet no other Air Force commissioning source was using rifles in its training. Thus there was ample room to argue that rifles were "not critical," a phrase used by cadets to describe various aspects of their training that they found hard to accept.[c]

The Academies as Others See Them

While Annapolis seems to have escaped much notice, a number of books were written about West Point and the Air Force Academy in

[b]The academy has expanded from two to eight or nine hundred graduates a year.

[c]Civilian readers may wish to refer to Appendix I for information on officers' ranks, insignia, and career progression.

the decade before 1976. In *Duty, Honor, Country*, Stephen Ambrose presents a straightforward account of West Point's history from its founding in 1802, through the MacArthur reforms of 1919–20, to the period following the Korean War. Factual, but without a theoretical framework, the account touches on hazing, on the treatment of blacks, on football, and on cheating. Ambrose generally accepts the academy's own premise and evaluation: what an officer needs is "character" and "that is what it [West Point] gives its cadets."[1]

J. Arthur Heise, author of *The Brass Factories*, served as an officer-librarian on the Air Force Academy faculty from 1962 to 1965. His study questions the wisdom of concentrating military power in the hands of an elite trained at the academies. It also questions academy training, which (Heise believes) emphasizes stresses and challenges unrelated to future duty. Heise's critique is principally of the academic training, but his analysis of the cost of educating a cadet, as opposed to offering ROTC scholarships or simply training college graduates, gives one pause.[2]

Against a background of inaccurate Vietnam body counts and the My Lai massacre and its cover-up, K. Bruce Galloway and Robert Bowie Johnson, Jr., argue in *West Point: America's Power Fraternity* that the West Pointer is taught to believe himself "morally and intellectually superior to those he is charged to protect." This belief, they say, separates the Army from the people and makes its defense of the nation and its citizens problematical. "Should Americans trust an institution that produces men who don't trust them?" ask the authors. Their answer is "No!" Else the men for whom "morality is their possession, order is their cry, and stability is their goal" are likely to bring their values home from the battlefield and possibly try to impose their discipline on the civilian population.[d3]

Richard U'Ren, the chief of psychiatry at West Point from 1970 to 1972, argues in *The Ivory Fortress* that the system which develops "obedience, group loyalty, cooperation, uniformity, competition and the importance of the mission" imposes its own reality and in doing so fosters "cover-up," "can-do," "careerism," "favoritism," and "elitism." U'Ren's descriptive work vividly pictures cadet life and training, the application of the honor code, and the dominance of engineering and military training in the educational program. U'Ren is also the only author who discusses sex and the academies. Even

---

[d]The analogy between home and abroad was also made on a popular (civilian) dormitory poster of that day. It shows police beating student demonstrators; a quotation from Lyndon Baines Johnson comments on the scene: "Our foreign policy must always be an extension of this nation's domestic policy."

though a West Point cadet's roommate is known as his "wife," U'Ren found that "sexual perversion is the ultimate violation" in a society that so cherishes the masculine image; thus, homosexuality was absolutely taboo in that hypermasculine but monastic setting.

U'Ren devotes a chapter to "West Pointers and Women" because women's exclusion, he thinks, makes them not just alien but "essential others." "The Academy" he says, "fosters both chauvinism toward and dependence on women. The Victorian world, where appearance and decorum force passion and feeling underground," has survived at the academies. Further, the weekend-only dating pattern followed in all single-sex colleges is exaggerated in a setting where not even every weekend is the cadets own, where only upperclassmen have the mobility offered by cars, and where dates, in fact, often do the driving to get their cadets "home" by the required time. The cadets are attracted to women. U'Ren says 50 percent of West Point graduates marry within a year of graduation; at that time, some are already fathers. Even after their husbands leave the academy, the wives of West Point graduates sometimes find it a competitor (class rings are worn on the third finger of the left hand), and all wives find themselves officially classified as "dependents" unless they, too, are military. Again, psychiatrist U'Ren sees officers as sometimes dependent and immature in their acceptance of military discipline and in their need for strong and periodically independent "dependents."[e4]

In the same year that U'Ren's book appeared (1974), Joseph Ellis and Robert Moore's *Schools for Soldiers* developed many of the same themes.[5] In particular Ellis and Moore note that even though most generals are West Pointers, most West Pointers do not become generals in spite of their rigorous training in order, detail, and responsiveness to authority—if only because so few are promoted to that rank. The authors note, too, that serious problems developed when the Military Academy began systematically recruiting black cadets in the late 1960s. Yet even though the Equal Rights Amendment had recently been approved by Congress, only U'Ren anticipated women's admission to the academies. To the other authors and to most Americans, the academies were simply assumed to be all-male institutions.

There are no accounts by women of the academies "before wom-

---

[e]Military wives routinely act as heads-of-household when their husbands are assigned to ships or remote locations. Having a dependent also substantially increases a service member's pay. The military does not provide equal pay for equal work *per se*; rather, it increases benefits according to the number of one's dependents.

en," but the Air Force Academy, at least, treated seriously the findings of Janet Lever and Pepper Schwartz. In their *Women at Yale*, Lever and Schwartz describe Yale's characteristics before women as consisting of (1) tradition, (2) residential colleges, (3) interior orientation, (4) male aesthetics, and (5) competitive selection. They described the "preppies" as "cool" and "totally self confident," as presenting a "self" for an audience of men only. In all these ways Yale and its student *persona* "before women" seem very like the pre-integration Air Force Academy. The first women to matriculate at Yale found themselves (1) self-conscious, (2) "tolerated," and (3) forbidden access to central activities. They also found that an expressed opposition to women was still acceptable. During their first year the cadet women were not asked their opinions much, but, if they had been, their responses would probably have been similar to those reported by Lever and Schwartz.

The Air Force Academy as Seen by Its Cadets

Cadets record their views in their (supervised) publications. These include *Contrails* and the *Contrails Calendar*, *The Dodo*, *Talon*, *Beast*, and *Polaris*. *Contrails*, named after the condensation trails formed by high-flying aircraft, is the 3″ x 5″, 187-page handbook new cadets treat as their bible; memorization of much of its content is mandatory. It is introduced by the poem "High Flight," by John Magee, Jr.:

> Oh, I have slipped the surly bonds of earth and danced
>   the skies on laughter-silvered wings;
> Sunward I've climbed and joined the tumbling mirth
> Of sun-split clouds—and done a hundred things
> You have not dreamed of—wheeled and soared and swung
> High in the sunlit silence. Hovering there
> I've chased the shouting wind along and flung
> My eager craft through footless halls of air.
> Up, up the long delirious, burning blue
> I've topped the wind-swept heights with easy grace,
> Where never lark or even eagle flew;
> And, while with silent, lifting mind I've trod
> The high untrespassed sanctity of space,
> Put out my hand, and touched the face of God.

Page one asks "To What Shall I Devote My Life?" (an answer is given); this is followed immediately by "The Cadet Prayer" and color photographs of U.S. military decorations. Sections of approximately equal length are devoted to the histories of flight and of the Air Force (entitled "Heritage"), the Air Force and its planes (aircraft, which do *not* all look alike), the Air Force Academy, and "Fourth Class Knowledge." The last section includes the oath of allegiance, mission statements, quotations (from Patton, Rommel, Kennedy, Churchill, but mostly Patton), and the code of conduct. Air Force as a second language is taught too: there are the phonetic alphabet, rank and ratings and their insignia, cadet rank and insignia, the chains of command, a glossary,[f] and abbreviations.[g] *Contrails* is mostly for literacy's sake. It prepares one to see and hear, read and understand.

Because *Contrails Calendars* are purchased for personal use or as gifts instead of being issued, they may be a good indicator of what cadets like to see and read about the academy. The quotations there are from Mark Twain, Oscar Wilde, Henry Thoreau, Voltair (*sic*), and Churchill. This time it is the Churchill of "If you have ten thousand regulations you destroy all respect for the law." Other quotes are in a similar vein: "I don't know," "I can resist everything except temptation," "Any fool can make a rule and every fool will obey it," and "Liberty of thought is the life of the soul." The photos are captioned with wry humor (under a photo of the chapel, "But will it fly?"), and every week each class is told how many days remain until its graduation.

Cadet expression assumes its least-censored form in *The Dodo*, a cadets-only, stapled-together, humor magazine that marks academy buzz phrases, such as "professionalism" ('73–'74), "decorum" ('74–'75), and "positive motivation" ('76–'77). Descriptions are also provided of academy wildlife (The Tourist) and mores such as "bracing" (exaggerated attention posture required of doolies) and chin "racking," the achieving of multiple chins by digging one's chin into one's throat (also required only of doolies).

The first issue of *The Dodo* to appear after the women arrived (August 1976) displayed acute male self-consciousness about their presence. An annotated dictionary definition proclaimed women as (1) "distinguished from man": comment, "at least"; (2) as "mis-

[f]Examples: Bogey: a member of wing or group staff. Buy the Farm: to crash. Ground Pounder: nonflying officer. Rock: superhuman, free from female entanglements. Magic: electrical engineering and all related hand-waving activities.

[g]Examples: CIC: Commander in Chief, ETA: estimated time of arrival, OIC: officer in charge, TDY: temporary duty, OTF: over the fence.

tress": comment, "they should be"; and (3) "a female person who cleans house, cooks, etc": comment, "don't we all wish." Fourteen pages featured "Women [already] at the Academy." Officers, airmen, and civilian employees, all young and smiling, and several in cheesecake poses, competed with the usual "Spacemate" taken from *Playboy* and several other bikini-clad women scattered through the pages.[h] Several grotesque female photographs appear, as does a cartoon in which a female cadet wins her pugil stick match by baring her chest before her dumbfounded opponent. The base Human Relations Committee was asked to consider the wisdom of the issue; it declined to act. However, the *Dodo* editor was dissuaded from doing a similarly irreverent issue on minorities planned for later in the year. The question whether what is offensive to minorities is also offensive to women, and vice versa, was not squarely addressed. Still, the council was dealing with an act completed and with another not yet begun.

By December *The Dodo* was reflecting a wider range of cadet complaints: (1) the public relations line on women that "everyone is pleased" and that "standards have not been lowered in any area" was joined by (2) the losing football team and (3) the new (positive) motivation. In March *The Dodo* noted that some squadrons with "negative" nicknames (e.g., The Dirty Dozen, Grim Reapers, Campus Radicals, and Ali Baba and the Forty Thieves) had escaped the "squadron-patch purge" and that unofficial nicknames (e.g., Seagram's Seven, Nooky Nine, Horny Eighteen, Playboy Nineteen, and Mellow 23) continued to flourish. Each of the forty squadrons has an identifying patch and a related nickname. Officials try to ensure that such names are positive and professional. Cadets have a stronger regard for the double entendre, the irreverent, the original. While the cadets were light-hearted about labeling, the staff was less so. When one patch was proposed with a large, full-faced male Viking and an inset showing the profile of a female Viking coming only to his shoulder, the deputy commandant disallowed it, saying "maybe the women don't see anything wrong with it now, but they will, they will."

Cadets memorialize their academy years more seriously in *Talon* (a slick-cover magazine), *Beast* (a first time yearbook for Basic Ca-

---

[h] Air Force recruitment literature for women follows a similar pattern. Men are always shown doing something, yet in the same brochures women in attractive poses are smiling at the camera. To be wholly fair, it should be noted that the USAFA information office entered five male cadets in *Seventeen* magazine's (1977–1978) Cover Boy Contest; one was a semifinalist! (West Point and Annapolis did not participate.)

det Training [BCT]), and *Polaris* (the yearbook). Even after women had arrived, these publications continued to reflect pre-female thinking. For example, *Talon*'s "Girl of the Month" commanded a four-page layout every month; cars ("he's a cadet and drives a "Vette") and airplanes (which women were not routinely eligible to fly) were major themes too. One message is clear: if one doesn't fly one misses the "peak experience" of the Air Force. Three pieces of literature that reflect the experience of those who fly are printed and reprinted in cadet publications. Those who do not fly, and they are numerous, must feel a separation if not a denigration. The first is "High Flight." The second is a letter by Charles Lindbergh, reading in part: "I began to feel that I lived on a higher plane than the skeptics on the ground. In flying, I tasted a wine of the gods of which they could know nothing. Who valued life more highly, the aviators who spent it on the art they loved, or these misers who doled it out like pennies through their antlike days? I decided that if I could fly for ten years before I was killed in a crash, it would be a worthwhile trade for an ordinary lifetime." The third is "Because I Fly," by Captain Brian Shul:

> Because I fly,
> I laugh more than other men,
> I look up and see more than
> they.
> I know how the clouds feel,
> What it's like to have the blue in
> my lap.
> To look down
> on birds,
> To feel freedom in a thing called
> The Stick. . . .
> Who but I
> Can slice between God's
> billowed legs,
> And feel them laugh and crash
> with his step?
> Who else has seen the
> unclimbed peaks?
> The rainbow's secret?
> The real reason birds sing?
> Because I fly,
> I envy no man on earth.

"That's freedom!" exalted the vice-commandant as he watched a jet streak by, and it is true that academy personnel seem to seek out every possible way of getting off the ground; in addition to flying, they parasail, soar, mountaineer, and parachute. As a psychological or physical test, as a risk, alone or in groups, cadets seem bent on challenging gravity. Even when cadets are being creative in a once-a-year, special issue of the *Talon*, the subjects are women, flying, and sometimes death. The medium is usually poetry or photography, and the mood is romantic, serious, or both. The style is rarely ironic; the lines are not cerebral and spare. There is no politics and not a hint of absurdism, of victimization, or of a foreign or a sub-culture.

Polaris (the yearbook) is the cadet's permanent record of his senior year. The 1976 edition is not untouched, for cadets knew women would be coming. In fact, the women Air Training Officers (ATOs) who arrived in January 1976 are noted in the list of significant events, along with items like making breakfast mandatory. Interestingly, about 25 percent of the news events listed for that year concern women: two are about Patty Hearst, and two more are about the California women who attempted to kill President Gerald Ford. Still, women appear principally as "Squadron Sweethearts" and as the admirers of cadets' performances.

The activities section of the *Polaris* is led by four pages of photographs of lovely ladies described as "motivation-plus . . ." and "and more motivation. . . ." Even the four-page section introducing the ATOs (whose job was for the 1976–77 year, although they were not included in *that* yearbook) is led by two pages of a pair of horizontal, bikini-clad twins eyeing the reader.

Positive cadet imagery focuses on the falcon's fierce beak, sports cars, guns, and the spikes of the chapel. The Bicentennial theme of freedom is illustrated by the career of Captain Lance Sijan, who died in 1968 as a POW in Vietnam and master of himself to the end. From the wall of the "Hanoi Hilton," this inscription is featured: "Freedom has a taste to those who fight and almost die that the protected will never know."

The 1977 *Polaris* belongs to the self-proclaimed "Pivotal Class." It was the last to enjoy the traditions of cannons at change of command, no "coke-break" (a recreation period) BCT, and short-arm (venereal disease) inspections. It was the last to wear meticulously polished leather shoes to ranks (cadets may now wear permanently polished corfam shoes) and to have pointy (hooded) parkas. On the other hand, it was the first class to do without winter parade dress and (quasi-official) leisure-time blazers, cross-country training flights, and out-of-continental-U.S. (OUTCONUS) Third Lieutenant summers. As first class men they found themselves administering men *and* women doolies in what they called a "Burger King" ("Have it your way") BCT at "Camp USAFA." Along with privileges gained, the class of 1977 was also the last to have the option of going to medical school or of majoring in General Studies. (By 1978 the medical school option had been reinstated.)

In their "Remember When" queries, the class of 1977 first asked, "Remember when men were men and so were cadets?" and quickly went on to "Doolies buffed upper class floors for stereo privileges?" "Doolies had to gaze at the floor when in Mitch's [the dining hall]?" "There was an acceptable double standard?" "You didn't have to wear anything in the hall?" and "Doolies had dancing lessons?" Other nostalgia items included "unmarked underwear," washcloths "on the other side of the towel," and a BCT that "drove the weenies out."

No women's photos appear in the photos of the superintendent's and commandant's staffs in 1977. A few appear in the dean's display. In the athletic section the first picture is of a female cheerleader, but men's sports are identified by name and women's as Girls volleyball, Girls cross-country, Girls basketball, Girls gymnastics, Girls swimming, Girls tennis, Girls outdoor track. ("Boys" was a word never used.)

Playboy Bunnies remained part of the morale-building program of the cadet rally committee, although squadron sweethearts did disappear during 1976–77. Still, the comments under the picture of each graduating cadet reflect a very male culture. Examples: "Likes to sleep in a mixture of digested food and Sangria." "Measuring in at a staggering 5'6", Chef strongly believes in the saying 'Great things come in small packages,'" "Don't let him alone with your wife or daughter." "Known for being the first out and last in on weekends, Garth looks forward to chasing women at Reese." "He came to the Academy to learn to fly and to get an education. One out of two isn't bad." "Took four years to convince him that airplanes aren't the only thing in the world with operational tails." Nicknames are common. One black cadet is referred to as "Black Magic," and a Chicano is nicknamed "Beaner." Even if the intent is to express affection, one doubts that such nicknames would appear in the yearbook of a co-educational or women's school, where formality or sensitivity would preclude the use of names that are informal tests and where nicknames are more likely to be self-selected than assigned.

Cadet Life: Predictability

Cadet life is shaped by the principles of predictability, pressure, and participation. More than anything else, a command structure must be able to count on its people; it must be able to anticipate individual and group response whatever the task, the place, the circumstance. Habit and uniformity are important elements of this effort to achieve predictability. For the cadet this means that the academy may prescribe clothing, personal possessions, and even room and drawer arrangements. It also prescribes behavior through training in decorum and through the Air Force Cadet Regulations, and it prescribes activities. For each class there is a carefully-worked-out daily schedule, an annual cycle, and a four-year program.

The uniform is the most obvious symbol of the prescribed way of life. It is not that the costume is so different from that of civilians,[i] but what is important is that each cadet is dressed in the same way. Yet each individual is clearly marked.[j] All cadets wear insignia showing their name, their year, their rank, their squadron, their achievements (Commandant's, Dean's, and Superintendent's Lists), and their special training (RECONDO, parachute training). In addition, signs on one's dormitory door yield such information as "academic probation" or that one is "out" and where one is. These features of cadet life tend, of course, to reduce privacy and guard against anonymity.

"Decorum" insures that good manners make military and social occasions run smoothly, because each cadet knows in detail what is expected. For instance, there is even a set of rules covering dining-out behavior.

> Prompt acceptance or refusal
> Arrive on time
> Greet hostess first
> Speak to everyone

---

[i]Cadet hats are an exception. These billed and triangular trappings are singularly military.

[j]So are officers. The first item in *Contrails* teaches a cadet how to "read ribbons," which can tell that one has been wounded, in what campaigns one has served, and if one entered the Air Force as an airman or as an officer.

Make introductions, if necessary
Offer to help the hostess
Remember your table manners
Thank your hostess
Make a timely departure
Send a thank-you note

With an explicit check list as a guide, a cadet can tackle the new with full confidence.

Air Force Cadet Regulation (AFCR) 20–1, which prescribed the organization, responsibilities, and duties of the cadet chain of command, was more than 40 pages long in 1976 and provided details right down to the seniority of the Wing Safety Officer (#6), the Honors Representative (#13), and the Color Guard (#25). It was but one of 90 regulations. Since that time the number has been reduced to 25. Nevertheless, their detail and comprehensiveness are likely to strike the uninitiated as overwhelming and invasive.

When women were admitted the cadet day began at 6:15 A.M. Room and self had to be prepared for inspection before a mandatory 7:00 breakfast. This was followed by four required-attendance classes. For lunch, cadets went into a meal formation and marched to Mitchell Hall, where the entire wing ate at once with cadet commanders, officers, and guests (who were seated on a balcony, "The Tower"). Two classes followed lunch, then intramurals, and (except in winter) ranks were sometimes formed again to march to dinner. At 7:45 P.M. study began and at 11:00 Taps was sounded. There was virtually no free time for 4° (entrance year) cadets, nor was there much free space. Most of the time the cadet had to be in a specified place, performing a specified activity. To sleep even ten minutes late could be to march two fifty-minute punishment tours.

The first or doolie year of the four-year cycle is unique. While the "seniority system" assigns different responsibilities and privileges to each class, the principal distinction is made between the fourth class and the three upper classes.[k] The four-year activity cycle begins in late June with in-processing of the arriving doolies. It culminates four years later with the round of festivities and cere-

---

[k] In 1976–1977 the privilege packet (a phrase no longer used) was considered a "carrot" by the administration but all too often a "stick" by cadets. As doolies, cadets had no privileges; with time their rights were progressively restored. This restoration gave cadets their time back, but it also rewarded differential achievement, provided for class distinctions, and gave cadet officers "a leadership tool."

monies known as June Week.[1] For many cadets, graduation, commissioning, and marriage occur on a single day.

Before each academic year the cadet has a summer of military training and a leave (vacation) period. The first, or doolie, summer is devoted to Basic Cadet Training (BCT). This is the period of imprinting at the academy. Entrance to the military in any branch or at any level includes an orientation or socialization period. Even if that orientation differs greatly from the Air Force proper or what a particular individual ultimately does in the service, it nevertheless gives the inductee a sense that what happens in basic training is what the military is really about.

And what *is* basic training about? Gary Wamsley has argued that in the past the Air Force has used both harsh and low-key approaches to basic training: the first, to instill heroic values; the second, managerial.[6] Yet he says there is no evidence that either harsh or low-key training produces the desired product, an officer who will "retain cool judgement in crisis." Actually, the academy's program seems to be something of a hybrid. It entails a great deal of classroom instruction, with emphasis placed on good management. At the same time, BCT imposes severity and stress to generate pride and comradeship. It appears that the academy program utilizes shared jeopardy to unify the survivors of what is essentially an individual and group trial by ordeal.

Another study outlines the elements involved in the rite of passage from civilian to military status. They are said to be: (1) disparagement of and isolation from civilians, (2) lack of privacy, (3) group evaluation (and punishment), (4) physical and psychological stress, and (5) emphasis on aggression and masculinity and a derogation of and a utilitarian view of women.[7] Wherever it is conducted, basic training is arduous. But it is designed so that most of the men undertaking it (recruits or cadets) *can* make it through. What keeps pride high is the firm conviction that most of the population (all women and many men) could not. Thus basic training can be simultaneously inclusive (of most scheduled for the training) and exclusive (of women and old, weak, or uncommitted men.) Again, if women do not do something at all, men are automatically in the "top half," even if they are not in the "top half" for men. Thus it can be more undermining to a sense of elitism to train five women than

---

[1]With the academy's new schedule the activities associated with June Week will in the future mostly occur in May. Nevertheless, a cadet referendum voted against changing the name of the week. Whether tradition overwhelmed reason or whether the reason for the proposed name change was unclear is unclear.

to train five men of exactly the same capacity. Doing so destroys the presumption that the trainees are by definition better than one half of the population.

The cadets' second summer is composed of three segments. One is leave, the second is Survival, Evasion, Resistance, and Escape (SERE), and the third is elective. The options for the third segment include Basic Airborne (Army parachute training at Fort Benning), selected by about 35 percent; Soaring, available to only 10 or 15 percent and in great demand; and Operation Noncom, taken by just over half the new second class men. The latter is an intern program with widely varying duties, conducted at bases throughout the U.S., intended to give cadets an understanding of what it is like to be an enlisted woman or man and thereby, it is hoped, to make the cadet a better officer two years later.

In their last two summers, cadets usually take the Third Lieutenant Program (an intern-like assignment designed to give them junior officer experience), leadership option, and two electives. The leadership option for most cadets is participation in the BCT or SERE training cadres. A limited number (under 100 total) serve as instructors in soaring, parachuting, or navigation. Electives include special training programs that accept between 50 and 150 cadets each, and competition for them is stiff. These include RECONDO (combat leadership training), Underwater Demolition Training (UDT), Free Fall Parachute, and Summer Research. All cadets going to pilot training after graduation take the T-41 (flight indoctrination) program during their first class summer.

At the end of the first summer's training (BCT), Acceptance Day is celebrated by the awarding of shoulder boards (epaulets) to the new fourth class men. This is rapidly followed by the beginning of the academic year. Classes resume, parents come for their weekend, and the football season begins.

Make no mistake, football is emphasized. It absorbs time, attention, and newsprint; the cadet wing attends each game in uniform. But the 1976 victories over the University of the Pacific, Wyoming, and Navy did not balance losses to Army, UCLA, Kent State, Colorado State, The Citadel, Arizona State, and Vanderbilt. If the purpose of football is to build morale for a military organization through the winning of physical contests, what is the effect of a 3–8 losing season? If cadet life is too rigorous to accommodate the training of the nearly professional athletes of some colleges, what should an academy do: select lesser opponents? focus on other sports? or do the conventional and fire its coach? (It fired the coach.)

Or if school spirit cannot be derived from a nationally dominant football team, where else might it be developed? One source is other athletic teams such as track, swimming, basketball, and hockey. (These academy teams had creditable but not extraordinary records.) Another is the national press coverage of other activities such as debate, ballooning, or the cadet chorale. In 1976–77 the academy did receive a lot of national coverage. But because this media attention focused on the women rather than the cadet wing, it was counterproductive for morale. This meant that the rally committee, charged with fostering cadet spirit through such events as homecoming, a Halloween dinner with cadets in amazing attire, a three-thousand-person circle in which each cadet sat on the lap of the cadet immediately behind him, and visits by Playboy Bunnies, had its work cut out for it.

The pre-Christmas period is filled with semester exams, a Blue Bards production, a performance of the *Messiah*, the traditional Lessons and Carols concert, and the first of a series of all-school formals, the Superintendent's Ball.

Until the late 1960s, doolies were not allowed to go home for Christmas. The Blue Bard drama group was founded to foster emotional survival over the holidays. It was the only cadet group to have women members before there were women cadets. (The Elizabethan solution for the filling of women's roles was apparently not acceptable.) Other balls are those of the dean, the commandant, and the Valentine Formal. In addition, there is a Ring Dance for second class men, a Recognition Dance for doolies, and a Graduation Ball for firsties. Attendance is not mandatory but "requested"; if *all* were to try to attend they could not. The ballroom is comfortable for fourteen hundred couples, although eighteen hundred did squeeze in for the Commandant's Ball in 1977.

In early January the second semester begins and the fall's career planning is put into practice with cadet Career Decision Week. Pilot-eligible cadets are expected to go to Undergraduate Pilot Training (UPT) and most choose to do so. The one-third of the class not eligible to fly choose assignments from a variety of Air Force Specialty Codes (AFSCs). In choosing, cadets are not committed to a separate corps as are their counterparts in the Army, and cross-training (moving to another specialty) is not difficult. Strategies are numerous even *within* a career choice. Thus one issue of the *Talon* delimits the pros and cons of the eight locations for pilot training, including such criteria for choice as "work for wife," "auto hobby shop," "auto insurance," "surrounding colleges," and "golf."

The Dark Ages is the affectionate term used for that long period in the second semester when gloomy weather and study seem to go uninterrupted. One observer of cadet life (a group sergeant-major) claimed that during the year of integration, the Dark Ages "didn't happen"—possibly because things never settled down enough so that the major complaint could become "routine" or "boredom," or possibly because cadets began practicing "positive motivation" on each other.

The Dark Ages are enlivened each year by the Dean's Ball, handball and boxing competition within the wing, rock and folk concerts, and Black Arts Week sponsored by the Cadet Way of Life Subcommittee, which functions as a Black Student Union does on some civilian campuses. In 1977 the program featured Julian Bond and a dining-out for black cadets with Generals James Allen, Stanley Beck, and "Chappie" James.

Spring brings the annual Assembly (a discussion program that in 1977 featured nuclear power), the Commandant's Ball, and Wives Recognition Week (which over the course of the year became Spouses Recognition Week). Finally, Retraining or Hell Week, exams, and June Week bring the second semester to a close. June Week provides "recognition" of the doolies by the upperclassmen, rings for the second classmen, awards for organizations, and graduation and commissioning for first classmen. For some cadets it all culminates in marriage, and for others in R Flights (a make-up period for failed or otherwise deficient cadets).

The second semester's Retraining Week for fourth class cadets requires elaboration because it is considered important to the cadets' performance as third class men. Also called "Hell Week," it lasts for only two-and-a-half days and is a reliving of the most strenuous pressures of BCT. Its purpose is to develop class unity, to make the transition *out of* fourth class dramatic and meaningful, and to put members of the soon-to-be-third class in a properly stern mood for training the next set of doolies. In 1976–77 it was the most recent escapees from the fourth class system, the third class, that had the primary responsibility for training the doolies. (This policy has since been changed.) Nevertheless, the third class does not usually approach the job with a single understanding. Indeed, one (ex-cadet) academy officer estimated that only about one-third of the third class really and consistently "trained" (that third was well known to the fourth class men), while the rest did not know how to, did not want to, or did not believe in it.

In the third class year, cadets are assigned to the squadron in which they remain until graduation. They receive a "privilege package" that leaves about 50 percent of their weekends free, are granted increasing control over their finances, and at the end of the year, after attending their first class in the fall, after their third class summer, make their military commitment.[m] That is, they obligate themselves to two more years at the academy and to five years of active duty service, increased to six if they take pilot training. As of September 1978, disenrollment without penalty will be permitted until the cadet begins his first class (senior) year.

By their second class year (their third year at the academy), cadets have chosen an academic major and have become eligible for a variety of squadron and group jobs (as cadet noncommissioned officers). The promotion list (called the "make" list before women arrived) lists cadet officers and is issued three times a year, although in 1976–77 the top positions (i.e., the Wing Commander and the four Group Commanders) were not rotated. One's chances for leadership opportunities also increase in other organizations and in athletics. Moreover, one is able to enjoy a stereo in one's room and to plan the purchase of the automobile many cadets believe crucial to their existence. At "car time" cadets may charter a plane to Detroit (at their own expense) to pick up their prized new possessions. Those possessions get well broken-in on the 1,000+ mile return trip to Colorado Springs. At the end of the same year, class rings (especially designed for each class) are received.[n]

In their last year cadets hold many responsible positions in the wing, enjoy a substantial amount of free time, and begin to look forward to their careers. In addition, many of them have gone on the chaplains' pre-nuptial retreat and made reservations for a chapel wedding. Such reservations are scarce enough that they are sometimes kept after a falling-out in hopes that a new engagement can be made before graduation.

It is important to note that as the cadet is prepared for the "real" Air Force, his life becomes more like that of civilians and less stereotypically military. Some argue that all training should be more like the service will be. Others argue that the rigor of the first years makes it possible to rely on older cadets and on graduates who only appear to have become civilian-like.

[m] There is a forced savings program for cadet salaries. Most of their first year's income goes for the cadet "issue" (uniforms and equipment). Some $1,000 is saved for graduation and $200 for June Week. Financial self-management really occurs only in the second and first class years.

[n] The class of '77 chose "Pride Rides" as its motto. The class of '79 would have no slogan; the empty space on its ring is said to stand for "Last Class with Balls."

Cadet Life: Pressure

The constant heavy scheduling of a cadet's life exerts psychological pressure. While no single part of a cadet's schedule may seem unreasonable, when one grasps the totality of regulation one understands that this is, indeed, another way of life. Intentional and unintentional overscheduling seem to be chronic, and cadets learn both to cut corners and to set priorities; they also learn to fail.

Another form of psychological pressure is called harassment or hazing by its opponents and discipline or training by its supporters. The idea is that individuals need to know their limits—to learn that they can do or withstand more than they had ever expected, but, also, that they cannot do or withstand everything.° Enduring a trial can yield personal satisfaction, especially if the ordeal is understood as relevant. However, the relevancy of tests and training is being increasingly questioned in society generally; and the military, too, tries to evaluate its programs with some regularity. Thus the requirements for the squaring of corners, for exaggerated posturing, for the reciting of unimportant information, as well as arbitrary, insulting, and bullying commands, are being questioned. To some degree they are also being eliminated.

Testing one's physical capacity and one's response to physical stress is less debated and is the analogy used to justify psychologically stressing programs. Programs with much physical activity are also among the most popular cadet programs. Those that involve risk as well as pressure seem especially popular. Still, while many programs do have a potential for risk, there is also meticulous attention given to safety; for example, parachutes automatically open at a given altitude even if the cadet fails to pull the cord, and the SERE trek requires check-ins every several hours. In a way the training can be described as being like that in a well-controlled, well-calculated Montessori school that provides a structured program to create an illusion of freedom and danger in order to teach thinking and safety.ᴾ

Punishment exerts pressure too. It especially does so because punishment at the academy is not automatic or wholly predictable. Every cadet and alumnus has a story. One faculty member remem-

---

°The testing of one's limits is unusual in women's activities and is uncommon even in the training of ROTC or OTS officers. On the other hand, Outward Bound is a civilian and co-ed program that does give women a chance to take their own measure.

ᴾThe soaring program lost its first cadet in the summer of 1977. That same year the academy soaring distance (220 miles) and time (six hours, seven minutes) records were set.

bered that as a cadet he had been required to do 2,000 pushups for reading a letter with a flashlight under his blanket after taps. He also told of committing more outrageous acts (e.g., provoking fights with "townies"—local civilians) that went unpunished. But, while discipline is supposed to teach obedience, initiative sometimes wins informal rewards. While one is taught to obey the rules, defiance can inspire a certain awe. In fact, spirit raids—actions that break regulations—are sometimes urged on subordinates because certain kinds of out-of-bounds behavior (caught or uncaught) command respect. Thus a successful night in town when one is supposed to be on base can evoke admiration. Similarly, Karl Richter, the youngest Air Force pilot to down a MIG, an officer who won numerous decorations before being killed on his 198th mission, has an academy lounge named in his honor. However, the story cadets tell about him is that while a cadet he rode a motorcycle into the cadet dining hall. And so it is that airplanes move to new locations, statues appear in bizzare attire, wondrous objects are run up flagpoles, and the yearbook features a picture of cadets jumping off the "Bring Me Men" ramp into a snowbank some 30 feet below, an event that resulted in Commandant's Disciplinary Board action for some thirty-seven cadets. Of course, there is no good rule for distinguishing between spirited pranks and disgraceful behavior. Even so, cadets are formally and informally taught decorum and honor throughout their four years.

Some exploits undertaken by men might elicit a negative reaction if carried out by women. For instance, the smuggling of a man into the dormitory for paid intercourse would almost certainly be more upsetting to administrators than the similar smuggling of a woman by men. Similarly, a promiscuous woman cadet might be less acceptable than a man with a reputation as a Don Juan. Indeed, the departure of one especially active woman cadet was arranged in the first year. Among other things, she was apparently using sex for profit.

A full explanation and assessment of the Honor System is impossible here, but its importance and the pressure it generates must not be underestimated. The code says simply: "We will not lie, steal, or cheat, nor tolerate among us anyone who does." The application of the code can be severe. Lying is a difficult habit to excise totally, as several recent studies have shown, but the rule is that "pop-offs" and social "tact" are not necessarily lies, while "quibbling" is.[8] The "toleration clause" (which Annapolis does not have) requires reporting each other and leads to a moral dilemma for cadets with a strong loyalty to one another. Further pressure was experienced at

West Point, where there was not only no toleration in reporting but also no discretion in enforcement. This meant any violation led to expulsion. An added complication was the fact that the honor codes are supposed to be a cadet tool for self-discipline, and they are not supposed to be used by administrators to enforce administrative regulations. Thus some questions are "proper and necessary," but others might use a cadet's pledge not to lie to entrap him and may, therefore, be inappropriate. Again, honor sets a minimum standard of conduct that is exacting and complex. It can add enormously to the pressure cadets feel, although it can also be a source of pride.

Finally, cadets compete and are evaluated. Sometimes it seems that they compete in everything, with everyone, and at every moment. There is many a trophy or award to win. Conversely, there are many kinds of loss to suffer and three kinds of probation (academic, conduct, and aptitude) to endure. (Some make "All-Pro"— all three kinds of probation.)

Cadet Life: Participation

Peer ratings are a particularly effective way of guaranteeing participation and interaction, but participation is also a basic value shared by most cadets. In fact, "woodworkers" (cadets who "go into the woodwork"), who keep a low profile and who do not develop a sense of teamwork and of cooperation, are objects of some scorn.

The squadron is the primary unit of loyalty. While a squadron is always "new" in that doolies are in a particular squadron for only one year and third class cadets are entering their squadron for the first time, a squadron is also always "old" because first and second class cadets have already been in it for two and one year(s), respectively. This rotation means that new energy and old alliances coexist, that vigor and experience are both provided, just as in the U.S. Senate. Squadrons (composed of some one hundred cadets) live together, participate in intramurals together, march together, and win or lose trophies and awards together. Athletes and members of certain special groups may have other important loyalties, but if those other loyalties are too strong, the cadets involved may suffer low peer ratings since fellow squadron members control these ratings. There is also a loyalty to one's class or year; indeed, classes are sometimes given names, and class reputations are said to affect class members throughout their military careers.

Participation pervades the life of the academy. Intramurals involve competition, but, more important, the rules for competition also require participation by every cadet. Drill (practice for parades and ceremonies) also requires participation; indeed, drill excellence is attained only as individuality is obliterated.[q] Conventional wisdom holds, in fact, that there are two kinds of cadets who do not make it through even the first summer: one is the introverted, who needs but cannot have private space; the other is the "hot dog," who is extroverted enough but is accustomed to only leading, and has rarely been either a follower or a failure.

The sense of being part of a whole is further enhanced by the academy's practice of providing everything a cadet requires including an ersatz family (through the Doolie Sponsor program) and a social life (through the Office of the Cadet Hostess). The incumbent in 1976–77 was also the original hostess, who retired after twenty-one years. The office continues even though many cadets now have access to cars and have more time to use them than before. Girls are also less likely to come to the academy by the bus load and to expect personal invitations; they do not like participating in the "cattle call" or "ghoul pools" of yore, nor do many submit pictures and résumés to the "date selection book."

One last item must be mentioned because it suggests that part of the cadets' unity comes from participating in and also beating the academy's "system." Tail End Charlie is the lowest ranking senior. At graduation he is singled out and honored with a silver cup filled with silver coins. This award does not signify that even the last is one of the best (because academy standards are so high), nor is it a compensation for being a good sport, working diligently, and finally succeeding. Rather, it is a tribute to the apparently shrewd cadet who meticulously calculates and makes the minimum effort necessary to meet graduation requirements. The 1978 "Charlie" did not like his "honor" much; academy officials have decided that cadets should not compete for last place. Thus the 1978 "Charlie" was the last one. Annapolis and West Point have also put an official end to the practice.

The Conundrum

The question remains: how can one distinguish between male culture and military culture, and how can one make female culture

[q]The academy has found that disliking drill is one discriminator for cadets who are likely to resign.

legitimate in a military setting? Military personnel accept the threat or use of force as a legitimate part of conflict. They learn the technology of force and prepare themselves mentally and physically to use it. They also recognize that force may be used on them.

Men more than women exercise to build their strength and endurance. They engage in physical contests (athletic competition and even fights) and pit themselves against the environment (rock climbing, spelunking). They use technology in accepting challenge (parachuting) and know more than most women about machinery (autos, radio). What is not clear is (1) whether these tastes and behaviors enhance military performance, (2) whether an attitude or action needs to be habitual or only within one's repertoire in order to be available (i.e., does a propensity toward or experience in violence make one more likely to follow an order to use force?), and (3) how new values and attitudes would affect military capacity (would the wearing of cranberry, mocha, and lime blouses, instead of only blue ones, improve morale? would it undermine discipline?).

Before 1976 cadet publications portrayed women as morale builders—whether as sex-objects or approving observers. "Commitment to Excellence," the academy's recruitment brochure, described the purpose of BCT as "the making of a man" and noted that during BCT "a girl's smile has become as inaccessible as the far side of the moon." Cadet candidates were also told that "We hope for your sake that she [your special girl] cares enough for you to understand why you have to challenge yourself" and that "Most parents need some preparation, too, especially mothers."

Query: is it necessary to end such stereotyping entirely to make it possible for women cadets to be accepted as peers? Or is it enough to enrich the variety of portrayals of women *and* of men, for instance, by picturing an admiring young man, on a visit to the academy, dancing (in his tuxedo) with his cadet date (in her dress uniform)? Further, let us suppose that ornamentation of oneself and one's surroundings is more a part of female than of male culture in this country. Does that make jewelry or flowered sheets unmilitary?[r] Again, if sensitivity to the feelings of others, to the visual and tactile, is more female than male, does that make women less military? Or could heightened sensitivity enhance certain military tasks (such as intelligence gathering and analysis)? Or does insensitivity (real or pretended) actually help officers by making it easier for them to

---

[r]One eighteenth-century feminist, Mary Wollstonecraft, argued that, in fact, women and military officers were alike because both value ornaments and physical appearance, and because both are social parasites—nonproducers.[q]

give and take unpleasant but necessary orders? <u>Does the apparent insensitivity of others teach a necessary stoicism?</u> Does male humor and nicknaming, which may vulgarly highlight difference and weakness, have a bonding effect important to group performance? Are women less humorous than men, or do they have a different kind of humor? Does it have the same or different consequences? How might that difference or similarity affect military performance? Perhaps we could gain a clearer idea of how hard it is to distinguish that which is military from men's culture by asking questions such as these: If young men were admitted to a nursing school for the first time, which practices should they be held to and which should be modified or ignored? Should men be allowed to abandon the caps that traditionally indicate one's place of training? Should the same kind of solicitude toward patients be expected of men as women? Would the diversity the incorporating of men entails weaken or strengthen nursing as a profession? <u>Sometimes a new context for an old question sheds light</u>. Indeed, I was taken aback when a young Air Force nurse described to me the male nurses who had taken training with her. She spoke as disdainfully and uncomprehendingly of them as any upperclassman ever spoke of the women doolies.

CHAPTER

3

The Fishbowl

An organization that carries out much of its activity under scrutiny may respond to being observed in one of several different ways. Sometimes this visibility encourages a self-conscious but nevertheless self-defined and carefully explained response. Sometimes it promotes an anxious conformity to what is thought to be wanted. Sometimes, especially when there are a number of interested audiences, the organization's visibility makes invisibility seem intensely desirable. This response becomes all the more probable when what will please one audience will almost certainly displease another.[1]

When the Air Force Academy admitted women in June 1976, it felt visible. Too cross-pressured to seek recourse in any kind of conformity and too exposed to achieve inconspicuousness, the academy responded carefully and explained its actions thoroughly. To do so meant addressing observers with varied kinds of interest. Congress and the Pentagon had official concern. Distinguished visitors and tourists were curious. The media wanted to tell the story of the first women cadets to the world. Even within the academy, a variety of observers with different duties and concerns were carefully monitoring the integration process.

The vulnerability and visibility felt by those charged with admitting women to the service academies cannot be overemphasized. To the taxpayer, the academies may represent a part of what is understood to be a relatively nonnegotiable defense budget. To academy staff, however, an academy is an imperiled species that is annually evaluated and funded by a legislative body that is itself subject to fickle public opinion. No matter that an academy is doing a good job and is currently held in good repute, it is still constantly exposed to the scrutiny of public agencies, official guests, and even American tourists. Nearly all these observers may approve of the academies' performance, yet their large number almost guarantees that some will not approve; and military leaders, like elected officials, know that an aroused critic can be more influential than numerous, but preoccupied, supporters. Disapprovers, then, are worrisome; thus, a great effort is expended in anticipating and averting criticism. In this vein, one officer who likened life at the Air Force Academy to life in a goldfish bowl observed that the public *does* affect life at the academy even if unknowingly. It often does so not by learning, responding, and acting, but by its potential for doing all three. Again, policy makers may not actually respond to the public, but they do try hard to anticipate and avert its disapproval.

Congressional Watchers

Congress (with the President) controls the academies' funding; with the assistance of the General Accounting Office (GAO), it exercises oversight of the schools. Before these routine ways in which Congress monitors the service schools are discussed, another way—unique and less formal—should be explained. That method involves the nomination system. Individual members of Congress nominate most of the young men and women who enter the academies; the academies do not fully control the selection and admission of their students. Instead, federal law provides that each senator and representative may have up to five nominees attending each academy at any one time. This would total 2,675 (5 × 535) or some 60 percent of the enrollment at the three military academies. In fact, some 80 or 90 percent of all cadets come from the pool of Congressional nominees, because alternate nominees are chosen through competition to fill remaining academy openings. But no candidate is accepted who is not qualified. Most members of Congress use a merit system to select their nominees, or they leave the ranking and selection to academy admission committees. Nevertheless, the typical cadet is conscious of having a Congressional sponsor who maintains an interest in him and in his experience at the academy.[a] (See Table III.)

Qualified children of Medal of Honor holders receive automatic appointments; American Samoa, Guam, Puerto Rico, the Canal Zone, the District of Columbia, and the Virgin Islands are each allotted one cadet per academy. Just over one hundred nominations per year are made by the President and the Vice-President. (Most of these appointments go to children of career military personnel or children of deceased or disabled veterans.) Children of "persons in a missing status" have a special allotment, and other slots are authorized for members of (1) regular and reserve components, (2) the Reserve Officers' Training Corps, (3) honor military schools, and

Table III. Typical Distribution of Appointment Categories in an Air Force Academy Entering Class*

Congressional	618
Qualified alternates	552
Presidential	100
Vice-Presidential	2
Canal Zone	1
Virgin Islands	1
District of Columbia	1
Puerto Rico	2
American republics	4
Regular Air Force	41
Reserve Air Force	111
Sons of deceased and disabled veterans	11
Sons of Medal of Honor recipients	0
Honor military schools	6
AFROTC and AFJROTC	14
Total	1464

Source: United States Air Force Academy, "A Great Way of Life," guide for students and counselors, 1976–77.

*American Samoa, Guam, and the Philippines may appoint candidates when vacancies are available.

[a] Imagine running a tax-supported school for the children of legislators or a private school whose student body is composed exclusively of trustees' offspring. The analogies are not perfect, but in either case one could expect to find extremely responsive administrators.

(4) the junior Reserve Officers' Training Corps. A handful of places also go to allied students from the Philippines and from American republics. Although all cadets must be qualified, they do not compete in a single pool. A few do not have to compete at all. (Special pools for women and "nonflyers" will be discussed later.) Most cadets, though, represent a constituency: they receive outside support for their endeavor.[b]

Congress collectively (as contrasted with the individual nomination process) audits the academies' budgets and programs through the GAO. In the eighteen months preceding the entrance of women, the GAO compiled three reports on the service academies: "Financial Operations of the Five Service Academies" (February 6, 1975), "Academic and Military Programs of the Five Service Academies" (October 31, 1975), and "Student Attrition at the Five Federal Service Academies" (March 5, 1976). In addition to the United States Military Academy, Naval Academy, and Air Force Academy (under the Department of Defense), the reports covered the Merchant Marine (Department of Commerce) and Coast Guard academies (Department of Transportation). The financial operations report emphasized savings that could be obtained by substituting a civilian for a military employee whenever possible, by contracting custodial and food services, and by reducing staff levels. In particular, the Air Force Academy was urged to use a civilian faculty, to reduce the size of its band, and to reduce overall staffing. This report did not attempt to estimate cost effectiveness or to calculate the cost of educating a cadet. Its only goal was to document costs, including those incurred by military retirement, faculty training, moving (for students and military personnel), and academy prep schools.[c]

[b]Parents are considered an important support group as well as more "eyes on the academy." While entering cadets are being processed, parents are given an orientation that culminates in an evening swearing-in ceremony, followed by a brief informal reception. Parents do not see their sons and daughters again until basic training is over. A Parents' Weekend is held in the fall, and Parents' Clubs in various parts of the country hold regular meetings for which the academy may provide speakers. The cultivation of parental support increased at about the same time that women entered. This change was probably motivated by high attrition yet still compatible with efforts to recruit women as cadets.

[c]Faculty openings each year average 190 for the Military Academy, 125 for the Air Force, and 69 for the Naval Academy, which has a substantial civilian staff. Most of the slots are filled by officers who have done graduate work and most will go on to other duty after a tour at one of the academies.

The one-year prep schools were intended to prepare selected enlisted men for the academies. Such students now make up approximately one-half of the Army's preppies, but only one-fourth of the Navy's and one-sixth of the Air Force's prep enrollment. The prep schools are also used to enable minority candidates and certain athletes to develop into eligible can-

The principal findings of the study of the academies' academic and military programs posited a need for a comprehensive examination before graduation and for a post-graduation assessment of individual and group performance. (The Navy was already conducting such evaluations.) The Air Force as a whole was also advised to define and communicate its needs to the Air Force Academy and its students to achieve better administration of the majors program. This study assessed the relationship between the programs offered and the military's stated needs; it did not examine the quality of instruction.[d]

The most thorough, and perhaps sensitive, study covered attrition. Published in the spring of 1976, the report and its supplements (1) described methods, procedures, findings, and interpretations; (2) reviewed previous studies of attrition; and (3) examined the reasons for the dropouts from the class of '74. While all the academies experienced moderately high attrition rates, the USAFA class of '75 had an attrition rate of 46 percent, the highest of the three DOD academies and the highest in USAFA history.[e] As a result, the academy came under strong pressure to reduce its attrition at the very time women were scheduled for admission. Some officers worried that women's entrance might increase men's attrition. Others feared that policy changes designed to reduce attrition would be attributed to the presence of women, especially any changes that could be interpreted as "softening" the arduous doolie year.

Institutions that have selective admissions policies and exacting performance standards have a special problem when it comes to attrition: they wish to justify their admission decisions by having their students do well. To do well, however, those students must be motivated. High motivation (at least at the academies) is rooted in competition, but competition requires that low rankings be given to some of the carefully chosen admittees. A somewhat similar dilemma is experienced in Marine Corps recruit training. There, the drill instructor stresses, drills, and trains recruits, always emphasizing that only the toughest will survive. At the same time, the instructor's goal is to prepare *all* his "boots" for military service. Tough as he may sound, he has a stake in passing his trainees. Thus

---

didates. Minorities represent about one-eighth of the Army's, one-fifth of the Navy's and one-fourth of the Air Force's prep enrollment. Athletes represent about the same percentage of each prep school class. Close to one-third of the Air Force and Navy students are "others" drawn from the civilian population.

[d]The DOD Committee on Excellence in Education (the Clements Committee) was conducting a concurrent study that *did* encompass quality.

[e]Indeed, Senatorial concern over the USAFA attrition was what prompted the GAO report.

competition and high standards are constantly evoked in order to motivate at the same time that the motivators are under pressure to have all or most of their trainees succeed. After all, officials are held accountable if too many of their charges (cadets, recruits, students, team, or union members) fail or leave.

Academy superintendents and commandants are thought to be especially influential in the matter of attrition. Once the cadets have been selected, these officials have two basic options. They can try to weed out poorly motivated cadets before much has been invested in their training (i.e., during BCT). But this policy can create a high attrition rate just at the time that officials may be trying to achieve an overall reduction in attrition. Or they can try to build motivation over the four years. Unfortunately, that effort must be conducted in the face of evidence suggesting that students' commitment to the service decreases the longer they are at the academy.[2] The Air Force chose the second option. Its principal manifestation was the philosophy of "positive motivation" introduced in the 1976 BCT.

Congress conducts its business specially as well as individually and collectively. Members of the Senate and House Armed Services Committees and, in particular, those serving on the Military Personnel Subcommittees have special concern for the military and its academies. Conventional wisdom holds that Congressional committees are chaired and dominated by conservative Southerners whose views might be expected to agree with those of military leaders. Since the hearings concerning women's entrance into the academies were held in the House, a close look at the 1976 composition of its Armed Services Committee and Military Personnel Subcommittee is appropriate. Melvin Price, Democrat from Illinois, chaired the forty-member committee. Twenty-seven were Democrats, including eight Southerners and five members from Missouri, Texas, and West Virginia. Thirteen Republicans included six Southerners and a member from Tennessee. There were two members of a racial minority and two women.[f] While the committee was rarely at odds with the military, its membership did include "watchdogs" Les Aspin of Wisconsin and Ronald Dellums of California.

The thirteen-member Subcommittee on Military Personnel was chaired by Democrat Lucien Nedzi of Michigan. It included four

[f] One woman, Marjorie Holt, who had Annapolis in her district, favored the entrance of women to the academies, even though she was not a strong supporter of the Equal Rights Amendment, according to an official of E.R.A. America. (Holt was not a member of Congress when the amendment came to a vote.) The other, Patricia Schroeder, who had a district contiguous to that of the Air Force Academy, was a supporter of women's entrance and some say was the first woman to eat on the floor of the cadet dining hall.

Southerners as well as recent appointees Aspin and Dellums. The ranking Democrat on the committee, Charles Wilson of California, was a strong supporter of women's participation in the military and even supported removal of the combat restriction. That an outspoken feminist had recently challenged Wilson in the Democratic primary may have made him especially conscious of and reflective about women's issues. In short, the full range of Congressional views was available to both committees, and it is possible that despite the military's opposition both would have approved women's admission to the academies if the legislation had been developed through the committee system instead of raised on the House floor.

The most attentive academy-watchers in Congress may be the legislative members of each academy's Board of Visitors. Each board consists of four Senators, five Representatives, and six civilians appointed by the President. In 1976 the Air Force Academy's Board of Visitors included the only woman Presidential appointee, Dorothy Nelson, Dean of the University of Southern California School of Law; others were attorneys John C. McDonald and Stillman D. Rogers, and businessmen John B. Wogan, Jr., James E. Brown, and Robert R. Herving. Congressional members were Senators Gary Hart of Colorado, Clifford Hansen of Wyoming, Ernest Hollings of South Carolina, and Ted Stevens of Alaska; Representatives Mendal J. Davis of South Carolina, Frank Evans of Colorado, John J. Flynt, Jr. of Georgia, J. Kenneth Robinson of Virginia, and David C. Treen of Louisiana. These boards meet only a few times a year at the academies they oversee and receive rather formal briefings. Their function is not really to investigate, but to observe. Nor are they responsible for programs or for budgeting, yet they are the very essence of planned fishbowl-watching; that is, they alert the academies to the concerns of the public and Congress. One might even say they are intended to serve as an early warning system.

Military Watchers

The Department of Defense watches the academies through the military chain of command and through the civilian secretaries and their staffs.[g] Decisions or wishes may be conveyed in a variety of ways,

---

[g]The Air Force Academy's chain of command: the President of the United States, the Secretary of Defense, the Secretary of the Air Force (all civilians), the Chief of Staff, USAF, and the Superintendent of the USAF Academy (both military).

but the Air Force unit with the major interest in USAFA affairs is that concerned with personnel. Under the Deputy Chief of Staff for personnel, the Air Force Academy Activities Group coordinates Colorado Springs's concerns with those of Washington, D.C., and defends academy programs to inquirers. One section of this group handles nominations procedures, a second handles Congressional liaison, and a policy and projects section handles items that require delicate treatment.[h] Coordination between the Air Force, West Point, and Annapolis desks is not routine, although the Department of Defense will sometimes ask them to develop a uniform policy on such items as setting a common day for graduation or establishing a single policy on cadet pregnancy. On occasion a problem of great concern will arise (such as the 1976 West Point honor scandal). Then the services make an effort to keep each other briefed.[i]

At the Defense Department level, the Asst. Secretary of Defense for Manpower and Reserve Affairs (especially the Office of Education) monitors the academies. For both offices, the academy population is a numerically insignificant part of their responsibility. The Asst. Secretary is tasked with providing, training, and maintaining military personnel for all services at all ranks; the Office with managing a worldwide education network that provides study from kindergarten through graduate work. As long as things are running smoothly, the academies, which are small but elite units, tend to be semi-autonomous. However, when an outside nonmilitary agency probes the service academies (e.g., the GAO for Congress), an inside study, such as Deputy Secretary of Defense W. P. Clements's "Excellence in Education Report," may be generated. Thus an outside inquiry can stimulate internal activity even if the stimulus is never formally acknowledged (or even if it is denied). This development makes it hard to assess the function of such observers. Often their very act of observing seems to create change, which makes pure or static observation difficult. For social scientists interested in policy making and implementation, the problem is that their monitoring generates self-monitoring that would not otherwise occur. The more general question is whether the existence of potential monitors stimulates high performance, even if the monitors never take an observable action or have an obvious impact.

[h]These are more often budgetary than political. Indeed, one officer commented that the pressure to promote and retain women academy graduates as career officers will come more from making good on a $105,000 investment than from legal pressure or feminist advocacy.

[i]In addition the DOD academies' superintendents, commandants, deans, and honor and ethics officers meet with each other periodically to discuss common problems (and to assess relative standing).

Another monitoring group that has not had its role well analyzed is the DOD's Defense Advisory Committee on Women in the Services (DACOWITS). Organized in 1951 by Gen. George C. Marshall and the Assistant Secretary of Defense Anna M. Rosenberg, this group of fifty women met twice a year to examine military women's (1) training and education, (2) housing, welfare, and recreation, (3) utilization and career planning, (4) health and nutrition, and (5) recruitment and public information. The first members were distinguished women, who were briefed by the Secretaries of Defense of the Army, Navy, and Air Force, and by the military chiefs of staff, personnel authorities, and the directors of the nine major components of women in the armed services. Its auspicious start coincided with a decision to double the number of women in the military; a new war (Korea) meant women were suddenly in demand. And men apparently felt a need for advice from women on how to recruit and manage them properly.

Over the years DACOWITS acquired the reputation with some of being a do-nothing committee composed of political influentials' wives who did not know exactly what they were there for. But in the early 1970s, DACOWITS minutes reflect a changing tone. Member Sarah McClendon, a WAAC during World War II, began to ask some tough and provocative questions that caused some defense officials the same discomfort President Lyndon Johnson used to feel when journalist McClendon worked his White House news conferences. By 1974 DACOWITS minutes show that it was making very specific recommendations, requiring very specific official responses, and inviting presentations from members of the public—in particular, members of the public who represented the Women's Lobby, the Center for Women's Policy Studies, the Center for Law and Social Policy, Women's Equity Action League, the American Civil Liberties Union, and the National Organization for Women.

In 1976 a funny thing happened. A grand twenty-fifth anniversary celebration was staged for DACOWITS, a silver cover was ordered for the minutes, and a reunion was held for past members. At the same time, the Secretary of Defense allowed membership to drop to twenty-three; twelve more members were scheduled to retire in the fall. The one-person secretariat came to an end in July, and clerical help had ended even earlier. Clearly a tug of war was going on. DACOWITS was acting vigorously: it was bringing together senior women officers, the news media, a variety of pressure groups, and civilian women. The meetings seemed to be serving as women's caucuses do in other organizations (i.e., as a communications center, as a place for commiseration and recharging, and as a place to learn new strategies in order to wage a more effective battle). Yet officially provided resources were withering away.

By early 1977 DACOWITS acquired a new lease on life. While new membership was limited to fifteen, Gen. Jeanne Holm, the first woman to win two stars, had been appointed to the committee, a lieutenant colonel who was the first woman to teach at the Air Force Academy was made Executive Secretary, and three other women (and one man) were assigned to administrative support. The group's current recommendations include increasing the percentage of women line officers to equal the percentage of women enlisted (scheduled to reach 11.1 percent in 1983), giving weapons qualifications training to all women, having the Air Force determine whether its "test" programs for women pilots and navigators have been successful, revising the U.S. Code to equalize all provisions that currently vary with respect to gender, and specifically repealing Section 6015, Title 10, U.S. Code and Section 8549, which prevent assigning women to combat aircraft and ships.

Visitors

Adjacent to the superintendent's office on Harmon Hall's second floor, the Protocol Office manages the calendar of guests. For any month this calendar is filled with the names of distinguished visitors whose greeting, escorting, housing, feeding, briefing, and entertaining are carefully arranged by a staff of officers, enlisted personnel, and civilians. In July 1976 the coincidence of the entrance of women and the nation's Bicentennial resulted in an unusually large number of visitors. On one day the entire Colorado Committee on the Status of Women and its chair, Dotty Lamm, wife of the governor; the head of the Japanese Air Force; Deputy Secretary of Defense, W. P. Clements; and William H. Oliver, Department of Defense Director of Equal Opportunity filled the academy's calendar. Other typical visitors that year included participants in conferences, such as the Military Aircraft and Design Conference, groups of USAFA Liasion Officers (LOs) who recruit cadets to the academy, officials from the Civil Air Patrol, NCAA football officials, and the U.S. Olympic soccer team. The total number of visitors for 1976 exceeded even 1975's record-breaking 12,400. Official visitors carry away opinions that circulate in a variety of informal and formal information networks. Gen. Jeanne Holm, for instance, visited the academy in June 1976, while serving as President Gerald Ford's Special Assistant for Women. She also had access to thousands of women as she criss-crossed the country on speaking tours.

Relations with the public are considered of great importance; after all, each academy conducts its affairs amid a constant flow of tourists (sometimes referred to as GNATS, Great North American Tourists). West Point's story has been told so well, so often, and for so long that it has become a focal point for northeastern vacationers. The Naval Academy's waterfront setting in the state capital of Maryland, with its easy access from Washington, D.C., brings many a family to nod at Tecumseh, admire the Nimitz library, and wonder at the chapel housing the crypt of John Paul Jones. Even the relatively isolated Air Force Academy enjoys overflowing parking lots on any sunny summer day. Indeed, in 1976 it welcomed more than 1.6 million visitors.

Air Force Academy tourists have access to a visitors' center and a number of picnic grounds; they may also drive through the installation's 18,000 acres of mesa land (elevation between 6 and 8 thousand feet), with its numerous viewpoints, extensive housing areas, airfield (with a 3,500-foot runway and parachute drop zone), cemetery, golf course, and bivouac.[j] The off-limits cadet area is compacted into a rectangle. One pair of opposite sides are dormitory and dining areas, a third side is the academic building, and the fourth is the portion open to the public. This area contains a planetarium, administrative offices, the angular steel-and-stained glass chapel, and a terrace from which visitors can overlook the Air Garden and the Terrazzo where the cadets line up for pre-meal formations. Lying outside the perimeters of the cadet area are a deer-filled ravine, the Rockies' Rampart Range, a parade field, acres of playing fields, a field house (basketball court, track, and ice-skating rink), a gymnasium, and thirty tennis courts.

Tourists who have driven across the plains on a hot summer day must be ambivalent when they reach this oasis. On the one hand, they must be comforted to see the precision and high performance required of their future defenders. On the other hand, they must wonder about the expense involved in educating several thousand young men and women in such a lavish setting. The model cadet

[j]The unremarkable visitors' center, with its trailer toilets, cannot compete with West Point's handsome museum. It has a lavish souvenir supply with many Falcon carvings, a map showing the hometowns of current cadets and an aerial map of the grounds. Like athletic facilities and the Officers' Clubs, the Visitors' Center at USAFA is maintained with nonappropriated funds, i.e., it is not supported by tax dollars.

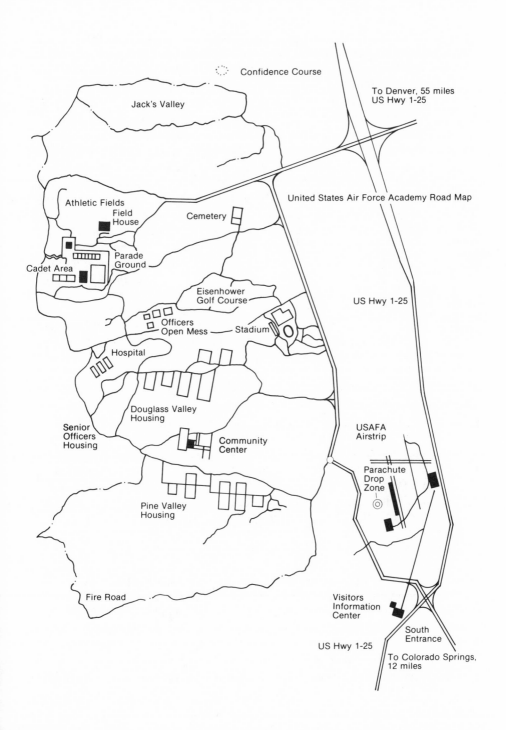

Confidence Course

Jack's Valley

To Denver, 55 miles
US Hwy 1-25

Athletic Fields
Field
House

Cemetery

United States Air Force Academy Road Map

Parade
Ground

Cadet Area

Eisenhower
Golf Course

US Hwy 1-25

Officers
Open Mess

Stadium

Hospital

Douglass Valley
Housing

Senior
Officers
Housing

Community
Center

USAFA
Airstrip

Parachute
Drop
Zone

Pine Valley
Housing

Fire Road

Visitors
Information
Center

South
Entrance

US Hwy 1-25

To Colorado Springs,
12 miles

room set up for the perusal of the tourists suggests discipline, control, and seriousness. But even if ornamentation and individual expression are limited, any "poverty" experienced by cadets does not involve actual want; instead (like the asceticism of some religious orders), it entails only a foregoing of the personal control of wealth. The academy does provide; indeed, it provides very well. Cadets are *not* deprived even if they are dependent.

Among those whom the academy encourages to visit are educators, especially those who may counsel students to become cadets; prospective cadets themselves; and local businessmen. The academy tries to be a good neighbor; when, for example, the wife of the mayor of Colorado Springs died, the ranking officer at the academy that day, Vice-Commandant James McCarthy, canceled all appointments in order to attend the funeral. Conversely, the mayor has a sign (on wheels) placed at the academy's entrance each year to greet the new cadets on behalf of the city. In the spring of 1977, it proclaimed: "Welcome AFA class of '81, Love ya."

Then there are the professional onlookers—the journalists, authors, and media personnel. Their tours and interviews are managed by professionals from the Information Office. As in most organizations, the Information Office oversees internal communications, community relations, and special projects; and it also handles requests for information from outside professionals and the public. As specialists, the academy's public information officers understand what is news, how a reporter is likely to tell a story, and why an attempt to cover up can simply balloon a story. At the same time, they know that many military officers believe they have had a bad press in recent years, that the media are not always interested in pursuing the whole truth, and that even if one tries to give journalists a full and interesting story, one cannot be certain about what will be written, much less about how what is written will be understood.

Grace Lichtenstein's article in the *New York Times Magazine* (September 5, 1976) is a case in point. Lichtenstein is an established writer, known for her account of the women's professional tennis tour. Her analysis of basic cadet training made it clear that participation in such an endeavor was beyond her comprehension, more or less her capacity; but the story was fundamentally accurate and straightforward. Nevertheless, few officers seemed to approve of it. Most of their disapproval was vaguely expressed, although one senior officer expressed a sense of near betrayal in noting that to report events without explaining their purpose was misleading. Later one information officer did say that he believed Lichtenstein had done a

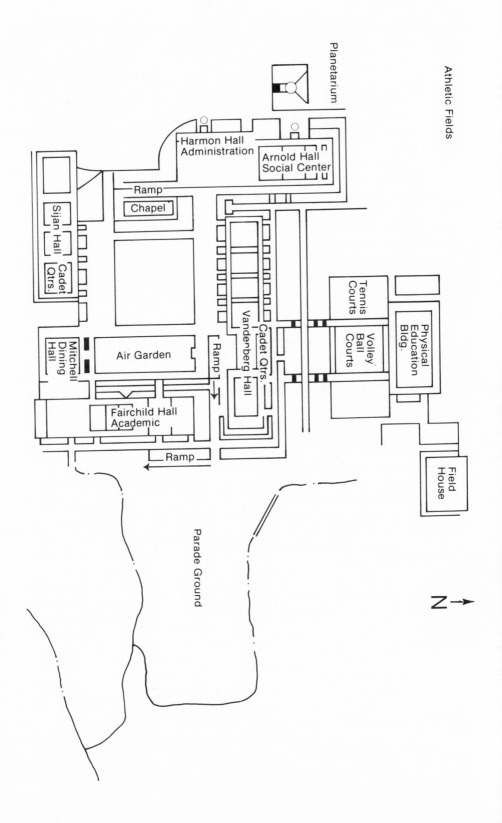

good job. When queried about what was troubling others about the article, he guessed that the problem was its headline: "Hate, Kill, Mutilate."[k] When the article was reprinted with a less provocative headline, "This Is the Air Force, Miss Jones," its effect was quite different, he felt. Still, the experience must have confirmed the views of a number of officers who are not ordinarily concerned with public relations that encounters with the press just are not worth the risk.

The advent of women at the Air Force Academy greatly interested the public, and women cadets became the stars of the biggest media event since its 1955 opening. The Information Office, nonetheless, soon found itself walking a tightrope. Its course had been clear in the fall of 1975: secure as much publicity as possible to get as many applications from women as possible. However, by June 1976 the class was both selected and inducted.[l] And while the press was anxious to continue its coverage, the academy was beginning to see that coverage as a two-edged sword. One, reporters inevitably disrupted the activities of what they reported (cadets had come to the academy to be trained, not to be media stars). Two, with the media's attention focused only on a small percentage of the entering (doolie) class, a negative reaction from the other cadets was inevitable. With the lowest of the institution's low appearing on network news, while deserving "firsties" were being ignored, cadet morale suffered. Cadets (and some officers as well) resented the media's emphasis on women and its judgments about their performance. Even though the academy was getting extensive coverage and considerable external approval, internal rumblings became severe enough that the Information Office felt it had to discourage coverage. It is not often that an information officer has that task; favorable coverage is usually coveted, not refused.

For whatever reason, the Air Force Academy had few self-appointed outside monitors of its integration of women. Perhaps its fairly remote location discouraged inquisitors, or perhaps it was seen as willing in spirit as well as in word. In 1976, though, a new group was formed that would follow the cadet women's performance with special interest, the Retired WAF Officers Association. Yet another group was based in Washington, D.C., the National Coalition for Women and Defense, and led by a Navy commander's

[k]Reporters do not write their own headlines. Copy editors do so.

[l]Intensive recruiting efforts, including a speaking tour by Superintendent Allen, resulted in more than 1,200 nominations for women by January 31, 1976. This number was up from 57 on October 31, 1975.

wife experienced in lobbying, lecturing, and litigation. At West Point some monitoring was done by a West Point chapter of the National Organization for Women (NOW). Of course, whatever power these monitoring groups had lay in their ability to generate "bad press." As one woman officer noted (about Congressional and other official supervision), "They may very well not be monitoring, but the military doesn't know it for sure and doesn't count on it."

The Other Fish

The view from inside the fishbowl was clearly different from that outside. An investigator trying to sample attitudes several months before the Air Force Academy's women were to arrive was told by the first officer interviewed that "You're already too late. It's been decided. The debate's over." In a sense he was right, for the day the Commander-in-Chief (CINC, the man civilians call the President) signed the legislation authorizing women's admission was the day official debate stopped—or at least shifted from "should we" to "how will we." In a military chain of command, once a decision has been made, dissent stops. But double messages are sometimes conveyed. For example, a commander can subtly indicate his own approval or disapproval of a policy at the same time that he hands it down. This can be done in a variety of ways: through repetition or failure to repeat, through emphasis, through follow-up or lack of it, through personal, visible effort. At the Air Force Academy the superintendent did convey the message that integration would not only occur but it would also succeed, and both ideas pleased him. Several Air Force cadets expressed it another way: "The guys at West Point and Annapolis *knew* their 'Supe' didn't want girls, but *our* 'Supe' didn't back us!"[m] Indeed, the Air Force Superintendent was fond of quoting from an Oklahoma newspaper interview with one of the new women cadets: "Well it doesn't really matter if the male cadets want us or not . . . the Academy wants us."

The chain constrains. So does the closed nature of an institution that brings its members and their families together often. Work, family, and social life are in large part conducted on base. Everyone knows a great deal about one another, and it is not considered inappropriate to know a lot. Rumors circulate among officers and ca-

---

[m] Army's Supe was seen as the male cadets' friend since it was made clear that women would conform to male standards even in apparently trivial ways. For instance, West Point women were said to have had to carry their books on their hips instead of across their chests.

dets and many a tale is told about illicit activities in the planetarium
or on the handball court. More important, one's personal life is considered relevant to one's job performance, and that performance is
regularly and formally assessed. For cadets this assessment is done
through the Military Order of Merit; for officers, the Air Force Officer Efficiency Report (OER). In 1976 the OER regulations forced
evaluators to distinguish among their subordinates' performances by
directing that within any unit only 22 percent of the officers could
receive a rating of "one," 28 percent could receive a "two," and 50
percent had to receive a "three."[n] This controlled distribution meant
that people who were working together were also competing against
each other in a zero-sum game in which if one wins the other loses.
Each fish certainly had good reason to watch the other fish.

Formal "in-the-bowl" watching is conducted by the Inspector
General's Corps (the IG), which is independent of the academy but
has an office on base where formal complaints can be filed. In addition, off-base IG investigators periodically evaluate various academy programs and policies. While the IG can provide relief, many
officers perceive that having to take a complaint there lessens their
effectiveness and may reflect on their own evaluation.

An informal and indirect way of exchanging information between
the academies occurs through an exchange of six cadets for one
semester a year. The 1976 cadets who were exchanged between the
Air Force, Naval, and Military Academies seemed to agree that
women's integration went least well at the Air Force Academy,
where they perceived the greatest resentment and lack of acceptance
by male cadets. Journalists and outsiders tended to see just the reverse. (For example, see Narda Zaccino's front-page story in the
Los Angeles Times, June 13, 1977.) Possibly both were right.

The Naval Academy admitted 81 women, the Army 119, the Air
Force 157. The Army and Navy women were fewer, were dispersed, and were intended to be unobtrusive. The Air Force women
were more numerous, were clustered, and were highly visible, because they were required to wear skirts much of the time. Their
presence, then, may have been more disruptive in that they were
harder to overlook, ignore, or forget. At West Point and Annapolis,
cadets and midshipmen could more easily avoid the women, and
they did not have to consider the women as a group. But while the
Air Force Academy's cadets probably experienced more dissonance, they also experienced more institutional support for the view

---

[n] This forced distribution was especially painful for academy personnel, who were supposed to represent the Air Force's best. In late 1978 the distribution controls were removed
for all officers.

that women had a right to be there and that a surreptitious entrance and a diffident blending into the institution were not required of them. The Air Force cadet resistance may suggest that cadets believed they faced a more serious demand for change in their institution than did their West Point and Annapolis counterparts.

Perhaps the contrast between the academies' responses was not so much one of no change versus change as it was one of seeking change through unconscious and slow conditioning versus seeking change through confrontation, which would lead to cognitive dissonance, which would ultimately reorder understanding and change behavior. The first kind of change is probably more palatable to a system administrator and to those having to accept the change, but it does not provide newcomers with much legitimacy and may place a special burden on them. This is so because the newcomers are called upon to educate their peers at the same time that they are working hard on their own education. This educative burden is especially heavy when administrators meticulously distribute women (or minorities) throughout a system in which others are assigned randomly. When this occurs the system is similar everywhere, but nowhere is it the same for the minority as it is for the majority. Who benefits and who is handicapped by such careful distribution? Is marginality unavoidable for the newcomer in any case? How do absolute numbers affect assimilation? Is there any way a limited number of newcomers can force acceptance of their differentness? Or is an easement policy a better strategy when institutional change is and will continue to be minimal? Are there any circumstances in which full acceptance is accorded a numerical minority?

One might have expected that as educational institutions the service academies would be eager to explore such questions and that each would have experimented with a variety of policies and housing arrangements to determine which produced the best results. The academies, however, are military schools. While they would have valued well-grounded answers to such questions, it was important to them to provide the same training to every cadet. Indeed, offering a uniform experience was so important that the academies were willing to forgo any systematic experimentation with policy alternatives.

Special Observers

Even if they did not experiment, the Army and Air Force Academies did provide for special, in-house observation during the process of

integration. A civilian woman sociologist, Nora Scott Kinzer, from
the Army Research Institute in Washington, D.C., was made a co-
investigator in Project Athena, a set of research projects designed to
study the effects of West Point on cadet women and of cadet women
on West Point.° These studies were undertaken by the West Point
Office of Institutional Research, an established part of the academy,
which began its study early enough to measure attitude base lines
some eleven months before the entrance of women.

The Air Force Academy had not been conducting the same kind
of institutional research. However, the new chair of the Department
of Behavioral Science and Leadership (DFBL) (a tenured position
held by a colonel) believed the development of a research program
on the integration of women to be a priority. He knew, too, that his
current staff could not undertake a large-scale project, since all were
officers with other full-time duties. He therefore took advantage of
a new Distinguished Visiting Professor (DVP) program to bring in
a woman sociologist from Washington State University, Lois De
Fleur (who must have seemed especially desirable since she was a
devoted pilot). The DVP program was a part of the academy's response to GAO's recommendation that civilian faculty be increased;
each year it provided generous salaries for three one-year visitors.ᴾ
The sociologist selected by DFBL worked with the department to
design and administer a longitudinal study of the women cadets and
of their peers. She found the military environment more of a contrast to university life than she had anticipated and discovered that
conducting research was harder than she had expected. Civilian
studies often must be cleared by a Human Use Committee, a requirement that makes work cumbersome. At the academy, however,
clearing the way to conduct research is not just a matter of justifying
the importance and validity of one's work; it also involves getting
access to cadet subjects. That access is controlled by the commandant, not the dean of faculty, and the commandant's concern is military training, not research. Further, an institution that aims to provide high quality academic training, military training, and an
introduction to airmanship finds that its scarcest and therefore most

---

°In-house researchers (and their critics) are sensitive to real or imagined pressures to be
either laudatory or confidential. Thus West Point must have increased its credibility by bringing in an investigator who, even though she had some stake (her salary), was well known for
her feminist convictions and a superb (though sometimes cutting) style.

ᴾSome believed this practice was subversive. It had the effect of making civilian instructors more expensive than military instructors, thereby undercutting the GAO recommendation
that more civilian appointments be made to reduce costs.

valuable commodity is cadet time. Providing the occasion for survey research just cannot have a high priority.

The DFBL chairman also cooperated with the Information Office in facilitating my work on this book. Supported by funds from the Ford Foundation, I spent some four months of the first year of integration at the academy, conducting interviews and reading documents.[q]

The Association of Graduates (AOG) was both in and out of the fishbowl.[r] It may be that the Air Force Academy had an advantage as far as fostering change was concerned because it did not yet have any graduates who were generals. Therefore, no top decision makers had to overcome intense personal feelings in considering integration. But the academy does have many of its graduates on staff. Thus many implementers (especially on the dean's side) did have to overcome their own memories. Furthermore, Colorado Springs has a number of civilian alumni who watch as well. The AOG magazine, published by the academy's Office of Graduate Affairs, presented positive accounts of the integration, although some debate appeared in the letters to the editor. From the magazine's articles, one might have thought that graduates were neutral or accepting and that loyal alumni would continue to enhance each other's careers and the academy's development without being diverted by the new gender of cadet. However, almost a year after the women had been admitted, a woman officer who had been invited as a dinner speaker to an AOG meeting in "the Springs" found herself on the hot seat. As debate escalated and decorum deteriorated, the presiding officer finally announced, "I'm a civilian and you can stick it [integration] in your ear." The woman's scheduled appearance at a subsequent Denver AOG meeting was quickly canceled. This incident suggests that correct military behavior may have controlled and concealed opposition that would have been expressed in a civilian setting. When discipline controls behavior and behavior results in good per-

---

[q]During that year the author often wondered how an officer whose instincts were quite different from her own felt about being her sponsor. Three things must have given him comfort. First, outsiders often do not acquire the most embarrassing information; second, as an academic she would be restrained by responsibility (and if she were sufficiently restrained the work probably would not reach the general public); third, the academy generally believed that it was doing such an excellent job that no full account of women's integration could be damaging.

[r]When Ivy League colleges integrated, many found at first that the alumni were the most opposed. The reconciliation that occurred later might have been predicted; after all, half the alumni's children are female.

formance, discipline is clearly a bonus. When it leads to a misreading of attitudes and emotions, it is a potential handicap.

As one reads the account of the planning, implementation, and evaluation of women's entrance into the USAFA, one should remember that the actors felt themselves to be performing in a public place and understood the audience to be both large and variegated. Consideration and calculation, then, were a part of every decision. There was an intense desire not to err and an awareness that criticism could not be avoided. The goal seemed to be to do as well as possible and have a good reason for what one did. Should results prove disappointing, one could still establish that one had done one's best.

CHAPTER

Plans and Plans
and Plans

The more complex the enterprise, the more planning is required for change without disruption. John Kenneth Galbraith developed this idea in *The New Industrial State*, using automobile production as his example.[a] Specifically, Galbraith explained how lead times and the scale of an undertaking affect the production process. Generally, the longer the lead time and the larger the scale, the larger the investment; the larger the investment, the less acceptable risk becomes. Indeed, risk becomes *un*acceptable. This unacceptability fosters great care in planning and encourages whatever follow-through is needed to bring a plan (and thus an investment) to successful realization. For example, if a company has guessed wrong on demand for a product, it does not simply abandon the product—it tries to create a demand.

The Air Force is not a business, but its scale and the complexity of its weapons systems make it like a corporation in requiring long lead times and enormous investments. The result is that minimizing or, better, eliminating error through careful planning is a basic goal.

---

[a]Adam Smith used an equally ordinary example—pin-making—in his examination of eighteenth-century capitalism.

In fact, the word "fail-safe" (which describes devices that prevent error even when failure occurs) is principally associated with the mechanisms that prevent the accidental or unauthorized use of nuclear weapons—weapons that largely belong to the U.S. Air Force.

The Air Force's desire to guarantee against error, then, derives from (1) the need to protect large investments, (2) the need for safety in an environment dominated by complex machinery, and (3) an apparent universal preference of bureaucrats for caution as opposed to innovation.

Safety reminders and posters catch one's eye on every academy elevator ride. The base newspaper provides columns of admonition. The academy's chief of staff has a safety office, and the cadet wing, too, has a safety office. Safety is not often stimulating, but in a profession that involves risking and taking life, it does command attention and respect. Of course, it must be remembered that in the Air Force risk occurs even when there is no war. No matter the absence of combat, officers pay a regular toll for presuming to hurtle through the atmosphere in a variety of fallible aircraft.[b] Moreover, meticulous care seems to be exercised both in using equipment and in caring for it. For example, the well-tended fleet of firsties' cars in dormitory parking lots seems to reflect a love of the machine as well as pride in ownership.

All this is prelude; it attempts to account for the elaborate planning that took place for the entrance of women. It attempts to demonstrate that anticipation and planning are part of the academy's normal routine. To be sure, there was an element of apprehension, if not of actual fear, involved in undertaking so novel and radical a venture as integrating women. In retrospect, one might wonder if the academy did not overreact. Still, long-range and comprehensive planning are integral to the institution, there are good reasons for it, and it is vigorously undertaken.

Early Planning at the Air Force Academy

The "plans shop" is located in the Harmon Hall office of the deputy chief of staff. There, a small staff maintains a file of publications and of long-range and contingency plans both for the academy and

---

[b]A visitor to the academy is struck by the strict compliance with both the letter and spirit of the law and by the extensive safety rules, even in mundane matters such as the driving of an automobile on academy grounds.

for other commands that affect the academy, such as the Air Force Training Command. These plans range from studies of returned prisoners of war and long-range plans for obtaining, training, and utilizing personnel, to plans for a period of civil disturbance or work stoppages. Plans may date from as early as 1970 and bear a variety of security classifications. Those dealing with the admission of women are unclassified. Long-range and, especially, contingency plans are more likely to be "for official use only," "confidential," or "secret"; the Air Force is, however, quite ready to tell everything one may want to know about how it will react to "oil and hazardous substance pollution," or how it will prepare for the funerals of general officers and other VIPs, or how it did prepare for the academy's participation in President Jimmy Carter's inaugural.

A digression is in order here. Before planning itself can be examined in detail, it is important to understand the pressures Air Force planners experience. Fortunately, events surrounding the inaugural activities illustrate those pressures well.

One of forty cadet squadrons, each composed of about one hundred cadets, was selected to participate in the inauguration parade. The choice was based upon its excellence versus that of the other thirty-nine squadrons. During the competition there were no women in the winning squadron. However, by the time of the inauguration several women had been assigned to the squadron and, therefore, made the trip to Washington, D.C. But because the actual parade unit had to be smaller than the squadron, some cadets could not participate in the parade. Their selection was made based upon yet another competition; still, the situation was awkward because none of the women, who had, after all, not participated in winning the original honor, was cut. Fortunately, the traditional principle that every squadron member belongs gave a palatable rationale for an action that necessarily disappointed some young men.

The second part of this decision was more controversial. Military drilling units are assembled by height (tallest to the left front and shortest to the right rear) to produce an aesthetic effect. In this case, however, the direction of march left no women cadets visible to the new Commander-in-Chief, who was understood to want to see women participating. An easy solution was simply to re-size the unit, from right to left. This step was taken, but it was counter to tradition, to normal operation. It was a change made because of the women—an excellent example of the kind of accommodating decision made every day in large organizations. However, because it involved a sensitive subject—women—it was visible, and the decision makers were vulnerable. Moreover, the cadet anger produced was likely to be directed toward the young women, who had *not* asked for the change and who quickly came to abhor any decision that singled them out and thus exposed them. Over and over again the women responded to such situations by asking that they *not* receive special treatment of any kind.

This incident nicely portrays the tensions that continued throughout the first year. While the academy administrators felt a need to let nonmilitary observers know that they were acting positively on their new charge—that they were ungrudging in their acceptance of women cadets—any conspicuous demonstration of their good behavior was seen by many inside the academy as "press agentry," as special treatment, as favoritism, sometimes even as hypocrisy or lying. These administrators, moreover, insisted that the women cadets not become "men." To a lesser degree the administration also understood that to treat the women precisely like men cadets would not result in their having "the same" experience as that of the men, if only because of their limited numbers. Thus women's "differentness" was partially acceptable to the administration. The deep resentment of their cadet peers to any differentness, however, made the young women feel they had to reject all specialness—even that which was clearly justified, which was to their interest, or which was simply something they would have liked.

Planning for the admission of women began in 1972. Col. Robert Hess, who was to become first the alternate and then the incumbent academy Project Officer for the Admission of Women, arrived in Colorado Springs without anticipating this part of his work load in the planning office. It came to hold a special interest for him, however, because he had been one of the young officers who had served as surrogate upperclassmen when the academy first opened and because his son would attend both the prep school and the academy with the first classes to contain young women.

Academy officials began to discuss the possible admission of women in March 1972, when Congress passed the Equal Rights Amendment (E.R.A.). In April the Academy Board of Visitors also discussed the issue, and in May Superintendent A.P. Clark suggested in a letter to his superior at Air Staff (Lt. Gen. Robert J. Dixon) that the academies jointly prepare for what looked like the inevitable entrance of women.[c] Clark's intent was to take the initia-

---

[c] It should be remembered that in 1972 the academy, the elite entryway to an Air Force career, was the only source of officer training still closed to women. The other routes, Air

tive so that admission could be done "right." He sought to control the timing and terms of women's admission so that their absorption would be smooth and "would not degrade combat capacity." (This phrase underpins the thinking of virtually every military official who contemplates women's role in the military. Even when it is not articulated, "combat capacity" is where military thinking begins.)

At the annual academy superintendents' meeting in late May, General Clark found that his strategy was not shared and that the Navy's representative was especially opposed to anticipating the admission of women and to any preparation for their arrival. The position of the Air Force was that, while it was not in favor of either the E.R.A. or of women in the academies, the Navy's policy was not supportable; and so planning began, but without the support of either Annapolis or West Point.

As a first step the Air Force staff appointed an *ad hoc* committee. Its first meeting was held in mid-June in Washington, D.C. Those who attended the meeting were from Air Force Personnel, from the office of the Staff Director of Women in the Air Force (then Col. Billie Bobbitt), and from each Air Force Academy unit—the faculty, physical education and athletics, and the commandant's shop. This committee focused on four subjects: (1) the utilization of women academy graduates in the Air Force, (2) the appropriate selection criteria for women, (3) the feasibility of a single-track program, and (4) the minimum number of women cadets and earliest entrance date acceptable.

In 1972 only five Air Force job classifications were forbidden to women; the most central, pilot, being one of them. However, in August of that year Admiral Elmo R. Zumwalt was to issue his "expanded role" memo on the Navy's utilization of women. Among his new programs was pilot training for women. This innovation was bound to have an effect outside the Navy by diluting the arguments of those who claimed women could never, never be pilots. Of course, the argument seemed weak in view of women's World War II performance as pilots, but the nonmilitary status of those women made it possible for some to ignore the precedent. Moreover, that status was a subject of dispute. More than a thousand women (thirty-eight of whom were killed) served as pilots in the Women Airforce Service Pilots (WASP) during World War II. They

---

Force Reserve Officers' Training Corps (AFROTC) and Officer Training School (OTS), had been supplying women officers for a number of years. Only the academy was exclusively male.

later argued that they ought to receive veterans' benefits. The Veterans Administration argued that they were never given military commissions and were, therefore, ineligible. Congress decided in favor of the women in November of 1977.

Utilization was controlled by an Act of Congress (Section 8549, Title 10 U.S.C.) that prohibits women from flying in combat and by a U.S. Air Force policy of not training limited-duty pilots and navigators. Moreover, the Air Staff took the position that even passage of the E.R.A. would not nullify the Congressional prohibition against using women in combat. Therefore, the planners were told to assume that women academy graduates would not fly. This decision directly affected the academy's planning for women by restricting the number of women who would be admitted. This restriction occurred because of the way the academy shapes its admissions decisions. First, the Air Force determines how many new officers it will require in any given year. Next, it decides how many of them "could be" women, given their nonflying status.[d] Third, a desired percentage of women officers entering officer ranks from the academy (as opposed to other commissioning sources) is set. Next, the academy considers the probable attrition rate and admits as many women as it believes necessary to produce the requisite number of graduates. The decision to admit, then, is one of "demand" and "use," not one of "supply" or "qualifications." Since the number of positions allotted to women so controls their opportunity, the precise method by which that number is determined is crucial (and is sometimes hard to pinpoint).

The planners reasoned that, since the academy was supplying 16 percent of needed male accessions each year, it should produce 16 percent of needed female accessions. In 1972 the Air Force anticipated a need for 600 women officers in 1976; 16 percent of that number would be 96. Male attrition at the academies over the four years had averaged some 35 percent; using that attrition rate, some 148 young women would have to be admitted if the goal was to graduate 96 of them.[e] But how to select them?

[d]This status means not only that women cannot fly but also that they cannot participate in a flying/nonflying rotation of assignments.

[e]When women entered the academy in 1976, there were 157 in the first class. That number was easily reached. Interestingly, however, there was little debate (or, at least, little that reached official ears) whether that share was fair or whether so many places should have been allotted to men. The debate that did occur concerned the reservation of slots for *women*, not for men. Many cadets apparently were persuaded that women could not have competed in open competition for the 4 to 10 percent of the slots held for them by the three academies.

Selection criteria had to accomplish several things. First, they had to ensure a minimum level of performance; second, they had to produce approximately the targeted number of women—that is, the number the Air Force wished to enroll; third, they had to be similar to those applied to men. If the criteria for the selection of women were too discrepant from those for men (no matter what the direction), controversy would result.

The selection criteria for physical fitness and aptitude were of particular concern because it would have been possible to end up with few or no female cadets if precisely the same physical tests and standards were required of women as were required of men. Moreover, Congress had specified that "minimum essential adjustments" in physical standards would be appropriate.

Criteria for leadership activities were assumed to be less difficult because "equivalent" activities could be found. The question of the equivalency of leading a single-sex versus an integrated group, or of leading an all-male versus an all-female group, did not arise. Indeed, given the opportunity structure of most high schools, the activities of young men and young women probably had to be valued equally even when the activities were very different from each other. At the academy, however, cadets would have to meet the *same* challenges, and it is not clear that Saturday mornings spent reading to the bedridden or teaching crafts to children would prepare a doolie as well as participating in a marching band or becoming an Eagle Scout.

Academic standards might seem to pose no problem at all: nothing is as easy to compare as Scholastic Aptitude Test (SAT) scores and grade points. Yet even these criteria were tricky, for the academy did not have a single academic standard. There are two. Unlike the other DOD academies, the Air Force Academy actually has two kinds of cadets—pilot-eligible and navigator-eligible (referred to as "rated") and cadets not eligible for flight training ("nonrated"). Over the years, their ratio has been approximately 70–10–20.[f] Because so many more candidates can meet nonrated physical standards, competition for those slots is more intense than for the rated slots and the corresponding academic standards have tended to be higher.[g] The question, then, was whether the women (who would

[f]For 1977 (class of 1981), the ratio shifted to 60–10–30 (pilot eligible-navigator eligible-nonflying), reflecting a decreased need for academy-trained pilots.

[g]In the guide for students and counselors (1976–77), the average Scholastic Aptitude Test scores for "flying" cadets are 544 verbal and 636 math. The scores for "nonflying" cadets are 596 verbal and 682 math.

not be rated even if physically eligible) should compete only in the more academically competitive nonrated category, whether those physically eligible (except for their sex) should compete in the pilot and navigator categories, or whether the women should simply compete separately for however many slots were available to them. If women were required to meet the scholastic criteria set for men not eligible to fly, all the women would have a standard met by only 20 percent of the men. Of course, even if the women did not have to compete scholastically for acceptance against nonrated men, they *would* have to compete against them throughout their careers; thus, if the women were chosen in a less selective way, they might suffer a long-run disadvantage.

The decision was to take "the best" women. As it worked out, 58 percent of the women would not be eligible to fly. Only 16 percent of the men would not be eligible.

The academy was committed to a single-track program from the beginning (i.e., it was determined to give women the same training men received). However, it was also understood from the beginning that adjustments would have to be made. Physical education expected to make the largest adjustment; in fact, it anticipated that as much as 50 percent of its program would have to be altered. The commandant's shop expected some modification, the faculty almost none.

One must remember that much of the Air Force Academy's motivation in launching its planning was to pre-empt judicial, legislative, or executive action to control better the circumstances of women's entrance. The Air Force believed a minimum of eighteen months would be needed to develop an adequate recruitment pool, and a twelve-month lead time would be required to design and procure women's uniforms. As far as numbers went, the Air Force wished to recruit a group of women as its first entrants rather than to receive a handful of judicially required admittees. The academy staff wanted the women to have a sense of group identification. Second, it believed that budgetary reasons dictated a large enough group that per capita costs for the women cadets would not be dramatically different from those for male cadets. Finally, the staff wished to determine for itself the number admitted, because the absolute number would affect the women's management. The numbers 100 to 150 consistently appear in planning documents. (The lowest number ever mentioned was 10, the highest 210.) The smallest number actually recommended for entry was 44. This figure represented the number that would be required to fill one flight after attrition.[h]

Deciding to write a plan for women's admission and establish criteria for it took several months of negotiations. The drafting itself was almost an anticlimax, for it involved little more than listing and assigning responsibilities. Indeed, the initial draft was completed over twenty-four hours in July 1972. Six individuals from the planning office, using the "Staff Reference Chart" to ensure that all aspects of cadet life were covered, simply outlined the decisions to be made, the actions to be taken, and the academy unit(s) responsible for each.[i] The draft did not discuss the moral or political aspects of sex integration; rather, it simply assigned responsibility for implementation, should such integration, for whatever reason, come to pass. Contingency plans, after all, exist to preclude embarrassment; they are not predictive, nor are they supposed to advocate or affect policy.

During July the draft was sent to all units for elaboration and response. Even though the planners' mode of thought was "what" and "how," the most important contribution of the drafted plan (and of women's admission) may have been that it forced consideration of "why." There were certain programs in which no one believed women belonged, but to justify their exclusion required a rationale. Thus assessment of those programs was begun and their very necessity, long unexamined, was scrutinized. For example, programs such as SERE (Survival, Evasion, Resistance, and Escape) and boxing were felt by many (maybe even most) academy officials to be "wrong" for women. The rationale offered was that women would never serve in combat and that the training was, therefore, unnecessary. Justifying why women should not do something often spoiled the logic of why all men should; in the Air Force many men know they will never see combat, and some women know that they may see it. If the logic for programs like SERE and boxing is combat preparation, then some women probably *should* receive such training and some men now receiving it should be free to abstain. The latter might contend, in fact, that when some males receive unnecessary and unpleasant training they are experiencing "reverse discrimination." This subject will be discussed later, but it should be

[h] The implicit reasoning was that women would be trained separately and would sometimes function as an all-female unit.

[i] The Staff Reference Chart is an organizational chart; an abbreviated version is found in Appendix III.

noted here that boxing represents a special hazard to an Air Force cadet. If knocked unconscious, he must obtain a waiver before regaining eligibility for pilot training. Further, it is dangerous for anyone. In the spring of 1977, a West Point cadet died from injuries sustained while boxing—an activity in which he would never participate in combat. At some point a male nonrated Air Force cadet will almost certainly challenge the boxing requirement as not being germane to training; his case will be strengthened if women are not participating in it.

Reassessment, the re-examination of purpose, continued from 1972 through 1977. While not specifically called for in the early planning, at a minimum, reassessment prompted a scramble for new rationales; at a maximum, a new spirit of inquiry. At the same time, resistance to change may have been heightened because of the fear that any change, no matter how sensible, would be attributed to the mollifying effects of women's entrance.

In August 1972 Superintendent Clark tried for the last time to elicit the cooperation of the other academies in planning for the admission of women. This action was probably provoked by Admiral Zumwalt's continuing activities in expanding the role of naval women. The action that was probably most unsettling to his naval colleagues (and their wives) was the decision to place women on ships by assigning them to the hospital ship *Sanctuary* (no longer in use). The experiment was a "success," but it had no immediate effect on naval policy. General Dixon of the Air Staff responded that there was just no pressure in Washington to admit women. In fact, he noted that Mr. William Hogan, Jr., had called from the office of Rep. F. Edward Hébert, Chairman of the House Armed Services Committee, to indicate that the Congressman would be very *displeased* if women were admitted and that the "intent of Congress" was "no, hell, no!" There was some positive pressure at Air Staff, however, for Gen. Jeanne Holm had argued strenuously that Dixon's letter to Clark did not reflect "our" policy and that the initiative to admit women remains with "us" and does not require Congressional action of any kind.

The Air Force decided to proceed with its own planning, and by late summer responses to the July draft had been prepared by various academy units. The plan was, for the most part, to be an in-house document. One external source of information was tapped, however. Eight academy officers, including one woman from the cadet records office, visited Lackland Air Force Base late in August to review the training programs for women who would become officers and for women who would become airmen. The first program had a product similar to that of the academy (second lieutenants); the second dealt with a similar age-group. Both had WAF (women) officers involved in women's training. (Indeed, one WAF squadron commander was Maj. Diane Ordez, who as a lieutenant colonel was appointed assistant dean of faculty when women entered the academy.) The two training programs differed at that time in that officer training was partially integrated, while that of airmen was completely segregated.

The trip was made to assess plans for facility modifications at the academy and to determine whether the USAFA plan had addressed all aspects of training. Of special concern was women's response to "stress training";[j] At that time there was virtually no information available on the subject. The 1972 site visit findings are important because they contrast with the follow-up visit's findings made in 1975. They are also important because they nicely foreshadow the academy experience that was to come.

First, the women and men in officers' training at Lackland agreed that their separate billeting isolated the women, even though the women were assigned to male flights (an organizational unit of officer candidates) for academics, drill, and meal formations. In fact, "integrated" billeting (which provides floor-by-floor separation) was then under study. Second, women felt they could compete, and the commanding officer believed the pride and spirit of units with women was higher than that of units without women. But some male trainees believed that women held their squadrons back and that the women enjoyed some favoritism. Third, the women's training did not include physical stress, verbally abusive confrontations, or weapons familiarization. Academy officials who prepared the trip report probably felt some apprehension because the minimal discipline and regulation they observed at Lackland *was* described by women trainees as "stressful." It seems likely, then, that because of their different prior experience women perceived the same training differently from their male peers. Thus academy officials would confront the problem of eliciting uniform performance from cadets with disparate understanding.

[j]Stress training encompasses both physical and mental stress. At the Air Force Academy, entering cadets experience the following forms of psychological stress: sleep loss, isolation, perception and information deprivation, time compression, exhaustion, possible failure, and loss of status. This stress is intentionally induced to teach cadets to handle, or at least endure, psychological stress. Tradition has justified such training for men, but tradition holds that women cannot endure such stress.

The younger women, the ones who were training as airmen, emphasized (1) their desire for "as equal" a program as possible; (2) their interest in soaring, jumping, and flying; (3) the low value of their physical conditioning program; and (4) the lack of time provided for participating in sports. Their comments suggest that they felt under-challenged and that they supported a single-track program. At the same time, however, none of the women objected to twenty hours of "personal development" (a charm course) or to the special "House of Fashion" for the sale of women's uniforms. Commanding officers of the airmen (women) emphasized that women responded best to positive criticism and that they responded differently from men.[k] Yet the training for women was completely separate from that of men, and "male" discipline had not been tried on them. There were, in fact, no "controls" upon which to base judgment.

The Lackland visit confirmed the planners in their preliminary decision to have a segregated female squadron with a woman AOC (Air Officer Commanding) and women ATOs (Air Training Officers). It also confirmed the decision to utilize segregated billeting, although the report did suggest that integration could be considered by the second class year, when a minimum of ten women could be assigned to each squadron. Thus the goal of avoiding tokenism in the entering class was to be applied to squadron assignments as well. Finally, the principle of women's fullest possible participation in all activities was emphasized again and again: the only limitations to be accepted were those relating to "upper body strength."

In assessing the provisional plan in light of the Lackland AFB visit, the staff's re-evaluation focused on what seemed to be the unnecessary exclusion of women from some aspects of physical education and basic training. Some additions were also recommended, such as course material on women in the Air Force and on sex education, full-length mirrors in women's rooms, and a charm school course. It became apparent, at last, that more study of women's response to "stress situations" was required, that an orientation for male cadets before the arrival of women might be valuable, and that participation by male cadets in the brainstorming and

[k]"Positive motivation" would become an academy watchword during the summer of 1976. All officials would vigorously deny that it had anything to do with the admission of women. Nevertheless, it was a style of military leadership that had been customarily practiced more on women than on men, and it would prove very hard to disassociate women from the new discipline in cadets' minds.

planning phases of women's admission would benefit both the cadets and the program.

The conclusions from the 1972 visit to Lackland were signed by all members of the team. There was, however, no agreement on the rightness of women's entrance. The commandant's shop, which would bear the primary responsibility for the women's training, found the prospect especially unsettling. Perhaps the moderate position was one that went, "It's fine, but not on *my* watch."[l]

The Pink Plans

In September 1972 the first pink-covered contingency plan was delivered to Superintendent Clark. (His copy had a special cover with a Playboy Playmate photo.) Revised but very similar plans were prepared in April 1973, December 1973, July 1975, and October 1975.

Over that period, the plans show only slight changes in detail and emphasis. The first (1972) plan contained more than 60 pages and was almost as complete as the last. Thirty-two officers were tasked by their divisions to plan the "Integration of Females into the Cadet Wing."[m] Three of the thirty-two were women, but they were assigned as WAF representatives, not as representatives of their unit. They included a captain and a major, both faculty members, and a lieutenant colonel from the Admissions Office.

After outlining the planners' assumptions, the core of the plan assigned particular responsibilities to each division; these were to "include, but not necessarily be limited to, the specific tasks that follow." A list of each unit's regular duties followed. The bulk of the plan consisted of eight annexes (chapters) prepared by the individual divisions. Each described what would be done during the stages of "preparation, transition, and execution." The transition stage was described as lasting from the time the decision to admit women became official until the day of their admission. The most thorough annex was that of the athletic department, which included no fewer than nine appendices.

It must be emphasized that each annex was the work of an already functioning unit. Each had handled a large number of cadets, and

[l]That is, "It's all right in principle, but I don't want anything to do with it."

[m]By the fall of 1975, the title and mission were changed to the "Admission of Women into the Cadet Wing." The goal was to accomplish all this "smoothly."

those cadets varied as to background, physique, temperament, capacity, and race. The divisions were asked to detail any changes that must occur because of the addition of women to the cadet wing. In theory, the changes, modifications, or both were to respond to physiological differences only. In fact, sociological and psychological differences had borne heavily on the responses from the beginning.

For instance, even though West Point went so far as to write a "justification for deviation" statement, arguing that "differences in the anatomy" made it "impractical" to have identical uniforms, the Air Force never even considered identical uniforms; and all three academies went far beyond anatomical requirements in attempting to design attractive, practical uniforms for the incoming women.[n] All provided uniforms with skirts as well as pants. The skirts were for women only—and obviously for sociological, not physiological, reasons.

The women's uniform issue totaled $237.93 more than the men's.[o] Many items cost the same for both sexes (e.g., "Cover, Raincap. 1 ea., $1.28"). A few items cost men more, but the difference was usually $5.00 or less. Some items, like handbags at $23.10 each, were for women only. Still, many apparently similar items cost women more. A good example is the white mess dress jacket, which cost women $41.00 as compared to $29.52 for men. Further, since women needed both skirts and trousers for summer and winter, while men needed only trousers, women's total costs were bound to be higher. The point is that all cadets would be receiving the same pay but women would have to spend more of that pay on required uniform purchases. It could even be said that the result was that women were in effect receiving less pay for performing the same duties. A lack of bulk purchasing, high start-up costs, and the need for extra tailoring and more variety (skirts and pants) all contributed to the women's higher uniform costs.[p]

Again, variations in the Pink Plans from 1972 to 1975 were few. Some involved word changes, as in the title; others involved a

[n]The Air Force Academy's women's uniforms were designed by a company specializing in band uniforms; their "attractiveness" was a matter of some debate. The original male cadet uniforms had been done by Cecil B. DeMille.

[o]Cadets purchase their uniforms out of their cadet pay.

[p]One solution might have been to establish separate uniform allowances and to give each cadet an allowance that would cover all required purchases. Another might have been to charge all cadets an average-cost-for-entering issue without distinguishing between women's and men's different costs. After all, the academy would spend more per male cadet than per female cadet on food each year.

change in nuance. For instance, an early plan promised women "as much privacy as possible." By the fall of 1975, women's billeting was planned to ensure "necessary privacy." Only a few modifications in the plan resulted from specific critiques. One such was the decision to require pre-marital counseling for both women and men or to abandon it altogether.

The overall pattern seems to have been one of tentatively exploring full integration, drawing back from it, and at the last minute moving toward it again. The plan shop's earliest draft emphasized the need for a single-track program, a consideration of "new attitudes on mixed use of dormitories," and the attainment of a "nonsegregated living and working environment." However, as other academy units began to contribute their appendices, separateness crept into the plan. Perhaps the plans shop's willingness to contemplate the kind of integration practiced by civilian institutions was the work of "theoreticians," while the units' responses represented the caution of "implementers." Interestingly enough, this caution was not sustained. In late 1975 (after Congress had approved the legislation authorizing admission but before the President had signed it), after the plans of West Point and Annapolis had been developed, the Air Force made a last-minute shift in the direction of "sameness." Thus the October 1975 plan again called for a single-track program, although only to the "maximum extent possible, while at the same time ensuring a sound logical program for the training of women officers." Furthermore, "the environment," which now entailed only cadet "working" (not living) areas, was to be "integrated" as opposed to "nonsegregated."

At the academy, differences over policy and policy modifications were worked out through debate, negotiation, and occasionally through direct order. For example, the planners strongly supported the idea of ATOs, but the commandant's shop did not like the idea of using women officers as surrogate upperclassmen. The issue was finally resolved by a decision of the superintendent. Even in a conflict like this, however, direct overruling can be and often is avoided. If an opponent of a plan, for instance, is in a position to recommend options to his superior, he can influence the selection by proposing five courses of action. Four of the five will include his preferred policy (no surrogate upperclasswomen); one of the proposals will include the use of ATOs. The proposer, then, can be over-ruled by his superior's decision to use the one program that recommends their use.

While most of the planning was done at the academy and in a

decentralized manner, the final plan was formally reviewed at the Pentagon by the Air Staff in the summer of 1975. Some changes were recommended. The first was in language. It was suggested that, because "woman" was less sexual and "limited to 'human beings,'" it should replace "female" in the title and generally throughout the plan. This was done. Also, the word "restroom" was recommended as a replacement for "latrine."[q]

Second, Air Staff urged full participation for women in SERE and their fuller participation in intramurals. Especially recommended was their participation in cross-country, soccer, flickerball, and handball. (Flickerball is a game played [at some military facilities] with a football but according to basketball rules.) The point was that women were *already* participating in these activities at Fairchild Air Force Base and at Squadron Officer School (SOS). (Squadron Officer School at Maxwell Air Force Base provides in-service training.) The academy's planning was behind existing practice; the Air Force's most visible and elite training institution was planning to do less than its other units were already doing.

A third recommendation made in Washington concerned summer programs. The Air Force was prepared to enroll women in all of its own programs and took the position that if RECONDO and UDT training were opened to women by their Army and Navy sponsors, then Air Force women should be permitted to elect them.[r] However, neither the Air Staff nor the academy apparently even considered withdrawing all academy cadets from activities or programs that discriminated against any cadet. Thus continuing the exchange program with the French military academy, which would not accept women, seemed no problem.[s]

In her comments, the Director of Women in the Air Force pointed out that if sex education courses were needed, both men and women should have them, and she added that the phrase "the problem related to" the selection of women cadets might be dropped.[t] She also

[q]Implementation is never perfect. There are still doors at the academy labeled "Women's Latrine."

[r]The Army faced a problem in that four of its five (summer) specialty training programs did not admit women, although the problem did not come up immediately since the programs did not take place until the end of the cadets' second year. Ironically, the one summer program open to Army women was airborne (parachute training)—a kind of training *not* open to Air Force women at that time.

[s]As it turned out, the French program changed (to admit women) before the issue arose.

[t]Even at this stage women were mostly understood as "problems" as far as most of the academy's staff was concerned.

reminded the academy that the cadet store would have to stock cosmetics and that the phrase "the maximum number" might lead to questions about quotas. Most important, she did not object to "separate units" for women nor to the withholding of "combat oriented training." This position might have been expected because the separation of "command and control" from training and work fit both her own experience and the current practice of the Air Force. Still, the concurrence of one of the top women officers in the Air Force may have given the academy undue confidence in its planning. In the planning and implementation phases, men seemed to gain assurance by having women officers concur in their decisions, even though there was little disposition toward seeing even military women as experts on women in the military.[u]

The fact was that the degree to which integration was to occur at the academy remained ambiguous, and in other Air Force training programs it fluctuated constantly. Commitment to a common program "to the greatest extent possible" left room for the same kind of debate that accompanied the phrase "with all deliberate speed"— used by the Supreme Court to describe the rate at which public schools should become racially integrated.

The office of the commandant prepared a thorough exposition of just how an integrated and yet separate command-and-control pattern could work. In fact, a preference for a "parallel and equal, not mingled and equal," organization was expressed in August 1972. Much of the argument rested on the idea that a separate program would benefit women by giving them more opportunity to acquire leadership experience and win high Military Order of Merit (MOM) rankings. Thus, according to the early plans, even if women were to train with men, the command structure was to remain distinct. In 1972, for instance, WAF personnel requirements listed by the commandant included one AOC "per separate female unit," one special assistant, one military training instructor, and one junior officer per ten female cadets. By the fall of 1975, the WAF requirements called for two AOCs, two planning officers, and one ATO (a junior officer) per ten women cadets. References to an all-woman squadron continued, although two alternatives were also being explored: (1) a women's squadron with male upperclassmen living in their area and serving as trainers, and (2) full integration except for billeting.

When the planning stage was over (by virtue of President Ford's signature on P.L. 94–106), the issue of command was still not settled. Ironically, it was probably the Air Force's preplanning efforts that led to this ambiguity and indecision. Separate organization was *de rigeur* when the planning began in 1972, and separatist assumptions underpinned basic decisions about staffing, billeting, and training. However, between 1972 and 1976 views on sex integration evolved rapidly outside the academy. Inside there may also have been some movement toward commonality; however, because integrated billets were never a real possibility and because there was never a conscious shift toward fuller integration and a restatement of integration policy, there was never a redefinition of staff and program requirements. Thus when early assumptions became outdated, the planning superstructure already erected on them inhibited their re-examination, even though later policy making proceeded from rather different assumptions.

Again, the academy's competing objectives were full integration in a single-track program and a group identity for the outnumbered women. But there was a third but latent objective, too: the academy's great desire to avoid embarrassing incidents—particularly those resulting from the physiological differences (and resulting affinities) between women and men.[v] This anxiety resulted in an unstated but constant conviction that young women's and young men's bedrooms simply should not be side by side. Until this sentiment was overcome, there was little chance that the principle of integration could be fully realized. Similarly, preserving women's identity as women would be difficult as long as only 150 women were to be admitted to a wing of nearly 4,500. Thus it was almost impossible to distinguish the component of separatism derived from administrators' fears from the component based on a belief that women needed a "critical mass." One simply could not say whether a separationist policy "really" existed because it was "what's best for the women" or whether it existed because of administrators' worries about "incidents."

The "final" decisions on the administrative responsibilities of command and control were not made until just before the women arrived. Although it had been decided as early as the fall of 1975 to

[v]All administrators must deal with "incidents." However, these physiological differences would create a new kind of incident for academy officials. This would be unpleasant for an administrator because no safe routine for managing them existed and because the media would be likely to publicize what it considered "news."

assign them to "specific, existing squadrons" for their training (as opposed to assigning them to "separate/distinctive female units"), that "final" organizational decision lasted for only one semester. Moreover, the second semester's reorganization solved some problems, left others untouched, and produced new ones. Even changes designed to increase stability are often times likely to lead to more change.

Plans and Views at the Other Academies

The completed and approved Air Force plan was sent to the other academies in the fall of 1975. The Merchant Marine and Coast Guard Academies responded with thanks. No acknowledgement came from the Navy.[w] The Army responded by noting how similar the Air Force plan was to its own (but did not send a copy).

A September inter-service conference on the admission of women was held at the Air Force Academy, and there the academies had the opportunity to test their thinking against that of their counterparts. The stated purposes of the meeting were to discuss "problem areas" concerning the admission of women and to learn as much as possible from Merchant Marine representatives, whose cadets had just completed their first co-educational year.[x]

Because the Merchant Marine Academy admitted women two years before the military academies (and without a Congressional mandate), its contribution came from experience. It had followed a liberal dormitory visitation policy; in fact, a bulkhead originally separating the men's and women's areas was soon removed. No quota was set for women's admittance, and a low-key approach was followed in inaugurating the new policy. Nevertheless, press coverage proved a constant irritant. Men were resentful (jealous?) and women annoyed (embarrassed?) by the media attention. That women's uniforms cost more than men's was considered a potential

[w]The Navy never did produce a public "ops plan," although at a September 1975 meeting on the subject of women's admission a cover for such a plan was produced. It featured two admirals crying over their beer and one saying to the other: "If God had wanted women in the Academies, He would have made them men."

[x]The West Point delegation pointed out that it did not use the terms "problem areas" or "females" in discussing the admission of women. The language had, of course, been altered in Air Force planning documents. Its reappearance in working papers suggests that officers were still talking to each other about a "problem."

source of trouble for the military academies, and the Merchant Marine also believed that placing more women in key positions would have made its transition smoother.

The Army's planning for admission did not really gear up until the Congressional legislation was passed in the spring of 1975, although a two-page plan on the "forced" admission of women was in existence as early as 1973. A more thorough study, dated September 1975, was made public and distributed at the conference. This plan differed from that of the Air Force in several ways. First, it assumed "a small number of women." Second, great emphasis was given to the theme of "equality": whether the subject was admission, training, education, or graduation, "equality" was the key, and "equality" meant "similarity." Any deviations from the "policy of equality" required "justification" and the approval of the superintendent, an approval that would be granted only on the basis of "physiological differences." Strong emphasis, then, was placed on equality as identity and on centralized decision making. Any variation had to be personally authorized by the superintendent himself; it was clear where inertia lay in such a process; still, some variations were permitted. For example, it was decided that women's haircuts need not be as short as men's; nevertheless, since the cuts would not be identical, the legitimacy of deviating from "equality" had to be explicitly stated.

In contrast, the Air Force was from the beginning concerned about having "too few" women cadets. There was a minimum number it did *not* wish to fall below. There was an assumption that the "successful" training of women would necessitate "a sizeable group with which [the women could] identify." "Success," then, was a goal from the outset. In the Air Force plan there was not only a sense of seeking a positive outcome but also a sense of trying to choose "correct" principles. Furthermore, the Air Force did not make "equality" a controlling objective, nor did it assume that identical treatment would necessarily produce identical or equal results. In fact, the Air Force did not want "equal" results in that it assumed that the academy's mission was to produce high quality men *and* high quality women officers. Thus when the Air Force drew up its plans for women cadets, its model was not only the male cadet, but also women officers. For example, the medical criteria for women's selection were not male cadet criteria, nor even "modified" male cadet criteria; they were the Air Force commissioning standards for women. Knowing that it wanted its women officers to be *women* officers helped the Air Force avoid debates about whether women should have men's haircuts. Yet, the image of a top-notch woman officer was hazy in most officers' minds. Indeed, none of the male officers involved had ever worked *for* a woman officer, few had ever worked *with* one, and only a handful had had one work *for* them.[y]

The chief concern expressed by the Air Force Academy at the conference was over the acceptance (or nonacceptance) of the women by the male cadets.[z] The Navy, on the other hand, was primarily concerned about the U.S. Code that severely limited the assignment of women to ships. The other worry the Navy expressed was over its company officers (those who held command positions over cadet units, similar to Air Force AOCs). Few of those officers would have had any previous professional experience with women, whether as superiors, peers, or even as subordinates; the Navy worried about how to prepare them to be effective commanders of women.

Other areas discussed during the counterpart sessions were pregnancy, sexual intercourse, fraternization, counseling, and visiting in rooms.[a] Each of these items was important to administrators, but not because physiological differences required modifications in the training of individuals. These problems were distinctly social and arose from the possibility that excessive interaction between certain individuals could produce an emotional environment disruptive to the training of all. Physiological differences *did* bear on the Physical Aptitude Examination (PAE), on basic (first summer) training, and on physical education and military training, but they had little to do with most of the items under discussion.

[y]One learns a great deal about the person one works for. Since virtually all of the academy staff's experience with women officers was limited to junior officers involved in auxiliary activities, the planners' thinking about what was required for the full development of women's talents was confined to the norms these women established. Had more of the planners worked under a senior woman officer, their expectations might have been different.

[z]They were right to worry, as it turned out. Still, the Air Force may have set its goal higher than the other academies in making acceptance a goal!

[a]The Department of Defense asked the academies to develop a uniform policy in several areas: elements of the Physical Aptitude Test (PAT), the methods of predicting female cadet attrition, and pregnancy. The latter proved difficult and Pentagon drawers began to bulge with sixteen months' worth of pregnancy "position papers." West Point wanted flexibility and was willing to consider abortion; the Air Force was less willing, and its line on both birth control and abortion was distinctly chilling. The Navy argued for a policy of disenrolling a cadet for being pregnant or causing pregnancy. This last position was the one approved by the Secretary of Defense, although some officials argued that the punishment would inevitably be unequal since pregnancy is a "fact" but paternity is only an "opinion." (The Air Force Academy had its last paternity case in May 1975. However, it was uncontested, and the ultimate reason for dismissal was not paternity but low grades.)

In addition, "manning" (staffing), psychological training, the impact of the media, and uniforms were on the agenda. But a strict interpretation of changes required by integration was simply not possible, nor were those issues the ones really bothering policy makers. A rigid policy of "no changes except for those necessitated by demonstrated physical differences" was too theoretical and simply not possible. If such a policy were followed too closely, female failure or withdrawal would surely result. If proclaimed and then not followed, charges of hypocrisy or deceit could develop among dissident cadets (and staff). To some degree, the first alternative was that adopted by West Point and the second that chosen by Air Force. By the end of the first year, however, their programs converged to a remarkable degree.

USAFA Singularities

The Air Force Academy proposed two policies that differed from any offered by the other academies: segregated billeting and the Air Training Officers (ATO) program. Dormitory accommodation plans show separate billeting from the beginning. In the first-draft plan, a need to explore integrated housing was expressed. The last (and official) plan stated that "further evaluation of integrated billeting will be considered at a later date." Both plans suggest some openness on the issue, but top administrators were, in fact, adamant about separate billets. Their motivation must partly have been old-fashioned and moral. However, the celebrated Merchant Marine incident (a male and female cadet were discovered in bed together) must have reinforced the authorities' desire to avoid trouble. (See Chapter 5.) The irony, of course, is that while only the Air Force billeted its women and men separately, only the Air Force was to have an officially known cadet pregnancy in 1976–77. (The circumstances were so unusual that even the Air Force's meticulous planning failed to anticipate them. See Chapter 7.)

In all the academy's plans, "manpower" requirements specified a need during the first two years for two women Air Officers Commanding (AOCs), two other women officers, and one Air Training Officer (ATO) per ten women cadets.[b] All these officers were to be

[b] AOCs command a cadet squadron of approximately one hundred cadets. The ATOs were to serve as surrogate upperclasswomen. They were to do this amid thousands of genuine (male) upperclassmen.

under the commandant; their need was predicated on separate female units. As the plans changed toward an integrated command structure, the ATO concept remained intact. However, the two women officers first planned as military training instructors were shifted to staff planning, and the two women AOCs continued to be written into the plans. By the June 1976 implementation, however, the women cadets were assigned to existing (male) squadrons, and *no* women were slotted as AOCs, as commanders of squadrons.[c]

Why? Two things probably happened. First, one of the individuals slotted to move into a female AOC position had been extensively involved in the preparation for women's admission. During the process she may have lost too many battles or the confidence of too many people. Whatever the reason, the administration seemed reluctant to give that individual the command of one of its forty squadrons of cadets. With the integration of women into existing units, moreover, no one squadron would have had very many women; specifically, none would have more than 5 percent women. This distribution meant that a woman AOC would command some 100 eighteen to twenty-four-year-old men, many of them deeply hostile to the very idea of women at the academy. It was a task that the administration was probably not ready to give to *any* woman, no matter how well qualified she was.

There are a number of comments that might be made about the academy's decision not to use women as AOCs. The first is that the academy gave the appearance of believing women good enough to command women, but not good enough to command men. One implication of such a sentiment was that women did not need the best leadership. Second, the "not ready" line of reasoning, as is often the case in discussing social change, is troubling. Cadets clearly were not ready for the change, but cadets often are not ready for particular academy policies and programs; they simply have to live with them. Only a very reflective officer could examine his thinking thoroughly enough to know whether decisions he made based on *others'* unreadiness actually involved his *own* unreadiness. (One Navy study showed that individuals regularly reported themselves as having more contemporary sex-role attitudes than others of their sex.)[1] Third, the concept of "ratio" was clearly at work in the academy's decision making. Specifically, one general officer explained that it would be artificial to have a woman AOC, since women represented such a small percentage of the wing. When the ratio argument was

[c] Two women officers ended up in staff planning and two in military instruction.

made using a different base, he seemed genuinely surprised to discover that one female AOC out of forty AOCs would be appropriate for the *first* year only, and that the correct proportion would quickly rise to as many as four out of forty. Another general officer pointed out that the job of an AOC was so sensitive that one simply could not "risk" putting a woman in the position. When asked how the academy first came to put a black into the job and whether that "first" did not entail similar risks, he replied, "Yes, but in that case we ran an even greater risk if we didn't do it."[d]

There are two important historical factors to be noted in analyzing why the Air Force chose the two singular policies of separate billets and junior officers as ATOs.

First, the Air Force began its detailed planning early. It did so at a time (1972) when there was a planned, rapid expansion in the number of women in the Air Force and a reduction in career fields closed to them. There were more women colonels than there had ever been (fourteen); one was selected for the National War College, while another was assigned command of a 2,000-member Air Force unit.[e] A recently integrated ROTC had recruited more than 1,400 women, pregnancy waivers were being granted to both enlisted women and officers, and dependency claims had been defined judicially as the same for male and for female members of the Air Force. Within the Air Force, then, there was increased acceptance of women, their role was being vastly expanded, and there was a thrust toward equality.

But a separate directorate for women in the Air Force continued to exist, OTS would not fully integrate or give women command of integrated flights until 1974, and most women commanders commanded all-WAF and, therefore, all-women squadrons. Furthermore, even though enlisted women might be assigned to a male commanding officer for duty, they were attached to a WAF squadron for "housing, counselling, off-duty supervision and discipline, morale and welfare."[2] Thus when planning began, the Air Force model

[d]Women's incapacity to make it seem risky for institutions to not respond to their needs and wishes makes them different from racial minorities, which are perceived as having limits and bottom-line requirements, and as being ready to punish if abuse or exploitation reach certain levels. It seems that, when it comes to retaliation, women have little credibility.

[e]By December 31, 1976, there were only four women colonels. This is an important pattern. Women were being invited to enter institutions (at the bottom) just about the time those who had entered during World War II were retiring (from near the top). As the number of women increased in entry level positions, the number at higher levels was actually decreasing. In between, in "the pipeline," women were few in number.

was to work together but to live and be administratively controlled separately. The academy's separate billeting, then, followed current practice. Ironically, the separate WAF squadron organization was phased out by the Air Force; indeed, it ended July 1, 1976, just as women entered the academy. Had the Air Force *not* planned so early, had it waited until Congress actually passed the legislation, it would have had a more integrated force as its example, one which would probably have led planners to a more integrated program. In this case, the early planning probably caused the Air Force to commit itself to a model that became *passé* before it came to pass.

There was an historical reason for the emphasis on role models, too. When the Air Force Academy was founded in 1955, it adopted much of West Point's philosophy and training techniques. One part of the training involved using upper class cadets as trainers of the entering class. Upperclassmen, of course are essential to the layered, "class" system. A cadet hierarchy is required; a dichotomous cadet-officer division is not enough. In 1955, therefore, the Air Force brought in a group of 134 young officers to serve as surrogate upperclassmen for its 600 entering cadets. It was a logical extension of that experience to assume that the separately billeted women would benefit from having a surrogate upper class for their training.[f] Studies of other institutions that had recently integrated women into their programs, moreover, drew attention to the need for female role models, although the emphasis was more often on the need for adult models rather than that of older siblings.

Teachers tell students they should first think through their goals, then develop a logical plan, and finally act. In fact, logic is more often used as an *ex post facto* tool, and proof is often developed to assess a program rather than to devise it. Thus the fact that the rationale for the ATO role models was developed (or perfected) long after the decision to use them was made should not create undue suspicion. The rationale was presented formally by an officer from the Department of Behavioral Science and Leadership (DFBL) at the September 1975 inter-service conference.[g] This presentation's title was "Integration of Females into Previously All Male Universities." It focused on humanistic and social problems, deriving its data from a search of professional journals, reports prepared by recently integrated institutions, and responses to queries sent to a va-

---

[f]The precedent was enthusiastically supported by the officer in charge of the planning for women who had himself served as an ATO in 1955.

[g]The department had been charged to explore the literature on sex and stress and to evaluate the need for a sex-education course.

riety of schools in July 1975.[h] These queries centered on (1) faculty acceptance of co-eds, (2) student acceptance of co-eds, (3) problems in classroom decorum, (4) fraternization between co-eds and faculty, and (5) pre-/post-attitude surveys of students and faculty.[i]

These collected observations and recommendations about the social aspects of integration might not meet the tests for adequacy applied to social science research, but they did represent the savvy judgments of responsible (because held-to-account) administrators.[j] A widely shared and fundamental proposition asserted that the male-female mix should be equal and that anything less than a 1:3 ratio created problems. This latter supposition put the Air Force Academy behind the eight ball. It would achieve a 1:10 ratio and that only after four years. Its women, then, would have to accept the status of permanent minority.[k]

Other major conclusions of the DFBL study were that after integration

(1) women were treated as different from men *and* other women;
(2) women were regarded as superior in intellect *but* inferior in most abilities;
(3) women were socially rejected;
(4) women attempted to make more men friends than women friends;
(5) women needed an unusual sense of self-order and self-respect;
(6) some women were content in a "minority, subordinate role," while others assumed a "superwoman" role.

Co-ed dorms were generally preferred by women at all the reporting institutions. One reason was security. It seemed that trashing, peeping toms, and similar harassment were more prevalent

[h]Responding schools included the Merchant Marine Academy, Princeton, Yale, Dartmouth, Amherst, Notre Dame, Virginia, and Phillips Exeter Academy. Nursing schools in Colorado Springs and Denver that had recently become co-ed gave insight because of the reversed nature of their integration. While the Yale experience was best documented, both West Point and Air Force Academy officials were particularly impressed by a personal letter of advice written by a sister at Notre Dame.

[i]Logically, a "co-ed" should be either a male or female. That the term refers only to women is a constant reminder that men got there first.

[j]This is all policy makers had to go on, whether accurate or not.

[k]The experience at OTS, ROTC summer camps, and the Merchant Marine Academy suggested that over time the importance of the social mix was reduced.

when the sexes were housed separately.[1] Also, strong pockets of resistance to women's entrance remained among students and alumni, while the faculty was more likely to support integration.[m] Still, faculty sometimes overreacted by asking for "a woman's point of view," by being paternalistic, or by giving extra attention. Classroom decorum seemed to improve and male endeavor in some areas increased, but male G.P.A. expectancies may have diminished because the women were perceived as academically talented.

DFBL concluded that there was

(1) a need for feminine role models on the academy faculty and in high administration,
(2) a need for a strong career counseling program,
(3) a need to consider how to win the "acceptance" of the dominant portion of the wing,
(4) a need to consider that women tend to be more internally motivated and men more externally motivated.

This was the basic information available to officials as they moved from planning to implementing.

The generally unfavorable attitudes of cadets towards women's admission and cadet insistence that there be no lowering of standards and no preferential treatment for women made attitude and attitude-change studies seem important. Also, each academy had to decide what effect informational programs about the integration of women would have on attitudes. Nonevaluative, nonargumentative dissemination of facts might preclude the spread of rumors, but would advocacy or programs designed to change negative attitudes have the intended effect? The specters of backlash and of polarization hung over any proposals for attempting to change attitudes about women cadets. Debates broke out over whether administering attitude surveys would be helpful (in that they would accurately portray the emotional environment of the academy) or unhelpful (in that the taking of a survey could solidify attitudes and thus strengthen opposition). West Point chose to find out and began surveying in 1975. The Air Force took a middle-of-the-road position by beginning some data collection in 1976. The Navy would have

[1]Women apparently understood that the way to security was to get as close to "the enemy" as possible. It is not clear whether they did so to enlist protectors or to disarm the hostile.

[m]These two findings might have been expected to neutralize one another at the Air Force Academy, where alumni made up a large percentage of the faculty.

preferred to skip the whole affair, but perhaps because the other academies were preparing studies for presentation at professional meetings and it did not wish to be left out, it permitted one study by the Navy Personnel Research and Development Center in San Diego. As far as affecting attitudes was concerned, though, the Navy developed an internal information program and provided officers a handbook on how to command women. West Point also conducted some training in integration. At the Air Force Academy, a proposal was made for an attitude program that would filter down—that is, would begin with the education of officers and then emphasize daily, informal interaction between men and women cadets to influence "the affective components of attitudes." From the top and low key, the Air Force thought, would be the best way.

Last-Minute Advice

The last outside source of information consulted during the planning period entailed an August 1976 return visit to Lackland Air Force Base. This time a new five-member inspection team was formed (the chief of plans and programs was the sole holdover); it included two young women officers, advocates of female accomplishment, who held special assignments concerning women's admission, the vice-commandant of cadets, and an officer from staff management. The official personnel briefing at Lackland included no woman above the rank of captain. Role models were apparently not considered important there.

The visit was made to assess the integration of women in the ROTC summer training program, which had included women since 1971. The ratio of women to men in the program was high, 1:3; nevertheless, both men and women reported that women's acceptance as leaders was marginal. Men disliked taking orders from women, and women who felt competent believed the men thought them incompetent. Men were not sympathetic to informally shortening the drill step and felt they were given demerits while women were given reprimands under the same circumstances.[n] On the obstacle course, women apparently were not pushed to challenge every obstacle, and "team spirit" (highly valued at the academy)—cheer-

[n]The solution to drilling women and men together, despite their different leg lengths, had been to "adjust" the step. Another solution could have been to revise the drill manual. Then men would not have felt they were being asked to do less (literally) to let women catch up.

ing for one another—was prohibited. Women complained that sexist remarks were common and that men evaluated them for their looks. Because their slower running times hurt squadron honor competition, women were forced or encouraged *not* to try the mile-and-a-half run but to elect an alternative exercise program provided for women. Women's conditioning suffered as a result. Even though the numerical ratio was 1:3 and that at the academy would be 1:10, and even though integration was routine (four years old), women's acceptance was low and the quality of their training lower than that of the men. These ROTC findings were especially interesting because OTS training was conducted at the same base and apparently going much better. There, men expressed confidence in the women, and women said they felt no prejudice. The 30-inch stride was reduced willingly. Women were assigned to the regular OTS staff instead of being "loaned" in a liaison capacity, and counseling was more informal and not controlled by detailed rules concerning witnesses and open doors.

One obvious difference between OTS (college graduates) and ROTC (college students) is the participant's age. Perhaps men between eighteen and twenty-one are at just exactly the wrong age to accept women as their peers, and perhaps women of that age are especially sensitive to men's assessment of them. The age cycle question requires more study. It may be that rules and environments intended to foster a spirit of equality may affect different age groups differently.

5

The Other Academies

As each academy planned for and then implemented women's integration, each also watched the other. Each knew of "foolish" decisions made by the others. Each knew that "they" did things we would not have done if we had been "they." And it is true that although P.L. 94–106 covered all the academies, their responses to it, in part because of their missions and in part because of their decision makers, were quite different.

The Merchant Marine Academy

The Merchant Marine Academy at Kings Point, New York (under the jurisdiction of the Department of Commerce), admitted fifteen women in the summer of 1974. (The total student body numbered about one thousand.) This action followed similar ones taken in 1973 by state maritime schools in California, New York, and Maine. Graduates of the academy receive a B.S. degree, a third mate's or engineer's license, a Naval Reserve commission, and can often command as much as $18,000 or $20,000 starting pay. The educa-

Documents of the United States Military Academy are cited herein with the understanding that they do not represent the "official position" of the U.S. Army.

tion is free and no active duty obligation is incurred, although three or four years of work and training in the maritime industry are required.

The nation would probably have taken little notice of the new admissions policy at Kings Point if not for one mishandled event. During the first integrated year, a male and female were caught in bed together. She was dismissed from the academy; he was not. One explanation for this seeming inequity was that he had not been identified; another, that since he was a senior and she only in her first year, the same punishment would have been much more severe for him. It was also said that his academic and disciplinary records were better than hers. This invoking of a double standard earned the Merchant Marine Academy ridicule, headlines, and an A.C.L.U.-sponsored court case. More important was its effect on the academies newly directed to admit women. At those schools administrators began their planning grimly conscious of how easily a mistake could make headlines and also conscious that mistakes were almost inevitable.[a] The result was that each academy approached women's admission with caution; every decision was made with great care. In short, integration, which might at first have been considered a joke, received very serious treatment indeed.

West Point: Circumstances

During late 1976 one observer was asked why she thought West Point cadet women were quitting at higher rates than Air Force women. She answered, "The uniforms are the wrong color." What may at first seem fatuous on further consideration may not be so far from wrong. West Point is often described as beautiful, and it may be that gray flannel is handsome and that pink sandstone buildings afford a relief from the overwhelming dourness of khaki uniforms and weathered, gray stone buildings. Still, the palette is so masculine and sober that even a glimpse of a Baltimore oriole is experienced as a visual assault. Similarly, the report of the West Point Study Group, which evaluated the academy following the Borman

---

[a]In the summer of 1977 the Navy spent several days in the news after two women were put on report (with the possibility of receiving a sentence that could include thirty days at hard labor) for removing their high-heeled shoes while standing in formation during an official ceremony at North Island Naval Air Station in San Diego.

Report, noted the "humorless atmosphere."[1b] Both of the above observations may themselves seem humorous; yet West Point's tradition and milieu may be so severe that jokes and women (or even
novelty, for that matter) are by definition disruptive and, therefore,
experienced as debilitating.

Women entered West Point just before its one hundred seventy-
fifth year. Many West Pointers regretted that that proud anniversary
would be overshadowed by the entrance of women. Yet they would
come to regret even more that the presence of women cadets would,
in turn, be obscured by the Electrical Engineering 304 cheating
scandal and, worse, that the scandal would be augmented by
charges that attorneys for the accused cadets were harassed and in-
timidated.[c] Indeed, one would suspect that, relatively speaking,
women became a pleasant topic for Army conversation during
1976–77. In fact, by midyear (just when the Air Force Academy
was attempting to de-emphasize its women) West Point officials participated in network television shows and the women's basketball
team was featured in a *New Yorker* article. One West Point public
affairs officer estimated that in 1976–77 one-half the academy's
public relations work dealt with cheating, and only one-eighth with
women. In "ordinary" times athletics would probably have been the
center of attention. The situation at West Point, then, was quite different from that at the other academies. Top administrators were
preoccupied with the cheating scandal; this preoccupation affected
women's integration because it had been decided to keep a tight and
central control over all decisions concerning women. Thus junior
officers and cadet leaders, who had once been anxious but without
responsibility, found that they sometimes had to take action without
expected supervision.

Another special circumstance was the public resistance to

[b]At the request of the Department of the Army, a commission headed by former astronaut
Frank Borman studied the cheating scandal of March 1976 and its aftermath. The West Point
Study Group was appointed in January 1977 and was directed to review all aspects of academy life: academies, environment, and professional development. Its report, which was "inevitably problem oriented," identified numerous areas requiring improvement.

[c]The final disposition of the scandal included asking 151 cadets to leave West Point.
However, 105 of them were allowed to apply for readmission under an unprecedented program. Ultimately, 96 did return. Their return meant that the effects of the controversy would
continue for another year, because many cadets did not want the honor violators to return. In
particular, members of the class of 1978 did not want their reputation "stained" by accepting
the returnees. This whole affair confounds comparisons that might be made concerning the
classes of 1979, 1980, and 1981 (the last all-male and the first and second integrated classes).

women's admission that West Point officials had displayed. At one point, Superintendent Sidney Berry had indicated that he would resign before admitting women. He later described that view as "rather adolescent." And in a December 1975 letter to graduates and friends of the academy, he noted: "The orders have been issued . . . . : The United States Military Academy is now co-ed." To Berry this was West Point's "most significant change since 1802" (the date of the academy's founding).

The Army's position seemed to be, however, that while the Congressional act permitted women to enter West Point, it did not require that they stay. West Point was determined that there would be no quotas, and no tokens. If all the women failed, that would demonstrate only that all the women had failed. After all, West Point could not be faulted if women failed to meet its standards.

The West Point position on "equivalent training," as outlined in January 1976, demonstrates how deeply the academy opposed change or accommodation. The policy held that equivalent training was to be considered only when and if "failure becomes the consistent mode for women." An adjustment might then be made if the following conditions were met: (1) when "it is obvious that repeated failure of the unaltered event will psychologically damage the motivated women," *and* (2) mastery is "not essential" to successful training, *and* (3) the equivalent "provides essentially the same type of training experience," *and* (4) the equivalent is considered by the "trainers and by *both men and women cadets* as an acceptable modification" (emphasis added). In April 1976 a quite different policy was established that no women making a serious effort would be separated for physical reasons during the first summer. They would, however, be given the same physical training as men. A need for modifications based on "physiological differences" would not be anticipated.

Because official resistance had been so strong, top Army policy makers thought a formal commitment to accept and train women was required. Thus a program for training cadets to train women was created and a research program on women's training was instituted. These efforts to make integration successful were carefully documented. If the program did not succeed, the Army would still be able to say, "We did all this, we did all that, we did all that we knew how to do. What would you suggest?"

The decision to give women and men identical training was made even though the West Point summer program was more physically demanding than those of the other two Department of Defense academies. In 1976 the West Point "day" averaged sixteen-and-one-half hours. During the summer four three-mile, two ten-mile, and one twelve-mile hike with approximately thirty pounds of gear were required, compared to none at Annapolis and two four-and-one-half-mile hikes with a fifteen-pound pack at the Air Force Academy. Navy middies spent no nights "in the field," while Air Force trainees spent two weeks in tents with wooden floors and cots. Army cadets spent ten nights in two-person pup tents. The relative rigor of the programs was reflected in "injury/sick" totals: 15 percent of Navy women; 25 percent of Air Force women; 33 percent of West Point women. This figure was the subject of some dispute. West Point medics argued that cadet sick slips were being used for "nonmedical" problems—to excuse duty that should have been excused on the basis of "common sense." Some officers thought that the "one-track" conception of the program was incompatible with the documented differences in Physical Aptitude Test (PAT) scores (men's mean 500, women's mean 273) and a legal recognition of the need to make allowances for physiological differences. The argument was made that many of the women cadets were neither ill nor injured but exhausted, and that performance standards should have been revised and scaled to "physiologically normal" and realistic levels.

There was another item that must have haunted West Point planners. Just as they were preparing to admit women, an Army cadet was convicted of raping a Wellesley co-ed. This incident must have affected the decision to install locks on (only) the women's doors. Later this decision was rescinded, but both Annapolis and West Point clearly felt a special concern for the security of the women cadets.[d] The Air Force did too, but it took care of the problem by separating and securing the whole women's area.

Finally, West Point did enjoy one advantage over the Air Force Academy. While it, too, had been examined by the GAO, West Point did not have as severe an attrition problem as did the Air Force. Nevertheless, Military Academy officials realized that great discrepancies between male and female attrition would be questioned. In its planning West Point estimated a one-third attrition rate for men over the four years and a one-half rate for women.

[d]Annapolis tried to ensure that no woman was alone in her room at night by shifting women about if their roommates were gone. Navy officials also contemplated but decided against locks.

West Point: Preparations and Implementation

Serious preparation of a women's admission plan began in May 1975; it was finished by November. (There was a two-page "plan" ready as early as 1973.) Instead of using young women officers as test subjects for its planning, West Point used local high school (girl) athletes to test different physical training programs in Project 60.[e] Fifteen of the Project 60 subjects also participated in Project 60A to test women's capacity for military activities, such as the manual of arms, dummy grenade throw, bayonet training, weapons firing, and foot marches.[f] Eight enlisted women, graduates of basic training, undertook cadet field training in the summer of 1976 to see whether that program would create any problems for cadet women during their second summer. It was decided that no alterations in the program were necessary. Meanwhile, a "natural experiment" was being conducted at the Army's prep school, which women had entered for the first time. That experience demonstrated only too clearly that men anxious to enter the academy were no more receptive to the entrance of women than were men already at the academy. Markedly antagonistic attitudes developed between the men and women at the prep school. But despite this strain, seven of the sixteen women "preppies" did enter West Point the following fall.[g]

The cadet attitude toward women was the first item studied in Project Athena, a set of cooperative research efforts undertaken jointly by West Point and the Army Research Institute.[h] All cadets were surveyed in August 1975; they revealed strongly negative attitudes. Prominent were fears of "reverse discrimination," a sense of loss of "pride and discipline," and literal interpretations of "equality" that used males as the measure (e.g., the idea that women's heads should be almost shaved, as were men's, was acceptable, while the idea of men's wearing women's haircuts or clothing was so unimaginable as not to be queried). Few differences in attitude

[e]The training of the Air Force ATOs for their duties was similarly intended as a test of women's capacity to undergo physical training.

[f]The only changes instituted for women as a result of the study were a shortening of the operating rod (for inspection arms) and the substitution of a (lighter) M-16 rifle (for the M-14) for reveille runs and bayonet drills. M-16s are the Army's standard weapon.

[g]Typically 15 percent of a West Point entering class comes through the prep school. In the case of women the proportion would be about one-half of 15 percent.

[h]Project Athena's first major report was issued September 2, 1977, and titled "Report of the Admission of Women to the U.S. Military Academy." Athena's purpose was to study both the effect of the system on women and of women on the system.

towards women's admission were found between cadets with high and low scholastic aptitude or leadership ratings, and attitudinal differences between classes were not large. Prejudice seemed general. One dramatic difference by class did show up, however, on an "attitude to casual sex" measure. The three-fourths acceptance rate among upperclassmen makes West Point cadets substantially higher in acceptance of promiscuity than other college males. Just how sexism and attitudes toward casual sex are related may be unclear but worth contemplating.[2]

The survey data defined a problem; they did not explain how attitudes might be changed, but they did suggest that the cadets' views were not linked to fundamental personality characteristics. All this meant that intervention might be productive, although the data also suggested that cadets believed women could best overcome any discrimination by quiet, individual achievement: "group action, protest, and system blame are not acceptable to a majority of cadets."[3]

West Point did not ignore its problem. Unlike the other academies, it brought in a number of civilian and military consultants; it also provided rather formal training to its cadets in preparing for the admission of women. The Office of Physical Education retained Dr. Jan Felshyn, a feminist spokeswoman from East Stroudsburg State College; Dr. Evalyn Gendel, a physician from the Kansas State Department of Maternal Health; and Drs. Ann Jewett and Waneen Spirduso, chairs of health, physical education, and recreation departments at the University of Georgia and Texas, respectively. Each visited the campus several times and commented on planning materials. The Office of Military Leadership consulted Dr. Morris Janowitz, of the University of Chicago, and Dr. Charles Moskos, Northwestern—both are military sociologists. Dr. Janet Spence, a psychologist from the University of Texas who specializes in attitudes toward women, women's achievement motivation, and sex-role stereotypes, and even "founding mother" Betty Friedan were asked for counsel. Moreover, six women officers were assigned to the academy by the time the class of 1980 was enrolled.

After formal training that included formal briefings, an information packet, cadet participation in Project 60, lectures on human sexuality, female physiology and reproduction/menstruation, and presentations on stress, counseling, and rumor control, cadet attitudes were retested in March 1976.[i] By then integration had become

---

[i]For a fuller account of the training see Appendix II.

an official policy, formal training of a professional nature had taken place, but no women had yet arrived. This time faculty attitudes were also assessed (something the Air Force never attempted) and their attitudes were compared to those of cadets.

The West Point faculty were far more accepting of women's admission than were cadets and also more accepting than their Army officer colleagues. Indeed, 44 percent of the West Point faculty said they would feel "as comfortable in combat" with a female commander as with a male commander, while only 18 percent of the cadets and 32 percent of a sample of other male officers felt that way. And 66 percent of women officers surveyed responded affirmatively.[4]

About 30 percent of the cadets surveyed volunteered spontaneous comments about the study or their attitudes. Only 9 percent (of the 30 percent) were positive toward women; 14 percent were neutral or ambivalent; 42 percent were opposed to women's admission. Only 12 percent expressed the "professional attitude" that "the law is the law, and I will do my best."[5] If the professional outlook was the position of the officers, it apparently had not been communicated to or internalized by the cadets.

The March 1976 data did show some change towards accepting women. The hope was that with women's entrance, with close association and shared experiences, attitudes would continue to improve. However, surveys in August 1976 and April 1977 suggested that this was not the case (see Table IV). Indeed, one of the more interesting findings from the later data was that women not only reported more instances of discrimination (both positive and negative) than men but they also reported more than they had some six months earlier.

Women's presence apparently set attitudes toward them back, although prejudice was lower in cadet units that had women than in those units that had none.[6] The failure of positive attitudes to blossom may have resulted from the great emphasis West Point placed on physical performance—the very area in which women found it most difficult to compete with men. Whether strength is understood absolutely to be important or whether it is valued only symbolically is not clear. (In the "whole person formula" used to select candidates for admission, physical attributes count for only 10 percent.) Nevertheless, the time and attention given to athletics and to competition in the academy schedule argues that strength and stamina *per se*, not fitness and attitude, are what matter. Whatever the cause, the

Table IV. Discriminatory Treatment of Women
Perceived by the Class of 1980

	September 1976		April 1977	
	M	F	M	F
Treated More Severely				
No, never	67	40	61	5
Maybe	13	12	17	9
Yes, once or twice	8	23	10	19
Yes, on several occasions	7	18	8	30
Yes, frequently	1	7	5	28[a]
Treated More Kindly				
No, never	83	27	76	15
Maybe	12	26	15	17
Yes, once or twice	4	24	6	42
Yes, on several occasions	2	19	2	20
Yes, frequently	1	4	0	6[b]

Source: Adapted from Alan G. Vitters and Nora Scott Kinzer, *Report of the Admission of Women to the United States Military Academy* (West Point, N.Y.: United States Military Academy, Department of Behavioral Sciences and Leadership, 2 September 1977), p. 134.

[a]The women report a significant increase in discriminatory severe treatment: $t = 7.15$, $p < .001$ by an uncorrelated means test.

[b]The women report a significant increase in discriminatory kindly treatment: $t = 2.08$, $p < .05$.

message from the data was clear. Contact is not a sufficient antidote for prejudice. Even though reserach on prejudice confirms this wisdom over and over again, policy makers somehow continue to believe that "getting together" will lead to harmony.

The Office of Institutional Research at West Point also analyzed American Council on Education data to determine how cadets differed from civilian students and how women cadets varied from men cadets, civilian men, and civilian women. While women cadets were more like men cadets than they were like civilians in categories such as family background and political conservatism, they were

Table V. Attitudes of West Point Cadets as Compared
to Attitudes of Other College Students
*(Numbers represent percent of respondents
that agreed with each statement.)*

	Men		Women	
	West Point	*Other Colleges*	*West Point*	*Other Colleges*
I expect to have two or less children.	60%	67%	70%	61%
I consider raising a family an essential or very important goal.	66	60	38	56
I believe that the activities of married women are best confined to the home and family.	41	37	5	19
I believe that I have a very good chance of getting married within a year after college.	30	16	15	19

Source: Adapted from R.F. Priest and J.W. Houston, "New Cadets and Other
College Freshmen Class of 1980," Report No. 77–013 (West Point, N.Y.: United
States Military Academy, Office of the Director of Institutional Research, March
1977).

more like civilian women than like any men in "cheerfulness" and
(low) mechanical aptitude. In their attitudes toward interpersonal
and family relations, cadet women were dramatically different from
cadet men. And when compared to civilians, the women and men
cadets often fell at opposite extremes. (See Table V.)

One might suppose that such incompatibility would put to rest
official worries about pregnancy and fraternization; however, availability is always relevant, and the male-female ratio at the academy
of more than twenty-to-one suggests that any interested woman
would be almost sure to find one compatible man.

West Point women were not quartered together, and while some
men believed women used the hospital as a sanctuary, the women
rarely came together in a way that lent them group support. Minority
cadets had achieved this camaraderie to some degree through a club.

The Contemporary Affairs Seminar functioned as a *de facto* non-white organization. Similarly, an effort was made to provide a legitimate opportunity for cadet women to come together by creating an organization called the Corbin Society. A woman counselor, who was also the women's basketball coach, met with the group weekly. Attendance was small. Moreover, attendance was mostly male, and upperclassmen at that! As the group evolved, however, some cadet women did begin to participate. Films from summer training and appearances by such guests as Jill Volner made the program attractive.[j] But any benefits came from male-female interaction: no haven for women developed. Even the local chapter of the National Organization for Women (NOW) did not attract a single cadet woman. It *did*, however, attract some officers' wives and some cadet men. It seems possible that the cadet men's interest in such groups was subversive.

West Point women cadets generally tried to be invisible. They thought that to be together was to invite notice and to ask for trouble.[k] Black cadets, in contrast, seemed to have enough self-respect, or commanded enough respect from others, to gather together with less concern about possible retaliation.

During the first year, the life of women cadets at West Point developed differently from that of their counterparts at the Air Force Academy. They *did* utilize counseling services almost twice as often as men, but they had no opportunities to participate in intercollegiate athletics. Four club teams were formed, however—basketball, volleyball, gymnastics, and softball. In fact, the "Sugar Smacks," the women's basketball team, won a fair amount of cadet approval.[l] Although regulations permitted cadet women to wear skirts in formation, cadet officers did not permit it, nor did they permit make-up. The taboo on skirts exemplifies the pressure on women to meet male standards and contrasts with the Air Force Academy policy of keeping cadet women in skirts (not very stylish ones) much of the time.[m]

[j]Attorney Volner's work on Watergate won her public renown. She later became counsel for the U.S. Army.

[k]If the women had not all been plebes, they might have found organization more feasible.

[l]Because the academies did not accept women over six feet tall, they might have suffered a competitive disadvantage had a height change not been made. It was. Now both women and men may be as tall as 6'8".

[m]At West Point the commandant did try to require skirts at dances but did not require them at chapel. At the Air Force Academy, women were not only expected to wear skirts to chapel but the deputy commandant also preferred high to low heels.

The West Point women did well academically but no better than the men. As the dean observed, their performance "did no harm" to the standards. West Point women *did* quit though. By the end of the first summer, West Point had already lost 15.9 percent, Navy 7.4, and Air Force 2.5.[n] At the end of the year, 27 percent of the West Point women had resigned, while 22 percent (but ten times as many) of the men had quit.

It would be presumptuous to guess why so many women left, and wrong to insist their attrition could have been avoided. West Point does train mostly infantry officers, even if West Point graduates customarily try to avoid that role. (Post-academy assignments are selected by class standing at graduation, and often the first choices are the Corps of Engineers.) Thus women cadets, who did not expect to serve in combat, may have found much of their training irrelevant to their vaguely defined future. Furthermore, the limited number of women officers at West Point and the jobs they had may have led women cadets to think that even if they did not quit, their reward would be limited. Women generally served as staff officers or teachers. Officials were not willing to ask other men to accept women's authority. Even the woman officer assigned to support the integration program was told that her recommendations would carry more weight if they were presented by her male (and also senior) colleague.

The West Point physical education program was designed to push male cadets to just the point where a few males would fail. During basic training runs in 1976, for example, male "fallouts" were over 1 percent on only three of twenty-three days. Women were asked to follow the same program, and on only one day did fewer than 10 percent fall out. Rates soared as high as 42 percent and often ranged between one-quarter and one-third.[o] The physical education department finally decided that women would have to be scored against other women admitted to the academy and be assigned points based on a female-only standard. Still, the approach was not systematically parallel to the one used for men because the scoring for men was based on a distribution of male *candidates*, not male admitees. This disparity meant cadet women probably had to compare better with other women than cadet men did with other men.

For the second year, a change was made in physical training that

[n]Ten percent of West Point men left before the end of the first summer.
[o]The 42 percent rate came from a very small group: three of seven fell out.

was designed to challenge but not exhaust cadets. All cadets (male and female) were placed in groups based on physical ability levels. These were called the black, grey, and gold groups. Even the lowest met a rather exacting standard, but because two "higher" groups were available, even the strongest cadet could be placed in a taxing situation.

In sum, West Point began serious planning more than a year before the women came. Officials committed themselves to documenting changes related to women's admission and seemed to take some pride in demonstrating their capacity to do something well, even if it was difficult for them to accept the decision to do it at all. They took pride, too, in doing what others had thought they could or would not do. The entering women also undertook a challenge they were not expected to meet. They attempted difficult tasks (e.g., basic training) they did not welcome (except as a means), and they took great pride in having succeeded. Yet neither the West Point officials nor the women cadets were seen by their respective critics as having done especially well. In each case the pride no doubt ensued from having come "so far" (the West Point staff in accepting women, and young women in having been plebes).

Women officers had suggested to West Point officials that women in the Army were generally under-challenged and under-utilized. This under-utilization was a fact at the academy itself, with its handful of women officers (the top-ranked a major). Indeed, at the time there were only eighty-eight women majors, sixteen women colonels, and one woman general in the *whole* Army. Nevertheless, academy officers *felt* and said things like: "You women are taking over." To them the salient data apparently were the 500 percent increase in women officers at the academy (from two to eleven in eighteen months) and the higher promotion rate for women, even though that rate still left women far behind in absolute numbers.

Finally, a number of observers commented that women cadets seemed to "speak up" and to express themselves more than male cadets. One suspects that their marginality permitted this openness and that they will be punished for such license if and when they are incorporated into the group. Women may not have feared the institution simply because it had not yet come down on them, because they felt they had other career options available, because they had not yet learned the system's values, or perhaps because they felt they had so little to lose.

Annapolis: Plans and Practice

The Annapolis 1976–77 catalogue is a handsome volume with photos that date back to the nineteenth century and a variety of historical and contemporary quotations as their captions. Blacks appear in numerous photos, and many of the captions speak to black consciousness; for example, "It is definitely not a copout for Blacks to go to Annapolis. America is my country and I want to get with it." Only two captions refer to women: "I've always believed that women should remain superior, rather than becoming equal to men" and "Being a woman is a terribly difficult trade, since it consists principally of dealing with men." Neither conveys the "come on in" message of the black captions; both suggest that becoming a midshipman would be degrading and/or difficult for women.

Three themes emerge in the Naval Academy's descriptions of women's entrance. The first is legality. While West Point adopted a good-soldier, "It-is-the-law-of-the-land; we-will-obey" posture, the Navy communicated a more knowing "We'll-comply-with-the-letter-of-the-law, but-meanwhile-do-what-is-best-for-the-Navy" position.[p] Of course, the Navy was legally constrained in a way the other services were not, in that an Act of Congress forbade Navy women's assignment to combat ships.[q] The Annapolis women, then, were to be trained for something proscribed. At West Point the situation was more ambiguous because Army policy (not Congressional legislation) governed what career fields would be available to women. At the Air Force Academy a large number of cadets ineligible to fly were graduated each year. Thus, the enrollment of women there had little effect on cadet military training.

Four enlisted women filed suit against the Navy in November 1976, charging that the combat ship prohibition violated their constitutional rights. In March 1977, three women officers joined them. One was the aide to the head of the Pacific Fleet Training Command and also one of *Time* magazine's twelve Women of the Year; another was one of the Navy's few women pilots. In all this the Navy gave the impression of not so much fighting the lawsuit but rather waiting to see precisely what the court would require.

[p]Rear Adm. C.N. Mitchell, Director of Naval Education and Training, wrote, in the cover letter to a memorandum in the fall of 1975, "We are continuing to try to comply with the language of the law, while keeping in mind the needs of the Navy."

[q]Civilian women could go to sea on Navy vessels; so could women from other services. Some NROTC women took an orientation cruise by taking leave, donning civilian clothes, and going as the guest of a Navy man.

After women entered Annapolis, the Navy proposed to the Carter administration that it ask Congress to change the law and permit women to serve permanently on noncombat vessels and temporarily (when not in combat) on combat vessels.[r] Once again the Navy Department appeared determined to force the civilian government to define the changes that must be made; Navy officials seemed to deliberately put the initiative into the hands of elected or judicial officials. In contrast, the Air Force sought to *take* the initiative, preferring to influence policy by acting rather than by reacting.

A second Navy theme was accommodation. Several middies said proudly, "Here, the women have had to accommodate to us—not vice versa." As will be shown, a great deal of educating men about women went on at Annapolis. Almost nothing was done (at any of the academies), however, to educate women about men and their norms and conventions. This negligence meant that those who entered the alien environment were supposed to assimilate without being taught about that environment; by contrast, those who were supposed to absorb the intruders were thoroughly briefed on them. Those who were supposed to accommodate were left unconscious and uninformed. Those who were supposed to remain unchanged were admonished and made highly self-conscious.

The third theme was "underkill." Perhaps the new superintendent, Adm. Kinnaird McKee, best summed up the Annapolis policy: "The whole business is the nonevent of the year."[s] He explained that Annapolis just let it "come naturally": "We tried not to plan anything we didn't have to plan, and not to decide anything until we had to."

The academy considered its major problem to be the number of women it would have to take. "How many nonsailors," the staff pondered, "can one have in a sea service?" To be more specific, officers who graduate from Annapolis are not permitted to enter the Staff Corps (supply, medicine, chaplains) or the Restricted Line (public affairs, engineering). They must enter the Unrestricted Line (aviators and "ship drivers"), which has few shore billets (principally administrative). The Bureau of Naval Personnel determined that the Navy could absorb forty-three Annapolis women graduates a year plus ten officers for assignment to the Marine Corps.[t] This

[r]Academy training calls for cruises after the entering and second class years. Nevertheless the Academy's administration did *not* endorse the change proposed by the Navy.

[s]Other Navy officers described it as a "headache" or "bad joke."

[t]To achieve this result, the Secretary of the Navy directed that some eighty women be admitted, twice as many as in-house planning had anticipated.

minuscule number may help explain how women's entrance could be kept a "nonevent."

Navy planning began late, never culminated in a formal, public plan, and was primarily the work of one brigade officer, Capt. William Holland, who worked directly under the commandant and with two civilian consultants, Dr. Edie Seashore of the National Training Laboratory and management specialist Allan Drexler.[u]

In his career Captain Holland had never served with, under, or over a woman. He began his formidable assignment by consulting his wife (who was pursuing an M.A. in counseling) and by raiding the library. He studied such works as Judith Bardwick's *Psychology of Women* and her *Readings on the Psychology of Women*, Simone de Beauvoir's *The Second Sex*, Alice G. Sargent's *Beyond Sex Roles*, Catharine Stimpson's *Women and the Equal Rights Amendment*, Beth Coye's articles on women's role in the Navy, and Ashley Montagu's *The Natural Superiority of Women*. He ended this study, he claimed, as a convert. He also left for Hawaii just before the women arrived.

Senior women naval officers were not given an opportunity to contribute to or criticize the Annapolis plans. One officer explained that the Navy benefited by not having to accommodate senior women officers who were survivors, who had made it in a nonintegrated context, and who did not necessarily agree with each other or with the "new generation."[v] Holland, then, felt he could plan with a relatively free hand. His civilian consultant began working with him several times a week in the late fall of 1975 and continued through the year, moving from a role as planning consultant to one as an educator when programs for preparing the midshipmen were begun.[w]

The brigade officers (cadet officers) and the plebe detail (cadets who would train the new midshipmen during the summer of 1976) were Holland's chief concern. These men would be the liaison, dis-

---

[u]Holland received advice from a small committee, which included one woman officer serving as a conduct officer. A midshipman Planning Review Board also existed, although its function was limited.

[v]By June 1975, there still had been no woman line officer promoted to the rank of admiral. Two blacks had won that rank. In February 1976, a woman was "frocked" as a rear admiral to take an assignment that calls for an admiral. She was later promoted.

[w]She not only made recommendations (even in such detailed ways as reminding Annapolis that women would expect diet drinks in the "Coke" machines), but she developed programs and her view carried an authority woman officers would have found difficult to achieve.

ciplinary, and role-model officers. Each was chosen for his job because he was in some sense "exemplary." To single out your most
outstanding cadets for special instruction and admonition might
seem awkward. Therefore, the Navy did so in its own, low-key
style. The tone of instruction was not one that presumed guilt or the
need for expert tutelage but one of intimacy, like saying "Hey, guys,
here's how we can cope with this." The principal document, a working paper entitled "Information and Education Program in Preparation for Women," was sent to the superintendent in January 1976
and proved useful to both cadets and officers. Its rationale was that

> Male officers of the background and experience of those
> assigned the Brigade are generally unprepared mentally
> and emotionally to lead women. Their base of experi-
> ence as husbands, lovers, fathers, brothers, and sons is
> generally inadequate because of its narrow base and
> scope.

One can understand why this document was kept in-house. It
was, basically, a set of tips for brothers, rather than a research or
policy report. In commenting on diet, for instance, Annapolis was
the only academy to urge attention to "overzealous" weight watching. The other two DOD academies worried only about weight gain.
And the Navy specifically warned women and their detail leaders
about menstrual-cycle changes. It also instructed male midshipmen
on women's grooming standards, so that men would assume their
responsibility for maintaining consistent standards on make-up and
"rigging" (appearance of the uniform). The goal was to teach men
to handle *all* personnel: the Navy did not want its men to look for
help or be dependent on help from women officers.[x]

During the planning the Navy's consultants had developed some
twenty-three "point papers" on issues they thought might arise. In
their educational handout they suggested appropriate comments and
behavior for dealing with most of them. They also set forth many of
the crucial ideas about sex roles from both the psychological and
sociological literature, such as the importance of role models, male-
female differences in self-esteem, and the harmony (or disharmony)
of men's and women's family and career goals.

Without citing any literature, the document outlined a number of

[x]Women officers at both West Point and Colorado Springs complained that men did not
"train" women in the areas of grooming and appearance because they had not learned to do
so.

complex gender differences such as levels of assertiveness and attitudes toward competition, it discussed chivalry, and it admonished
men that military courtesy took priority over social courtesy.[y]

The document warned that a "lack of straightforwardness" was
associated with women's sociological role and that women would
have to be taught to be direct. Officers were advised not just that
women tend to personalize failure but that officers were responsible
for reversing this tendency. They learned not only that women were
vulnerable to criticism but also that an officer must learn to criticize
constructively and avoid responding to women's hurt as men typically do: by either placating or ignoring them. Women, the paper
went on, needed to cultivate friendship, develop group identity, and
express affection (or frustration) through "zingers" (pointed, personal remarks). Men needed to learn never to goad other men by
pointing to women who were performing better, to praise rather than
demean or belittle women's high performance, and not to react to
tears when they represented anger or frustration.[z] In conclusion,
Holland and staff delineated the stereotypes described by Kanter of
"mother," "mascot," "seductress," and "iron maiden"; and officers
and midshipmen were reminded that plebes were "misses" with a
wide range of talents and interests who should not be forced into
any of the above-mentioned roles.

The staff at Annapolis was quite specific in detailing the various
academy groups to be educated and in designing training sessions
for them that would educate without triggering resentment. The primary method chosen was nonrequired closed-circuit television. Superintendent's letters, an information pack, articles in the *Log* (the
Annapolis cadet magazine), and bulletin boards were also used.
Again, the primary target was the plebe detail and the class of
1977.[a] The purpose was to inform midshipmen of decisions as they
were made and of changes that might have to be made.[b] Two pro-

[y]One senior officer (not at Annapolis) who was deeply involved in women's admission
confided that he found it so embarrassing to have a young woman officer open the door for
him that he made it a practice of hurrying ahead as they approached a door, quickly opening
it, then slipping through leaving her to open the door (only) for herself.

[z]One officer remarked that, although his basic rule was "what's good for the men is good
for the women," he thought opposite strategies were appropriate for crying. "When men cry,
I lay off: they've reached a limit. When women cry I go right on—they're just angry."

[a]Because they would be most influential. West Point and the Air Force Academy to some
degree left their first class men alone because they were assumed to be the most intractable.

[b]The other academies experienced problems as a result of the contrasting interests and
understandings of their external and internal audiences. The Navy partly resolved this dilemma by ignoring the external audience. Nor did the Navy paint itself into a corner by

grams, "Channel Check" and "Soundings," produced a number of offerings related to women. These included two half-hour interviews, one with three women stationed at the academy and one with Capt. Dixie Kuhn, commanding officer of the Officer Candidate School in Newport, Rhode Island. *Pride in Belonging*, a Navy film featuring one of the women officers who had served at sea (as a navigator in the U.S.S. *Sanctuary* experiment) was also televised, as were a fifteen-minute program with the director of physical fitness and a phone-in question-and-answer session with Superintendent McKee; the retired Dean of Admissions, Adm. Robert McNitt; and Lt. Sue Stevens, then a conduct officer, the model for the women's uniforms, and soon to become the Naval Academy's first female company officer.[c]

Regulation changes were kept to a minimum. As at the other academies, upperclassmen were not permitted to date plebes nor to "spoon" them. "Spooning" is an Annapolis tradition in which personal recognition is granted to an individual plebe by an upperclassman. This practice is often observed by members of an athletic team to other team members. Furthermore, at Annapolis intraplebe dating was much more controlled than at either of the other academies, and free weekends were restricted to four a year. "Berthing" at Annapolis was less problematic than "billeting" had been at the Air Force Academy, because there was only one (thirty-acre) dormitory; and since each room had its own sink and shower, only toilets had to be shared, altered, or alternated. Twenty-four companies (of thirty-six) received three room-sharing women, and the rooms were assigned at the end of each company's area so two women's rooms would be together. This pattern placed women at unit "junctions."[d] Women's rooms were identified with reversed-color lettering, but a knock and wait for acknowledgement *or* for a "reasonable period" (at least ten seconds) for entry gave male cadets the feeling that women's privacy was being excessively protected.

denying that "changes" would be made; it simply de-emphasized the changes and said the issue was *not* change or no change, but good versus bad programs.

[c] As such she was the only woman to hold a command position at any of the academies during the first year of integration. Neither West Point nor the Air Force Academy placed a woman in command during the first year. In an early release to the *Naval Institute Proceedings*, Annapolis had said it would not make such an assignment since such slots had to be filled with warfare specialists. The same release indicated that no women faculty would be hired "merely" because they were women, but their numbers did increase consistently from 1975 to 1977, when there were twenty women officers as faculty and staff.

[d] It was decided to assign rooms randomly the second year so women would not literally be at the margin.

While attire requirements were not changed for men, men were required to close their bathrobes in the hallways and modesty provisions were enforced.[e] "Sexual activity in the hall" and "sexual solicitation or coercion" were specifically prohibited as conduct "unbefitting an officer of the naval service," and a substantial number of demerits (50) was prescribed for failure to have the door open when opposite sex midshipmen occupied a room.[f]

Although the Annapolis "dean of women's office" went out of business in June 1976, differences in the Naval Academy's approach to integration remained evident. First, most changes in its preparation for women took place during 1975–76; changes in plebe summer (responsive to the GAO attrition study) had taken place the previous summer. Thus few program changes coincided with the women's arrival. Indeed, more changes probably occurred because of the new superintendent, who was a cigar-smoking, "back-to-basics" officer who conveyed traditional attitudes and spoke "Navy" (rather than academy or management language), than because of women's entrance.

Women's athletics had not been fully planned because of the small number of women entering, but, in fact, their success in athletics turned out to be a most important way for women to win acceptance. One woman plebe won the state foil championship. The volleyball team had an 11–0 record in a state "B" league. A one-woman swimming team named Peggy Feldman won thirteenth place (of forty-eight) in the eastern swimming championships and was paraded through the dining hall on midshipmen's shoulders—an honor usually reserved for the likes of Roger Staubach.

The cadet magazine, the *Log*, is a slick paper, thirty-two page monthly with a little news, a little sports, four pages of photos of girls, and a fair amount of humor. It also includes the (anonymous) column of "Salty Sam," who serves as an institutional gadfly. Individual foibles receive attention and institutional weaknesses can become the "joke of the month." In one issue an officer who dozed in public was named, the lack of chocolate milk lamented; dried out sandwiches at the supe's reception were booed, and midshipmen's views on the "ploobs" or "plebettes" reviewed. For example, it noted that 25 percent of the diet table were female (and cheerleaders

[e]This change was made during the 1975–76 school year so that it would not coincide with women's entrance. It was part of the Navy plan to make all changes *before* the women's arrival.

[f]In contrast, fifteen demerits were charged for "failure to shave," and five for "failure to have door open when room unoccupied."

at that), and it alluded to a host of other sore points: illegal kisses, girdles, shoes being tied for women, grades of "A" given in a "benefit of the doubt" situation, and special assistance rendered at the tailor shop.[g] The *Log* goes further than either the Air Force *Talon* or West Point's *The Pointer* in using ridicule and laughter to help set group norms. It goes further, too, in permitting sore points to surface and a certain ventilation to occur.

Co-ed schools choose prom queens and campus beauties; military barracks post pin-ups. In the first case, the chosen are students themselves and often participate in the selection. In the second case, glamorous females often unknown to the picture possessor are displayed as though they were trophies won or to be sought. The *Log*'s "Company Cuties" were not part of the choosing community nor were they chosen because they were valued as peers. It seems reasonable to ask how more than 10 percent of an educational institution's magazine can be devoted to nameless portraits of lovely ladies. Perhaps the amazed reaction of a cadet officer to the proposition that women midshipmen might find such pictures silly or even offensive may be as sure a proof as can exist that the academy was simply not understood to be a co-ed institution (either because of the women's numbers or because of the role adopted by the women there). When queried further the mid said: "If the Cuties were taken away, the girls would be run out of here in two weeks."[h] Should men be added? "That's absurd!" When told that at the Air Force Academy a complaint had been filed with the Human Relations Committee over a similar practice, he assumed that nothing happened and observed that the woman who complained would have been wiser to overlook the issue.

Civilian women have easier access to Annapolis than to Colorado Springs or West Point because it is set in a town adjacent to St. John's College and near the Maryland state capital. When the women entered, civilian women were displaced as cheerleaders and supplanted in such activities as dramatic productions. (In 1976–77 mids produced *The Girlfriend*, in which twelve mid women joined twelve mid men in a cast of twenty-four).[i] But civilian women continued to participate in religious programs and other cadet functions.

Favoritism was clearly the hottest issue among midshipmen. To

[g]That issue also claimed that a third class man had been named as a father, although the *New York Times* reported that no violations of the paternity regulation were ever established.

[h]Perhaps only because such a small number of individuals should not be able to effect such an enormous change in tradition.

[i]"Midshipwomen" is incorrect. Midshipman is a rank held by both men and women.

some it meant "fabricating" slots for women, as distinct from "tokenism" that reserved or guaranteed existing slots for them. As
women officers at Annapolis saw it, Navy women seemed to be
tokens but not "favorites": they were few in number and picked
because women were coming, but they *did* have "real" jobs. From
the beginning in fact, Annapolis meticulously avoided assigning responsibility for the women to women; men were always required to
manage mids of both sexes, and the few women officers there had
regular responsibilities. The latter condition meant not only that
women had military role models but also that men saw women in
command and in professional roles. One did not hear that some
midshipmen refused to salute women officers as one did hear at the
Air Force Academy.

Favoritism was not just the work of officials. Middies saw it in
themselves and assumed it about others. Middies worried (as did the
cadets at the other academies) about their own capacity to discipline
a good-looking, smiling, young woman; officers, too, worried more
about their chivalry than their chauvinism. This disbelief in their
own capacity to be even-handed may have led them to suspect one
another. If so, women's presence could be said to have created division—even if the women did not want special treatment, men
were prepared to believe they were getting it.[j] Further, the uncertain
enforcement of social prohibitions between women and men mids
made most men stop initiating contact with the women; this lead to
an isolation made even stronger by the very limited number and
wide dispersal of the women. One woman wryly reported, "the only
way they [men mids] know how to relate to a woman is through a
Form Two!"[k]

Navy Research

Navy research on the new kind of midshipmen did not come out of
the academy. The Annapolis Department of Behavioral Science
came under the Division of Naval Command and Management
(along with Navigation, Seamanship, and Tactics), although it had
a civilian chairman. Its mission was considered training, and during
1976 it was formally transferred from the dean's to the comman-

[j]Most women argued strongly that they did not want such treatment, and they appreciated
that penalties would be attached if they were to get it anyway.

[k]And the women *did* receive at least their share of demerits.

dant's jurisdiction, much to the surprise of the newly chosen chairman, who learned of the reorganization only after his arrival.[1]

The Annapolis administration was not interested in research on women's integration, even though the Department of Defense did favor some kind of systematic reporting. Both West Point and Air Force made a commitment to document their experiences. And professional associations such as the American Psychological Association and the American Sociological Association had indicated an eagerness to schedule presentations about women's integration. The Academy finally yielded and the Navy Personnel Research and Development Center in San Diego was permitted to send two attitude surveys (in October 1976 and May 1977). However, on-site research was discouraged and questionnaires sent for the class of 1981 were never administered.

The primary research question was whether and when contact reduced prejudice. Other scholarship has outlined certain conditions that appeared to reduce and other conditions that seem to enhance prejudice. Apparently prejudice is increased when: (a) the contact involves competition, (b) the contact is involuntary and/or unpleasant, (c) prestige is lost by the contact, or when one group is of lower status or lower in any relevant characteristic, (d) the dominant group is frustrated, and (e) the groups hold different moral standards. Contact seems to decrease prejudice when: (a) an egalitarian relationship exists, (b) authority encourages friendliness and egalitarianism, (c) background is similar, and (d) contact extends from a role to a personal basis.[7] To some degree, *all* of the above seemed to characterize women's academy admission. Thus prediction would seem nearly impossible!

The most interesting research finding was that midshipmen's attitudes converged.[m] In the fall those with the most contact (participating in mixed small units like platoons or squads) had the most positive attitude, those with least contact (members of companies without women) were second, and those in companies with women but *not* in squads or platoons with them were least positive. (A company has 120 members.) However, by the end of the year, attitudes became slightly more positive and also more homogeneous. (See Table VI.)

---

[l]This shift is exactly the opposite of the West Point shift. At the Air Force Academy, the Behavioral Science Department features an all-military cast but it comes under the dean and is clearly an academic, not a training, unit.

[m]Perhaps this convergence should be expected in a military institution that imbues "The Brigade" or "Mother B" (like "the wing"), with an identity of its own.

Table VI. Attitudes of Male Members
of the Class of 1980 toward Women
(Divided according to contact group)

Group	N	*Attitudes Toward Women* Mean Score
Level of Contact, Fall only	*October 1976*	
All male company	199	41.50
Mixed company	262	40.70
Mixed platoon or squad	249	42.65[a]
Level of Contact, Fall or Spring	*May 1977*	
All male company	178	42.67
Mixed company	116	42.00
Mixed platoon or squad	377	43.29
Total Resurveyed Group		
October 1976	661	41.45
May 1977	661	42.77[b]

Source: Adapted from Navy Personnel Research and Development Center,
1976; Durning, "Assimilation of Women into the Naval Academy: An Attitude
Survey," paper presented at the seminar on Armed Forces and Society (Chicago:
20–22 October 1977), p. 7 and Table 4.

[a]$F(2,707) = 3.156$, $p < .05$.
[b]t(correlated) $= 5.24$, $p < .0001$.

Women's views were examined separately. They believed attitudes toward them were negative; 40 percent of them said they were
not treated "as full team members" by their companies, and 20 percent said they were not accepted by other midshipmen.[n] In contrast
to some experimental findings that women performed better in
single-sex groups, 82 percent of the women said competing with
men enhanced rather than decreased their performance.[o8]

Overall, the egalitarian views of women concerning the sexes

[n]Ten percent of male plebes reported not being treated as full team members, and five
percent of the males said they were not accepted by other midshipmen.
[o]Close to two-thirds of the men denied that cross-sex competition enhanced their efforts.

ranged from 82 up to 100 percent on seventeen items; male views ranged from 82 down to 32 per cent on the same items.[p]

Other research on sex roles demonstrates the discrepant perceptions of women and men, and the Annapolis study did so too. Specifically, women and men midshipmen differed on all "impact" items, although they came closest to agreeing when they said that women may have had a positive and at least no negative effect on academic standards. A large minority of women agreed with a large majority of men that women had decreased physical performance standards. However, perceptions on discipline, overall image, and "pride in being a part of the brigade" diverged dramatically, with a large majority of men seeing a negative impact on discipline, about half on image, and a large minority on pride.[q][9]

Similar divergences appear in the class of 1980's perceptions of "favoritism." Women generally perceived fair treatment, although one-third admitted receiving favoritism in physical education, and about one-half believed men received it from upperclassmen. In contrast, close to half the men saw women favored in P.E., and by upperclassmen, company officers, academic instructors, and executive departments. Only 39 percent believed squad leaders favored women, and only 23 percent thought that company commanders did so. The most favoritism men admitted receiving was said to come from upperclassmen. Only 17 percent reported it, but 56 percent of the women believed they saw it.[10]

In describing the sources of their first-year problems, some two-thirds of the women referred to (1) being an object of publicity, (2) resentment of male peers, and (3) male traditions. The lack of senior female role models was *not* considered a problem by 78 percent, and 88 percent did not feel there were "too few other women as support group."[11] These perceptions appear consistent with views of women in the other academies and seem not to provide support for the concern among advocates and planners of women's admission to the academies that there be role models and peer networks at the institutions.[r]

Two other personnel studies (neither done at the academy) bear

[p] Scores fell as items came closer to midshipmen's experience and to the use of women in warfare.

[q] Male views, including those of the class of 1980, were quite negative overall; this is fundamental to any consideration of women's opportunity within the institution.

[r] This subject will be discussed later in connection with the roles played by the Air Force ATOs.

on women's future at Annapolis. They are the work of Lt. Cdr. Beth Coye, who in one study analyzed the theoretical and real roles of women line officers and assessed officers' attitudes toward new roles for women.[12] In the second she surveyed 343 (one-half of the universe) WAVE line officers and 303 male officers attending the College of Naval Warfare and the College of Naval Command and Staff classes of 1972.[13] In this study, women expressed confidence in their capacities to accept new challenges and, except for the captains (the highest rank then held by a woman), believed women were under-utilized, needed viable career lines established, and should become eligible for sea duty. Male officers were more uncertain and inconsistent about women's status and potential. Three-fourths disagreed that "women officers should be given the same opportunities as male officers, including sea duty and flying status."[s] Only 50 percent disagreed that "if a woman were promoted to flag rank, she should be assigned only to the billet of Assistant Chief of Naval Personnel for Women."[t] (That office has since been abolished.) Yet only 30 percent disagreed with the statement that "women officers can give orders as effectively as men."[u]

Perhaps the *Sanctuary* experiment represented the most interesting potential for study. From October 1972 to October 1973, women served at sea aboard the hospital ship *Sanctuary* (which has since been decommissioned). Lt. Susan Canfield (later an Annapolis instructor) served as a navigator, thereby becoming the only woman line officer on active duty with sea duty behind her.[v] Among the *Sanctuary* enlisted personnel, 1.8 percent of the men were discharged "for the convenience of the government" while 3.6 percent of the women were discharged, if pregnancy discharges are ignored; otherwise, 12.7 percent of the women were discharged.[w] On the other hand, men were not trouble free, for they committed twice as many disciplinary offenses as the women. The full report has not been made public, but newspaper and informal accounts suggest that traditional views and behavior remained strong and that the "experiment" changed few views.

[s] One-fourth of the women disagreed.
[t] Ninety-three percent of the women disagreed.
[u] Four percent of the women disagreed.
[v] Other women officers had served at sea in the past.
[w] At that time, pregnancy meant automatic discharge. In 1975 pregnant women were permitted to apply for a discharge *or* for "convalescent leave." In the first year under the new policy, 1,000 pregnant WAVES stayed on duty, and 450 were voluntarily discharged.

The Coast Guard Academy

The Coast Guard Academy (under the Department of Transportation) offers a sea-going civilian career specializing in search and rescue.[x] Both these characteristics may make it more attractive to women than a military defense mission would be, and women have done well in the Coast Guard. More than 10 percent of the class entering in 1976 were women. At the end of the fall semester, a woman was first in academic standing. Active duty Coast Guard women began to go to sea in the fall of 1977, and the first woman Coast Guard aviator won her wings that year. The Coast Guard's apparent success without fuss was sure to pressure the Navy to let its women go to sea. Similarly, both sea services' "successful" female aviators had to pressure the Air Force to declare its experiment with women pilots a success.[y]

The Coast Guard's first research effort involved a study of an active duty male crew and of male and female cadets at sea in the summer of 1977.[14] Several observations bear on decisions administrators had to confront. First, crew attitudes were found to be both more favorable and more heterogeneous than those of men cadets. Apparently young men who (1) understand themselves to be assuming grave responsibilities, (2) are competing directly with women, and (3) feel strong pressures toward uniformity may be *maximally* resistant to women. Second, a strong stereotype attributed "moodiness" and "emotionality" to women. But does this allegation represent a "female" characteristic or does it represent women's response to differential and contradictory treatment? Is it something women must work at, or something men must work at? Does it exist?

In thinking about the meaning of "sexism" or "stereotyping," one should recall that the Civil Rights Movement of the 1960s finally established that white racism was the root of the "Negro problem." Out of that developed the understanding of two different kinds of racism: discrimination and paternalism. In the same way male sexism seems to have (at least) two components: chauvinism and chivalry. This is elegantly demonstrated in an experiment conducted by

---

[x]Some Coast Guard cutters were deployed to Vietnam during the war there. Those so assigned patrolled the coastline and provided naval gunfire support.

[y]Each service seemed reluctant to admit women to its core activity. To avoid doing so, it admitted women to an ancillary activity. However, what was ancillary to one service could be the core of another. Thus in protecting its own core, a service sometimes made a sister service more vulnerable to criticism.

Shomer and Centers that showed men's attitudes toward women fluctuated widely depending on group composition. Men were overwhelmingly chauvinistic in an all-male setting. They were more feminist than any group of women in a setting that included many men but only one woman.[15] Chauvinism is usually admitted as unjust; chivalry is frequently complained about by women, but it seems actually to be a major concern of men. Paternalism probably did not worry whites as much because blacks were in fact a minority. However, even though women and blacks may enter many arenas in similar numbers, the *potential* number of women entrants is so dramatically different that their entrance may cause more latent fear in men who must feel that they cannot afford to be even a little bit chivalrous or they will be totally engulfed. Again, chivalry may well be a more pervasive and intractable form of sexism than chauvinism. It may be particularly difficult to overcome in the military, where officers are by definition gentlemen.

Conclusions

The Merchant Marine Academy went first. Its experience helped the other academies plan with some confidence. The Coast Guard's effort probably represented what all the academies desired—quiet success. The military academies, however, could not avoid public scrutiny. Annapolis kept the lowest profile, but an outsider must have wondered why at-sea integration of its cadets was so much more difficult than for those of the Merchant Marine and Coast Guard.

The Defense Department academies responded to the same mandate in rather different ways because of their different missions, staff, and histories. West Point, thinking infantry, tried to make its women cadets as similar to its men as possible. Annapolis, responding to the women not so much as antagonists but as beneficiaries of a bizarre Congressional decision, sought to submerge its women and treat integration as, after all, incidental. At the Air Force Academy, officials accepted the mandate as a challenge and set out to do it "better than anyone else." Whether the spirit was one of sober compliance, cool managing, or enthusiastic purpose, all three academies permitted the continued expression of a male culture that may have seemed "natural" to insiders but that outsiders might have found surprising. One of many examples was the Annapolis class ring selected by the class of 1979. It read "Last all-male class." This recorded a fact, but it also drew a boundary. One assumes that a ring saying "Last all-white class" would not have been permitted. Even if women's integration was accepted as legal, it was still not felt to be right; moreover, that feeling was rooted in physiological differences—especially those related to strength.

6

Upper Body Strength:
Physical Education and Athletics

Athletic competition is a cherished part of U.S. culture. James Michener, who himself got to Swarthmore on a basketball scholarship, argues that the basic principles of sport are fun, health, and entertainment and that if sport degenerates into the kind of production associated with ex-Ohio State coach Woody Hayes, "our democracy is doomed."[1] But athletic competition is mostly male, and Michener's elements of health and recreation do not provide enough of an explanation to account for male dominance in athletics and athletics' continuing importance in the military. Harry Edwards goes further by arguing that the American sports creed is nothing less than an ideology and that athletics is not only associated with character development, discipline, competition, and fitness but it is also linked to religiosity and nationalism.[2] Violence is central both to the military and to the most popular U.S. sport, football, but the crucial commonality may be that of *ordeal*. An ordeal involves victory, but it also tests limits. Either an individual's or a team's physical and/or mental resources are pushed to exhaustion to prove one's worth and even one's moral rightness, whether it be through an individual's challenge to nature or Air Force's challenge to Navy. Other observers have described male athletics generally, and the whole first year at the military academies specifically, as a masculine rite of passage.

Whereas tribal analogies may be relevant, what is clear is that in both instances physical tests justify a social role.

The military competes on behalf of a nation just as an athlete competes on behalf of a school, yet women are not often included in either of these forms of ordeal. Is this so because women only represent women? Is representation of a nation or an institution basically a male prerogative? And why are athletic tests usually of hard-hitting, high-jumping, and quick-running—undeniably things at which men as a group are better than women? Are the tests of "manliness" and, therefore, of things men do better than women? Or are hitting, jumping, and running of intrinsic value? What if the tests were of floating, flexibility, and balance? Is it possible that women's participation is limited because they are required to fill the roles of spectator and supporter? Why should Air Force cadets training to become career officers regularly be subjected to physical and mental ordeals? Why should they participate in competitive athletics? What level of accomplishment should be required of a cadet? What value is there in exceeding some kind of physical strength minimum?[a] These are ultimate questions and ones academy physical educators eventually asked themselves as they worked out the integration of women into their programs. However, when first told that women were coming and that there was to be a single-track physical education program, the colonels in charge were stupified. They soon recovered and sought to find out just what women could do athletically and to inform the rest of the academy about what they had learned of women's physiology.

The Code Word

The Department of Physical Education outlined the areas that would require research and compiled a reference bibliography as early as May 1972. Their attention focused on the need for new measures of women's capacity. Both pushups and pullups were assumed to be "too strenuous for females," and it was also assumed that a new method of scoring would be needed for those physical tests that could be used for both women and men. Since the three military academies use the same Physical Aptitude Exam (PAE) to test admissibility, reconsidering its elements and scoring had to be a co-

[a] Annapolis set a minimum Physical Aptitude Exam (PAE) score for entrance and that was that. West Point graded on a curve for admission. The Air Force set a minimum for principal appointments and gave bonus points to higher achievers.

operative effort.[b] Items on the Air Force Academy's Physical Fitness Test (PFT), however, were completely under academy jurisdiction because the PFT was used only to monitor cadets' physical condition during their stay at Colorado Springs.

The physical education department's educational effort involved first its staff, then the upper class cadets who had regular teaching and administrative duties, and finally the new cadets themselves. What is interesting is the topics the department selected for education; they were rather different from those chosen by Yale when it went co-ed in 1970.

Yale's student Committee on Human Sexuality published a pamphlet, "Sex and the Yale Student," for members of the Yale community. The cover featured a photograph of a Brancusi sculpture from the Philadelphia Museum of Art representing an embracing couple, and it contained sections entitled "Anatomy and Physiology," "Questions Students Ask," "The Morning After Pill," "Venereal Disease," and "Campus Groups Related to Sex." Yale's concern was clearly copulation and procreation; its response was to educate and to "provide you with some practical ways in which you can cope with your problems (and pleasures) if and when they arise." The Air Force had concerns about conception, too, but handled them with studious neglect.

The pamphlet the Air Force Academy would issue in 1976 was an instructional booklet authored by two junior officers, one male and one female. Its title was "Sex Differences in Response to Physical Activity," although the cover showed three drawings of women and none of men. Inside, the physiological differences between women and men were meticulously described. These were not the differences between the reproductive systems, however; they were primarily the differences in the aerobic and musculature systems. The concern was not sexual but athletic; specifically, the emphasis was on the different capacities of women and men as they related to physical training, the PAE, and the PFT.

The intended audience was mostly male, and it was assured that there were no gynecological considerations of any consequence, that the menstrual cycle need not interfere with training (even with

---

[b]Reaching unanimity was not always easy. For instance, one of the test items was the basketball throw for distance. The Air Force argued (unsuccessfully) that, because of women's hand size, a volleyball throw would be more appropriate as a strength test for women. Interestingly, though, the use of a volleyball rather than a basketball showed little change as far as the weaker women were concerned. Only the "better" women changed their scores with a ball more suited to their hand size.

swimming), and that "possible" stress associated with premenstrual and menstrual days should be of no "major" concern to instructors.[c] What the book failed to say that might have been of concern to women cadets was that intensive physical training sometimes disrupts the menstrual cycle. Because a missed period or periods can be emotionally devastating to a young woman who has engaged in intercourse, this omission would seem most unfortunate. Given that some Air Force administrators seemed to hold the traditional belief that to give young people too much information about reproduction was to encourage immorality, their circumspection here may seem misplaced. In this case, however, the omission of information was based on the belief that information about the effect of exercise on menstruation was still uncertain and should not be treated as though authoritative.

The section on physical differences began, "Anatomical differences favor the male." It acknowledged that women can withstand colder temperatures "far easier" than men and that woman's lower center of gravity "gives her an advantage in balance."[d] Overall, however, the data on oxygen consumption, heart weight, skeletal size, and body fat percentage left the nontechnical reader with the impression that a woman's physical capacity is just about 85 percent that of a man.[e]

The study of capacity was crucial because P.E. philosophy was going to evolve to one requiring "equal effort," and, to measure effort, capacity had to be known. While national studies suggested

[c]This section began, "Studies have indicated that 49 percent of female medical and surgical hospital admission, most psychiatric hospital admission, and 62 percent of violent crimes among women prisoners occur on premenstrual and menstrual days"—a rather awesome beginning to a benign conclusion.

[d]In the post-Vietnam era, a toleration of cold temperatures might not seem important, but in other wars in other places it could be relevant. The question of balance seems more problematical. The female's center of gravity is at 56.1 percent of her height, while that of the male is at 56.7 percent of his height. Since women are shorter, their "centers" are absolutely, as well as relatively, closer to the ground. Still, one has little sense of how or how much the woman is advantaged. In spite of the wondrous accomplishments of women gymnasts on the balance beam, for instance, women did not perform noticeably better on the horizontal log crossing in the obstacle course. Possibly, the males' practice outweighed any female advantage in structure.

[e]Women's track records are around 85–90 percent those of men's. Swimming records seem to be converging: in 1924, the women's 400-meter free-style record was 16 percent less than that of men's; by 1976 it was 7.7 percent less. The academy's 7,250-foot altitude was an added concern because some research suggested that women conditioned more slowly than men and, in particular, adjusted to altitude more slowly.

something like a 15 percent overall physical differential, the Air Force Academy would find that its female population could narrow that gap to about 10 percent. Based on this information cadet women would be asked to run two miles in eighteen minutes in 1976; men would be expected to run them in sixteen minutes. In 1977 these standards were changed to seventeen and fifteen minutes.

The Department of Physical Education wanted its staff, military training officers, and supervising cadets to know just what kind of performance they could expect of the women cadets. By providing the best information available, it sought to avoid abusing the women by overextending their capacities and to prevent coddling them because of underestimating their strength and endurance. The department also hoped to demythologize menstruation and to prepare men to handle possible "emotional outbreaks."

Even the "best" information was meager and tentative. In the face of profound ignorance, the Air Force took the position that one's policy should be guided by what was known, but that policy makers should be open to new information and be prepared to adjust their policy to it. West Point took the position that data on women's physical performance was so inadequate that no policy could be based upon it. Therefore, West Point chose to inject its women cadets into the regular physical training program, to observe them, and only later to determine what adjustments would be necessary. In a curious way anti-feminists and some pro-feminists were in accord with each other and with West Point (i.e., in urging that women meet male standards).

The booklet was generally well received: officers and cadets felt they knew what to do. For the most part women, too, responded positively; they had a sense that goals established for them were appropriate and that their disciplined efforts were "successful" even when they did not match male achievement. Only a few were offended by what they saw as an implicit message that women were but eighty-five one-hundredths of a man. Only one woman noted an analogy to the slave who was considered "three-fifths of a man" in the 1789 Constitution, although another did argue that the net effect of the booklet was to undermine women's confidence and to buttress men's disdain. After reading it she said, "I was amazed I could get up in the morning!"

The booklet emphasized the ways in which men were the superior, because it was based on physical tests in which men were superior. When pressed, the physical education department's chair and his head of research were able to think of training and tests at which women would excel. They even contemplated the benefits for women (esteem) and men (perspective and humility) of incorporating such activities in the physical education program.[f] That idea, however, had only a brief existence.

The academy's physical education testing may distinguish men with higher overall strength and endurance and with more positive attitudes from "lesser" men, but the tests make little pretense of relating to professional needs.[g] While good health and a positive attitude may be prerequisites to a successful career, competitive strength and endurance tests are not used to select officers for admission to the service *or* for promoting or continuing them in service.[h] Physical size is not controlling in technological, conventional, or guerrilla warfare. Thus the continual testing of items in which men excel and the continual referring to women's "lack of upper body strength" may render that phrase a virtual code word that suggests women are inferior, just as "law and order" has been said to mean "anti-black and poor."[i] That is, repeated reference to women's "lack of upper body strength" implies a female deficiency in something Air Force officers *do*, even though that "doing" may be totally apart from the demands of duty.

[f]Items might have included measures of buoyancy, or flexibility, or both.

[g]After efforts to shift enlisted women into a variety of nontraditional career fields resulted in some mismatching (i.e., slight women being expected to perform tasks they could not manage physically), the Air Force developed a set of physical requirements for many enlisted job classifications. These requirements now apply to both men and women. Previously, small men had been "carried" (and probably, to some degree, tormented) by their larger co-workers. As women entered jobs that were physically demanding, a potential developed for having many small individuals. Assisting them became a burden. As a result, the women's lesser capacity was resented. A long-term solution might involve equipment redesign. Two small tool boxes could replace one large one. The purpose of machines and tools is, after all, to create a mechanical advantage so that the operator can accomplish a task with little effort. If machines now emphasize the use of upper body strength in amounts available to an "average" male, there is no reason at all for not (1) redesigning them for the "average" female, and/or (2) switching to the application of "lower body strength." In World War II, Korea, and in Vietnam, U.S. servicemen fought smaller men. It was never suggested that because our men were bigger and had more "upper body strength" they had an advantage over the enemy.

[h]The Air Force does require "fitness" of its officers; both men and women must annually report their weight, and men must report their time for the mile-and-a-half run. These tests, however, are rarely used to force discharge or retirement, nor were they used to accomplish a "reduction in force" following the Vietnam War.

[i]The literal or intended meaning of such phrases may not be an issue. Nevertheless, the meaning attributed to such phrases by listeners and readers is of great importance.

Personnel and Programs

Although Physical Education and (intercollegiate) Athletics share one director and some personnel, they operate different programs from different buildings. In contrast to P.E., Athletics thought it could play a waiting game. While efforts were made to recruit women swimmers the first year, any women's team would necessarily be an all-freshman team and therefore (it was thought) would not require full and first-class scheduling. It was also thought that coaches could be borrowed from the P.E. staff. Thus the Director of Athletics mostly just waited to see who turned up and what talents they had.[j] Athletic "planning" primarily consisted of stating an assumed sequence for women's participation, which went from support (cheerleaders, managers) to co-ed (but mostly male) teams, to women's club teams, to interscholastic competition. The timing remained unspecified.

Physical education *had* to plan because no matter what their talent, women would be in P.E. courses and in intramural programs. The head of P.E., a West Point graduate from a small town in Georgia (he retired after women had been at the academy one year), was fundamentally troubled by the prospect of women at the academy and the possibility that they might enter combat.[k] Pieces of calligraphy by his son—"Women are necessary evils" and "There's only one way to handle a woman but nobody knows what it is"—were casually (though not prominently) displayed in his office.

The head of research for P.E., freshly returned from a stint in Southeast Asia, was almost bewildered by the prospect of rapidly developing a program for the relatively frail individuals his data told him that women cadets would be. Senior staff members tended to agree with their boss. The (Olympic) wrestling coach in charge of evaluation, the swimming coach who was also deputy head of the department, and the martial arts instructor who managed the intramural program saw little to recommend women's integration—even though one of them had met his wife in a judo class, one had coached girl athletes, and another had a teenage daughter deter-

[j]Potential women coaches eagerly watched in-processing from a convenient balcony, mostly to see how tall the new women were. As it turned out, there were enough athletic women to field teams in basketball, volleyball, track, tennis, gymnastics, cross country, and swimming.

[k]He also thought they would later regret the "fun" they had missed by not attending a civilian school and that they would not live up to their commitment.

mined to become a star basketball player. Women athletes were mostly beyond their experience. One found the expletives he had heard from professional women athletes distasteful and astonishing, and another said he found it hard to accept Micki King Hogue's competitive ferocity.[1]

Junior faculty in physical education included Captain Hogue and three other women officers, one of them a P.E. professional; the other two officers were not P.E. specialists. In fact, one of them was a naval officer on special assignment. These officers were more sanguine about the capacities of young women. So were the more junior male officers—especially those trained in physical education—who seemed to have attitudes somewhat different from those of the "fly boys" assigned to the department for one tour of duty. Their views also seemed to differ from those of the civilian football and hockey coaches, who were hired by the athletic department in hopes of creating winning varsities in two of the three revenue-producing sports.[m]

Three women officers, then, were brought to P.E. in anticipation of the coming of women cadets. Hogue, however, had come there on a routine appointment in 1972. Even though she was a world champion, almost a year passed before officials assigned her to teach diving to male cadets. (One result of Hogue's academy assignment was the chance to help coach a fellow officer to a 1976 Olympic gold medal; a second was her marriage to a newly graduated ex-cadet, James R. Hogue.)[n] Because she was a champion, Hogue was in a somewhat special category. She did a lot of public relations, and while she generally advised on the integration of women she was not involved in the day-to-day development of the women's program. Hogue, a person who makes stringent demands of herself and expects others to do likewise, described herself as "amazed" by the number of "weak" men at the academy. Still, her position on

[1]Captain (now Major) Maxine (Micki) King Hogue was a 1972 Olympic gold medalist in three-meter diving.

[m]The football and hockey coaches had no contact with women athletes, although both selected women as managers for their all-male teams. The athletic director was especially interested in revenue because he hoped to recover some four or five hundred thousand dollars of nonappropriated funds invested with but lost through a stockbroking firm. Yet even under this financial pressure, he did not fall back on what was (and is) frequently claimed in civilian schools—that funds generated by male athletes (usually by football and basketball players) should be used only to support other male athletes in "minor" sports such as tennis or golf.

[n]The novelty of the marriage, with its differences of age and rank favoring the woman, was unsettling for some; but, because the courtship was so discreet and the individuals so respected, it was generally accepted.

women cadets was that they would have to be carefully selected, that they must perform excellently, and that they would have to outdo men. She expected the best of anyone associated with her, and her own experience suggested that, realistically, the only way a woman could survive in the military was through overachievement. From the beginning Hogue argued that women should do everything in the regular program unless there was clear scientific evidence that they could not or should not. Hogue's field report on the Women's Physical Education Department of the University of Northern Colorado might have been used by the P.E. department to justify a rigorous program for women; however, P.E. officials were suspicious about advice from other schools that ran "We don't do it here, but in *your* kind of institution. . . ." In the early planning her views were overruled; it was at first thought that women should not even attempt pushups. As time passed views changed, and by the end of BCT in 1976 women were exempted from only two elements of the summer training—the rope climb (for which they could volunteer) and the wall climb. (Most women were too short to climb the eight-foot wall unaided, but if wall-climbing had been considered an important skill, one might think that P.E. would have followed Hogue's counsel and built a shorter wall for all short cadets or followed the Annapolis policy of providing a stool for short cadets.)

The other women's P.E. specialist was an educator; she had competed nationally in track and had had four years of teaching/coaching experience. Still, she found herself starting as an "assistant instructor," just like the "fly boys." In many ways her views were not congruent with those of Hogue, but both women did have higher expectations for the women cadets than did their male colleagues.

The variety of views about women in the P.E. department reflected heterogeneous personalities and backgrounds. The staffing goal was to have:

60% advanced degrees in physical education
77% annual staff holdover
33.3% service academy grads
25% rated officers
10–13% minority officers[o]

A ratio of one woman officer per one hundred women was considered appropriate to provide role models. It was assumed, however, that all women's classes *could* be taught by men; the converse was

[o]Not a quota and not achieved.

not considered true. As compared to civilian schools, such staffing represents low professionalism and high turnover. It emphasizes amateurism (one of four is "really" a pilot or navigator) and institutional loyalty (one of three is a DOD academy alumnus). It does so because the academy has long emphasized role models by regularly using pilots and graduates as instructors in all aspects of cadet training.

Physical education programs at the academy have as their goal fitness for leadership. They are designed to develop maximum physical endurance, agility, and coordination while instilling competitive, aggressive attitudes.[3] In an institution where courage is a prime value, self-confidence must be a behavioral norm; thus, the physical education programs at the academy seek (in MacArthur's words) "to sow the seeds on the fields of friendly strife, which on other days on other fields, will bear the fruit of victory." Skills and participation but also coaching, organizing, and refereeing athletic activities are essential parts of the program.

There are four kinds of required P.E. courses: (1) aquatics, (2) body development, (3) recreational or carry-over sports, and (4) "competition," which was called "combatives" before women arrived.[p] The name change is not trivial, even though the men's "combative" courses were changed in name (and in the catalogue) only. They encompass boxing in the first year, wrestling in the second, judo in the third, and self-defense (which, according to cadets, is supposed to enable a man to go anywhere in the world without fear) in the fourth (first class) year. Academy administrators were unwilling to enter women in two of these, boxing and wrestling. Although women were not eligible to serve on combat planes, they could not just be excused from "combatives," because then a number of men could claim exemption, too. The solution was to develop substitute courses for the women based on physiological differences and to use the general term "competitives" for both the women's and the men's most rigorous courses.

As compared to many P.E. programs for women, the academy's programs were quite competitive. Also, while other institutions have frequently emphasized individual performance, such as in gymnastics, the academy was quite ready for team sports like bas-

[p]Some believe the single most fear-inducing event at the academy occurs in aquatics: the required jump from the 10-meter platform. Stories of frightened cadets and the pressures used to make them jump are part of cadet mythology.

ketball.[q] Individual sports can be quite narcissistic; team sports require others both to cooperate with and to compete against. Sports like water ballet and dance, which emphasize participation, are sometimes preferred for women over a sport like track, which involves competition against a standard as well as an opponent, or sports, like volleyball, that pit a team squarely against an opposing team. At the academy competitive team sports are important for men, and women participate too. Still, "contact" sports seem to have an especially high value for men, and are almost unknown for women.

"Combatives" seems to be the special case that incorporates both contact and competition. They also comprise a will to dominate, not just to win. Combatives involve a special psychology, for they almost explicitly serve as "trials by ordeal." They are not just a test of "doing better"; they show who *is* better. In military combat one's purpose is to beat, to defeat, to overpower; and in P.E. male cadets are explicitly taught controlled forms of combat.

Some men cadets do not want to box, and wrestling produces a number of injuries. Yet the academy insists on the importance of each man's being tested in a "fight." Boxing instruction is given during the cadets' doolie year, when one complies or quits. One wonders if there would be more resistance if it were not offered until the first class year. Boxing is popular with spectators, however, and the Wing Boxing Tournament is well attended—the 1976 yearbook says especially by "pretty girls." Again, however, there was no debate at all about putting women in boxing or wrestling: the idea was unacceptable. Even the possibility of a weight-class or women-only competition was unpalatable.[r] While some staff believe boxing and wrestling are more important than ever because there has been a decrease in the number of cadets who remember "fighting" as they grew up, none believed such skills were important to women.[s] Therefore, wording in the catalogue was changed; "competition" replaced "combatives," and in the women's curricu-

---

[q]Women's team sports have sometimes been suspected of fostering lesbianism; at one point, in fact, this suspicion was raised in early planning at the academy.

[r]A woman cadet at the Department of Public Safety Academy in Texas sustained a brain concussion while boxing a male cadet in July 1978. A department spokesman said at the time, "because a girl is a girl, she is not exempt from the boxing portion of the training." There were only two women in a class of eighty cadets. Admittedly, the Texas woman was outclassed by a man who was almost 40 pounds heavier.

[s]In one P.E. class six of twenty men reported never having been in a fist fight.

lum (foil only) fencing replaced boxing, while track and field replaced wrestling.

"Self-defense" was put off until the last year for women, although the commandant's "Sexual Assault and Rape Training" (SART) course, which recounted in detail what could happen to young women (and men) and even delimited (on a map) the highest risk areas surrounding the academy, was given after the first summer's basic training. Two crucial issues are involved in offering a sexual assault course. First, there is the question of whether such a course increases women's competency, confidence, and freedom to move in public places, or whether it increases their caution and constrains exploration. Does knowledge that one is considered "fair game" when alone in public handicap an individual, or does it prepare one to assert one's right and while apparently increasing the risk actually decrease it? If social attitudes and physical size make women more likely victims and if the Air Force expects its officers to be confident and coping, should not women be given extra and special self-defense courses—and at the beginning of their training rather than at the end? If they begin disadvantaged or with a "victim" complex or image, do not women need remedial combatives to make them feel as effective as the men with whom they compete? In short, might not women need *more* rather than less combative training?[t]

Second, who should get what training? Most courses like SART are designed for women. Sometimes men are made privy to what women are being taught, but is there something else men should be taught? Should they be taught how effective a trained woman prepared to maim can be? Should they be trained to respect and teach others to respect the right of every woman to have access to all public places without loss of respect? Should they be trained to assist and defend physically or verbally any individual being victimized? Susan Brownmiller has studied the link between women and war; she suggests that women are both war's victims and in a way its justification.[4] If the enemy's women were not "legitimate" rape victims, would men be as quick to assume the role of "their" women's "protector"? How is one's image of oneself as a protector affected by having potential "protectees" as one's peers?

The Air Force Academy staff might profitably have asked if a special experience can be derived from combatives that cannot come from competition. If so, is that experience important to training as

---

[t]SART included a voluntary section on self-defense, which 90 percent of the women indicated they would like to take. However, by the time the course was finally offered only a handful took the time for it.

a military officer? If so, how can a policy of refusing that training to women be justified? If not, how are the injuries to men induced by boxing, wrestling, even football, justified?

The P.E. department had its own Women's Integration Committee, which began a January 12, 1976, report by observing that women not only "have their foot in the door, but a slender leg, hopefully attached to an attractive torso, topped by a comely face."[5] Even if that apparently somewhat insensitive committee had worked out a set of consistent principles with respect to combatives, it probably would not have been allowed to implement them. To have killed boxing or wrestling for men would have created furor in the academy and among its graduates; to put women into boxing or wrestling would have created a public furor and led to accusations that the academy was trying to drive women away. Of course, the committee did not want to do either. The fact was all too clear that the detested "dual track" *was* more palatable than any single track. This reality was especially true of combatives, but it was also to some degree true for recreational sports and body development as well.

The point must be made once again about the purpose of the physical education program. Because programs consist of skill-learning, testing, and competing, even the faculty sometimes has to remind itself that physical education programs are means, not ends. The ultimate goals are said to be health, discipline, confidence, leadership, appearance, and safety. There is no strength requirement *per se* for joining the military, only size and health requirements. The aim is not to meet an absolute strength standard, but to be able to do one's work and manage one's body weight. This point was acknowledged in an early position paper that declared the training purpose to be improving flexibility, muscle tone, and aerobic capacity. After the department had gained some experience in training women by training the ATOs in early 1976, it further refined this training goal. That refinement involved a new criterion (which might be interpreted either as a clarification or as a modification of the "body-weight" aim): "equal effort." The physical training programs were said to have as their purpose not attaining equal absolute strength, not managing one's own body weight, but giving equal effort. Physical education was to challenge cadets and test their commitment; it was not to ensure that each could press 300 pounds.[u]

___

[u]With equal effort as the criterion, the handbook defining women's capacity became a very important basis for establishing what the criterion meant in practice.

Optimally, an "effort" test would be individualized and allow a number of variables to be taken into account so that even the finest specimens, those who could meet every challenge with ease, would be pushed to their limit. In fact, all men undertook the same program and were measured by the same criteria. Women had different programs and/or criteria. The intent was to let every cadet experience some success, but also to let each one experience at least a potential for failure.[v] Meeting adversity, dealing with inadequacy, and confronting one's weakness were considered as important to building cadet confidence and character as constant success. Indeed, it was an academy (not particularly a P.E.) axiom that high school "hot dogs" who had never experienced failure were especially prone to first summer attrition.

Physical Education and Athletics directs three different kinds of programs: P.E. instruction, intramurals, and intercollegiate competition. Each cadet takes four P.E. courses a year. There is a core curriculum for the first year and one or two electives during the last (first class) year. Even though the academy was committed to a single-track program in the women's entering year, swimming was the only co-educational course.[w] Both women and men took a class in physical development and one in gymnastics, but they took the two separately.[x] Finally, women took fencing when men took boxing. In the second year, two of four courses would be co-ed (sports such as tennis, golf, and volleyball), but women would play badminton when men played handball, and they had track when men had wrestling. It was thought that women's smaller and more easily bruised hands justified not making handball a required course. However, women were allowed to play it for recreation and intramurals. In the second year of integration, racquetball was made mandatory for all, and handball was dropped. Only in the third year would

[v]A third training goal is to develop group unity. Thus most activities are organized by squadron, and squadron spirit is assiduously cultivated through competition and recreation, and BCT unit names manifest this spirit: "Aggressors," "Bearcats," "Cobras," "Demons," "Executioners," "Falcons," "Guts," "Hellcats," "Invaders," and "Jaguars."

[w]Segregated courses, combined with the low number of women cadets, meant that women often took very small classes—sometimes as few as three students to a class. It is also interesting that in the *one* integrated class, swimming, when male-female grade points were compared at the end of the year, they were within one one-hundredth of a point of each other.

[x]Physical development is a classroom as well as exercise class that focuses on conditioning, nutrition, and weight control. Men and women practice different gymnastic events. Although both share floor exercise, the style of even that exercise is rather different. Women often approach a dance style; men's style is more acrobatic.

cadets have wholly integrated P.E. courses. In the last year it was planned to give women racquetball rather than squash.[y]

All cadets (except those on athletic teams) also participate in an elaborate, three-season, squadron-organized, intramural program that cadets organize, coach, and officiate. Since even the least adept must participate, strategy can become complex. For instance, all of a squadron's nonathletes might be bunched on a team acting as a "loss leader" to build a championship team in another sport.[z] Women were "fully integrated" in the program, but "cadet interests and squadron needs" were deemed to preclude the use of women on a squadron's football team. (Two women did ask to play football, but when they found out it was tackle, not touch, and that they would be legitimate targets for every hostile cadet on the opposite team, they were dissuaded.) Because choices for women were fewer than for men, and because most of the women were on a varsity team, a ruling was made that permitted women to participate in an intramural sport they played (in another season) as a varsity team member. Men were not permitted to do so, but because the policy did not upset the intramural balance and gave the squadrons more options in making assignments for women, little opposition was registered to what was a clear dispensation for women. In early plans, all-women intramural competition had been considered.

Women's participation in intramurals was hardly tested in 1976, since so few women participated.[a] Only 24 women were in fall intramurals, 62 in winter, and 66 in spring. When there are 3,000 or 4,000 men in a program, 60 women scattered through several sports have little impact. One intramural officer noted, however, that the women did produce an "observer" effect. According to him, the women "added a little electricity, produced better sportsmanship, and lifted the level of language." Why were so few women in intramurals? Because they had discovered one important benefit deriving

[y]The net result was slowly increasing integration. The effect of this process is unknown. Some studies suggest that if change is to be accomplished it is better to effect it quickly and cleanly. Other studies suggest that if women are to compete with men in an activity men dominate, they do better if trained in all-female practice sessions so that their confidence is high when they begin to compete with men. Women, the study goes on, should begin any competition as full equals. Early ideas about emphasizing "grace" in women through dance or synchronized swimming were never developed.

[z]Or in the fall all doolies might be assigned to cross-country so upperclassmen could play football.

[a]The best (or most ambitious) women played varsity sports; thus those "left" for intramurals were not only few in number but they also tended to be the less athletic as well.

from their minority status: it was easy for a woman to make an intercollegiate athletic team![b] And if one did make a team, one not only got out of intramurals but also did not have to eat with and be hassled by the upperclassmen in one's squadron. One also got to travel, a pleasure not usually available to a doolie.

Some tension has always existed between athletes and the cadets in their squadron because a certain amount of privilege is thought to accrue to athletes, whose coaches monitor their academy experience and pressures. Thus when so many women made one athletic team or another, some cadet unrest (and disparagement) was inevitable. Some women made three teams, one per season. Fortunately, even though the teams were selected from fewer than 150 doolies, their creditable records against even four-year schools protected the women athletes; the women's track team placed the first women's trophy in the field house display case in the spring of 1977.

The Learning Process: Preppies, ATOs, and BCT

The athletic department's integration committee had two pre-entry experiences to learn from. First, it learned from the Prep School (where only seven of fourteen women finished) that women were not well received by their peers.[c] Then, in the ATO program, academy personnel were given the opportunity to try to teach and train women.[d] As is thoroughly reported in an academy report titled,

[b]Each year, as women increased in number, competition to make a team would also increase. Nevertheless, the odds for making a team are better for those who are one of 600 rather than one of 4,000.

[c]In 1976–77 things went more smoothly. A woman's athletic trainer was available, women cadet candidates were admitted to the "Blue Chip" (athletic program), and women were more integrated in physical training and intramurals. Only wrestling was for men only. It should be noted that the prep program is one year long, so the women associated solely with peers. There were no upperclassmen—male, female, or surrogate.

[d]At West Point, Project 60 was in progress at the same time. It involved sixty local high school girls selected for their "responsibility" and "physical activity"; each had passed the West Point physical entrance exam. Project 60 was designed to assess two kinds of training programs: a three-day-a-week strength training program, and a four-day-a-week reveille exercise program similar to Basic Cadet Training (BCT). (A control group was included.) At the end of seven weeks of training, physical testing was conducted and the opinions of the young women and of their male cadet trainers were collected.

While its results were not definitive, the program gave staff and cadets experience. The findings were similar to those the Air Force Academy would generate, but the training observations are important, too, and they gave some reason for continued concern. Among the findings: (1) instructors believed that the women performed better when pushed in a demanding but enthusiastic way; (2) an initial low tolerance for pain was overcome during the training

"Women's Integration Research Project, Project Blue Eyes, Phase I," the ATO training program involved putting fifteen young women officers through an abbreviated, one-semester form of the four-year cadet cycle of physical and military training. Because officers are college graduates, no academics were included. Short versions of BCT and SERE were included (the BCT being conducted in unpleasantly cold, rather than hot, weather). First class cadets (under supervision) did much of the training, and here the "contrasting perceptions phenomenon" first emerged. The women were pleased with themselves and believed that they had successfully completed the training. Some respect was accorded them because many men had not expected them to finish at all. However, the basic male evaluation, which inevitably compared the ATOs to male cadets, was that the ATOs had fallen short.[e] (See Deaux for experimental evidence showing that a woman's performance may be highly valued when compared to that of other women but devalued when compared to that of men.) This ATO training evaluation confirmed the P.E. department's decision to teach physical development to the women and men separately, and to teach the women skills men did not seem to have to be taught (e.g., how to fall and how to jump). The need to teach became apparent when women tackled the obstacle course. Stiff-legged jumps and backward falls demonstrated some of the women's profound ignorance about how to handle their bodies. The department realized, as well, that specific standards to represent an "equivalent effort" would have to be established.

The ATOs were carefully selected, but they had not been chosen for athletic accomplishment. Indeed, 6 of the 15 were judged as athletically deficient, although none were removed from the program for lack of athletic ability.[f] It is also important to remember that the training environment of the small group of ATOs was quite different from that of the 150 women who would be trained alongside 1,500 male peers. In the ATO setting, small group interaction was important; individual injuries, illnesses, and moods seemed to

---

period; (3) these relatively athletic women displayed a surprising lack of form, even in running (this, of course, raised the possibility of improving performance simply through instruction); (4) a "fatigue syndrome" was manifested even in the seven-week test programs, as was a decrement in "positive attitude"; and (5) boots were so hampering that they had to be eliminated from training. These last three findings suggested long-term and cumulatively negative results.

[e] One faculty member said, "After seeing the ATOs, I thought we were going to have to conduct all women's training in secret!"

[f] As a group, the prep school women had averaged 460 on the PAE and the ATOs 480. The entering class of women would average 588.

affect the whole group.[g] Staff-trainee ratios were exaggerated, and trainers observed great swings in group motivation. Whether the variability derived from the intensely personal teaching or from differences in male and female culture is unknown, but it was not catered to. Generally, staff officers assumed that women at the academy would have to respond to the academy's way of doing things. Only in brief moments of contemplation did the staff consider that their job entailed eliciting the best possible performance from each cadet, or that the range of their motivating techniques might have to be extended as the wing became more heterogeneous.

The problem of how to motivate women was generally solved by assuming that their motivation was the same as that of men. Still, those who coached both women and men agreed that "in practice" men's and women's teams responded and worked differently. For instance, one male officer who had coached the men's junior varsity tennis team in 1975–76 and the women's team in 1976–77 agreed with a woman officer who coached volleyball and track that women athletes were less compliant than men, were less likely to do precisely what they were told, and were more likely to insist upon reasons and explanations. Thus instructors recognized the risk of creating a double standard by instructing cadets according to their gender. The same coaches also believed the women were more verbal, interacted more with each other and the coach, and enjoyed their sport (as manifested by singing and chatting on bus rides)—win or lose. As the tennis coach put it, "For them it seems to be enough just to be *on* the team; winning doesn't seem to matter." He was one of the officers who also admitted that he could not really grasp just why a "girl" would want to come to the academy anyway.[h]

Research on the ATO program was the first part of a physical education longitudinal research program called "Project Blue Eyes" (a name that would be changed before attaining too much publicity). The items that it assessed over time included (1) women's performance on the Physical Aptitude Exam (PAE) used by all three military academies, (2) performance on the Physical Fitness Test (PFT),

[g] ATO medical excuses ran as high as 20 percent of the group in the conditioning phase of the program and 33 percent in the weight training. Sprains, strains, and other injuries were also common. In fact, only four ATOs went without injury.

[h] He was an ex-cadet, and he and his wife had enjoyed many academy dates. They regularly mixed with cadets and their girl friends and extended themselves to the women cadets as well. Nevertheless, the women's motivation eluded them. All this is important because the academy was trying hard to manage cadets through "positive motivation." Thus a widespread failure to understand the motivation of any group of cadets could have serious results.

which consisted of five items and was taken by cadets at least twice a year, (3) results of various physical conditioning programs, including items such as calisthenics, group continuous running, interval running, weight training, and aerobics, (4) somatograms, which show (quantitatively) body shape based on the percentage of deviation from the individual's body radius, and (5) body composition.[i] The net result of the research on the ATOs and on cadets during BCT was to demonstrate the great variability in women's athletic performance. In a sense, both those with low expectations and those with high expectations could claim they had been right. Many women could not; however, many women could.

The ATO experience confirmed the academy's wisdom in sending letters to incoming cadets urging that they undertake a vigorous conditioning program. A particular program was specified, in part, because women's views on adequate conditioning were not necessarily congruent with those of academy instructors. For instance, one ATO described preparing for her academy assignment by "walking a mile a day," another played "some tennis," and a third joined a YWCA "Fat Fanny" club.

In Basic Cadet Training the athletic department had its first opportunity to see "real" women cadets in action (35 percent of them reported that they had followed the suggested conditioning). The decision to use the performance of only the top nine ATOs as a guide to developing the female cadet program proved sound.[j] The women cadets entering in 1976 chin hung eleven seconds longer, long jumped 4 inches further, pushed up one more time, sat up six more times, and ran 600 yards in half a minute less than had the ATOs.[k] In addition, 92 percent of the cadets were in the less-than-ten percent of U.S. women who could do a pullup. The cadet women, then, were much more fit than the average woman. On five items, they ranged from the 70th to the 99th percentile for women;

[i]This data would be used to "prove" women cadets had not been "masculinized" by their strenuous program. The body composition test was used to make individual "body image decisions", i.e., to determine whether a cadet was too fat.

[j]On the PAE the ATOs had performed at the 50th percentile for women nationally; the entering women cadets would perform at the 75th percentile. Further, in the first several days of training, the class of '81 looked even stronger than that of '80. Many of the women of '81 (60 percent) had obtained and broken in their combat boots before arrival. None "fell out" on the first mile run, and pushups and pullups did not seem to faze them. Presumably, the even more vigorous six-page letter from the athletic department about pre-entry training had been taken to heart. Thus the fears that the "pioneers of 1980" would set standards that would later be found "too high" seemed incorrect.

[k]The decision to have women cadets do pushups was made just before they entered.

that year male cadets ranged only from the 30th to the 75th for men. A general goal of the academy has been to admit men who are at the 50th percentile or higher and to graduate cadets who perform at the 75th percentile and up. In 1976, women actually entered at the 75th percentile (for women); thus, no improvement would be required of them for graduation if the same standard, one of relative fitness, were to apply to them.

However, when women's and men's performances on four of the five physical fitness test items were compared, the actual performance of women was .5 (pushups), .8 (600-yard run), .8 (standing long-jump), and .9 (situps) that of men.[1] Men's perception that women were not doing as well on test items as they was accurate.

Data were beginning to accumulate that would help the academy determine realistic standards for women, to what degree the distribution of male and female performances overlapped, and whether cadets could be treated as a unit with women clustered in the lower half of the distribution or whether the two groups would better be treated separately.[m] The fact is that the overlap was not large. In West Point's Project 60, for instance, the male cadet mean for the block shuttle run was the same as the best time for a woman participant; the slowest male cadet time was the same as the average time for the Project 60 women. On the West Point physical fitness test, the highest women's score would have been a (man's) C −, and 87 percent of the women would have flunked. Comparable statistics were hard to obtain at the Air Force Academy, where the chairman of physical education had declared, "There are two things we do not want to do—compare men to women or make Amazons out of women." Nevertheless, cadet women were reported to have 92 percent of the men's cardiovascular fitness.

Women's scores during BCT were not as reliable as the men's; and even though women's effort (as measured by average heart rate)

[1]Pullups are omitted since women were tested on the flexed-arm hang, instead. This test was given at the end of four weeks of training. The only major change since entrance was in pushups; on entrance, women had done only .35 as many as men.

[m]Because women represented such a small percentage of the whole, the number of men with the physical aptitude of women could yield a co-ed, but predominately male, ability-grouped class at the lower end of the scale, all-male classes at the upper end, and *no* all-female classes. To illustrate: 10 percent (147) of the entering male cadets swam less than 500 feet in the five-minute swim; 16 percent of the women did so. But since the absolute number of women was only twenty-six, when they were grouped with the "slow swimming" males, they were *still* outnumbered six to one. Thus men would not seem to have their egos jeopardized by being in a "women's" class. Conversely, women would not feel collectively incompetent since most of the members of the class would be male.

was almost identical to men's, dropouts were higher (averaging over 5 percent for women and under 1 percent for men). Drills designed to teach falling and body control to the women were deferred from the summer to the fall because more training was required than there was time in which to give it.[n] In fact, the specialized conditioning course previously required of the cadets who failed on the PFT was canceled in 1976. Presumably this cancellation occurred because the (worst) men consigned to this ignominy would correctly argue that they were in an absolute sense better than women who had escaped it.

The careful evaluation of BCT caused by women's presence made the athletic department newly aware of something they may have already known but not acknowledged: the rigorous summer program did *not* condition the cadets. In fact, it caused an actual deterioration in condition, especially in explosive power (jumping), because of excessive stress and fatigue. Varsity coaches had complained of this phenomenon previously, but their suspicions were not confirmed until the 1976 record keeping. Because of this finding, the athletic department was charged with developing a more moderate and better integrated physical training program for BCT in the following year.

Pugil stick fighting and the assault course were probably the two BCT activities in which people found it hardest to accept women participating.[o] The first involves two-person combat with long, padded poles that resemble a kayak paddle. Each cadet is matched for size (and in 1976 for sex) and wears a protective helmet and a groin or breast protector. (The "breast protector" was a catcher's chest protector. Solid, cup-shaped protectors were rejected by the women officers, who said the edges cut and actually did more damage than the activity itself.) Because a marine recruit had recently died in pugil stick combat, the weapon had been eliminated in most military training. At the Air Force Academy it survived. The assault course was conducted under mock battle conditions. It included crawling under barbed wire, dodging explosions, enduring verbal harassment, and carrying weapons with bayonets.[p] When these activities were treated as "expected behavior," women participated in both

[n] Culture seemed to handicap women physically in two ways. First, they were in poor condition; second, they did not "know how" to do things the Air Force had never thought of as needing to be taught.

[o] These BCT activities were supervised by the commandant, not P.E.

[p] In 1976, training began with bayonets. Without explanation they were removed halfway through, and male cadets believed it was because one of the women had cut her finger.

without adverse results. Perhaps the whole BCT experience was so novel to doolies that no single item seemed especially bizarre. One BCT change was made: the title awarded to the fiercest participant in basic was changed from "Bad Mother" to "Bad Basic."

In sports events during the summer, women participated in only six of the eleven activities. Football and wrestling were clearly ruled out by departmental policy, but women did not participate in basketball, soccer, or water polo either. Conversely, the limitation on women for contact sports almost certainly accounts for the women's low, 6 percent as compared to the men's 9 percent, injury rate (mostly to lower extremities). In fact, football, soccer, and wrestling produced 50 percent of all male injuries.[q]

In assessing changed performances over the summer, two differences between women and men need to be observed. First, some dramatic changes like the women's 46 percent increase in their capacity to do pushups may have occurred more through learning than through conditioning. Second, in most conditioning programs variability is reduced; performance becomes more homogeneous. Women, however, increased their variability in two of five items. This increase suggests that as a group women may have been farther from their physical limits than were men, or it may suggest that some women were more responsive than others to the short period of conditioning provided by BCT.

By the conclusion of the summer, the P.E. unit was ready to advocate replacing the flexed arm hang in the PFT with pullups.[r] Since 91 percent of the women could do a pullup with a range from zero to ten (the men's range was zero to nineteen), this test did yield a discriminating distribution for women and also made possible the same measure for all cadets. The pullup, since it involved movement, was clearly more related to the ability to manage body weight

---

[q]Officials worried about injuries because they understood women to be more susceptible than men. (They must have felt justified in that belief when this author suffered a sprained ankle and ended up on crutches after failing to rise properly from a chair to a standing position.) However, it was also clear that while officers were always concerned about safety, they felt a special anxiety about women. Partly they did not want bad publicity, but they also felt a degree of protection and chivalry. Four male noses were broken during the summer. If a woman's nose had been broken, there would certainly have been some formal response—if only a reminder to all concerned to be extremely and consciously reasonable about such events. Clearly, men would have felt worse about a woman's lost tooth or facial scar than about a man's comparable injury, and it is even possible that a woman cadet would have "suffered" more than a male from the same injury.

[r]It would take two years for this change to be effected.

in a vertical plane.[s] The women's dramatic improvement in pushups made the staff confident that pullup scores, too, were probably more related to "cultural deprivation" than they were to "physiological limitation."

Intercollegiates

Women cadets did not "evolve to" an intercollegiate athletic program—they plunged in. It was originally thought that they would begin in "support" roles, but in fact women's participation in those roles caused great dissension. In contrast, the women's athletic teams often created a good feeling within the academy (and good publicity as well).

Cheerleading and team managing are the usual support roles. Before 1976, freshmen had not served as cheerleaders. But in 1976 the policy was changed with the approval of cadet leaders. Under the new policy, doolie men and women became eligible for these positions. Many male cadets, however, believed that the intent was to give those slots to women, that the change favored the women, and that the wing as a whole should have been consulted before such a change was made. As a result, the women met resistance. The cheerleaders were booed, and the crowd sometimes cheered only when led by a male.[t] Other women won managerial slots for men's varsity teams, which also caused negative comment. Women no longer manage men's teams. Manager positions are customarily filled at the discretion of the individual coach, and often they go to the "last-cuts." In this case, a series of separate individual decisions gave the women what may have been "more than their share" of total managerships; once more, male cadets charged "reverse discrimination" and groused about women's privileges.[u] (One male did serve as a manager for the women's basketball team.)

[s]In the flexed-arm hang, the cadet is positioned as though she were at the top of a pullup. She remains stationary in that position as long as possible. Interestingly, the correlation between performance on the flexed-arm hang and chinups was not high, and women frequently did as well on the "hang" as males. In fact, one young woman did better than any cadet or faculty, reaching close to two minutes.

[t]Required attendance at rather dismal football performances probably enhanced the crowd's listless and negative response.

[u]It is always more difficult to balance the result of a series of individual decisions than that of a single collective decision. Thus a woman or a minority may be more likely to win a

When women stayed in their places—that is, on women's athletic teams—men seemed to support and approve them. Doolies have to attend one athletic event a week. and often, they attended women's events. They held a "march on" for the women's volleyball team (which achieved a 7–6 record) and led cheers for the basketball team. Only one athletic team incident floored the staff. They adjusted when women rejected breast protectors and coped with female figures in revealing tank suits and loose-legged gym pants, but they could not comprehend one decision of the women's cross-country team. In a dual match the Air Force women were doing very, very well. So instead of running to exhaustion for optimum times, the team engaged in a brief snowball fight, then ran with their slowest sister, and with joyous unity ran across the finish line hand-in-hand—the whole team tying for first place. It was the mind-boggling kind of performance that no coach would have forbidden in advance, because he could not have imagined such an event. The women were thoroughly reproved ("fried") and removed from the team.ᵛ Their display of unity was unacceptable. Why it was unacceptable is still not crystal clear. Was it because of their failure to compete to the limit even against each other? Or was it because by holding hands and running across the finish line they had "embarrassed" their opponents by emphasizing that their worst runner was better than their opponent's best—that is, they were ungraciously competitive versus their foes? The second explanation cropped up most often. Yet it may be that the coaches themselves did not really know what was wrong, but they *did* know that athletes should not hold hands, smile, and frolic across a finish line.

Everyone realized that many women who made teams in 1976 would not make them in 1977 since the pool of women athletes would be doubled. To the degree that athletic participation enhances a woman's academy experience and to the degree that the improving of one's position as one progresses through school is important, some women were sure to encounter discouragement in their second year. Some would be demoted, or perhaps even cut just as they were to begin their second or even their first class year. A negative effect on morale was almost inevitable.

---

state office when a slate (governor, lieutenant governor, attorney general, secretary of state, and treasurer) is put together than when each office is separately contested. In the selection of managers, individual coaches' efforts to be responsive may have resulted in a collective "over" responsiveness.

ᵛThey were permitted to try out for the track team when that season started.

The Fat Machine and Femininity

Just as West Point began to enjoy talking about their women when it meant they would not have to talk about the EE 304 scandal, the athletic department found a new focus for its attention once the women were doing well. That subject was fat. Fat became a concern because of a dispute between the academy and the Air Force Training Command and because of a Congressional special inquiry.[6] At issue was a cadet considered overweight and unfit by his pilot trainers, yet considered a fine specimen by his academy football coaches.[w] The question then became "How do you measure fatness?" The fat question was inevitably associated with the women cadets. They had been gaining weight, and to many of the men (from cadet to general officer) they looked fat. One officer argued that cultural stereotypes were built into "eyeball" appraisals, that most men "just don't know what women look like." Among other things, the academy's boxer gym shorts (a style eschewed by most women) emphasize thighs, which is one of two measures absolutely as large (or larger) for women as it is for men.[x]

If the male cadet's standard for nonfatness or good appearance can be estimated by looking at the women who appear in the *Dodo*, the academy calendar, *Talon*, and *Polaris* (yearbook), their preference is clear: it is for women with fat in the breasts and on buttocks but with thin arms, legs, and torsos. The question here becomes "Is the 'aesthetic' woman a fit or unfit woman?" Cadet taste seems to run to the emaciated-seeming mesomorph rather than to either lean ectomorphs or well-developed mesomorphs. But how would those women do on a physical fitness test? PFT tests scores showed that the cadet women were becoming more fit; scales showed they were getting heavier. Since lean muscle is 25 percent heavier than fat, both findings were perfectly expectable. The women could simultaneously be heavier, healthier, and *less* fat.[y]

In a somewhat defensive mood, the academy began to assess the

[w] Cadets become commissioned officers upon graduation and must therefore meet Air Force commissioning standards. In 1975 five first class cadets failed their graduation commissioning physicals.

[x] The other measure is the buttocks.

[y] West Point's Project Summertime reported that men's weight decreased over the summer, while women's increased. Specifically, the women increased their lean body weight, but decreased their fat body weight and percentage of body fat. (They still had twice the percentage of body fat the men had.) In general, these findings were similar to those of the Air Force Academy.

issue. The purpose was to establish "optimum" weights. At that time Air Force weight and height tables for men were based on averages drawn from raw data on U.S. Army recruits in 1950. The women's height/weight table was created by figuring a percentage (approximately 85) of the male weight.[7] In addition, the tables made adjustments in the height/weight ratio so that less relative weight was required of the younger and taller cadets. The P.E. department's position was (1) that an average weight was not necessarily a good weight, (2) that one's percentage of body fat was the best indicator of fitness, and (3) that different percentages were appropriate for women and for men.

How does one assess body composition? P.E. researchers used three methods on the ATOs: circumferences, skinfold, and body diameters. Since no one method was considered more reliable or acceptable, an average of the three was computed. In developing a "role model body image," a desired percentage of fat was assigned each ATO, ranging from 19 to 24, depending on her bone structure, and a recommended weight was then calculated. By the time women cadets became subjects, a new method was available using "the fat machine," otherwise known as Dr. Allen's Human Body Volumeter.

The rather elaborate procedures involved were made possible only by computers. Each cadet is weighed once a week during BCT and once a month during the fourth class year. All cadets are weighed in September and February, when they take their PFTs. At each weighing, change since last weighing, change since entry, and variance from Air Force standards are assessed. When a cadet is over her or his limit, intervention by P.E. officials sometimes occurs. An exercise program can be assigned, a diet table prescribed, and (since 1977) privileges can be withheld.

To obtain data that would make possible the setting of appropriate standards, research was conducted that included the meticulous measurement of fifty body diameters. Pinching occurred. Finally, a swimsuit-clad cadet would exhale vigorously, climb onto a small elevator, and gently descend into a column of water so that his or her body volume could be calculated by measuring the water displaced. Unfortunately (but typically), the formula for determining the percentage of body fat as related to total volume and weight seems not to work as well for women as for men. Nevertheless, P.E. argued that the crucial ratio was that of body fat weight to lean body weight, not height to weight (the traditional and Air Force measure). Take the case of Man A and B, for example:[8]

A	Dimensions	B
36	Age (years)	45
180	Height (cm)	174
79.3	Volume (liter)	77.4
82.2	Weight (kg)	82.6
24.8	Fat (kg)	13.4
57.4	Lean body (kg)	69.2
0.43	Fat burden (ratio of above)	.19
14.0	Percent overweight (height: weight standard)	24.0

Both men weigh about 82.5 kg. According to the standard table, the taller (A) is 14 percent overweight and the shorter (B) is 24 percent overweight. However, 69.2 kg. of B's weight is lean body weight, compared to only 57.4 kg. of A's. A's fat burden, then, is almost twice that of B's! Which man needs to diet? (Maybe both— but maybe A more—in spite of the height-weight tables.)

The average female's percentage of fat is 24, the male's, 16. The academy's goal is about 12 percent for men and 21 for women.[z] All this seems reasonable in seeking "fitness." What is important is that the goal is fitness for everyone—not a particular fat-lean body ratio for everyone. Again, the measure is relative to one's sex and body; it is not a single standard required of every officer.

The academy was also very sensitive to any suggestion that its women were not "feminine": "It is not our policy to turn our women into men" was fundamental P.E. doctrine.[a] Indeed, the P.E. department conceived an ingenious way of demonstrating that it had not rendered its women masculine—through measurements. These were not just 36-26-36 measurements, but "scientific" ones that included carefully taken diameters. When the women cadets' diameters were compared to those of men, it was found that they had similar thigh and hip circumferences, and chest depth. Compared to men, the women's smallest relative measure was a 91 percent waist depth and an 86 percent neck circumference. Compared to "refer-

---

[z]Minimum essential fat is considered to be 3 percent for men and 14 percent for women.

[a]Which would be hard to do even if it *were* policy, since women apparently do not "bulk up" the way men do. Swimmers do build shoulders, but the colossal (and winning) ones of the East German women are alleged to be the result of hormone stimulation.

ence" males, male cadets had larger knees and ankles and smaller abdomens. When compared to "reference" women, female cadets also had larger knees and ankles, *but* they had 6 percent smaller waists and 7 percent larger chests. Thus if the hourglass look is pleasing and "feminine," women cadets had it. If thin arms and lower legs are crucial, they did not.

Queries

The first summer did not begin to answer all the questions officials had about women's athletic potential and the conditions that enhance it. Despite careful thought and research, questions seemed to multiply and at the same time to become more subtle. Could the academy expect improving performance from each year's new women cadets, or would the pioneers of '80 prove to be the sturdiest? Should minimum performance standards be set for all cadets, even if only the top quartile (or even higher) of women could meet those standards? What is a standard's purpose? How does it relate to an officer's work? How should academy standards compare to those used in other commissioning sources? If an emphasis on sex differences in upper body strength results in a generalized contempt for women as officers, does this contempt differ from that expressed toward "wimps" (frail men)? Why is the shoe and boot problem for women so hard to solve? Does it not get enough attention? Is there a lack of expertise? How does women's presence affect male performance?[b] If women are treated as observers, how does that affect the way men behave? In some situations women have complained that even one male observer "spoils" women's interaction and whether intended or not exercises undue influence. What is the role of the women co-performer? Does her presence produce a self-consciousness that enhances accomplishment? When does a co-performer become a competitor? How does that affect behavior? If women have "low" strength, is it expected that they will be "high" on intelligence, just as small bespectacled males are expected to be "brains"?

In concrete terms, what is meant by "feminine"? What makes a woman appear "masculine"? Is it size, grooming, voice, attitude

[b]For instance, did the "joint" gymnastics, track, and swim teams have better (or worse) performance and morale than the all-male tennis team?

toward men, off-duty behavior?[c] Is discrimination against "masculine" women acceptable? Does this concern reveal a latent fear of having lesbians as officers? Does the concern disappear as women's number and variety increase? Are women more likely to assume protective "male" coloring when they are few in number?

How should grouping be carried out for P.E.? At the Air Force Academy, grouping was once determined by swim test scores; at West Point, by weight. (By a previous method a cadet's whole life had been organized by his height!) Random assignments would result in women being so distributed that they would never compose a "critical mass" anywhere. Because of the separate dressing rooms and the reduction of formality in the P.E. setting, the gym may become a special refuge for women. Is that good or bad for discipline and for morale?[d]

Every BCT squad has a weak or small man who cannot climb the wall or rope. Until women came, the group routinely helped him. When women came, instead of being included and assisted, they were excused from the wall and the rope. Thus male cadets were *not* taught to assist, help, and include women as they did men, but to remain separate from them. Does such separation, which limits first-hand information about female performance, lead men to judge military women not by their own accomplishments and attitudes but by their wives, mothers, dates, and daughters?

Cadets project an overwhelming omnipotence. But if one should chance to observe one of the senior P.E. electives—ice skating—one is reminded that they are normal. To see a rink full of blue-clad cadets solemnly heeling-out and heeling-in in an effort to move backwards is to remember that much of academy training is not directly related to professional work but is designed to produce certain habits and attitudes, and that many of the training settings are male not out of necessity but because men designed them. What "female" training settings would accomplish the same ends? Should men be expected to perform in them?

Women instructors and coaches were brought in and Captain King did coach male divers. Still, there was a feeling that women instructors did not know how to coach "male sports" but that "with their broader experience" men could instruct women. Thus a pattern similar to that in military instruction was established. Male officers

[c]One is easily caught off guard the first time one sees a woman officer (one previously seen only in uniform) in formal dress with elaborate hairdo, jewels, and make-up.

[d]In a class at the University of Southern California, a large number of women admitted to having been student body officers in high school. None had even sought such an office at the

were considered able to handle either men or women, while women officers were assumed to be valuable in working with women, but their capacity to fill any slot a male could fill was doubted.[e] Was that doubt justified? What information or experience could change that attitude?

The Army worked its women to their limit and had a relatively high attrition rate. By the end of the first year, it found itself easing women's requirements by using a different scoring system for them. In contrast, the Air Force consistently moved toward being more demanding. Nevertheless, the Air Force planned to continue to separate incoming women and men cadets in their physical development courses in the second year of integration. West Point's modification decision was to try (at least in BCT) three levels of ability-clustered running groups. One (the "grey") would maintain the traditional distance and pace; the second (the "black") would increase the pace in order to challenge the strongest cadets; the third (the "gold") would be "just a cut below." Presumably most women would be in the third, with a small percentage of men, who would nevertheless represent a substantial absolute number. Presumably, too, those men would work hard to get out of the group.[f]

This last point raises a final and crucial question. Women may compete fiercely against other women but still "accept" defeat by a man. Men may compete strenuously against other men, but outdo themselves in competing against women.[g] Presumably these responses carry over to areas outside athletics. The result is that

---

university. When asked what had happened to them between the June of leaving high school and the September of entering college, one observed: "Well, you know, we don't have gym class any more and that's where we used to organize everything."

[e]For instance, one female coach had been a track competitor at the national level and coached the women's team. Undoubtedly, she was valuable in that assignment, but what would have happened if she had been assigned to coach the men's field events team? Then her function as role model would have been to command, not to consult—it would have been mainstream instead of "special." If she had "succeeded," what would that have meant? If she had failed, what would that have meant? How many or what percentage of women must succeed to change expectations about women in general? How many or what percentage can "fail" without a generalization being made for "all" women?

[f]When I proposed grouping by ability at the Air Force Academy, many officers vigorously opposed it, believing that it would be too degrading for the males. James Michener, too, argues that permitting women to compete against men for "their [the women's] convenience" takes a "heavy psychological cost" and that separating the sexes between ages twelve and twenty-two "conforms to some permanent psychological need for the human race."

[g]One Air Force officer wryly described his Pikes Peak run. At about the time he was sure he would have to quit, he looked over his shoulder. There was a mature woman hard on his heels. He finished, and he stayed just ahead of her.

women and men experience the same situation differently. Both must compete and most of their competitors are men, but for women there is a special problem: as soon as they enter a competition they inspire their competitors to superhuman efforts. That is, their very presence stimulates others to an unnatural, excellent performance. While this may be functional for the group's performance as a whole, it is hard to win yourself if your very presence so consistently brings out the best in others!

Again, it sometimes seemed that women and men were, in fact, engaged in constant competition. Women sought to show they were equal, men to prove they were better. But in doing so they were not playing the same game. Moreover, the women played it all day every day. Individual men (because of their numbers and ability to substitute endlessly) played only sporadically, when they wished to, and on terms they defined. Can that be called sporting?

7

Leaders and Surrogates:
The Commandant's Shop

"Bring Me Men" summons the chiseled granite beam over the ramp leading to the Air Garden. Few 1976 visitors could resist inquiring about the future of that inscription. To appreciate the academy's response, one needs to know that the phrase is the title of a poem by Sam Walter Foss:

> Bring Me Men
> Bring me men to match my mountains:
> Bring men to match my plains;
> Men with empires in their purpose,
> And new eras in their brains.
> Bring me men to match my prairies,
> Men to match my inland seas
> Men whose thought shall pave a highway
> Up to ampler destinies;
> Pioneers to clear Thought's marshlands,
> And to cleanse old Error's fen;
> Bring me men to match my mountains—
> Bring me men!

Dismissing claims that the slogan, "Bring Me Men," needed rephrasing, the academy officially decided to follow "common English usage" and interpret the word "men" in the generic sense. That decision was not made on linguistic grounds, however. In fact, no effort was made to examine the meaning of "men" in context. Instead, the criteria underpinning the *status quo* were an interesting amalgam of extra-lingual concerns: (1) changes must not be detrimental to academy tradition, (2) changes must be standardized, (3) changes must be minimal, (4) changes must not be grammatically awkward, (5) changes must be cost effective, and (6) changes should promote positive attitudes toward women cadets.

The last criterion was taken quite seriously. But judging what would or would not promote "positive attitudes" was difficult. In this particular case no one argued that a cool and unhesitating change to "Bring Me Men and Women" would enhance women's acceptance; although, at least in theory, incorporating the new order into a prominent academy landmark might have emphasized the inevitability and, more important, the permanence of the change. Instead, it was decided that such tampering would be perceived as "catering to women" and would negatively affect attitudes toward them.[a] A consensus of decision makers thought that civilian critics were implacable anyway, that attempting to please them would be foolish if doing so increased resentment within the academy.[b]

Many women's organizations (e.g., the League of Women Voters) are criticized for their timidity in pressing social change; their fear of creating a backlash is sometimes described as debilitating, and some think them foolish for believing that they can win change either without discomfiting their opponents or without threatening coercion. In the case of "Bring Me Men," however, (mostly) male officials made the decision to try to avoid what is perhaps the necessary dissonance of social change. The basic question is, can a result that is achieved through pressure and coercion have also been achieved without them? Or can education, positive motivation, and

[a]Displacement of hostility is a common phenomenon. In this case, where hostility would be directed against women for something done by administrators, cadets would be discharging their aggression on a vulnerable rather than a powerful group—a traditional form of displacement. In addition they would be directly showing their power versus that of the women who could be said to have challenged them indirectly, through Congress and academy officials.

[b]Some even argued that women did not "seriously" expect such changes. Of course, what women expect, what they would like, and what they would consider "right" are not necessarily the same.

Another highly visible academy inscription refers to "Man's Flight Through Life." This motto appears on the "Falcon and Fledglings" statue in the Air Garden. Presumably the falcon is female; it is a tribute to knowledge.

leading by example wholly substitute for direction, punishment, and discipline?[c]

Leading by Example

Leadership is crucial to military organizations. Its importance is demonstrated by the fact that the concept permeates every aspect of the Air Force Academy's program, although the office in charge seems to shift between the military and academic quarters with some regularity. At West Point, "Leadership" has been an office on the military side; since 1977 it has also been a part of an academic department. At Annapolis, leadership had been a part of the (civilian) Psychology Department, but in 1976 it shifted to the military side. At Colorado Springs there is now an academic Department of Behavioral Science and Leadership, but its history is short too. While anxious to study and learn about leadership, the academies are most interested in producing it. Therefore, much of the daily schedule includes activities designed to make cadets practice leadership; for example, intramurals and P.E. emphasize organizing and coaching almost as much as they do the improvement of skills.

Practice is thought to be enhanced by imitation. Thus the presence of good role models is considered essential to good training for leadership. The Air Force Academy uses officers almost exclusively as classroom teachers, and a certain part of each period is legitimately used to talk about career experiences, commonly called "war stories," and life in the "real" Air Force. (In 1976 the ultimate in heroes, ex-POWs, held several important and highly visible posts at the academy—head of military instruction and head of the ethics committee.) Moreover, a new discipline system based on "positive motivation" was begun during BCT 1976 to emphasize the burdens of leadership and the importance of leading by doing, of teaching by example. Whatever their views on "positive motivation," even

---

[c]Academy decision makers were operating in an environment that afforded more support for coercion as a legitimate way to affect behavior than is usual in our society. But officials must have been considering that they must lead the academy on a variety of issues; and they must certainly have been aware that the larger the number of disagreeable experiences a leader imposes on his followers, the more he diminishes his power. Thus officers may not have opposed the changes so much as they were unwilling to use up any of their "good will" on them. The dilemma was formidable: How do you insist upon providing opportunities for women to lead without diminishing your own capacity to lead by making your followers unleadable?

the hardest-nosed "brown shoes" agreed that commanders should ask of others only what they would do themselves.[d]

A strong belief in role models, in leadership by example, and in a "total training environment," combined with the administration's desire to separate the girls' bedrooms from the boys' and its wish to turn girl cadets into women (not mannish) officers, were the impetus behind the academy's strong commitment to the ATO (Air Training Officer) program. This program and the development of detailed policy papers concerning cadet life were the responsibility of the commandant and his staff.

The Commandant's Shop

The commandant, assisted by a vice-commandant, is in charge of cadet life and military training.[e] This enormous responsibility also takes in a number of small units that provide administrative and support services such as the cadet store, the dining hall, cadet scheduling, and cadet media (publications). Two deputy commandants direct (1) military instruction, which includes airmanship, navigation, and military training (both in summer programs and the classroom), and (2) the cadet wing. The latter is directed through four group AOCs and their ten squadron AOCs, each of whom has responsibility for some one hundred cadets that compose a squadron. Thus there is an officer chain of command for the cadet wing. This hierarchy is paralleled by a cadet chain of command; for in order to practice leadership, upper class cadets assume many duties handled by staff in a civilian school. While the academy's mission of providing "the knowledge and character essential to leadership" is shared by all units of the academy, the commandant's shop provides the uniquely military aspects of cadet training.

At the Congressional hearings Superintendent Clark had testified against women's admission; but if it were to be mandated, he said, *he* preferred to define the terms and timing. He demonstrated this preference by having his commandant, Gen. Hoyt S. Vandenberg, Jr., bring to the academy a young woman officer who was to initiate

[d]Leadership is also taught informally in offices filled with uplifting quotations, by the telling and retelling of the heroic exploits of academy graduates, and in the daily news report's "Quote for the Day." Further, *Contrails* (the doolie handbook) has three pages of quotations about leadership to be memorized.

[e]See Appendix III for an Academy Organization Chart, and Appendix IV for the Organization of the Academies' Student Bodies.

planning for women's possible entrance as it affected areas under the commandant's jurisdiction.

In mid-1974 a new superintendent, Gen. James Allen, came on board along with a new vice commandant, Col. James P. McCarthy. McCarthy was unenthusiastic about women cadets and might be said to have agreed with the "let 'em grunt with the rest of the grunts" school of thought. His views were not crucial at that time, however, because Vandenberg and his assistant were the officers chiefly responsible for the commandant's Women's Project. But one year later (July 1975), Vandenberg was replaced by Gen. Stanley Beck, McCarthy was appointed chair of the commandant's Committee on the Integration of Women, and Capt. Judith Galloway (from Vandenberg's staff) was made a member of McCarthy's special planning staff (for the admission of women).[f]

McCarthy seems to epitomize the Air Force response to the change mandated by Congress. He was not enthusiastic about the program originally, and he still may not care to contemplate "a woman flying on his wing." From the start he had opposed the ATO program. Still, he was a "fast burner" with strong management skills and a penchant for innovation. (A "fast burner" is one who receives early promotions.) As an AOC (ten years earlier), he had written one report urging the abolition of punishing cadets with physical exercise and another urging the gradual phasing out of compulsory chapel attendance.[g] McCarthy also started the popular soaring program. Since women were what was "new," it was logical that he would be interested in the program and would see that it succeeded. Thus the "unbeliever" became a veritable "missionary." McCarthy assumed the task, prepared intensively, placed implementation in the hands of the chain of command, and left the academy in the spring of 1977 with an apparently successful program in place. He did what he was told to do well, and the reputation he established was the one he wished to establish—that of being an excellent implementer. He did not become a "woman's expert" or advocate. Indeed, among women officers one's views on McCarthy

[f]It is said that Allen and Beck were chosen for their capacity for flexible management. Their appointment represented a change in leadership style and might have been unsettling for the academy even without any program changes. Indeed, one long-time civilian woman secretary observed that more ferment and change occurred as a result of the new command style than from women's entrance.

[g]Physical education staff believe in cadet discipline but feel that the use of physical exercise as punishment destroys motivation for P.E. programs!

The U.S. Supreme Court abruptly phased out compulsory chapel soon thereafter.

became something of a litmus test indicating whether one understood what was going on or not. Most of the women understood him to be trying to do the right thing, but neither for the "right" reason nor with much sensitivity.

Women did not wholly trust McCarthy. They observed that his chauvinism took the form of chivalry, that the ATOs he once opposed in effect became his daughters, and that "his" women were paternalized if not patronized. Among the adjectives used to describe him were "brilliant," "manipulative," "a ladies' man," "super pragmatic," "timely." Even if he finally "believed," many perceived that he did not "understand."

This last reservation raises an important question about the implementation of change. Does one have to understand a goal to accomplish it? Or can nonbelievers do *more* because they are sensitive to the resistant environment? What *are* the elements of success in creating social change? Perhaps McCarthy's views on the elements of his own success are instructive: first, the manager must have a strong, positive, optimistic, confident approach that sustains both him and those working with him.[h] Second, change requires thorough planning that anticipates every possibility. Such planning calls for a special staff with anticipation as its primary duty. Third, a philosophical underpinning must explain any particular decision and also guide other decisions. A principle or a philosophy enhances consistency and, therefore, acceptance. It also enables the staff to make decisions and recommendations with confidence. McCarthy also advocated low-key management in which officials never overreacted (even if they did overanticipate), and did not bully, although they were capable of repeating, again and again, "this is what is expected." McCarthy preferred *not* to meet resistance head-on. For him the key to women's integration was "winning acceptance."[i]

McCarthy's chief assistant, Captain Galloway, had been brought to the academy by General Vandenberg, a man with an uncompromising style, a man she emulated.[j] As one of the most junior officers on the commandant's staff, she was placed in a very political and

[h]The positive use of the self-fulfilling prophecy seems to have been a technique of the whole command.

[i]At one point, a "Subcommittee for the Acceptance of Women Cadets" was actually appointed. However, it never became active.

[j]Galloway's commitment to academy principles can be demonstrated by her refusal to lock her car on the academy grounds because that would demonstrate lack of confidence in those bound together by a sense of honor. Many officers *did* lock their cars. (At some military bases, it is a court martial offense not to.)

emotional situation. Moreover, after Vandenberg left she reported to a man whose style of managing was quite different from that of her previous superior. The commandant's Committee on the Integration of Women made her work difficult, too. Slightly more than half of the fourteen members were lieutenant colonels or above, and the rest were majors, except for Galloway, who was not only the only captain but also the only woman. When the committee began its work, an all-woman squadron under the command of a woman was still planned and a commitment had also been made to the concept of ATOs. Still, numerous details needed definition, debate, and resolution. The committee's primary activities were (1) to obtain more information (mostly through trips to the field), (2) to monitor the training of the ATOs, and (3) to develop "issue papers" recommending policy over a wide range of areas—from haircuts to decorum.

Major Field Trips

McCarthy and Galloway went on the fall field trips in the role of implementers. The field trip mode of gathering data was beneficial in that it emphasized the current social climate and looked not just at co-ed situations but at those in which the change to co-education had just occurred. The library prepared a research bibliography on women in the military, but McCarthy and Galloway had little recourse to library materials.[k] Sometimes such material can be very helpful because seen in retrospect problems achieve a proportion that they lack in the present. For instance, one can develop guiding principles without getting bogged down in personalities (including one's own). In particular, a reading of Treadwell's account of the second year "slander campaign" might have led the Air Force Academy to prepare for the second year with as much care as the first, even if the first did turn out successfully. Also, if the problems Treadwell documented had been analyzed and discussed with the entering women, they might have been better prepared for the maleness of the environment they entered. The problem was that if preparing women had required sessions separate from men such action would have been considered impermissible double tracking. On the other hand, if the male cadets were taught about what "might" hap-

---

[k]Even Mattie Treadwell's *The Women's Army Corps*, an 800-page volume that focused on World War II, went unused.

pen, that teaching could *cause* it to happen. Basically, the academy chose not to discuss or prepare for negative outcomes; that is, cadets were not told not to put beans up their noses.

Galloway and McCarthy's trips took them to (1) Maxwell Air Force Base's Air Command and Staff College and Squadron Officer School (SOS), a service school for training captains and lieutenants (the occasion was a series of lectures and seminars on the role of women in the Air Force);[1] (2) the Merchant Marine Academy (then integrated for fifteen months); (3) the Los Angeles Police Department; and (4) Texas A. & M., a civilian school with a recently integrated student cadet corps. The cadet clinic's flight surgeon, Col. Edward Jenkins, who was quite persuaded that women's physiology was a bar to their piloting of jet aircraft, visited Pensacola Naval Air Station, where the initial eleven women naval aviation cadets had been trained. Jenkins also visited an environmental physiology laboratory in Seattle to study decompression sickness.

The trip reports are interesting because they show what was on the minds of the implementers. The first item noted at SOS was numbers and spouses. McCarthy and Galloway found that women were less than 2 percent of the class (13 of 800) there, only 5 were married, and none was accompanied by her spouse. About one-third of the males were accompanied to the eleven-week course. This matter of accompaniment was of interest because participating in social affairs is often part of an officer's "work." Some women officers participated in the social gatherings; others did not; some said they found their colleagues' wives so "cool" that it was easier just to restrict their social life.

A second important observation was that women, male minorities, navigators, foreign officers, and so on are "deliberately split among the sections as evenly as possible." The reason for doing so was to maintain a balance between squadrons since they competed with one another in a variety of ways. Making each section similar, however, also had the effect of isolating members of any small group. This meant the "different" officers were constantly having both to prove themselves and to educate their unit. Doing so can be exhausting under already stressful and competitive conditions.

Third, the report described what seemed to be the criterion for high peer acceptance: an all-out effort to perform. Although peer ratings did not demonstrate sex bias in either direction, some men

[1]Among the speakers were Gail Thayne Parker, president of Bennington College, Lt. Col. Diane Ordez of the USAF Recruiting Service, and Col. Bianca Trimeloni, Director of Women in the Air Force.

said that they had been "easy" in their ratings of women. One study of these ratings shows that men, in fact, *are* easier on less able women than they are on less able men. It also shows, however, that they are *harder* on able women. Thus women end up with mid-range ratings.[1] Also, while women *thought* they were accepted by the men, men reported that, in fact, they were not.[m]

The question of counseling was explored with care. At SOS men were considered fit to counsel women, and no woman liaison officer was formally assigned to each unit. As it worked out, however, male officers informally asked female officers for advice on how to motivate their women.[n] Women students, however, did *not* seek out women staff for advice or support. This finding may have weakened the academy's commitment to role-model theory. Why was this the case? Do women hate women so much? Were the women staff at SOS perceived as negative role models? Or did young women officers find that to associate with women officers was somehow to admit a differentness and that by *dis*associating themselves from women they could win credit with men? If so, did they secretly emulate the senior women they did not seek out?[o]

Discrepant expectations among a population are always a problem for an administrator. So is the lack of any data on which to base uniform, realistic expectations. The women at SOS consistently thought they had performed well in physical training, while men considered their performance mediocre. Administrators, meanwhile, had little idea about what women could do yet were gravely concerned that women trainees not be viewed negatively for not matching men's physical standards.[p] Male administrators, espe-

---

[m] At least one study shows that men report more discrimination against women than women perceive. Philip E. Converse and Jean M. Converse, "The Status of Women as Students and Professionals in Political Science," in *Women in Political Science*, studies and reports of the APSA Committee on the Status of Women in the Profession 1969–71 (Washington, D.C.: The American Political Science Association), pp. 19–20. They should know. But are women so ignorant? Perhaps women who want to get ahead do not level charges they cannot prove, or the women who survive and are studied may be those who have not been discriminated against.

[n] At some point this practice could become burdensome if the women officers were sought out frequently while having a regular (and competitive) full-time assignment of their own.

[o] The crucial element in a woman officer's ability to serve as a role model for women is, obviously, her ability to command men's respect, since men constitute over 90 percent of the military.

[p] A number of women officers believed current standards for women did not sufficiently challenge them. A smaller number thought women should (and that some could) meet existing male standards.

cially, worried that they would not be sufficiently exacting in other areas of training if they eased up on the physical standards women had to meet.[q]

The Merchant Marine Academy had fixed no quota for women, but only fifteen had entered in 1974. One would think that so small a number (1.5 percent) would have made little impact on the institution as a whole and that there would be no reason for male cadets to resent such an insignificant number.[r] However, acceptance *was* a problem; cadets perceived (1) that lower standards were set for women, and (2) that men's standards also fell.

Even while Merchant Marine reports described "acceptance" as tenuous, a problem with fraternization continued.[s] This may mean that what is needed is simply *more* women. With the first-year ratio, 98 percent of the men would necessarily be "rejected" by the women as boy friends. Those rejected might, in turn, reject women at the academy. The point is that both rejections would be strongly influenced by the ratio of men to women, although individuals might not understand this.

Male cadets most often cited (perceived) lower standards for women as their reason for rejecting women; but here, too, numbers are important. Women's high visibility made any deviation from standards or any other difference dramatically evident. The lack of a bill on their hats and lack of buckles on their belts meant they did not have the same dusting and shining chores, and this difference aggravated the men. They perceived that women had it easier; women resented that perception, and they responded to it in their second year by holding the entering women to even higher standards than they had met.[t] What is unknown is if women, as outsiders,

[q]One senses that women's advocates found themselves arguing for women's compensatory superiority in other (often scholastic?) areas. What they may not have considered was that the "other" areas might not be valued or tested at the academy, or that the physical drain on the women might diminish the time and energy they had for those "other" accomplishments. Another element is involved here, too. Male critics of women often expressed doubts, not about the women, but about themselves and their male peers. They doubted their own and other men's capacity to train, discipline, and judge women.

[r]Because women are in fact a majority of the population, their participation in an institution must always represent a threat different from that of minorities, who, even if fully represented, would, nevertheless, remain a minority. Lebanon, Cyprus, and Northern Ireland provide examples of the special hazards of societies encompassing two groups with similar amounts of power. Calm comes more easily when dominance cannot be questioned.

[s]Which may only mean that the young women were being accepted as dates and mates at the same time that they were being rejected as peers.

[t]In any profession the best performers respond thus as they bemoan the lack of excellence and dedication of the young.

were trying to meet *all* formal requirements while male insiders knew the informal rules well enough to distinguish between what really had to be done and what could be "shined on."[u] Or it may be that individual men frequently escaped scrutiny instead of always meeting it, or that any lowered standards for women were actually caused by the failure of the male "enforcers" to enforce. Whatever the case, the women seemed to accept the male perception of their low performance instead of challenging it. Their number, their status, and their newness probably kept them from even imagining a positive counterperception of themselves.

A new item appeared in the Merchant Marine trip report— weight. In the first year the minimum women's weight gain was 15 pounds, and one of the fifteen women gained 35 pounds. Another item surfaced too—debate over when, where, and why women were to wear skirts (as opposed to pants). Mostly men wanted the women in skirts. Women found marching in straight skirts difficult and preferred pants for warmth. The symbolism of a skirt apparently provoked strong feelings. When women were given discretion over what to wear, they were likely to get contradictory cues from their environment. When the administration prescribed their dress, however, the women could and did complain. The point is that uniforms are much more than clothing. They make a group a whole. They signify group membership and evoke a variety of feelings.[v] As it turned out, the clearest way of communicating that women were *really* entering the academies (and, incidentally, of recruiting women to be applicants) was to show pictures of women's uniforms. Thus before women arrived at Colorado Springs, the cadet store displayed women's items as part of the effort to make the wing realize that the admission of women would soon be a reality; also, logistics planners emphasized having all items ready for the women so they would feel "welcome."[w]

The Air Force team visited the Los Angeles Police Academy because publicity concerning its successful recruitment and training of women had come to the academy's attention. Ironically enough, the

[u]Cadets are taught the importance of learning what is important by being given such rigid time constraints that they must set priorities and frequently choose between them. Even some "requirements" have to go by the wayside.

[v]Wearing pants seemed to imply a fuller identification with male cadets. Sometimes this seemed desirable to men and to women; sometimes it seemed undesirable.

[w]When the women's uniform prototypes were first displayed in the Air Force Academy library, they were removed by unreconciled cadets, who left in their stead a note saying, "Forgive them Lord for they know not what they do."

Los Angeles Police Department was then and is now engaged in litigation and negotiation over its alleged sexist practices. Its colorful chief, Ed Davis, made no bones about his view of women officers: they were limited in capacity, were not assigned to patrol (the police equivalent of combat), and therefore lacked experience crucial to command. The plaintiff against Davis, Fanchon Blake, however, *had* had patrol experience. She predated him and got that experience before it was denied to women.[x] No visit was made to the Los Angeles County Sheriff's Office, which was utilizing women in every capacity and which was thought of by local feminist groups as the "good guys," in contrast to the city police, who were regarded as "bad guys."

Texas A. & M. is a unique institution. Until 1963 all of the several thousand students at this public, male, civilian university were also members of "the corps" and usually ROTC cadets. Since then A. & M. has grown to over 25,000 students and gone co-ed. By 1976 only 10 percent of the students were members of the corps and some 30 percent of the students were women. When ROTC became co-ed in 1972, a plan was devised (mostly by male members of the corps) for admitting women to the corps.[y] The transition was to be very gradual: women were to be assigned to a separate unit (without housing), could enter only as freshmen under ROTC contract (not requirements for male admission), and would be limited in their leadership opportunities and in the activities in which they could participate. (Denied to women were the freshman drill team, the mounted cavalry, the Aggie Band, and the upper class honor guard.) The plan was approved by the commandant at one point, although much of it did not ultimately stand. Neither did the women stick. Forty-six women entered the first year, 1973–74, but only twenty-three remained in 1974–75, when only eighteen new women entered the corps.

At Texas A. & M. the first year women lacked housing and uni-

---

[x]She had also served in the military and (most unusual for a woman) had been recalled to service during the Korean War because of her special skills. Typically, too, she was devoted to, even loved, the institution she was suing. The Los Angeles Police Department never conceded a point, but its academy did start graduating more women. Three questions arise: (1) to what degree does the squeaking wheel *not* get the grease (senior women sue and junior women gain entry); (2) is the opening of entry slots really a "change" resulting in a potential for a "regular" career for the new trainees; and (3) will the new entrants' numbers inevitably so diminish that other young women cease to seek entrance and the cycle repeats itself until a few frustrated survivors once again sue, and once again create opportunity and hope for another group of young women, even though they gain little for themselves?

[y]ROTC contracts would have been voided if the corps had not admitted them.

forms. Rules for "Frogs"—individuals who enter the corps as up-perclassmen—differed for women and men, and upperclass harass-ment seemed to be directed toward driving women cadets out, rather than toward strengthening their resolve to succeed. The nearly self-governing student corps did its own recruiting, set its own priorities, and hazed women and any male inclined to speak up for them.

This situation differed from the academy in several ways. First, responsibility for direction and control rested almost entirely with student members of the corps, and they strongly pressured each other not to accept women.[z] Second, all this took place on a civilian campus where civilian men and women rejected the idea of women as cadets. Third, the presence of stylishly adorned noncadet women dramatized the question of "femininity" as it would not at the acad-emy, where all the young women would have short hair and would strive to develop an assured manner that withstood both physical and verbal harassment. Academy women could define themselves as women and as feminine by contrasting themselves to academy men. A. & M. women cadets were constantly contrasted, not just to men but to the ever-present civilian women, and seemed some-times to be treated as though they belonged to some unspecified third category. For any institution interested in the successful inte-gration of women, A. & M. represented a most unsatisfactory ex-ample; in particular it demonstrated how easily male peers can un-dermine a policy they do not accept.

The ATOs

Outsiders may perceive military assignments as ordained by a mys-terious order-issuing command system. In fact, a personnel center (at Randolph Air Force Base) maintains job listings and an inven-tory of Air Force officers of different skills. Self-directed officers seek out and apply for the best opportunities; leaders in turn recruit the officers they think will best fit their needs. Officers may even travel hundreds of miles at their own expense and on their own time to interview for jobs. In the past, Air Force Academy jobs have been considered especially desirable and recruitment of the best of-ficers has not been considered a problem.

---

[z]The question arises again: Is women's acceptance as peers (rather than as juniors) always problematical, or is it especially difficult at certain ages—for instance between 18 and 25, when men first feel strong pressures to support themselves and a family?

By September 1975 the ATOs had become something to recruit and to train. McCarthy and Galloway had an attractive location and a unique job to offer. They began the recruiting by listing 268 women officers with fewer than eighteen months of service as of January 1976.[a] Of these, 220 were single or divorced.[b] An intensive screening began that focused on the 183 who were "most eligible."[c] Qualified candidates were personally interviewed (usually at the academy) by McCarthy, Galloway, and Maj. Jack Smith, who would be in charge of the ATO program until training actually began. By mid-November 1975, 50 women had been contacted, 25 interviewed, three "hired," and 3 selected. By January a contingent of 15 was ready for training.

An early policy decision had an important influence on the program: it was decided to recruit only as many women as would actually be needed.[d] There would be no screening after hiring, even though the first half-year would involve the rigorous kind of training that ordinarily produced substantial attrition among cadets. This circumstance put McCarthy in the position of managing a "no-cut" (no-failure) but highly competitive program at the same time. Other institutions find themselves in a similar position. If they apply highly restrictive admissions policies, they feel duty bound to guarantee the success of their selectees in order to justify the admissions decisions. Thus they tend to make whatever accommodations and adjustments are necessary for the admittees' success—even the kind of accommodations they would find wholly improper in a pre-selection record.

The pressure on the academy to see that all of the ATOs "fit" their jobs was especially intense because the ATO recruitment was done at the same time that the job, which had never existed in quite the same form before, was being defined. Moreover, it was being defined by an officer who had the highest respect for flexibility. This

[a]This meant that they would remain lieutenants through their two years as ATOs (until June 1978).

[b]Only one married woman was selected. (Her husband was on remote assignment.) It was thought that single women were more like upper class cadets than were married women and would probably tolerate the twenty-four-hour rotation more easily. However, their singleness may also have suggested to young women cadets that the price of a military career would be no marriage and no family.

[c]Preference was also given to younger women (22–24), especially those who had entered service directly out of college.

[d]This would save "overage" costs. Total costs were estimated at $442,471 for the two-and-one-half-year project. There was to be one ATO for every ten women.

situation created a potential for difficulty. As the job definition developed and evolved, the young officers (who were submitting themselves to very rigorous training) sometimes wondered if anyone knew exactly why they were doing what they were doing. Some misunderstanding is inevitable in a quickly changing situation, but sometimes the young women described themselves as feeling betrayed. Several factors may have contributed to this feeling. First, it would be easy for some of the ATOs to have accepted a job that, from the onset, they understood differently from their recruiter.[e] Few of them could have fully appreciated what academy life would be like. Moreover, as circumstances developed, the officer in charge was quite ready to redefine the job. Indeed, he felt it his duty to change the ATO job description any time he thought doing so would enhance the program's goal—the integration of women cadets into the wing.

Major Smith, an ex-AOC, was in charge of the ATO program from September 1975 through February 1976. After that (during the training period), command passed to Galloway. With the arrival of the women cadets in June, control passed to the four group AOCs with whom the ATOs worked.

The fifteen ATOs had excellent though brief service records. One was recruited while she was on a tour celebrating her selection as the outstanding officer in Alaska. Another came straight from a university ROTC program, where she had been commander of her unit. The selection interviews were designed to assess the candidate's potential as a role model, with particular emphasis placed on communication and human relations skills. The selectees represented a variety of shapes and styles, although some officers felt too much emphasis was placed on appearance and vivacity.[f] Physical aptitude was tested, but it was not used to screen candidates. In retrospect the people in P.E., at least, considered this omission a mistake. Of course there were no specific physical standards set for the cadets who were to come. The planners' idea was to let cadet selectees set the physical baselines; this is what the Air Force had done in 1955 in accepting its first class; for it had not simply borrowed West Point's standards, but had allowed its own entering class to set its norms.[g]

---

[e] Nor would there be any real data for recruiter and recruit to cite to substantiate their interpretation.

[f] The selectees included one black officer.

[g] The altitude of the Air Force Academy is more than a mile; thus sea level standards would not have been appropriate. The criticism of such a policy is that when norms become

As explained to the ATO recruitees, one part of the job was simply to "be": to be an example, to be a model, to be "feminine," to be capable. The ATOs were also to be responsible for training the women cadets in such areas as hygiene, dress, inspections, and counseling. Specifically, all in-dormitory training was to be in their hands.[h] In out-of-dormitory training, the ATOs (who were officers) were to "assist" the (male) cadet chain of command.[i] Becoming an ATO meant sleeping in dormitory rooms four nights a week, eating all meals in the dining hall, and being on duty from 0600 to 2300 on weekdays and to 0130 on weekends. The long hours were required because the male-female dormitory separation meant that officers had to substitute for always present squadron members. A variety of administrative duties that ordinarily fell to upper class cadets also would be handled by the ATOs; they included counseling, maintaining supply and logistics, arranging transportation, and keeping records.

It was hoped that the ATOs would perform several other important functions as well. One was to demonstrate to male cadets and officers their (and therefore women's) competence in difficult and demanding tasks. Of course, the women officers who were assigned "regular" slots in the academy would do so as well, but the cadre of fifteen ATOs would be the group with the highest visibility, both because they worked as a unit and because they would have undertaken a rigorous half-year training course before the women cadets arrived. This training was intended primarily to educate the ATOs, but it educated wing and academy officers as well. By watching the ATOs they hoped to preview what it meant to train women some six months before they would have any women as cadets.

---

goals, excellence is not achieved. Still, standards are not engraved in stone; P.E. standards are routinely adjusted to elicit maximum cadet effort. For instance, the distance to be swum in the five-minute swim was actually increased the year the women entered.

[h]When one holds a nominal position of authority, the loss of any responsibility—no matter how minor—can create a perception of decreased status. Since in-dormitory training is usually the province of cadets, the transfer of that responsibility to the ATOs triggered dismay among the male cadets. Although the superintendent insisted that no men would train women in the dormitories, when cadets regained dormitory inspection rights, they had a "foot in the door." Some status was restored. Subsequently, the ATO's role was diminished from that of "trainer" to "coordinator," and male cadets felt even better.

[i]At the Air Force Academy, the third class assumed a primary role in the training of fourth class men. Thus cadet women would be able to fill that role after only one year. At West Point, most training is done by first class cadets, and it would take three years for women to become involved in training.

Because the ATO training program was "identical in concept" to the cadet program, ATO training was expected to indicate what, if any, modifications and changes should be made in the academy's program before cadet women undertook it.[j] The bottom line, however, was cost-effectiveness. Advocates argued that the ATO program would reduce attrition, and the academy *did* reduce attrition considerably in 1976–77. Just how it did so is not clear.

The ATOs' training (from January to June 1976) included a mini-BCT, followed by four weeks of the fourth class cadet curriculum.[k] This included instruction (decorum, heritage, first aid, map reading), mastery of the manual of arms, inspections, morning runs, and shower formations. Wing orientation, airmanship, and navigation followed.[l] They were given "motivation" flights and navigation training, although as women they were ineligible to fly or navigate as part of their regular duties. The ATO program also included a sixteen-hour course in counseling techniques taught by the Department of Behavioral Science, and provided opportunities to audit regular academic and military courses.[m] The Jack's Valley (field) portion of BCT and SERE course concluded the program.

The role of the women ATOs was inevitably different from that of the male ATOs of 1955. Not only were they to be officers behaving like cadets but they would also be acting as upperclassmen in the presence of real (male) upperclassmen. This difference meant that the ATOs' interaction with male cadets was almost guaranteed

[j]Most changes for the ATOs abbreviated their training. No elements were left out because of "difficulty." For example, every element of the SERE program was included. But critics, nevertheless, argued that six months could not approximate four years, whatever the intent. Moreover, the meaning of "identical in concept" left room for misunderstandings that did, in fact, develop.

Even though women were admitted to the nearby Air Force Prep School during the second semester of 1975–76, their performance was not treated as a dry run and was not carefully monitored.

[k]Actually the ATOs took the "old" BCT, which included physical punishment (e.g., squat thrusts) for imperfections. By June 1976 the new cadets (both men and women) were given a training period that exacted no punitive physical exercise.

[l]Wing orientation included receiving demerits and serving confinements just as cadets do.

The airmanship and navigation training included parasailing (in which a parachute on one's back permits one to sail through the air while being towed from the ground by a truck), soaring (in gliders), a T-41 (propeller-driven plane) orientation flight, and a T-37 (two-person jet) flight.

[m]A shadow program, in which an ATO followed a squadron and its leadership through all the activities of one week, made the women feel that they better understood cadet life, just as a teacher-in-training profits more from observing other teachers all day than from visiting one class a day for fifty minutes and then leaving.

to be awkward because they would simultaneously (1) be "inferiors" (as women and as ATO trainees), (2) be peers (as surrogate cadets), and (3) be superiors (as officers). During the month they acted as doolies, the ATOs had minimal contact with the male cadets; professional contact *was* encouraged, however, when the ATOs were acting as upperclassmen.

The guidelines prepared for the ATOs emphasized their role as officers. They were admonished (1) to refrain from discussing other officers in a cadet's presence, (2) to refrain from using first names with cadets or with ATOs in the presence of cadets, (3) not to pass on rumors, and (4) not to date cadets. They were to be treated as officers in not being bound by the honor code, but as cadets in being asked to comply rigidly with regulations. Their role was additionally (and most) complicated during the training period of January-June 1976, because during that time cadets actually administered parts of the ATO training, temporarily making the women officers their official subordinates.

The monitoring and evaluation of the ATO program was done by the commandant's Committee on the Admission of Women Cadets, which began meeting in July 1975 and continued until June 1976. A planning staff of five had the responsibility for staffing and coordinating policies on the ATOs, for conducting a cadet information service on the ATOs, and for directing the program itself.

Meanwhile, a cadet committee had also been studying the ATO program, and in November 1975 it asked that cadets serve as the BCT cadre for the ATOs. Cadet involvement was considered a good strategy, but even those who most skillfully practice cooptation are not necessarily comfortable about giving responsibility to potential critics. Furthermore, the BCT training period was the most pressured and intense part of the training—the period in which attrition is usually highest. Because of the winter weather, field portions of BCT would not come until May, but the ATOs' first two weeks at the academy would involve a lot of military training and rugged physical conditioning. The commandant's committee was hesitant. Authenticity required cadet supervision; control called for arguing cadets had "too many other full-time duties." Nevertheless, since acceptance was the key worry, and since Texas A. & M. served as a negative reminder of what *could* happen, some degree of risk, of relinquishing of control, did seem called for.[n]

[n] In discussing "acceptance," policy makers sometimes spoke of "The Wing" almost as a living, breathing being—a monster to be pacified—a creature that responded to stimuli in a

By the time the last of the ATOs arrived in January, the cadets had won. The cadre, a group of cadets responsible for training doolies, was divided into dormitory, escort, and athletic units, and these groups were given an important training role.° They would see for themselves what women could do and how they could best be trained.

Perhaps the most important element of the ATOs' training was their survival. The cadets learned that motivated women *could* endure—few of them had seen this before, and many had not been able to imagine it. This survival won the ATOs a measure of respect; it changed some cadet attitudes. Of course competing, not surviving, is the academy standard, and a rather different conclusion was reached when the women's performance was measured *against* that of men.ᵖ Then the women's efforts rapidly diminished in the eyes of cadets. The prevailing view seemed to be that the women deserved credit for doing the program "at all." They deserved respect for their effort. However, they were not thought to have done excellently *except* "as women."²

The cadre reported that ATOs kept their rooms neater than men's rooms and they acquired technical knowledge faster than men did; moreover, they retained knowledge as effectively as men and during BCT maintained an equal appearance, decorum, and spirit. But their stamina and rate of injury gave cause for concern. The cadets also noted (1) that the wing orientation phase of ATO training had been awkward because of an ATO's dual identity as cadet and officer, and (2) that discipline, conduct, and privileges were griped about in the "usual" way. The cadets also believed that the ATOs were reluctant to enforce discipline within their unit. This perception may have influenced later beliefs about the lack of discipline demanded by ATOs in the "girls" dormitory area. The ATOs were anomalous, after all: fourth class men do not enforce "the system" against each other. It is principally enforced by third class men, who have only just escaped it themselves.

In recounting their experience, the cadre also reported that the

---

single way. Cadets share a great deal and enormous pressure to conform does exist, and perhaps in the academy days of many current officers, a single, collective response even existed. But the expansion of the academy reduced its intimacy, and while cadets who are attuned to their peers' views may not speak up or out, a diversity of views does exist.

°Five of the cadre members withdrew from competition. Forty first and second class men participated.

ᵖThe ATOs did not, of course, actually compete with any men; therefore, many of the relative measures were subjective.

women were more talkative, used a personal tone of voice, "over-reacted" to praise, and took criticism too personally. Crying, which had been a source of anxiety for some men, occurred infrequently, and, having been carefully briefed, the cadets did not find it hard to deal with. Correct management called for an insistent "Crying is not acceptable."

In the second portion of wing orientation (after the spring break), ATOs ate with a particular squadron for a week (to develop continuity) and then "shadowed" key squadron members through their entire day (except that they were not allowed in the squadron meeting rooms in the evening). In turn, ATO ispections were conducted by (male) cadets (and an AOC). This practice led cadets to think that they could inspect cadet women as well. By this time two of the ATOs were "rumbling": they wanted out. The program was not what they expected. "Extensive counseling" was employed in an effort to remotivate them, but they were not persuaded. By the time the cadet women arrived, these two, and a third ATO as well, had left the academy.[q]

Major Stephen Ramsey of the Department of Behavioral Science and Leadership counseled and taught counseling to the ATOs. He found their ability to role play "amazing," but noted that the ambiguity of their roles and their embarrassment over their poor physical condition were chronic problems.[r]

During the late spring ATO physical fitness was to cause increasing concern and a controversy as well. Flu hit them hard; five ended up in bed. Stress fractures and mononucleosis took their toll, too. The fitness controversy developed over the running and training requirements for parachute instruction.

Parachuting is an attractive activity for cadets, and the ATOs had been promised an opportunity to participate in it. Some cadets go to the Army's jump school for summer static-line training; too many others choose the academy's free-fall program. Since only a certain number can be accommodated, entrance is won by competition.[s]

In 1976 a cadet became eligible by running three miles in twenty-four minutes and by being able to do eight pullups as a demonstra-

---

[q]One had a profound fear of water that inhibited her performance. She also developed doubts about the military's mission; sometimes the word "pacifist" was associated with her. The second had a back problem.

[r]Their wish not to participate in regular P.E. classes with male cadets was viewed as "prima donnaism."

[s]In 1975–76, 600 applied and 390 were assigned to the program. In 1976–77, the total trained was cut back to 300.

tion of upper body strength.[1] Training included classroom instruction, an exam, and then some sixteen hours on "training aids," such as the parachute landing fall and the suspended harness. Two failures on any of the training devices meant expulsion. Five jumps completed the program.

Captain Galloway was occasionally used as a guinea pig for the ATOs, just as they sampled programs for the new women cadets. Galloway had decided to obtain her parachute wings, since there was no chance for her to become either a pilot or a navigator—and she did win them, becoming the first woman Air Force officer to complete the free-fall parachute program.

She won and proudly wore her wings, but a great deal of resentment circulated among cadets who believed her wings were not earned. The official position held that "all elements of the program were successfully completed" (and apparently they were). The cadets argued that, because she was allowed to work on the training aids until she had mastered them (instead of having only two chances on each one) and because she had not made the three-mile run in twenty-four minutes, she had not "passed" the program. (And they were right in saying that a cadet who "completed" it as she had completed it would not have passed.)

The physical education department had decided earlier that, given their physiology, women would be doing as well as men if they were allowed 15 percent more time to run the three miles. Academy cadets were briefed on the reasons for this decision, but many did not accept it. The issue came alive again when the ATOs passed their written exams; some of them then passed the run with the 15 percent handicap; but *none* of them passed the run by the cadet standard. A deadlock ensued over which should prevail: a single standard of performance or a requirement measuring equal endeavor. In this case (the first clear test), the administration backed down; the provision for the 15 percent bonus was eliminated, and no ATO had a chance to win her wings. For some of them, this was "the first great betrayal." It was argued that, while the academy did need the flexibility to revise its programs, promises also should be promises. The ATOs would experience other policy changes as the year progressed. Some they would accept, others would have a negative effect on their morale.

[1]The flight surgeon argued that the need for upper body strength was absolute, not relative to body size. He claimed that of sixty female (civilian) parachute fatalities, three-fourths had not had the strength to pull their rip cords. The older Air Force chutes required 20–27 pounds of left-hand pull.

The obstacle course in Jack's Valley presented two problems to the ATOs that led to adjustments. One obstacle, "the weaver," consisted of five elevated, horizontal logs forming the skeleton of a pyramid. A cadet was supposed to jump up to the first log, go over it, under and behind the second, emerge over the top one, only to have to go under the log on the other side and proceed down in the same over-and-under fashion. All short cadets needed assistance. Since the 150 women increased the number of short cadets, it was decided to erect a second "weaver" of nine logs of much reduced circumference.[u] Each cadet could then choose fewer logs with large circumferences or more logs with reduced circumferences. Almost all would be capable of one or the other.

The other troublesome hazard required making a running leap, grabbing a rope, and swinging across a water hazard. The women fell into the water "in extremely hazardous ways, never before seen with men cadets." Chiefly, women tended to extend their feet forward to their maximum (with the rest of their bodies behind the feet), release the rope, and fall flat on their backs, sometimes with head and shoulders in the water. There was some speculation about lower centers of gravity, but ultimately it was decided that women just did not know how to swing and release. Here, the "modification" took the form of a walk-through of the course, where detailed instruction was given on the level at which one should grab the rope, optimum body position, and when and how to release. In addition, padding around the barrier and the water depth were increased. The result was that more women got across; those who did not suffered only the ignominy of having to climb out wet from mid-thigh down.

The ATOs survived SERE in good form, but it was decided to use noncommissioned officers as "guards" in the POW compound "for reasons of privacy." In "leadership reaction," which involved the solving of practical problems, cadets "were impressed with the imaginative ways in which the ATO had resolved the problems." "What women may lack in strength," one cadet observed, "they make up by thinking of different ways to solve the problem."[v]

There were some ATO "projection" problems. One ATO initially refused to complete the bayonet assault course. In the POW compound, the women found it hard to be consistent in their roles, and

---

[u]The first year minimum male height was 5'4"; the minimum female height was 5'. The second year there was one minimum: 5'.

[v] What large people see as "imaginative" small people undoubtedly see as "natural." The solutions of large people are probably *not* seen as "imaginative" by small people but as "impossible."

they were also reluctant to become adversaries in the pugil stick competition. Since the ATOs were found to be "exceptional" in role projection during counseling training, the question was whether cadet women would also be slow to adopt traditionally male roles, or whether their youth and the peer pressure they would experience would make them more malleable than the ATOs.[w]

The preparation for women's entrance sometimes meant experimentation. Questions about rifle drill led to a "study" using four enlisted women as volunteers who trained with the M-1 (an obsolete weapon in today's military) as fourth class men were trained. Officials' anxieties about injuring the breast and encountering emotional responses to setbacks were allayed by a twenty-minute videotape demonstrating the women's satisfactory performance. Only two problems were noted: (1) when they drilled in lightweight blouses, the women bruised their collar bones, and (2) they had some difficulty with the stiff chamber action of the M-1 (the spring tension of the ejector mechanism was reduced as a result).

The officer in charge of the ATOs' physical conditioning program was a wiry weightlifter, whose eyes lit up when he described the physical conditioning programs he had developed and the usefulness of his "street-fighting" course. He planned his program with no information on the ATOs' athletic ability and was dismayed to find how little endurance and strength the women had. He found two in "very poor" condition; one was to quit, and the other was removed from any duty that could require her to be a "physical" role model. Sadly, in the area of physical training the ATO experience may have made acceptance of the women cadets easier by creating such low expectations that the women doolies were easily able to surpass them.

Position Papers

The commandant "owns" the cadets. He controls their scheduling and the rules surrounding their lives. Colonel McCarthy, the special planning staff, and the commandant's committee had a second assignment during the school year 1975–76 to develop a set of issue papers that established or modified academy policies touching on the admission of women. McCarthy and the committee proceeded

[w] The women cadets would be training as a minority of 10 percent with fourth degree men cadets. The ATOs had no male peers at all.

by identifying issues in brainstorming sessions and then assigning them to an appropriate office of primary responsibility (OPR) to be "developed." Development involved (1) describing the problem; (2) enumerating factors bearing on the issue—including facts, assumptions, and criteria, (3) discussing all possible alternatives, (4) reaching a conclusion, (5) recommending action; and finally (6) obtaining approval of a course of action. This procedure worked to produce solutions; it also provided a record of current thought on various issues and kept senior officers informally briefed on the planning process.

The first ten issue papers pertained to the ATO program. The more important items involved fraternization (forbidden), off-base living allowances (granted), academic opportunities (*not* permitted to take courses but could audit them), manning (six were to be on overnight duty each night), and Jack's Valley duty.[x] Analysis of the discussion of this last item, Jack's Valley duty, reveals that as policy was worked out the role of the ATO was diminished as compared to the initial conceptions of the job. For example, one policy paper stated that "overinvolvement of the ATO would detract from the objective" of having cadets "perceived as conducting most of the actual training." It was also made clear that women cadets were to "identify with" their cadet element leader; the ATO role was only to be "supportive."[y] One form this support was supposed to take was CQ duty (in charge of quarters) for the women's empty tents. This duty was assigned the ATOs in their capacity as surrogate upperclassmen. On the men's side two cadets handled CQ. It was thought that to assign men cadets to the women's side might "cause resentment among cadets and hinder the acceptance of women," but if the role was thought too demeaning for men cadets, what were the ramifications of assigning it to commissioned officers?

The second set of position papers concerned the women's dormitory area, access for maintenance and supply personnel, women's access to the men's area (required to reach cadet furniture supply), privacy, and modesty. The minimum dormitory dress was changed from undershorts and footwear to footwear and bathrobes. Even ci-

[x]Even though fraternization was forbidden, by the end of the academic year 1976–77, there was one wedding, one engagement, and an unspecified number of romances between ATOs and cadets.

[y]A "supportive role" was not in the original job description; because it is sterotypical of jobs given women, many women wish to avoid such an assignment. Further, because ATOs were "to be available for problems," women cadets might have to admit having a "problem" to avail themselves of an ATOs assistance.

vilian clothing was "authorized" or "unauthorized." Thus males could wear regular T-shirts as outer shirts, but women were forbidden cut-offs, halter tops, and faded or tie-dyed dungarees. Needless to say, doolies' clothing was even more stringently specified. Drawn curtains were required when cadets were not dressed (no change), and sun bathing attire minimums (no bikinis and outer garments were made necessary to and from designated areas) were established. The problem of dress and appearance standards was not as simple as it first appeared. The male cadet regulation was almost identical to the Air Force regulation. However, to adopt the Air Force regulation for women would permit women cadets to wear wigs while men could not and would permit women Air Force Academy cadets to wear their hair much longer than women at Annapolis or West Point.[z] Nor does the Air Force regulation for women forbid pony tails, braids, pigtails, or cornrows or specify what cosmetics may be used. Thus in April 1976 it was decided to write an academy regulation for women that would be specific and that would establish a "more military" standard for women cadets than is set for women officers.[a]

More important, a mandatory knock and verbal request to enter a dormitory room were established—but only when seeking access to an opposite sex room.[b] Doors had to be open if both sexes were present in a cadet room, and the only reason for them to be there at all would be for inspection by upperclassmen. The "free access" policy was, in fact, limited to daytime hours and then only for personnel carrying out official duties. It was also made official that fourth class women would (like men) be housed three to a room and not be permitted to "float"—to eat with another squadron in the dining hall when there were not enough seats with their own squadron.

The issue paper on menu requirements recommended continuing the current policy of giving nutrition education and of assigning a limited number of overweight cadets to special diet tables. The dis-

---

[z] During their training, all the ATOs save one had their hair cut very short. The one was a test case. Her long hair was worn on top of her head and presented no problem except during physical conditioning.

[a] It was thought that following the "regular reg" would appear to be showing favoritism to women.

[b] At the other academies, the effect of the pause before entering was to make male fourth class cadets feel they were being discriminated against because their rooms could be entered without pause. Upperclassmen also felt the women might use the time to put something over on them.

cussion of women's and men's nutritional needs was thorough. Still, a special problem with weight gain for women was anticipated, "even if they eat only a proportionate quantity" of food because of "their hormone structure." Women's caloric requirements were said to be only 80 percent of those of men at the same age and weight.[c] A fourth class male cadet was assumed to need 4,200 calories daily, while the daily menu provided him with 4,800. (A typical airmen's dining hall offers only 3,200 calories daily.) Among the reasons given for not modifying the menu for women were (1) the possibility of reducing the total calories available below the minimum for some individuals, and (2) the effect on cadet morale if quantity were reduced or popular ("usually higher caloric") items eliminated.[d] The same issue paper assumed that peer pressure and availability would lead to weight increases for women. However, women also experience pressure from peers *not* to eat, and in an institutional setting availability is restricted to three short mealtimes. Room and home refrigerators, in fact, would seem to provide much more availability (and temptation) than institutional dining.

Hygiene and grooming are (like food) sensitive areas for morale—and, some would say, especially so for women. It was decided that permits would be required for any electrical appliances (hair dryers, curling irons) and that hair was to be washed only in showers (to prevent clogged sinks). Protective clothing (for breasts) was an issue that was listed but never worked up; it was also quickly decided not to have a menstrual-cycle policy.[e] There was some concern that dysmenorrhea would be an excuse for malingering, although there were also reports from AFROTC summer camp that women were reluctant to seek help for fear of being thought of as seeking special treatment. But debilitating cramps are not common *nor* the only problem; more distressing to young women would be irregular or suspended menstruation. There was some discussion that it would be important to brief women on the causes of such

[c]Absolute cost-effectiveness might dictate hiring more women because their metabolism makes them cheaper to feed.

[d]The problem of reducing the menu below the minimum for some individuals could have been managed by allowing unlimited "seconds." In 1977–78, in fact, there would be a dramatic drop in the daily calories provided in the interest of better fitness.

Food *is* closely associated with morale, yet not to eat a meal placed before one is wasteful, conduct the Air Force disapproves. Thus small portions would seem to be a sensible solution so that the "norm" could be the average rather than the "big" eater.

[e]At one time someone suggested that all women cadets be put on the pill and cycled so they could menstruate at the same time.

suspension and perhaps on birth control methods, and to provide them with easy access to medical advice. Neither became policy. ATO counseling may have provided some informal information, but one squadron commander admitted that he just did not know whether women in his unit had had any education in these areas.

A mandatory personal development course had been dropped by both ROTC and OTS by the time women entered the Air Force Academy, and at least one study showed that women already knew most of the items taught, and that there was no correlation between grooming, training, and self-esteem. DFBL was specifically asked to consider the need for such a course. It found no need, although it suggested that demonstrations by commercial agents might be offered on a voluntary basis.

The initial response to issues concerning BCT had been that it would have to be completely separate; however, by June 1976 a position paper approving women's participation in *all* summer activities was adopted. "All activities" included mess detail, tent setup, security guard, shower formations (conducted by ATOs in their own area), and morning runs. Policies concerning command were not as sweeping. In assessing the various duties associated with running a wing, the commandant's task force followed a general policy that men *could* perform all duties related to women (except train them in their dormitory area). However, strong reservations about what women could do remained, and not just at the academy. For example, at OTS male and female military training instructors (MTIs) were not always available in the same ratio as male and female trainees. Thus a man and woman team was occasionally used to train women. In late 1974, moreover, six women officers were lent to a male squadron. When "higher headquarters" learned of this loan, it was abruptly terminated; and the word came down: women were not to train men. What is interesting about all this is that something that was considered a temporary expedient, as assistance in a pinch, as help but not competition, seemed to have worked quite smoothly.[f]

The context for asserting men's "ability" to command women was usually one in which it was proposed that "a woman" should be on, for instance, the honor and ethics committee. However, when it did not mean yielding a desirable slot, men were quite willing to get advice from women officers, and top administrators were more than

[f]It should be noted that the officer who lent the women and was overruled was later assigned to the academy as commandant. Under his command, two women became AOCs.

delighted that a woman lieutenant colonel was available to handle the stickier aspects of the pregnant cadet. The contrary view, that "women can handle all problems of male cadets," was never formalized, and in the context of AOC slots and of teaching in physical education, an *opposite* (though not official) conclusion was reached. Again, the proposition that men could adequately command and represent women even though they were housed separately, was applied to all cadet committees, councils, and boards—whether "assigned," "elected," "selected," or "mixed." Mandatory inclusion of a woman cadet (or an ATO) was not even considered important to the dining hall menu planning board or the cadet uniform board![g]

The congruency for men but not for women between the dormitory unit and their squadron assignment made equitable Military Order of Merit (MOM) ranking difficult. In 1976–77 six items were used in rating a cadet. Three were objective: grades in military studies and wing training, and demerits. Three were subjective: performance reports (by cadet element leaders), AOC ratings, and peer ratings. "Peer" could mean either squadron or dormitory peer. For men the two were congruent; for women they were mostly different. For women it was therefore decided to omit any dormitory-based rating, either by peers *or* by ATOs.[h] The formula was unchanged, of course, but the basis for rating was in fact different for women and for men. Still, the system was described as "equal." A check of the rating system as applied to women was planned: a separate correlation of the three subjective ratings would be made for women and for men so that the commandant would know whether these ratings were significantly different.

In discussing motivation, the committee concluded (from the ATO experience) that the same items motivated women that motivated men. This motivation was principally related to flying. Indeed, two ATOs applied for and won entrance to Undergraduate Pilot Training. This new opportunity was "an experiment." It would seem that if the experiment "failed," the Air Force would experience severe demotivation on the part of women, yet no contingencies

[g]The decision not to ensure women's representation did not have an "equal" result for women and men. Women could often go unrepresented. Because there were so many more men, however, men had *no* possibility of delegating away any decision-making powers to a woman-dominated body.

[h]Planners worried that when women evaluated other women, the rating factors would be "different" and a dual rating system would emerge. Thus the ATOs were given no input. They were almost the only persons with supervisory assignments whose opinions on cadets' merit were not asked.

were provided for alternate positive motivators. The "results" of the experiment were still not determined by 1979.

Consistent policy was followed in providing for cadet women's membership in all clubs, including competitive clubs like rugby, even though women could not compete with the club (by the second year they could). A more Solomonesque decision was made concerning the choirs and chorale, where the number of women could not provide adequate balance. Women would be permitted in the Catholic and protestant (folk) choirs, and a woman's chorus would be organized that would give women an opportunity to sing and yet permit delaying a decision on the cadet chorale until interest and ability were assessed.[i]

The hitchhiking policy revealed an effort to be consistent, even though concern about hitchhiking was increased by women's entrance. Cadets are forbidden to hitchhike; nevertheless, cadets can accept rides. Indeed, there is one "Give a Cadet a Ride" site in the cadet area, and certain locations are known by cadets as collection centers for trips to and from Colorado Springs and for trips to Denver (sixty miles to the north). The academy's position was that the top priority was safety, that hitchhiking continued to be prohibited, that maximum publicity would be given a new (April 1976) bus route between the academy and Colorado Springs, and that cadet safety programs would "continuously" outline the dangers of hitchhiking.

The most troublesome issues involved counseling, fraternization, and pregnancy. "Counseling" covers a wide range of academy activity from selecting courses to a strenuous chewing out to the delicate managing of a personal problem. From the beginning it was decided that men would counsel women. What remained to be decided was whether any special arrangements would be required when men counseled women (as opposed to men).[j] A special committee that included NCOs and officers with graduate degrees in counseling worked the issue. They found a great deal of anxiety existed about cross-sex counseling and that the anxiety was not confined to men. They also found that much of the concern focused not on what to advise women but on how to counter women's "capacity to manipu-

[i]Past experience showed 50 percent of cadets were "interested," and 20 percent "interested and competent." Attrition during the first year was about one-half (10 percent), and another one-half were lost as upperclassmen. Thus about 5 percent of the seniors maintained their participation in choral activities.

[j]In the first year, women received counsel from, but gave little counsel to, men.

late a situation" and to gain advantage through tears or emotionality.[k] Ultimately, the decision was made that men of all ranks (including third degree cadets) would have to conduct themselves professionally. They would have to generate trust and use privacy where appropriate, but they would not be required to keep the door open or to have a third party present—even though such practices were followed in some Air Force commands.

"Brotherliness" (fraternization) was the second area of concern. There, the tension was between a desire to maintain proper superior-subordinate relationships and the need not to look absurd or to invite willful violations by establishing an unenforceable policy. With only one woman for every thirty men at the academy, women had many opportunities for fraternization. Even if cadets overwhelmingly rejected them, a large residual pool of approvers would exist. Policy makers decided to continue the prohibition against fraternization between fourth degree and more senior cadets. One might suppose that with a ratio of one to ten even among doolies, women could overcome the temptation to fraternize, especially when they knew that officers, civilian instructors, coaches, and cadets were all charged with the responsibility of reporting anyone who broke the regulation. But one would suppose wrong.

The maintenance of a proper superior-subordinate relationship was one of the institution's long-standing policies. Even the cross-sex superior-subordinate relationship was new only in that it now involved women cadets and in that these women were exposed to a great deal more temptation than male cadets confronted. But the women were all new and did not know the "informal" rules. Further, they could have a very active and still "legal" social life (with classmates), without even having to use a "privilege," because they could meet other doolies on campus. The fraternization policy was uniform, but because of the disproportionate numbers between women and men their experiences differed.[1]

To repeat, fraternization was seen as a "major" reason for the

---

[k] This fear, this attribution of power to calculating women, surfaced periodically. Its theme is very much a part of severely segregated Muslim cultures, too, where men fear their own susceptibility. Presumably the remedy is to gain experience and to understand tears as one way of expressing emotion (like cursing or driving 90 miles an hour), a way to try to control (like resorting to flattery or threats) an unstable situation.

[1] A loophole in the fraternization policy was left for kinship and friendship prior to entrance. Thus the entering cadet engaged to an upperclassman was not required to disengage and siblings enjoyed a dispensation.

"lack of acceptance" of women at the Merchant Marine Academy. The question may really have been one of jealousy rooted in the absurd ratio that gave great visibility to any woman's contact with an upperclassman. But when fraternization did occur, was it the (subordinate) woman's fault or the (superior in rank) man's fault? Was it a one-year problem or a perennial one? As the women became upper class cadets, would the problem expand to include cadet-officer relationships? The issue was definitely not settled just because a policy had been made.

Conduct on dates and sexual relations was left to the general code, AFCR 35–8 and 522–1, as well as to AFCR 35–6, which includes as offenses (1) public or improper display of affection, (2) conduct reflecting poor judgment, and (3) conduct unbecoming a USAF officer candidate (as well as fraternization). Promiscuity clearly would not be tolerated, but no regulation forbade sexual activity *per se*. Decorum, custom and discretion, and "the same standards for men and women" were the principles informing policy on these matters.[m]

Pregnancy. The most perplexing issue. The official files that deal with pregnancy can best be measured not by pages, or even inches, but by feet. Should all pregnant cadets be penalized? Should all cadet contributors to a pregnancy be subject to discipline? Is pregnancy solely a medical problem? Is it social misconduct? Is an aborted pregnancy of official concern? Is what may be good policy also good law? Would a policy withstand judicial testing?

Pregnancy was one of the few items on which the Department of Defense wished a united front. The three defense academies were asked to establish a common policy, but agreement could not be reached. Thus there was no set policy even when the women arrived.[n] Administrators probably expected that if a cadet became

[m]The phrase "same standards for men and women" does not appear in the regulation but does appear in policy papers. However, some academy staff believe that women will in practice not be granted the same sexual freedom as male cadets, that their actions will always be more carefully scrutinized.

[n]The Air Force had long had a policy of disenrolling a cadet for paternity. Its reasoning was that cadets are forbidden marriage to ensure against competing responsibilities; and even if a child born out of wedlock were not a responsibility, it would surely reflect on a cadet's "morals, character, or judgment." This policy was not enforced—at least one academy graduate could name a father-classmate of his. Of course, in the face of a tenacious denial, a legal finding of paternity would probably be needed before a cadet could be dismissed. Nevertheless, cadets had been disenrolled for paternity (the last one in 1973). Thus it was not wholly farcical to say women would be discharged or permitted to resign for pregnancy and men for making someone pregnant.

pregnant and wished to stay at the academy she would simply see to it that no one found out, and that if a cadet brought her pregnancy to notice she was probably looking for a way out. The situation that actually developed was one no one had imagined—a cadet who became pregnant but who did not look much like it and who absolutely denied it until six days before delivery.[o]

[o]Apparently her plan had been to go home on spring vacation, have the baby, and return without interrupting her doolie year at all. She missed pulling off the "Great Train Robbery of 1976–77 " by only a couple of days—acting in a cadet play, swimming, and even running a mile the day she entered the hospital. The academy news release was buried locally by stories about a 19" spring snowfall and nationally by a black militant takeover of several Washington, D.C., buildings.

CHAPTER

8

Immune Intellects: The Dean
and His Faculty

"If there is a problem it's 99 percent in the com's shop or in P.E.,"
said one senior faculty member; he, like most of the faculty, seemed
to consider his unit immune to changes associated with sex integration.[a]

"Immunity" can mean that one is free of and protected from disease (in this case, sexism). Thus "no change" would represent a
healthy, vigorous state. But "immunity" can also suggest a sense of
exemption, of privilege, of not being tied to the same rules, of not
having to be responsive when others are responsive. Both meanings
seem to have some application to the faculty's reaction to the advent
of women.

The faculty's strong belief in its intellectual objectivity is prob-

[a]This statement also hints at the "terrazzo gap" between the goals and the values of the
faculty and those of the commandant's staff. In the past this gap had represented a significant
difficulty, but in 1976–77 the units were working in relative harmony. They worked at it. A
group of officers called "Bridgers" met on Friday evenings at the Stag Bar (women officers
were welcome, but not wives) in the basement of the Officers Club. Typically, thirty or forty
(mostly rated) officers would gather. Regulars who contributed to cooperation between the
units had their names engraved on a plaque. One woman officer who flew came with some
regularity, but another who held a position of some responsibility in the commandant's shop
didn't even know the bar or the "Bridgers" existed.

ably linked to the nature of the school, its faculty, and its curriculum. Explorations of subjectivity, which can be either elegantly abstruse or vulgarly political, are not commonplace at the academy. There, the style and curriculum, the habits of the faculty, and the goals of the students are focused more on answering questions than on asking them. Both the faculty and the students are "on duty." One's duty is to teach; the other's is to learn.

The Department of Behavioral Sciences and Leadership (DFBL)[b] rightly played a special role in the integration process and actively cooperated with the various commandant's planning and implementing committees, although it had only limited interaction with physical education. It was also the office of primary responsibility for the Human Relations Education Committee. Views on human relations training and on the usefulness of the analogy between women's integration and the integration of blacks varied, but few staff members seemed to feel the urgency or the same sense of morality about the need for women's integration as at least some expressed about racial integration.

The School, the Faculty, the Curriculum

A military academy is not a liberal arts college plus. "Leadership, Military and Aviation Programs" precede "The Curriculum" and "The Academic Program" in the catalogue just as "Air Force" precedes "Academy" in the institution's name. The academy's purposes include career motivation and leadership training. Still, the Air Force Academy is more "civilian" than the other two service academies in that it offers its undergraduates some breadth of education.

West Point offers a forty-one-course core curriculum that results in a B.S. in General Studies. Only six elective courses are permitted over eight semesters. Annapolis has "breadth requirements," and each midshipman does choose a major; however, 80 percent of them must choose engineering, physical science, math, or operations analysis. (Annapolis' faculty, however, is approximately one-half military and one-half civilian.) The Air Force Academy does have a core curriculum, which includes three-fourths of a cadet's units (thirty-five of forty-six courses), but it is only about one-half tech-

---

[b]The correct acronym for the Department of Behavioral Science and Leadership is DFBL, derived from *D*ean of the *F*aculty, *B*ehavioral Science, and *L*eadership.

nical in nature; and about one-fourth of each cadet's program is
alloted to the study of an "academic major." About half the cadets
major in humanities and the social sciences; the other half take science or engineering. Still, there is a heavy emphasis on technical
training. Every student takes several math, science, and engineering
courses. At the same time, humanities offerings are limited. At the
Air Force Academy (in 1976–77) the only humanities departments
were foreign language, history (with emphasis on military history),
and English (with only a limited number of upper-division classes).
History was the only humanities major available.

In 1976–77 the academy's faculty of about 550 was divided thus:
145 in engineering, 154 in basic science, 136 in social sciences, and
117 in humanities. Virtually all faculty members were military, and
most were Air Force (as opposed to Army or Navy) officers; close
to 40 percent were military academy graduates, especially in engineering and in the basic sciences. But there was only one academy
graduate in the forty-person language department and only four
among twenty-nine behavioral scientists. Only 28 percent of the
faculty held Ph.D.s; most of the teaching was (and is) done by captains holding master's degrees who spend a three-year tour at the
academy.[c]

A core of some forty permanent, tenured professors and tenured
associate professors head the various departments and provide continuity, especially at the top. This hierarchy puts the faculty at an
advantage in bargaining with physical education or the commandant's staff, because those units have a policy of regular rotation,
which leaves them with only a limited institutional memory. Moreover, the faculty's dean had been at the academy since the day it
began. (He began in 1954 as a chemistry instructor, became dean in
1968, and retired in 1978.)

In talking about their own and their institution's response to the
entrance of women, faculty regularly expressed the view that there
was no need for change in programs under faculty jurisdiction. This
"clean hands" position rested on the argument that the material
taught was sex neutral and that it was unnecessary and even inappropriate to consider the kinds of bodies encasing students' minds.
Engineering, basic science, and even language instructors rarely
grapple with the subtleties of subjectivism, thus such views were
almost certainly sincere.

[c]Thus most of the officers on the academic side are outranked by the commandant's
AOCs, who are primarily majors.

Conversely, English and history are two fields in which feminists have severely criticized the selection and interpretation of traditional subject matter. Although each of these departments did have women instructors in 1976–77, they were low in rank and in no position to be critical even if they had been so inclined. Furthermore, neither department offers the range of courses one would find in a comparably sized college. English offers only sixteen courses in all. History offers twenty-two, but these include five on warfare and five dealing with regional history. Since the History Department did have a course on the "history of minorities" (in the U.S.), one might expect that a parallel course on "women's history" would at least have been considered. If it were, there was no demonstrable result. The department's principal contributions were a Saturday morning military training lecture on women in aviation and the military and a recorded interview with Captain Galloway for the academy's oral history collection.[d]

The training lecture was developed in the department but presented, under the auspices of the commandant, in a nongraded context that necessitated some superficiality and some catering to a reluctant (and probably hostile) cadet audience. Each viewer perceived the presentation differently. Readily available materials were sparse, which limited what could be done; nevertheless some women viewers found the lecture degrading and unserious. They deplored the emphasis on nonmilitary women like the "Donut Dollies" and Mata Hari of World War I and said they would have emphasized the contributions of women like the nurse POWs in the Philippines during World War II. Obviously, different people would have emphasized different points, but a feminist might have stressed that women have always fought and died in wars even if they have not been in the military; thus if women were trained for combat, the principal difference would be that some would be prepared to fight back. Or emphasis could have been given to Brownmiller's account of the attacks on women that war sanctions, or to the restrictive legislation that limited women's numbers and ranks for so long. More attention could have been given, too, to the degree of women's contemporary participation in the Air Force and the point made that their absence from the academy was anomalous—out of step.

The social sciences is the one area in which women necessarily compose part of the subject matter and in which the study of sex

---

[d] It also contributed a faculty daughter to the class of 1980. Soon after women's admission, a bloc on women was included in the department's course on minorities.

roles would seem mandatory. However, neither the Department of Law nor the Department of Political Science and Philosophy saw any need to acknowledge or respond to women's entrance. In fact, the latter was uncategorical in its statement that absolutely no changes had been made solely because women would enter the academy.

That department actually hosted and co-sponsored a five-day national assembly on "Women and the American Economy" in March 1976. Speakers included Martha Griffiths, Antonia Brico, Betty Friedan, Phyllis Schlafly and Jean Lipman-Blumen. Participants included cadets and more than sixty student-guests, the majority of whom were women, from all over the country. The prepared discussion questions were pertinent and sophisticated.[e] Nevertheless, the chairman (of Political Science and Philosophy), a father of seven daughters and a son, made it clear that the choice of topic was the American Assembly's (the co-sponsor) and *not* the academy's.

Generally, that department has a reputation for stimulating inquiry.[f] It also administers the "Distinguished Speakers" and the "Cadet Forum" programs. Except for the assembly programs, there were no "distinguished" women speakers during 1976, nor did any speaker discuss any aspect of women's changing role. Among the speakers were Colorado's governor, Richard Lamm; Adm. Noel Gaylor, Commander-in-Chief, Pacific; and Michael Novak, philosopher and columnist. Forum speakers included: Adm. Elmo Zumwalt, Julian Bond (a black Georgia legislator), and Thomas Schelling of Harvard. The department was accurate in claiming that it had taken no special interest in women's impending arrival. Its position was that to do so would be an inappropriate overreaction, for women were not excluded from the curriculum nor was the curriculum anti-women.

Only two academic units remain, both of which might be supposed to have a substantive interest—the Department of Economics, Geography, and Management; and Behavioral Sciences and Leadership. The former did bring some new materials to existing classes. The latter involved itself in women's integration to such a degree that it will be discussed separately.

[e]For example: "How will a continued increase in the proportion of women who work affect the distribution of income between high, middle, and low income groups?" "When is seniority and when is the affirmative action goal to be honored?" "How are changes in women's work roles affecting labor force mobility and work schedules?"

[f]The chair brought anti-war resisters to his classes at the height of the Vietnam War; he also teaches a class called the "Morality of War," and was nationally honored as a distinguished teacher.

Students and Teaching

The academy works hard to recruit talented and committed young men and women. Candidates are usually contacted as high school juniors by one of some sixteen hundred liaison officers (this makes a ratio of one officer per enrollee). Every three years each liaison officer spends one week at the academy, and local coordinators are updated each year. An important theme in recruitment is the presentation of a realistic picture of what being a cadet is all about, and cadets are regularly used in a grassroots recruitment program in which they visit high schools to provide students with a cadet's point of view. The Academy wants good candidates, but it also wants to be sure that applicants know what kind of school they are coming to and what will be expected of them. Special programs are directed at minority cadets, and in late 1975 a highly successful campaign was directed toward the rapid recruitment of women candidates. That recruiting effort utilized academy personnel, the Secretary of the Air Force and his staff, and various media. Distinguished visitors, including 110 school district superintendents, were briefed. Interviews with the academy's superintendent, the athletic director, and nationally known women staff reached national audiences. Cadets made public appearances during their Thanksgiving holidays. News releases saturated "women's" magazines: *Girl Scout Review*, *Vogue*, *Cosmopolitan*, *Essence*, *Good Housekeeping*, *Harper's*, *Ladies' Home Journal*, *Mademoiselle*, *Ms.*, and *Young Miss*. The national press published and broadcast articles and segments aimed at getting women to apply. By the end of January 1976, 1,202 women had become candidates; this compared to 625 women applicants to West Point and 532 to Annapolis. On June 28, 1976, 1,593 cadets entered as the class of 1980.[g] Almost ten percent (157) were women. Seventy percent of the class were medically qualified for pilot training and another ten percent for navigator. The class was drawn from a pool of 9,468 "candidates" and 2,669 "qualified candidates." (The latter represented a twenty percent increase over the year before, that is, before women applied.)[h]

Since the academy has always been interested in the size of its cadets, it is worth noting that the entrance of women affected mean size very little. Average height remained the 5′10″ it had been for

[g]The Air Force Academy got a one-week head start on Annapolis and West Point.

[h]Regardless of the attitudes of cadets already in training, the prospect of co-education must have made the academy more attractive overall. The next year (1977) there was some dropoff in the number of candidates but not to the pre-1976 level.

the previous sixteen years; average weight fell from 154.9 pounds to 152.3, and perhaps the 2.6 pound decrease should be attributed to women; but since a 1965 average of 162, there has been a steady downward trend in cadet weight. The male range from the previous class had been 106 to 238 pounds, with twenty-one men weighing less than 120 pounds. The point is simple: there have always been small cadets. Women's entrance barely affected average size.

As in many other professions, cadets are often following in their parents' footsteps. For the class of 1980, 211 cadets' fathers or step-fathers were on active duty, and 296 more had fathers or stepfathers who were retired military personnel. (No data were available on mothers and stepmothers.) About one-third of the cadets came from military families. Of these, 60 percent came from officers' families and 40 percent had enlisted fathers.[i] The number of cadets from military families represented a 20 percent increase (89 cadets) over the previous year and may indicate that women cadets especially tended to come from military families.

The first and standard screens used by admissions officers in making college entrance decisions are the College Entrance Examination Board aptitude test and related achievement test scores. As a group, cadets scored about 550 on verbal aptitude and English composition and about 650 on math aptitude; 5 percent scored over 700 on the math achievement.[j] The higher math scores only partly represent an academy preference; they also reflect the fact that math-oriented students apply to the academy.

Selected students must show academic promise, but it is the whole "person" formula that is the criterion for admission. This selection tool includes academic performance (ACT and CEEB scores, rank in class), athletic aptitude, and leadership activities, which run the gamut of high school activities, but athletic letters are considered especially important.[k] Participation in other particular groups such as Boy Scouts, ROTC, Junior ROTC, and Civil Air Patrol are also thought to have special bearing on success at the academy.[l]

[i]This shows that upward mobility exists; but, of course, the 40 percent are drawn from a much larger pool of potential candidates than are the 60 percent.

[j]As a result of these scores, the Air Force Academy was described as "very competitive" in Barron's *Profiles of American Colleges* (1976); this was embarrassing because both West Point and Annapolis were rated "highly competitive"—one full ranking higher.

[k]In the class of 1980, 89 percent were in the top quarter of their graduating class, almost two-thirds were in the top tenth, and 8 percent were number one in their class. A minimum score was required on the Physical Aptitude Examination, but higher scores won higher credit.

[l]Close to half of the class had been Boy Scouts, and 202 had been Eagle Scouts.

Given that all the cadets were good, were the women and men similar? The admissions committee hoped that about 10 percent of the class of 1980 would be women. Did that mean it would be "harder" for a woman to enter because there were fewer women's "slots," or "easier" because only a few women were interested in entering?

While women averaged 5 inches shorter and 27 pounds lighter than the men, other data suggest a rough similarity between the sexes. (See Table VII.) It seems that the major difference lies in men's obtaining an athletic letter while women were joining the National Honor Society, women's becoming publication editors (or business managers) while men ran for class president, and men's attending Boys State while women wrote valedictories.[m] It is also pertinent to note that women's academic scores were slightly higher than those of the men.

Students at the academies encounter a faculty highly committed to teaching; research is not central to faculty concerns. In fact, less than 30 percent of the faculty have Ph.D.s. What faculty do all day is teach. Most meet four classes a semester; these typically include fewer than twenty students and may require only one or two different preparations.[n] Instructors are also expected to give cadets as much E.I. (extra instruction) as they need—this may mean giving as much as an hour a day in special help. In addition, faculty are encouraged to undertake modest research projects if they are "blue" (related directly to Air Force activities) or if they emphasize cadet participation. The faculty is also expected to participate in nonacademic programs (including various aviation programs), act as advisors or as squadron assistants, associate with athletic teams, and participate in club activities.[o]

As an indication of the importance assigned teaching, it might be noted that new instructors typically have a ten-day orientation program. In 1976 the program in DFBL for some eight new faculty included participation by as many as twenty onboard officers. It included a tour of the academy and briefings on the cadet profile,

---

[m]This is very much in keeping with conventional wisdom and with research results that show girls as the superior in elementary school, girls and boys in good balance (but in different activities) through high school, and men moving into better positions from college on. The question, of course, is 'why?'

[n]Courses taken by many students typically have a director who designs the course, who may make up a mimeographed text specifically for the course, and who monitors as many as thirty-five instructors.

[o]As a counterpart to the "whole man," the "whole officer" not only instructs; he plays and is military. In doing so he demonstrates the "unity of military and intellectual activities."

Table VII. Comparison of Selected Characteristics and Activities of Men and Women Cadets in the Class of 1980

	Men	Women
CEEB mean scores		
Verbal aptitude	550	587
English composition	539	579
Math aptitude	647	642
Math achievement	647	668
ACT mean scores		
English	23.1	24.7
Social studies	26.6	26.9
Math	29.5	28.3
Natural science	29.9	29.6
Physical Aptitude Examination (PAE)	557	595[a]
Medical qualification at entry		
Pilot	1053 (73.3%)	57 (36.3%)[b]
Navigator	150 (10.5%)	9 (5.7%)
Air Force Academy— nonflying	233 (16.2%)	91 (58.0%)
All sports—team captains (one or more sports)	29.3%	28.7%
All sports—letter winners (one or more sports)	78.9%	55.4%
Class presidents	11.2%	4.5%
Publication editors or business managers	5.3%	14.9%
Boys/Girls State	19.1%	10.8%
Valedictorians	7.1%	12.1%
National Honor Society	56.9%	78.6%
Boy/Girl Scouts	46.0%	27.4%
Civil Air Patrol	6.2%	5.7%
Private pilot's license	3.3%	1.3%

[a]Women's and men's tests and scoring were not identical. Also, as noted before, the women were "better" physical specimens as compared to U.S. women than were the men as compared to U.S. men.

[b]Women were not permitted to train as pilots when this selection was made, so no selection was made based on medical qualifications for flying.

administrative procedures, honor and ethics, decorum, test security, teaching styles and preparation, the how-to-study program, and practice teaching and critiques. The last consisted of a twenty-five-minute presentation on a psychology topic. New instructors criticized each other and were also videotaped. After the final debriefing, two days were allowed to elapse. Then the tapes (which were seen only by the performer) were erased.

This kind of attention to teaching and to the training of new faculty does not occur in higher education with any regularity. Undergraduates usually do get more attention when there are no graduate students on campus, but a professor's course offerings are usually very individualistic; faculty feel few pressures to conform. The purpose of education at the academy is not exploration, as compared to that of a liberal arts college, and the disinterested judgment of a researcher is not the supreme value. The classroom is not used to stimulate, to unleash, to encourage doubt and curiosity. The goal of instruction is to impart a large quantity of technical information. Each lesson has an assignment, an objective, a list of key concepts, and a set of discussion questions. The purpose is mastery, confidence, and commitment. Elegant mental constructs are not of prime importance. Nor is the process the message.

Officer-instructors are expected to produce informed cadets who have mastered specified material and who have also learned to be effective leaders by modeling themselves after the role-model officers around them. Part of the learning entails discipline, drill, and memory; part, intuitive modeling. The development of creative and critical thinking receives less emphasis.[p] Teaching is so important that monitoring what the student has learned actually becomes the measure of the teacher; students' evaluations of the teacher, now used so extensively in civilian colleges, are not even sought. Student performance, not opinion, is the measure.[q]

Even if the material taught is understood to be sex neutral, two other considerations would seem to have occurred to the faculty: (1) are female role models essential, or are male models sufficient; and

[p]Creative and critical thinking are more often exalted than achieved, even in liberal arts colleges.

[q]However, qualitative teaching comparisons are directly available since large courses are taught in sections, and students take the same exams. Thus the relative success of different instructors' students is known to all. An instructor whose students are doing poorly can expect a discussion with the course director. Students who are doing poorly can expect a discussion with a number of people. Again, as military cadets, it is the students' *duty* to learn.

(2) could different teaching methods improve the learning of women students?

The role-model debate was settled in early planning: women were needed. Although one woman officer had worked in the admissions office as early as 1959, the first woman faculty member was not hired until 1968. Her selection was not made "because she was a woman," but because she had applied several times and had more qualifications and a higher rank than other applicants. It seems to have been a "cannot-be-denied" kind of appointment. In the next several years, two other women officers served as faculty members; they served well and without incident in the teaching role. Yet being "good" and "first" exacts a toll.[r] For example, as an extra duty, one of the women was asked to train upper class cadets to give academy tours to incoming fourth class men. During the instruction, she accompanied the cadets on the prescribed tour. When part of the tour passed through the "Air Garden," which was, incidentally, just below the commandant's window, he happened to glance out and see her on territory reserved for men only. He raised havoc. The general's precise words have not been recorded, and his final disposition may even have been to overlook the whole affair. Nevertheless, no professional officer relishes upsetting the boss merely by doing her duty. Even if the word of his anger comes to her only informally, she feels pressure—a pressure that is increased because she has no opportunity to explain or justify. The first women instructors did not extend their tours at the academy as many men do. The total experience was not the same for them; compared to their male peers, they seem to have experienced more pain and less pleasure.

Anticipating the arrival of women cadets, the dean and his chairman did increase the number of women faculty to 8 or 9 out of about 550. Nevertheless, the role-model problem was the same as it was throughout the academy: most women were working one to a department, and all were at a very junior level.[s]

[r]Even if one becomes impatient with the lamentations of the rich ("taxes" and "the servant problem") and powerful ("all that responsibility"), one should remember that "first" women lack a support group and persons with whom to identify. They depend almost exclusively on their own self-respect and professional identity.

[s]There were two notable exceptions. The first was Lt. Col. Diane Ordez, who was brought in for one year before she went to the War College. Hers was a "made" administrative job (it is not even listed in the 1976 catalog), and while this assignment gave her an excellent opportunity to learn how the academy worked and to serve as an ombudsman for women, her stay was brief, she was not replaced, and she did not hold "regular" institutional power. The second was Dr. Lois De Fleur, who received a one-year appointment to DFBL as a Distinguished Visiting Professor. That department apparently did not know of the existence of the

It is true that many of the fields taught at the academy are not "women's fields," but in some ways faculty recruiting at the academy offers more opportunities to integrate than at civilian universities, if only because more than 70 percent of the academy's faculty do not hold doctorates. (Nationally almost as many women hold M.A.s as men.) Also, more than 60 percent of the teachers are captains or lieutenants—ranks that many women hold. However, one department chairman noted that too many of the women had "poor" or "square-filling" masters degrees. By this he meant on-base or correspondence degrees that one undertakes to upgrade oneself. To him a "good" degree would be one earned by attending a civilian university full time (probably at Air Force expense). The catch is, of course, that one cannot just choose to do so. One must be selected, and it is not clear that women are as likely to be selected as are men. Furthermore, when a certain (large) number of slots are reserved for alumni and for rated officers (who are considered especially good role models), the number of slots women can even compete for is dramatically reduced. There are, after all, *no* women alumni; and at the time of women's entry there were no women rated officers.[t]

In the faculty's top ranks were fifty-nine lieutenant colonels. None were women. Many of these men instructors had taught at the academy early in their careers. They were then sent to civilian schools to obtain Ph.D.s in preparation for a second appointment to the academy. Women with the right academic qualifications would have been difficult to find; they were impossible to find if a particular career pattern as well as particular credentials were stipulated. This is an endemic problem. If hiring is based on both past performance and on one's promise for the future, women and minorities can sometimes manage to lose both ways. If they have performed well by following the conventional pattern, they can still be beaten out by a "promising, fair-haired fast burner" whose future looks more certain.[u] But if a woman or minority enters a highly selective competition with a superior record, either often arrives at that point in

woman lieutenant colonel who held a Ph.D. in psychology; but even if it had, she would have been considered too senior to be recruited if routine hiring practices were followed.

[t]If women role models for women cadets are to be provided at the same "rate" as those cadets, there should be about fifty women instructors soon.

[u]Predictability becomes more important as one moves up the command structure, because each selection represents an increasing investment for the military, and any performance errors can have wider and/or more serious consequences.

an ingenious or irregular way. This means their *records* do not read the same as their competitors'. Some squares have not been checked. Even if the candidate looks very promising, what is missing from the record—previous teaching experience at the academy—can hurt.[v]

In the Air Force Academy faculty, the pattern was the same as elsewhere. Women were mostly apprentices (for some unspecified future) or auditors (serving as consultants or consciences).[w] They were not mainstream, they did not make policy, and they did not provide cadet women with a full range of role models.

Do some teaching methods work better on women and others on men? What setting and motivation maximizes intellectual performance—in general and for specific groups? Educators would like to know the answers to these questions, but effective teaching is such a slippery subject that most institutions follow a strategy of providing a variety of teachers and formats and letting students seek out the instructors who best meet their needs. In a structured institution like the academy, however, there is relatively little student choice, and instructors have the responsibility of teaching every student who comes their way. They must assess each cadet's background, use enlightening analogies, and give whatever emphasis is required.[x]

At one point, planners considered programming women cadets so that they would be clustered in their academic classes rather than randomly distributed. The goal was to avoid making them "tokens," that is, to avoid their being only one or two members of a class. Clustering was not effected, principally because of the complexity of the task. However, in following the dictates of practicality, offi-

---

[v] An irregular record should be an advantage—it should represent an overcoming of odds. It should reflect one's extra capacity. The fact remains that it still does not read well enough. For example, because of past discrimination women academics are likely to have degrees from less prestigious institutions than their male counterparts. It might be argued that, by arriving at a mid-career decision point *without* the "best" training, a woman has done more and demonstrated more promise. Nevertheless a competing male's record that shows the "right" school and scholarships (even if women had been ineligible for those scholarships) often is read as showing the higher accomplishment.

[w] It was almost as though their role was to be (for male officers) the gift "the giftie gie us / To see oursel's as ithers see us" (from Robert Burns's "To a Louse").

A constant complaint of women officers was that their job description called on them to act as advisors but no one asked their advice.

[x] The most conscientious efforts can backfire. One chemistry professor (not at a service academy) told of his efforts to encourage and elucidate freshman lab to a young woman who was clearly bright and trying but not mastering. Urging her on, he noted, "It's really just like cooking." Her eyes showed that instant clarity had been achieved. "That explains it! There is absolutely nothing I despise more," she replied.

cials were able to avoid having to choose between two principles: one that sought to enhance women's performance by providing them an environment more like that enjoyed by the men, and one that afforded no cadet any kind of special treatment.

For the most part the faculty assumed that teaching women would be the same as teaching men. Were they correct? Did the women learn the same amount in the same way? Apparently they at least learned the same amount. After two semesters, the G.P.A. for fourth class men and women was quite similar, although men did better than the women both semesters.[y] For the first semester the difference was .05; the second it was .07. This difference is not statistically significant, yet one cannot escape feeling that it made a political difference. There is no question that the men felt great satisfaction at having done "better."[z]

Some staff were disappointed by the women's performance. Perhaps it was simply a matter of a failing of symmetry—that if men had "done better" in the physical activities of the summer, then women should have "done better" in academics. Perhaps the women's slightly better college board scores had led to an unfulfilled expectation that they would do better. Some argued that it was the women's poorer performance in military studies (although those topics represented only two of the twenty-two semester hours) that hurt women's G.P.A. Or as an Annapolis dean suggested, perhaps it was women's lack of experience in mathematics, their lack of applied science and of equipment manipulation, that hindered their achievement. Another Annapolis theory held that the women experienced a social isolation that interfered with a better performance. That is, informal peer teaching was reduced for the women as compared to the men. A counter-theory at the Air Force Academy proposed that women were *too* involved, active, and participatory— so much so that their efforts had been insufficiently focused. One keeper of statistics theorized that the (insignificant) difference in G.P.A. might be attributed to the small but consistent edge given to

[y]An examination of mid-semester grades, however, tells a somewhat different story. In both semesters, mid-term grades revealed that the women were doing better in academics than the men. Although the difference was small, the fourth class men were "very ticklish" about the matter, especially after it was announced over the wire services. Semester grades were just the opposite: men did better than the women, although the difference was only .05. Even though the "powers that be" notified the Associated Press of this it did not publish the results.

[z]At the end of the first year, 30 of 135 women were on academic probation and 262 of 1189 men (22.2 and 22.0 percent); by comparison, 34 percent of the men and 33 percent of the women were on the Dean's List.

students of the same sex as the instructor—a factor working to girls' advantage in early education and to men's in advanced and professional training. A social scientist argued (half seriously) that the women had collectively and carefully contrived to do just slightly less well, and pointed out that in both semesters the women had had the higher grades at mid-semester and then had slipped behind when it counted—when grades went on permanent records.

DFBL

The Department of Behavioral Sciences and Leadership looked to the future rather than to the past for its legitimacy. At the founding of the academy, there had been a Department of Human Relations, which encompassed philosophy, geography, and psychology. By the next year (1956), psychology stood alone, philosophy had dematerialized, and geography had become part of military history. Two years later, psychology was eliminated, and a Department of Leadership Studies was created on the military side of the academy. Then in 1961 "leadership" as subject matter was moved from the commandant's side to the faculty's, where it came under the auspices of the new Psychology Department, which emphasized management. The next year the department became Behavioral Sciences; in 1965 it became the Department of Psychology and Leadership. In 1971 there was a merger with the Department of Life Science. One more name and emphasis change brought the department the title it held in 1976—Behavioral Sciences and Leadership, a department primarily composed of psychologists, but with representation from sociology and anthropology.[a]

When the current chairman of Behavioral Science and Leadership took over, he wished to make his mark by contributing to both his discipline (psychology) and the academy itself. The department's major noninstructional contribution to the academy was in providing counseling.[b] It also played a role in educating cadets about women's new roles and served as an information resource on women. The commandant's staff drew on these resources, especially when it was

[a]The constant change, in part, reflects the importance placed on leadership and the uncertainty over how best to create it.

[b]The department works both in competition and in cooperation with Cadet Counseling, a separate administrative unit that has operated under the handicap of a cadet's having to acknowledge that something was wrong before receiving its services.

developing the ATO program and formulating its position papers.[c] The department's fourth major activity in 1976–77 involved the coordination of all research on women's integration.

Training in counseling began with the AOCs, who were given a sixteen-hour course by the department. Next, cadet counselors for the summer "R" (rehabilitation) squadron were given special training through the department, as was the cadet cadre that trains fourth degrees.[d] In preparation for the summer of 1976, more than seventy officers took part in the training of the BCT cadre. The next year the program shifted to the use of more audio-visual aids and fewer officers. In particular the program used a videotape entitled "Motivation Follies," featuring the academy's drama group, the Blue Bards. To "unfreeze" cadet emotions and to stimulate discussion, women were made a prominent part of the tape, which showed a great deal of negative training—pushups, squat thrusts, reference to weaker men as "these sisters," and, during a scene depicting physical activities (like shower formations), a superimposed mouth yelling such statements as "My sister can outrun you!" and "We don't want any weak sisters around here." The officer in charge of the training observed that the tape produced shock its first year. The behavior it portrayed was recognizable but taboo. The second year it produced protest: cadets denied that they were like their electronic peers and asserted that they did not like to see such barbarity, even for purposes of negative illustration. The officer's appraisal of the two responses was that over the course of the year there really had been a change in the direction of acceptance of women. "The women probably still feel they're not accepted," he observed, "and that's how they *should* feel, but attitudes have changed a lot. There's now maybe a 50–50 acceptance rate."

This officer, who had made a personal commitment to the program yet was moving to a new assignment, worried that further change might not come to pass. He worried that self-satisfaction or simple boredom would lead to a "failure to nurture" and that follow-up programs would not be supported.[e] An important cue, he

[c] The department educated cadets on women's new roles mainly through its two core (required) courses: General Psychology (for fourth class cadets) and Applied Behavioral Science in the Military Environment (for second class cadets). Each year fifty or more cadets major in behavioral science.

[d] The rehabilitation squadron (1) isolates cadets who wish to quit, (2) handles adjustment problems, and (3) maintains a program for injured cadets who cannot keep up with their programs.

[e] More than one officer observed that what we need is "a sabbatical from women."

thought, would be how third class women related to fourth class women. Many of the staff and faculty worried that third class women would be "too tough."[f] One prediction of such behavior was that women would be "too good," "too military," that they would not distinguish between form and reality. A second one that worried him was that they would overidentify with male cadets and, in fact, come to dislike "women as women." They would try to separate themselves from other women as part of their personal effort to gain acceptance. This kind of group self-hatred must ultimately be destructive, although an overwhelmingly strong military commitment could lead to high achievement and success for a limited number of individuals. Distinguishing between the two sensibilities, strong professionalism and self-hatred, may require careful evaluation.

Education, however, came before evaluation. The year before women arrived, DFBL had incorporated materials on sexism in its core course, Behavioral Science 302. While cadets expressed a feeling of saturation with the subject of women, the evidence does not suggest overemphasis. The "leadership" course, while subject to continual revision, basically covers theories and applications of leadership and counseling. The "Cadet Handbook" made up especially for the course consisted of forty-five lessons. Two dealt with "Racism, Sexism and Human Relations," for which two articles were assigned: Robert Terry's "The White Male Club" and William Blakey's "Everybody Makes the Revolution." Both pieces consider racism and sexism and make these points:

1. "The myth of achievement by bootstrap" and "the myth of individualism" have "no foundation in fact."
2. "Integration by race and sex is . . . racist and sexist insofar as it means 'you can make it in the club if you act like white males.'"
3. Some officials fear the voluntary military is attracting "too many" minority people.[g]
4. Only white males at the bottom of the organization are "bearing the brunt of social change."
5. Racism and sexism are perpetuated more "by everyday role definitions than by the psychic needs of individuals to be superior."

[f]This had been the Merchant Marine Academy experience.

[g]Anxiety about "too many" seems to encompass a worry both that the arming of a large number of minority people could endanger the majority and that a disproportionate number of minorities should not be called upon to sacrifice themselves for their country.

6. "For most men, pro-woman means anti-male."
7. As Bobby Seale said, "In the Panther household everybody sweeps the floor, everybody makes the bed, and everybody makes a revolution, because real manhood depends on the subjugation of no one."[h]

One of the two class periods Behavioral Science 302 instructors devoted to racism and sexism was used to show a 1972 Army training film entitled *Games*. Portraying a hypothetical job interview, the film depicts a variety of racist and sexist behavior on the part of a white male interviewer. Later he repeats the interview in a dream; however, this time he experiences the treatment he had given. All this is clearly an attempt to demonstrate "white racism" through role reversal. Yet when the film stopped and the lights went on, numerous cadet hands were waving.[i] The first to speak seemed to speak for most, "I sure am glad to see that someone is finally talking about reverse discrimination!"

This interpretation of the film may seem incomprehensible, but what it suggests is the overwhelming cadet preoccupation with what they perceived to be discrimination against them. When the "need" of the Air Force dictates that 90 percent of the appointments be reserved for men, it is hard to believe that men could genuinely or intensely feel discriminated against. But as one listened to the cadets talk, one began to understand that they (and many other) young white men do feel that they must compete with women and minorities, and that having to compete represents a loss to them, even if that loss is only a loss of privilege.[j] This loss is especially felt when young white men compare themselves to their fathers and older brothers, or when they contemplate being expected to support not only themselves but a family as well.

The classroom response, which at first seems shallow, selfish,

[h]The arguments are well made and the link between sexism and racism is addressed. Yet somehow one is sorry that men are once again speaking on behalf of women instead of permitting women to speak for themselves. One senses that impassioned and radical rhetoric would almost surely have been dismissed out-of-hand, but one wonders why black militants are understood to be "telling it like it is" while women militants are perceived as "Crazy Libbers."

[i]In a class of thirty-one, there was one black cadet.

[j]When women enter a competition from which they have previously been excluded, they double the competition. Today's extraordinary competition for entrance to law schools is principally the result of a dramatic increase in women's applications. When the number of applicants with resources and with access to the dominant culture doubles, furthermore, minorities may find doors suddenly closed that had just begun to open.

and ignorant, also reveals a fundamental and profound reality; numerous young men who may in fact be privileged are feeling relatively deprived. And if their reference individuals (role models) are their fathers and older brothers, they may be right. Perhaps they *are* the first group of young men who must compete with all their peers. Since relative deprivation is one explanation commonly advanced for social unrest, academy officials may have been wise indeed to anticipate this reaction to women's admission by male cadets.

One Behavioral Science 302 instructor, who had been "on remote" (and thus unaccompanied by dependents) in Alaska, asked a woman officer (married to a civilian and with one child), who was also "on remote," to discuss her career with him on tape with the understanding that he would use it later in the classroom. Their recorded interview covered: (1) her longer testing by subordinates and their doubt as to her knowledge, (2) her peers' resentment because they assumed she would be promoted first "because," (3) her need to demonstrate professionalism *and* femaleness, and (4) the doubt and suspicion of her expressed by the wives of male officers, which resulted in her believing she had to defend her morals—which "really hurt." (The last is a recurring theme in conversations with junior women officers. They seem to accept blame for jealousy, for others' marital problems, and to feel they must walk an especially narrow line.) To the cadets, this woman officer's matter-of-fact account of her role was almost incomprehensible; it was hard enough to grasp the idea of two or three tours on remote for themselves, and still *more* difficult to imagine that a woman would be given such assignments and have to leave her husband behind. The subjects of women as pilots and of women in combat were too absurd to even talk about. Women as officers was an unpleasant enough subject, one that cadets preferred to ignore. In 1976 only a handful had accepted or made peace with the idea of having women as their peers.

The cadets' fundamental incapacity to understand "why any woman would" was shared by officials at every level. When men described what they could not understand women's wanting to do, they mentioned things like being knocked around in intramural football, absorbing verbal abuse from angry superiors, or risking capture as a POW. Sometimes one would almost begin to agree and one would certainly better appreciate that, while men are sometimes almost entrapped in military service, women who enter the military truly *choose* to do so. Our service women have not been pressured into military service, although men often feel some sense of compulsion or obligation, or at least a resignation that refusing military service could lead to worse consequences than accepting. On the other hand, when they discussed women's motivation few officials mentioned the pay, the exhilaration of flying, the sense of duty and pride, and the glory of risk and sacrifice—all positive factors and beautifully articulated by men in explaining their own commitment to military service. Either they did not see these motives as applying to women or they understood them as related to combat and, therefore, as opportunities offered to men and still denied to women.[k]

The gap between the cadets' assumptions about women and the new acceptance expected of the cadets was too broad to be bridged in a single albeit direct discussion. Still, one woman officer deftly handled her invitation to speak to first class cadets in their "military career" class. In a low-key, gentle way she wondered why anyone would suppose that she had anything special to say about women "just because" she was one. Appealing directly to the cadets' interest and immediate future, she suggested that she got calls to give talks on women because others were not facing up to the challenge of commanding all their own troops. In the "real" Air Force, she noted, cadets would be working for and with women and would also be supervising them. A "good" officer, she pointed out, handles all his troops himself and would not have to go to a woman officer for advice; a good officer does not ask others to take on a sticky problem for him; he knows the regulations himself and is equally effective in leading and counseling women and men.

Her second point addressed a fundamental cadet concern. She described a variety of ingratiating forms of behavior, such as smiling, cajoling, and teasing, and noted how some could be taken in by these practices. When the room was with her, she tossed in a couple of syndromes well known to cadets—"black tongue" and the "moth."[l] It suddenly became a simple matter: womanly wiles were no longer a sexual mystery; they were just another manifestation of favor-currying, something cadets have long observed, disdained, and practiced.

One male officer made an effective point in his classroom when he asked if a woman could ever become a part of "us." After the cadets expressed some doubt, he was able to convey how gravely nonacceptance can affect one's behavior by showing that when he had studied for his Ph.D. at a civilian school, *he* had been one of

[k] If the most positive aspects of an Air Force career are in fact unavailable to women, one must expect a great deal of demotivation when they finally appreciate this.

[l] The first, the wages of boot-licking; the second, one who hangs around generals and full colonels.

"them"* rather than "us" and felt just as cadets do when they go to town on weekends: alienated.

In the behavioral science introductory core course, a new text was ordered—*Psychology: A Basic Course*, by David Krech et al.—that used gender in a random way and that included a section on motivation that encompassed both Matina Horner's work and that of David McClelland. DFBL professors' bookshelves suddenly sprouted numerous books on sex roles. Generally, then, DFBL faculty made a serious effort to be educationally responsive to and responsible about sex integration.[m]

The entrance of women seemed to trigger a new receptivity to advice and to research on the part of the commandant at just the moment when the new head of Behavioral Science was anxious to develop a service and research program. Over the year, DFBL prepared as many as fifty projects or reports related to sex integration. Some were as small as a briefing on sex-integrated billeting; others were as ambitious as the hiring of a Distinguished Visiting Professor (DVP) to design and monitor a four-year research study.[n]

Specific service projects assigned to DFBL during 1976 included redesigning the recruitment brochure "Commitment to Excellence," considering the need for a personal development course (possibly including sex education), studying cadet motivation, planning Saturday morning cadet training on sexism, and participating in the sexual assault and rape training program provided to ATOs, AOCs, and cadets. Although the committee considering anti-rape training was chaired by someone from the commandant's side, a DFBL faculty member developed the training course, and both cadet counseling and athletics staff members made important contributions to the program.

Although some research was done on the women cadets in the office of admissions and in cadet counseling, and although the English Department gave one captain time to write a doctoral dissertation on the planning for women's admission, the two major re-

[m]Some consideration was given to introducing a new course on "The Family, Courtship, and Marriage," but new courses are always difficult to justify because cadets are already so overburdened with courses. Indeed, putting new material into old courses or coordinating with other departments to ease new material into several courses are more likely modes of curriculum change. A course on the family, moreover, would have had a problem of content. A conservative institution like the academy would find it awkward to offer much more than traditional views. Yet women cadets must, almost by definition, make nontraditional decisions or, as male cadets now seem to see as required of them, give up the idea of children and perhaps of marriage, too.

[n]West Point's study had already begun and gave impetus to the Air Force endeavor.

search projects came under the sponsorship of DFBL.[1] The first (which resulted in this book) was done by an outsider who had obtained support from the Carnegie and Ford Foundations. The second was directed by the DFBL Distinguished Visiting Professor, Lois De Fleur, a sociologist from Washington State University who specialized in the sociology of deviance.[o] She was chosen specifically to design and conduct a longitudinal study of the women cadets.[p] In addition to her research, she was expected to participate in the more humble departmental activities (such as teaching sections of the introductory course and signing in and out on the duty board), yet at the same time she was treated as an honored visitor at social affairs and featured by the academy in numerous public appearances.[q]

As an employee of the Air Force, the DVP had to submit to a double clearance procedure in order to conduct her work. The clearance for access to her sample and to academy data banks was the same as would be required of any researcher; however, because she was sponsored by DFBL, her research was somewhat constrained by the department's view of what was appropriate and wise. She may have gained some leverage from her "outsidedness," from her naiveté, from her capacity to bargain; but for the most part the timing and content of requests to other units were managed by DFBL according to its broad interests, its reading of the acceptable, and through its bureaucratic channels. Several short studies that would aid policy making were requested of her. Often they were needed so quickly that constructing the kind of research design that makes a professional proud was impracticable. There were other inconveniences as well. Before-publication clearance was required by the department, the dean, and the Information Office, each with slightly

---

[o] It was tempting to guess whether she considered the women who wished to become cadets deviant, or whether she thought *anyone* in the military by choice deviant. Her other work had been on criminals and athletes.

[p] Two captains were detailed to assist in the study, one a new recipient of an M.A. in Sociology from Brigham Young University, the other, an officer skilled in the use of the computer who would leave after one year to work on a Ph.D. at Northwestern.

[q] The DFBL chairman is a conservative and cautious man; the style and independence of the two women researchers associated with him must have made him uncomfortable on more than one occasion. Still, he was game and professional enough not to say so. Other faculty confirmed, too, that he "let his pushers push."

For this researcher, at least, any pressure to please was more internal than external, that is, it came from anticipating how officials would feel about conclusions, rather than from any request to change those conclusions. The situation was much like that experienced by the administrators who planned women's integration. In both cases we felt that we were "in a fishbowl," and, knowing that what we did would never win unanimous approbation, we settled for careful work and hoped for respect.

different interests and concerns. Still, censorship was never exercised, although some discussion about the tone of drafted articles did occur.

Four research projects were conducted during the first year. The initial effort surveyed cadet attitudes toward BCT. The second asked 289 members of the class of 1980 about their views on the femininity of the women cadets.[r] Among the interesting findings was the discovery that cadet women were split about 50–50 on women's being trained for combat; their male peers were opposed 80–20. While BCT was both physically and psychologically more demanding than the women had anticipated, they agreed with men that it increased their confidence. The femininity items showed that men were somewhat more concerned about the women's femininity than were the women themselves, although neither thought women should have a different training program. Two items assumed significance later: (1) while women thought they had been "capable of doing everything," men did not think so and (2) while women were certain BCT had increased class solidarity, men were unsure.

The longitudinal questionnaire first given in December 1976 to a 300-member matched sample of the class of 1980 was the third project. (Men and women were matched for military background, academic achievement, and athletic accomplishment.) The questionnaire was also administered in May and December of 1977, and was scheduled for December 1978, December 1979, and May 1980. The four-year study will make it possible to examine myriad background factors, although the principal items to be examined are (1) attitudes toward women, (2) patterns of association between the sexes, and (3) the development of military/career orientations.[s]

The fourth project involved a study of "attitudes toward women." This was accomplished by surveying (1) upper class participants in BCT 1977, and (2) a sample drawn from the class taking that BCT—the class of 1981. Generally, the findings accorded with officials' perceptions. First class cadets were more opposed to women than were fourth class cadets (who had applied to the academy and come knowing that women would be there). The squadrons that had

[r]This action was precipitated by the comments of a DACOWITS member as reported in a local newspaper. Officials feared that she might report to the Defense Department that the women were losing their femininity.

[s]A data packet will give the researcher access to the registrar's information on demographic background, grade point average, activities, squadron, and Military Order of Merit. The annual questionnaires vary in content to enable the examination of more variables; however, each variable is examined at several different times. The Air Force Office of Scientific Research is the funding agency for this research.

no women were more opposed than those that did. (In one orientation session for new faculty, the presenting cadet volunteered that
his squadron would have no women and he was glad it would not.
Even as he spoke, one had the sense that he was speaking from a
sense of squadron pride and that, if his squadron had been assigned
women, he would have been glad of *that*!) One interesting finding
concerned the views of cadet officers. As compared to other cadets,
they were supportive of women, indicating they understood the acceptance of women to have become a requirement of leadership, a
new group norm.

At the academy, as at most institutions, the junior white males (at
the academy, cadets) are required on a daily basis to be most responsive to and accepting of the claims of new entrants. The higher
ranks (officers) maintain their personal immunity to change, although they may have to make or pass on policy changes. Still, the
idea that it was important to test, educate, and monitor the faculty,
staff, and AOCs was quietly overlooked. No attitude questionnaires
were circulated to officers, even though doing so had been recommended and even though West Point did do so.

In April 1976, DFBL hosted the fifth annual "Psychology in the
Air Force" symposium. At least 10 percent of the participants were
women, and paper sessions considered "family separation," "quality
of life survey," and "women in the military," as well as "training,"
"human factors," "cadet attrition," and "motor learning and visual
processes."[1] Three panel sessions were devoted to "women in DOD"
(the Department of Defense).

Some of the research findings presented at the symposium bore
directly on integration policies; other findings raised points for consideration by academy officials, even though the examined situations were not fully comparable. For instance, a Navy study of the
attitudes of enlisted women and men toward the Navy showed that
with promotion women experienced increasing disillusionment,
while men felt more and more a part of the Navy. Women's attitudes
toward their peers especially deteriorated. On a number of indices,
moreover, entering women were more positive than reenlistees. The
reverse was true for men. This disturbing pattern would seem to
forbode long-term problems in assimilation that first year integration
euphoria would conceal.[2]

An Air Force study of women in traditionally male career fields
also produced discomfiting results. First, nonsupervisors (both male

---

[1] In the "Quality of Life Survey," military spouse data were collected but not used.

and female) uniformly reported discrimination. However, males reported more discrimination and reported it more often as favoring women, while females reported it as being against women. Second, supervisors reported that women (1) were not as capable, but (2) learned well and progressed as well, (3) required less attention, and (4) were equally motivated. These same supervisors also reported *themselves* as practicing leniency toward women.[u3]

Finally, the all-female panel on women in the Department of Defense, chaired by the academy (male) officer who had made the strong arguments about the need for a "critical mass" of women, pointed to a variety of post-1970 changes. As compared to the past, 1976 was clearly a banner year for women. By absolute standards, however, they were nowhere near equality.

The Human Relations Education Committee

Superintendent Clark directed that a Human Relations Education Committee be established in November 1974; it held an organizing meeting in August 1975.[v] As a part of Air Force policy, all personnel receive human relations training at the point of accession. For cadets that means the academy. In addition, there is a goal of fourteen hours per year of training for all personnel. The base social actions office is responsible for training officers and enlisted personnel; the Human Relations Education Committee (usually chaired by a DFBL faculty member) was made responsible for monitoring the training of cadets as it occurred in the academic core curriculum, in military studies, and in wing training.

From the committee's inception, its relationship to and responsibility for the integration of women was a matter of discussion. The feeling that "the attitudes of the officer corps should be addressed first" did result in an invitation to John Gray, a human relations specialist from Kent State University, to present his provocative program. Gray, "a black American whose skin is white" (i.e., a man whose appearance gives him the option of "passing"), begins with

---

[u]Research confirms that administrators are dealing with a supremely difficult situation, namely, one in which each group member holds a different perception of the same phenomena. It should be noted, however, that the Air Force was always willing to put its best foot forward. Less than two years after presenting this paper, the black woman officer who authored it became one of the first two women AOCs.

[v]It also had three different chairmen in three years; it was clearly not a top priority assignment. In 1976–77, it included some twenty members, one-half of whom were faculty members.

a racist, sexist monologue that deprecates many different groups and provokes anger, rage, disbelief, sickness, and hatred in his audience.[w] It is strong medicine even when seen on videotape.[x] After the uproar Gray leaves the stage and returns as "a black man" (changed only in style and mannerisms) to discuss the audience reaction to his first performance and share his genuine views on race and human relations. His role playing lets many members of the audience actually experience belittlement. The dichotomy between his appearance and professed identity demonstrates to the audience its own "color conditioning."

A second project of the Human Relations Education Committee provided for the development of a special collection of books in the cadet library on women and their role. (The library also produced a special sixty-page bibliography on "Women in the Military.") This collection of some forty-seven books is difficult to evaluate because it is usually checked out. Whether because of cadets' intellectual curiosity or because a number of cadet academic assignments are made on these topics is not clear.

The Human Relations Education Committee also solicited suggestions for research projects that should be undertaken on the admission of woman cadets and worked with the base human relations officer to assess the "learning outcomes" of human relations training.

In 1976–77, the committee's principal achievement was the creation of a cadet wing social actions officer.[y] This action meant that the responsibility for cadet human relations training would be shifted to the wing and would become an integral part of its organization. (Actually, the responsibility for this training was transferred over the course of the women's entrance year; it first changed from an extra duty for a military instruction officer to a primary duty

[w] At his West Point performance, his attack on women was said to have produced vigorous applause. Only when he took up the subject of race did the audience begin to disassociate with him.

[x] The tape I saw begins by proclaiming that "God created Adam and Eve, and that was the start of the white race. He also created the ape, and that was how the black race evolved. I feel that if . . . we know our places in society, we won't have the types of conflicts that are going on today. . . . I tell those of the Jewish faith to stick to working in the accounting departments. . . . You can't expect women to be able to handle positions of leadership. . . . I realize there are some women who can handle men's jobs . . . and if you want to know the truth most of them are lesbians."

[y] This took a long time to accomplish. Apparently part of the delay was due to several complaints by black cadets. The administration did not want to appear to be creating the position in response to their complaints so it had to let a period of time elapse before creating the slot.

for a senior enlisted woman, and then passed to the cadet officer.) The social actions officer and five other cadets were sent to the Defense Race Relations Institute for a summer training program in 1977. That program had three principal components: human relations, drug and alcohol abuse, and human sexuality and sexism.

Human relations mostly means race relations. That minorities and women are put into categories comparable to that of drugs and alcohol is not lost on minorities and women. In the same way, the linking of sexuality and sexism seems awkward. Sexism is social behavior, akin to racism, which the Air Force seeks to eliminate or at least to control by teaching correct behavior. Sexuality has always proved hard to control, and just what correct sexual behavior is and whether it is the same for women and men has always been controversial.

At the academy no one seemed eager to deal with sexuality. DFBL was specifically asked by the commandant to consider the need for sex education for cadets, but with the creation of the cadet wing social actions officer, the reluctant "Sex Education Committee" went out of business.[z] With sexuality tacked on to sexism and included in human relations training, the issue could be dropped. The problem was that it was perceived as a "how to" course, and no one wanted to teach it—not only because it was embarrassing but also because it seemed to condone unbecoming (even immoral) behavior. In fact, the Human Relations Education Committee was so eager to avoid the issue that at one point it even voted 6–4 against inviting a scientist (presumably a biologist) to become a member of the committee so the issue could be discussed more thoroughly.

The committee also asked each academic department to describe in detail how its curriculum incorporated materials on women and sexism. A few (e.g., English) produced elaborate accounts of how everything discussed involved the subject. Others tersely replied, "this is not relevant to our activity." At best the committee raised some consciousness. By the end of the 1976–77 academic year, most of the committee's activities had been transferred (along with its budget) to the commandant's side. The committee continued to exist, but, unless new personnel or new problems materialized, it

---

[z]DFBL apparently took the position that sex education was unnecessary. HEW data showing that half of the young women in high school have experienced sexual intercourse might suggest that no further education was necessary. However, that more than one-third of the high schoolers used no form of birth control and that one million out of eleven million female teenagers become pregnant each year suggests that education may, in fact, be quite necessary.

would meet rarely. Expectations for it and interest in it were not high.

Again, human relations were mostly considered race relations; while matters involving sex discrimination were subsumed by human relations, they were handled quite differently. Officers trained in race relations were likely to have had some training in sexism. Still, the same officers who expressed enthusiasm for Hispanic Week and the Black Arts Festival saw little merit in a Woman's Week. Indeed, some believed it would create a backlash and perceived that the appearance of Betty Friedan early in 1976, for instance, had been counterproductive.[a] A feeling existed that having men like John Gray and Robert Terry analyze sexism, that is, having men describe men's responses to women, was "better" than having women make their own case. As a tactic this principle is understandable; as a strategy it seems questionable, for it does not require male-female communication and it leaves women dependent on spokes*men*. No interest whatever was expressed in providing an equivalent to the Cadet Way of Life Subcommittee, the officially sanctioned organization of black cadets, and no satisfaction was given concerning the *Dodo*'s portrayal of women, even though a formal complaint was made to the human relations office.[b] Ironically, those most responsive to black complaints were frequently cautionary about women's making arguments equivalent to those of blacks. They warned of the potential for backlash, and described symbolic grievances as nit-picking. Others remarked that they were not "going to make the same mistakes" with women as they had with minorities; namely, give them any kind of preference.

It would be interesting to try to recapture the experience of the first minorities to enter the academy. The first black graduated in 1963. Active recruitment brought minorities in the entering class to 192 for 1980.[c] The minority experience has not been recorded, but officers who were cadets when integration began indicate that it must have been difficult. Still, in 1976–77 women found that men were permitted to express, even to flaunt, their sexism, while similarly racist behavior or language would have been taboo. Certainly no racial slurs would have been condoned in the classroom, but

[a]In the pre-admission year, the academy had actually honored Jacqueline Cochran, whose views on women as cadets (as presented to Congress) were not unknown to the wing.

[b]That year the office also received a complaint of reverse discrimination: it was alleged that men cadets were being allowed to quit more easily than were women.

[c]Blacks numbered 68 or 4.3 percent of the total.

cadets were allowed to laugh at and to hoot about women cadets. Women were treated to regular verbal abuse in one-on-one situations (e.g., a whispered "What are you selling it for?"), and while one supposes that the same did not (or at least does not) happen to black cadets, one must be realistic. In one conversation I had with four "hand-picked" cadets, an otherwise glib senior referred to black cadets as "niggers." When asked if that was not an unusual choice of words, a second cadet replied, "Oh, we'd never say that when they're around." A third said, "We're friends, we kid them about their shadows, and tell them to smile so we can see them in the dark."

Again, in racial matters, human relations training tells specifically what is and what is not acceptable behavior. Minorities often conduct the training, and transgressions receive a punitive response whether formal or informal. Even so, some racism remains. In contrast, out of all the officers interviewed only two (both male) spoke of sexism with anywhere near the understanding or intensity of feeling with which a number of officers spoke of racism. Only two could summon anger and describe vigorous counseling they had given cadets about sexism. One was a faculty member who had just come from a human relations slot; the second was a black (white-appearing) officer in the commandant's shop.[d]

The hard-line position taken by some members of the commandant's staff was that women cadets *should be* like men cadets. Some faculty thought they *were*.[e] Even if the faculty's teaching materials were "neutral," however, the environment in which women attempted to learn was patently different from that enjoyed by men. Indeed, some members of the human relations staff assigned to the base reported that the faculty was the group least receptive to its training. They said faculty members tended to reject the very idea that they were racist or sexist and to be critical of the evidence used to support human relations instruction. A few officer-instructors were openly recalcitrant, saying in essence: "male chauvinism and male language are essential to the rapport I need to deliver my message, and I'm not going to change anything I do unless I'm caught at it."[f] Although one department, Behavioral Sciences and Leader-

---

[d]Like John Gray, this officer must sometimes have been in a unique position to observe, experience, and recount instances of racial discrimination. The same phenomenon accounts for the insights of John Griffith, in *Black Like Me*, and Grace Haskel, in *Soul Sister*.

[e]Some feminists also take one of these positions.

[f]One officer said he only appreciated how "male" his teaching was when his wife visited one lecture and he found himself constantly restraining his performance.

ship, assisted integration by reviewing scholarly materials and by sponsoring research on the subject, even in that unit no one seemed eager to deal with sex education. Nevertheless, one of the most convincing pieces of evidence that Air Force personnel believed the Air Force wanted integration to succeed was the number of officers willing, even eager, to associate themselves with the women's integration program.

9

Implementation, Feedback, and Modifications

Cadets are the implementers of policy. In particular, they are the academy's liaison with the entering class; during Basic Cadet Training (BCT), first class men (and some second class men) have a primary role in training. They hold such responsibility because BCT is considered leadership training for them as well as introductory testing (and motivating) for the doolies. There is, of course, supervision, and in 1976 there was a good deal of it. Officers were nervous about possible "incidents," the press and electronic media seemed omnipresent, and the presence of women officers made many men self-conscious. In fact, because the ATOs' role was poorly defined, they sometimes appeared to second-guess or even negate cadet directions. Further, a new system of "positive motivation" made the trainers' job seem more complex and uncertain than ever.[a] (By the end of the summer, in fact, "positive motivation" had

[a] When the academy was founded in 1955, the West Point graduates on the academy's staff imposed a class system similar to the one they had known. Even the first superintendent found their zeal excessive, and attempts to reduce hazing and harassment have been almost continuous since that time; indeed, attempts to reform discipline are almost a tradition! A 1961 effort prefigured the 1976 program. It called for teaching and training with a "positive emphasis" that would *not* be "softer" but that would be "mentally tougher." This program, which was aimed at AOCs as much as at cadets, achieved one desired result—50 percent decrease in attrition that summer.

developed such a negative connotation that the officer in charge of the next year's BCT emphasized what he called "good leadership" instead.)

The first class men were articulate if not always consistent about their views on the academy and women's presence there. The following excerpts from a single interview with a high-ranking cadet officer are representative: "I came here for an education and to become a combat leader. I want to fly and to get people to do things they may not want to do." Sometimes a proprietary tone entered the conversation: "They want to be a part of *my* Air Force. . . . When I commanded a squadron, there was a standing rule that no outsiders could enter *my* area. . . . My attitude in June 1976 was that it was my job to run those women out of the academy. I had to fight it out with the ATO so she understood that those were *my* cadets."[b] Yet self-described conversions to the acceptance of women were also the order of the day. A number of cadets could pinpoint a particular vignette—a "girl" running the assault course while enduring what they termed "a gastro-intestinal upset," a "girl" who commanded absolute silence when she spoke. As time passed cadet officers began to feel that they knew how to manage women. One said that he hand-picked "nonmanipulable" men to train his women and that he had learned that while a "chewing out" altered a man's behavior, "isolation worked better on women."

Still, even those cadet leaders who were the most effective in working with and training women could comment (as did the cadet above): "There was never a time I was not conscious that they were women. . . . They want to please and they especially want to please me as a male. . . . I was lucky, my ATO was gorgeous and feminine, and the women thought she walked on water. . . . Five of the women in my unit will really be sharp, but I don't want any of my women in combat. There's no need to send that special group to war. . . . I had one super girl, gave her the name 'squad cheerleader'—that gave her a sense of identity. . . . I like women; the ones on my committee follow me around. . . . I don't think there'll be very many here three years from now, but those who are will really be something. What? Studs!"

The newly appointed cadet social actions officer explained that his job had not existed before because the quality of cadets was

[b]He did not run out (or lose) any of the sixteen women under his command. Ironically, this student had been determined to come to the academy ever since age eleven, when he read his sister's academy catalog. She had an ambiguous first name, and the academy had tried to recruit her because of her high SAT scores.

thought to be so high that it was unneeded. As he described it, the job focused on drugs and alcohol and racial issues, not on women, because: "We haven't been told there was any problem," and "We handle crises—and women aren't a crisis."

To the cadets the analogy between racism and sexism seems to have made only limited sense. Women were seen not so much as "underprivileged" but as either overprivileged or as inhibitors. Even in so small a matter as classroom discussion, one cadet described the freewheeling debate of all-male sections and contrasted it to the reserve of mixed-sex sections. Thus women were seen as constraining, as having influence, as exerting a negative kind of power.[c]

Policy implementation began with the ATO training in January 1976 and proceeded through 1976 BCT, the academic year, and into the second year's summer programs—in particular, to SERE. Feedback was continuous, and most "changes" were a matter of fine-tuning or making practical adjustments. As in driving a car, most accommodations were made unconsciously; some, however, resulted from complaint, reassessment, and new calculation. Some of the changes were fundamental, indicating that the original decisions were "wrong" or else that the academy had an unusual capacity for accommodating to rapidly changing conditions.

The ATOs

The ATO program was multi-purpose: first, the ATO training was to be a preview or dry run for the training of cadet women; second, ATOs were to provide women cadets with training and counseling usually offered by upper classmen; third, ATOs were to be role models for the women cadets, and they were especially supposed to demonstrate that officers can be feminine; fourth, they were to foster the acceptance of women cadets by male cadets. These aims sometimes worked at cross-purposes.

For instance, if the ATOs were to be "guinea pigs" in an experiment to determine women's capacities in and responses to a physi-

[c]Because women had no way of knowing how things *were*, they may incorrectly have believed that their presence had no impact at all. It would be hard for them to appreciate that some of their male peers really did believe that women's presence (1) hurt the 157 men who would otherwise have been there, (2) was contributing to the coming of socialism, (3) would lead to the destruction of the American family, (4) destroyed cadet pride, and (5) made men cadets feel guilty for "having let it happen."

cally and psychologically stressful environment, their weaknesses and vulnerabilities would be exposed. But to do so would not foster cadet acceptance since it would diminish cadet respect. Their role as surrogate upperclassmen (in an environment filled with genuine upperclassmen) required them to identify with cadets, yet at the same time they were supposed to be model officers. Then too, their primary interaction was to be with women (as trainers and counselors), but their primary evaluators would be men (who would accept or not accept them). Thus the ATOs' acceptance as role models by the women cadets would ultimately depend on their first being accepted as good officers by men cadets—the very men cadets the ATOs were supplanting, even though they (the ATOs) had virtually no authority over anyone or anything.[d] Even if male cadets were able to accept women as officers (and the women in well-defined roles, such as military training instructors, were accepted), men found it almost impossible to accept the ATOs as surrogate cadets. Above all, that required a shared experience, and there was no way of creating that sharing between upper class cadets and women officers.

There was a further complication. The ATO concept was adapted from a time when no upper class existed (the beginning of the academy in 1955) to a time when it was assumed that women cadets would receive separate training and have a separate chain of command (in the early planning of 1972). However, the training and command of Air Force women was progressively integrated from 1972 through 1976; and, in fact, the WAF structure formally went out of existence July 1, 1976—three days after women entered the academy. During that period, academy officials were also thinking more and more positively about the possibilities of integration, but because they made their final decision about the command and control of cadet women only at the last minute, they probably failed to realize how much a viable ATO role depended upon separatism.

The ATOs were not selected for their physical and athletic prowess and did not do remarkably well during their BCT, with its heavy emphasis on building and testing strength and endurance. The male cadets knew the ATOs' limitations and doubted that they could adequately serve as BCT trainers. The cadets also doubted that the ATOs *would* give the specific training reserved for them—that which was supposed to take place in the dormitory area. One reason

---

[d]To be without authority in a hierarchical organization is almost to be demeaned.

for this doubt was that the cadets thought the ATOs did not exercise enough authority over each other when they rotated commands during their training. But there was another reason too.

Male cadets had limited access to the women's area; even those who had official reasons for being there had to coordinate their visits with the woman officer serving as CQ. Thus women were almost exempt from dormitory training by upperclassmen. By contrast, male doolies lived with their squadrons and could not even visit another squadron area without reason. They lived with and were outnumbered two or three to one by their trainers, while the women, who had *no* upperclassmen or officers living with them, outnumbered the two ATOs who slept in the dormitory each evening by seventy to one! For numerical reasons alone, their training could not be identical.

The ATOs met with cadet hostility and resentment from the beginning. This aggravation was probably exacerbated by the male cadets' dislike for the ATOs' woman supervisor, who was considered "too military."[e] ATOs were subjected to comments ("I hear you give it away." "ATO stands for 'Are They Officers?'" "Here come the A.T. Zeroes"), some cadets vowed never to salute them, and jokes were played on them. They may, then, have had another unmentioned function—that of serving as shock troops, or even as lightning rods that absorbed the first wave of cadet hostility, thus making the entrance of women cadets easier.

Even as the ATOs were preparing to assume their duties, cadets began to request some or all of those duties. Indeed, it could almost be said that senior male cadets came to see the ATOs not as women officers with a job to do but as their competitors! They saw them not as filling a new and unique assignment but as outsiders who had been given part of the male cadets' job. Moreover, some came to feel that the ATOs had been given this job because administrators did not trust the cadets to do it right. At one level, administrators who insisted that young men not train young women in dormitory areas could be interpreted as saying, "You are potential rapists. We can't trust you. You will take advantage of young and defenseless girls."

No one would deny that as a group cadets are competitive, proud, and industrious. Here, then, was an incentive (a positive motivation) for them to treat the new women cadets professionally and

---

[e]Holding this view did not seem to preclude also holding the view that women generally were not "military" enough, and in particular that they would not hold women cadets to high standards.

well. By doing so they would "show" the administration; at the same time they would wrest control from and supplant the ATOs. By relating correctly to their women subordinates, cadets could show up women officers.[f] (Perhaps the motivation is best described as both positive *and* negative.)[g]

By the time the women cadets arrived, two of the fifteen ATOs had departed and one was soon to go; also a decision had been reached that there would be *no* woman AOC. Thus ten of the ATOs were assigned one per BCT squadron, while the other three formed a staff.[h] On the day the ATOs formally began their jobs, those jobs had been reduced to little more than in-dormitory training, sitting CQ, counseling, and "monitoring" training given by male cadets. The last duty sometimes involved dispute; but if men cadets did their work reasonably well, they were likely to win disputes with the ATOs because there was no real ATO authority or territory; and even if they were not supposed to be "run out," the ATOs were eventually supposed to be put out of a job. The program was designed to end with a whimper, not with a bang, with which it had started (a January press conference). The ATOs' goal was to make themselves dispensable; ultimately they would "succeed" by becoming superfluous.

One could say the ATOs did their implicit or long-range job so well during their own training (by teaching men that men *could* train women) that they never really got to *do* their explicit or short-range job (of being surrogate upperclassmen). Again, by the time the ATOs had finished their training, their job was diminished almost beyond recognition because male cadets had demonstrated a "much greater capacity to train women than previously expected."

No matter how well they understood the program's purpose, the ATOs must have become demoralized by never having been employed in the way they had anticipated. While their vanguard activity may have speeded up the integration cycle, it also left the ATOs underemployed, bored, and without direction. Even their counsel-

[f]In this the Air Force Academy was different from Annapolis, where one middie observed, "There's just no positive incentive for a midshipman to relate to women at all."

[g]By this time, cadets may have begun to think they could pressure women out of positions of authority. Galloway was moved out of an assignment as an assistant AOC during the 1974 BCT apparently because of cadet objections. In 1976 ATOs were not allowed to take free-fall parachute training because of cadet objections, and the woman tentatively slated as an AOC was "vetoed" by cadets. Thus even if women cadets were there to stay, cadets may have thought the ATOs could be run out.

[h]Their superior officer was a group AOC, but in the summer they were supervised by the BCT commander.

ing role was minimal. Contrary to expectations, women cadets seemed to require less rather than more counseling. Morale sagged further as the ATOs' lack of challenging work made them poor rather than good role models.[i]

Ironically, the ATOs' mediocre physical performance and their suboptimum utilization may have assisted women cadets in *their* integration. The cadets, after all, looked good by comparison, and came to believe they could enhance their own acceptance by disassociating themselves from the ATOs—by saying that there was no need for ATOs, that the ATOs certainly were not *their* idea of role models. This disaffection is important to note: some women cadets regularly argued against the ATO program, separate billeting, and other attempts to give them group support. By doing so, they were able to establish their preference for being identified as cadets and not as women; but meanwhile they could enjoy the privacy, communications network, and benefits of the special provisions. They had their cake and ate it too.

One other point should be made about the role-model concept. In the academy, men were offered many models at every rank. The women had few models and almost none were senior officers. When they discussed the theory of role models, an interesting pattern emerged. Most women seemed to think "younger" women (whether cadet, lieutenant, captain, or major) *did* need models; but most of the women also denied that individuals of *their* rank benefited by having role models senior to them. It was almost as if they understood that "women" were not accepted, even though individual women could be. Thus while they could consider themselves "integrated" and "accepted" (and therefore worthy models for their subordinates), they also knew that the women senior to them were not generally respected, would not go to the top, were not good role models, and were not necessary as such.[j] It was almost as though the women applied an individual analysis in thinking about their own careers, but a social analysis in thinking about the careers of others.[k]

[i]Some tried to fill their time constructively by auditing courses, learning to soar, or by taking on extra duties. Two were accepted for pilot training and left the academy in January 1977.

[j]Role-model theory describes an imitative process in which individuals copy the behavior, or aspects of behavior, of the superiors they emulate. One wonders, however, if there is not an important top-down dimension to the process in which superiors note, approve, and promote juniors with attributes similar to their own.

[k]Even the best thinkers use different modes of analysis for different problems. John Stuart Mill noted that it would be helpful if people assumed "free will" in assessing their own

In trying to think through the ramifications of this attempt to apply role-model theory in a specific situation, one must remember that the ATOs were young women trained in other fields and with limited work and military experience. They were having trouble establishing their own identities. During ATO training, they had only one woman model, and they needed some time to understand that they were expected to provide a variety of attractive models, not all to imitate her. Even the DFBL memo on role models noted that it would be important to educate the ATOs about their own motivations (no mean task). The ATOs also needed, the memo went on, career counseling of their own since they were very junior officers placed in a most sensitive and quickly changing environment. As it turned out the ATOs were right to worry about their Officer Efficiency Reports (OERs) under the forced-curve system. And while they may have been (as they had been told) the best women officers in the Air Force, they were in a most competitive environment, one that could affect an OER adversely. Their supervision, furthermore, had been transferred from the officer who had recruited them and had some personal stake in their future to an officer who was not sympathetic to the program and felt no special responsibility for its participants.

At the end of the first semester, half the women cadets were relocated and assigned to groups three and four (during the first semester they were assigned only to groups one and two). Half the ATOs went with them and thereby acquired a new function: "to insure the uniform treatment of cadet women throughout the wing." However, with only ten ATOs left (two-thirds of the original group) and with three-fourths of their planned two-year tour still ahead of them, a thorough re-evaluation of the ATO assignment began. Most of the young women began looking ahead too. They had come to understand that just because one is hired as an adviser does not mean that anyone will ask for, much less use, one's advice; and they knew that informally arranging for the sex education the academy had decided to ignore, advising on the importance of attending academy balls, and seeing to it that black women cadets got appropriate soaps and conditioners, as well as permission to go "downtown" for beauty parlor treatments, did not constitute a real job.[1]

The choices were to carry on, modify, or end the ATO program.

---

behavior and "social determinism" in thinking about that of others; he also observed that all would benefit if kings believed in democracy and people in the divine right of kings.

[1]Even though they served as element leaders within the dormitory, the ATOs were not asked to rank the women cadets for Military Order of Merit (MOM) purposes.

Just before the class of '81 arrived, a decision was made to let three of the ten incumbents move on, to retain three at the academy in other but "regular" jobs, and to assign the remaining four as assistants to the four group AOCs. Shortly thereafter, officials decided to proclaim the program "successfully concluded" (one year early).

The ATOs survived or fell individually. They had undertaken a no-win job. They were called in because men feared, first, that some men would try to run the women out, and, second, that other men would be paralyzed by chivalry. The original plan was to let women handle the women. However, reports from the Merchant Marine Academy suggested that women might be too harsh; at the same time, Air Force Academy men suspected the women of excessive leniency. Eventually, having seen that women were trainable, the men cadets and officers reclaimed the ATOs' authority almost before they had a chance to exercise it! Thus at the beginning of BCT 1976 all "specialists on women" except the ATOs were returned to their regular duties, and all staff members became responsible for whatever women-related items fell "naturally" under their purview. With the beginning of BCT 1977, even the ATOs were removed from the scene and women had become "just" cadets.

Basic Cadet Training

Basic Cadet Training is an ordeal commemorated for the first time in 1976 with a popular ninety-six-page yearbook. Conducted in large part by first class men, it entails two three-week segments. The first three are spent in a classroom-dormitory setting, and the first day of that session is spent in "in-processing," which transforms more than fourteen hundred lively, active, self-directed teenagers into a group of uniformed, other-directed, sworn-in cadets.

Haircutting is perhaps the most visible symbol of the uniformity and wholeness of cadet submission. There is also a total equipping of cadets for the training to come, including dental checks and mouthguard fitting. As part of its commitment to consistency, the academy followed its rule of providing for all cadet needs, right down to bras and sanitary supplies for the women. The chosen "one-size," stretch bra, however, was quickly found not adequate, and a supply officer soon found himself at a local department store purchasing shopping carts full of bras of different styles and sizes. Sanitary needs, too, were *not* uniform, and supplements were soon provided. Thus did the first modification based on feedback occur. A policy change followed: the next year the Air Force let practicality overrule ideology, and women were permitted to bring their own bras. (West Point had done so the first year; Annapolis had not.)

The efficiency and thoroughness of day-one processing is considered an important part of the cadet's socializing experience. Therefore, it is supposed to happen without snags. In rapid sequence new arrivals deposit baggage, recertify their nonuse of drugs, obtain medical records and immunizations, establish their cadet records (from this point on a card is tied around the cadets' necks to record all subsequent information—giving them the appearance of Christmas gifts), obtain bank accounts, record the make and model of their calculators, receive linen and post office boxes (and stamps), have height and weight recorded, place valuables in lock boxes, take and sign their oath, have their hair cut, and receive a complete uniform issue, including pre-sized uniform trousers (women's uniforms are tailored that day). Lunch and water breaks are programmed, and after the evening meal the new cadets, in formation, take a public oath (with parents invited to the ceremony).[m] Training begins the next morning.

Reveille is at 0600 (6:00 A.M.) and breakfast assembly at 6:20. Some ten training periods (day and night) keep the new cadet busy until 2200 (10:00 P.M.) Taps. The first days include organizational and training functions. Clothing fitting and exchanges occur; drum and bugle corps tryouts are held; swim tests and academic placement exams are taken; orientation is given by various units including the chaplain, commandant, financial officers, and planetarium staff; and physical and professional training begins. The latter includes formal instruction in first aid, honor (sixteen hours), heritage (thirteen hours), drill (thirty-three hours), and ethics (eight hours).[n] Motivational activities include parasailing, a jet flight, and a navigation orientation flight. Practice inspections, traffic safety, and

---

[m]The oath is actually given individually as an "administrative" detail early in the day. This procedure seems to reduce the early resignations of cadets overwhelmed by the awesomeness of their promise.

[n]Decorum for the "cadet officer and gentleman" had to be taught without the usual thirteen-chapter handbook on military customs and courtesies and social etiquette. It was recognized that the chapter on "The Ladies" who "in spite of the women's liberation movement—still consider themselves members of the fairer sex and enjoy the treatment accorded that status" in the 1975 handbook would not do. Advising young officers to find out the commander's views on an officer's wife's working also seemed out-of-date. However, a new handbook had not been compiled.

care/cleaning sessions are conducted. Map reading and functional leadership are taught in labs, and the obstacle course ("Hell's Half Acre") is mastered.

Slightly under three weeks are spent in "second" BCT, which is held in Jack's Valley, a four-and-one-half-mile march from the dormitory area.[o] There, cadets live in large, platformed tents, and training becomes more physical. Leadership reaction and tactical leadership decisions are tested in the field. The confidence course and land navigation are undertaken, as are the assault course, the weapons range, and unarmed combat training.[p]

The head of the BCT that summer was, as he later described himself, "Anxious as a mother hen." He sought "naturalness" but felt he was sitting on a "powder keg." The ATOs worked for him and were intended to ease the pressure. He, however, found the whole women's program discomfiting and unnatural. His administrative style was one in which he felt the need to know "everything." Yet administrators are sometimes better off not knowing, for instance, that when one young woman was ordered out of her tent "now" she emerged in only a T-shirt, or that two male cadets nearly came to blows over whether a woman cadet had been smiling when she was being dressed down.

At the same time that the commander was trying to treat the women "naturally," he was trying to elicit "positive motivation" from cadets, some of whom doubted its efficacy and most of whom believed it was for the benefit of women.[q] He also had to explain why bayonets were removed from rifles after one of the women (supposedly) cut her finger, and why resigning women were interviewed by the superintendent when men were not.[r]

And there were some subtler questions regarding motivation that were overlooked. For example, if flying programs were used as "motivators," was it possible that women, who were not eligible for pilot training, would be *de*motivated by being shown what they would never be able to do? If movies were shown as motivators,

[o]Jack's Valley was dubbed "Jack and Jill's Valley" in 1976.

[p]Confidence course obstacles include the "Slide for Life" and the "Tiltin' Hilton." Both involve the possibility of a fatal fall. The goal of the course is to teach cadets that safety lies in calm and correct execution.

[q]"Positive Motivation" was not seen as wholly efficacious, and midway through BCT the marching of "tours" was reinstated as an appropriate punishment.

[r]Even in the 1950s some top administrators felt bayonet training was an absurdity for the Air Force. Still, it took twenty years and, perhaps, women's entrance for the absurdity to be removed.

could *Tora! Tora! Tora!*, *Bridges of Toko-Ri*, and *Patton* have the same effect on women as on men? If Doolie Dining Out was designed to give doolies a chance to relax in a home atmosphere, what would the effect be on the women to realize that only married couples could host doolies, making many women officers ineligible and implying that they were *not* a good influence on cadets.[s]

BCT featured an evening talk by Gen. Chris Mann. After the formal Arnold Hall address to the whole fourth class, General Mann met with the women cadets only.[t] The 150 women sat erect, four to a table, and listened to a second (brief) address that urged them to "look like a girl, act like a lady, think like a man, and work like a dog." A formal question and answer session followed, and the Air Force's only woman line general then departed.[u] As one cadet observed, "It's pretty exciting to see the Air Force's only woman general even if she is a Mann!" Part of the meaning of the bad pun was that even in the "all-woman" special session, the general's bearing was official, businesslike, and military.

The design of the women's uniforms had been developed in-house. Most decisions were made by men, and much emphasis was given to the reduction of costs for the women's issue, since all cadets received the same uniform allowance but the women's clothing tended to cost more. Even though there had been women in the Air Force for years, there was difficulty in getting small socks, the women's fatigue jackets were inadequate, and their boots lacked corrugated soles. No cadets liked to buy uniform clothing from their own funds, and some would try to stretch the life of an item of clothing to the very last day that it could hold together. But women had a special problem. One characteristic of a cadet's activity-filled day is numerous clothing changes, and at least once a day the women's uniform was sure to call for hosiery. The ten pairs issued did not last long, and subsequent pairs had to be paid for by the cadet.

The test of usage also demonstrated that the women's short, straight skirts were neither attractive nor comfortable; a decision

---

[s]When the author heard about this practice she specifically inquired whether it was the policy (several single women officers had complained about the discrimination). The next day she was told the policy had been changed, apparently as a result of her inquiry. If this is true, it illustrates how an observer can unintentionally influence the observed.

[t]A violation of the no-separation policy.

[u]Soon there would be two.

was made to provide women with longer, gored skirts and with uniforms with more trousers and fewer skirts. (Colorado is both cold and windy.) The straight, side-seam pant pocket also gaped unattractively and caught on things like doorknobs, so diagonal pockets were recommended for subsequent years.

Most anticipated problems were managed smoothly: gun bolt springs were loosened. But unanticipated lessons were learned quickly too: the right "handholds" for assisting a woman on the obstacle or confidence course. But perhaps the most interesting aspect of implementation during BCT was the rapidity with which official concerns changed. As it turned out, the ATOs were not the only ones with special assignments that did not really materialize. For example, the Air Force's top enlisted woman came to the academy in the summer of 1976 expecting to advise and assist with the women cadets. By September 1976 it was established policy that women required no special assistance, and she was assigned to social actions work, where she found that her chief concern was not the integration of women but the managing of complaints of "reverse" discrimination.ᵛ

As BCT progressed, administrators learned that their planning had been thorough but conservative, that "kid gloves" were unnecessary. They also learned that extra attention to or any special treatment of the women was deeply resented by the male cadets.ʷ The attention showered on the women by the media was especially resented by upperclassmen, who believed they had done it "before" and "better." Even at the end of the first year, a high-ranking male officer who had given an academy tour to visiting women Air Force officers described himself as "really turned off" when the visitors kept asking about the women cadets instead of being absorbed in what *he* wished to show them. Men are accustomed to audiences,

ᵛSomehow reverse discrimination is understood to be different from your plain, old, everyday discrimination, and somehow worse. In the early 1970s, when HEW was deluged with charges of sex discrimination in higher education, the complaints made by women were merely filed. Those by men were handled separately and given priority. The idea was to head off charges of reverse discrimination by providing a quick response. An alternative would have been to say, "We're very interested in assisting you: please get at the end of the line, and when we get to you we will see if there is a legally provable case." Men would then have had a more realistic view of what legal redress is all about, and they would also have received nondiscriminatory instead of privileged handling.

ʷAs one listened to officers discuss the handling of the male cadets, one sometimes had the sensation that one was actually listening to Dr. Benjamin Spock discuss sibling rivalry, or "what to do when the new baby arrives."

and they often are used to having women listen. When women begin to watch and to listen to other women instead of always men, men may suffer a relative loss of audience and may feel deprived relative to their previous state, at least to the degree that an increased interest in women represents a decreased interest in men.[x]

The year of the women coincided with a number of environment-enhancing efforts and increased freedom for cadets.[y] Arnold Hall game rooms and food facilities were improved, clothing regulations were relaxed, and the "privileges packet" was dramatically improved.[z] Even BCT was interrupted by a special Bicentennial Fourth of July air show, Doolie Dining Out, and a chaplain's picnic. During the year other activities sponsored by the chaplain would become a problem; military standards were not supposed to be suspended for chaplain-sponsored events (as they *are* supposed to be when cadets "cross the North Drive" into the athletic area). Still, the relaxed and nonmilitary purpose of the activities inevitably led them to be described as "hot beds for fraternization," and undeniably the choirs, the liturgical dance group, the retreats, and the "cheese cellar" discussions sought to offer fellowship. The question of when fellowship meant fraternization was unclear, and its resolution was left to disciplinary boards to decide.

Formal reports were filed on the BCT experience, and an attitude survey was conducted on the summer training. Consistent but small differences were found between men and women fourth class cadets, and larger differences between the women and the training cadres—especially the second cadre, which had done the Jack's Valley (as opposed to the dormitory-classroom) training. While both

[x]Women officers found that the assumption that women are supposed to listen (and sympathetically) applied to them in a variety of ways. Men sometimes volunteered details of their personal life and sought personal advice. Some men even felt it appropriate to explain their views on women in the military to busy women colleagues. One woman, "especially recruited" because of women's entrance, was told by an officer in a health counseling field that any woman in the service by definition "had problems." Another woman received two Christmas tree balls from her departing superior, who noted he had been "castrated" by her. While it is important to be able to laugh at and discuss differences when such interaction is reciprocal and understood in the same way by both parties, in an ambiguous situation levity is better initiated by the "inferior." Too often jokes or one-sided "serious" discussions are presumptuous. They assume sympathy in an audience that may in fact be unsympathetic but may not be permitted to say so.

[y]The latter were part of the effort to reduce attrition.

[z]These steps were part of a program to provide more positive motivation for upper class cadets. Later the term "pass authorizations" would be substituted to eliminate any intimation either that "rank has its privileges" or that it is a privilege to leave the academy grounds.

men and women thought the program should be equally stressing for both sexes, men were more likely to think that women should take a different course of training and that it must be "almost impossible" to take BCT and yet retain one's "femininity."

Once more, the most striking aspect of the survey findings lies in the discrepant views of men and women. Women believed they had succeeded. A significant minority of men were persuaded that women had not had the same training experience, that women were *not* capable of doing everything, and that the experience had not created group solidarity.[a]

During the summer the positive motivation policy was accompanied by a "hard-out" resignation policy (which gave the BCT commander some anxiety about causing excessive psychological stress). In combination the two policies *did* cut attrition. Even though some seventy-five cadets quit after BCT but before academics began, the overall attrition was still 5 percent lower than that of the previous year, giving rise to the hope that this represented a real decrease and not just a shift in time of resignation.[b] The women's attrition was lower than the men's and remained so until the end of the first year. At that time, however, the rates began to converge; the women's rate was about 19 percent, the men's 23 percent.[c]

BCT ended with a great and collective sigh of relief—and a wondering why "everyone" had been so worried. Officials looked forward to the school year when physical and combat-related training would be diminished and (they anticipated) things would become "normal."

[a]Some subjective responses were unambiguous. "BCT was a waste—the girls slowed down the pace—they weren't treated like men, men were treated like women." "It seems a little weird that over one-half the people on sick call were women." Perhaps the most Freudian, "I believe the change of going from negative motivation to passive was a great change."

[b]So much was new in 1976 that it is impossible to assign a cause to the decrease. One aspect may have been that the men "could not" quit because the women would not. This argument was absolutely taboo, but it could be sensed even if it were not expressed. In fact, one major, age thirty-seven, who had been perfectly happy navigating planes, suddenly took up parachuting that year. When asked why he suddenly craved jumping out of planes, he ruefully admitted, "I guess I did it because Judy (Captain Galloway) did it."

[c]One cannot say, however, that women's attrition had become "the same" as men's, since the reasons for women's resignations may have been quite different from men's, and the end of the first year may have represented the intersection of an accelerating attrition curve for women who at that point could then credibly say, "I could have stayed—I didn't want to." It should be noted, however, that in explaining their resignations, women did give responses very like those of men.

The School Year

During the school year a number of small modifications occurred, negative opinion seemed to ebb and flow, and separate billeting, like the Air Force's other unique policy (the ATOs), was constantly discussed, reviewed, and ultimately modified.

One modification involved women's hair length. Short hair was thought appropriate to discipline and also practical.[d] Many of the short cuts were distinctively unattractive, too, and longer hair would seem to have been an improvement.[e] A clarification was finally issued that permitted hair to reach the bottom (rather than the top) of the collar and to have 3 inches of bulk. However, various kinds of pins were forbidden, which made it virtually impossible to grow the hair long and convert it to a pinned-up style favored by a number of women officers. Interestingly enough, even the hardest-nosed male cadets hesitated to enforce women's hair regulations. As the year progressed, in fact, more make-up and curls appeared as women found they were acceptable to men cadets.

During the year, a controversy arose over travel for women's athletic teams. The volleyball team was told that fourth class cadets could not travel overnight and that neither Annapolis nor West Point permitted doolies to go out of state. Women swimmers, however, had been recruited to the academy and had traveled to Georgia with their coach and the men's swimming team. A distinction between teams partly and wholly fourth class was proposed, and the volleyball team did not get to make its trip. But by spring, all-women, all-fourth class teams did get to make overnight trips.

The policy of having "only cadets" (not women and men cadets) sometimes led to administrative inconvenience and confusion. For instance, minority cadet performance was carefully monitored, but one AOC admitted that he really did not know if women's perform-

---

[d]Nevertheless, women spent a lot of time on hair care. A survey showed that twenty of thirty-three women set their hair every day, and twenty-seven of them washed their hair each day. Professional care was available. For $4.00 per month, women could have as many wash/cut/blow dry appointments as they liked.

[e]After all, permitting long hair would be a very easy way of achieving one official concern—feminine appearance. Letting women wear nighties instead of plain pajamas and giving them something other than dark tennis shoes would also have helped. The obstacle was the desire for uniform appearance. Men were first; therefore, their uniforms were controlling. Women's items were, as often as possible, scaled-down men's items. Other options were considered. For instance, at one time the Air Staff favored a woman's parade uniform with high, white boots and cullotes or a skirt. Academy officials, who preferred white trousers because they resulted in a more uniform appearance, prevailed, however.

ance was or was not supposed to be noted separately in his squadron report. In the first semester, grade sheets had no way of identifying women cadets on the printout, and hand tabulation was required. By the second semester a cadet's sex was noted.

One fourth class 0730 (7:30 A.M.) Saturday training session was devoted to issues of sexism. The goal was to promote class unity. The program consisted of a skit, a lecture on language (for example, discussing the different meanings of apparent synonyms such as *stud* and *whore*), humor ("Who has an I.Q. of 200?" "The combined class of '80"), and male penalties for sexist behavior (heart attacks, repressed emotions). Discussion in small groups had uneven results. Men tended to be hostile or defensive, while women seemed to feel, "Glad *you* said it not me." What was most interesting was the make-up session given to students who missed the training. This group was composed mostly of athletes and was about fifty-fifty male-female. There the response was quite different: the women absolutely dominated the discussion.

What really counts as the measure of success at an academy is the Military Order of Merit (MOM). The MOM is modified from time to time, and various items are assigned different weights depending upon the cadet's class. For fourth class men in 1976, MOM ratings incorporated the following scores: AOC (commanding officer), 40 percent; peer ratings, 20 percent; performance report, 5 percent; military studies (grades), 15 percent; cadet wing training (grade), 5 percent; and conduct and discipline (demerits), 15 percent.

Planners had anticipated that subjective scoring and separate billeting would hurt women's ratings—especially the 20 percent done by peers.[f] They decided, however, to leave the system unaltered, at least for the first semester, and to see whether their expectations were true. If "too true" they reserved the option of handicapping or modifying the women's ratings by shifting the curve upwards.

Women's MOMs *were* lower. By March 1977, 403 (37 percent) of the men were on the Commandant's List, as were 38 (28 percent) of the women. It was decided that the ratings would stand, that the women *were* performing "as well as the men considering" the various socio-cultural disadvantages women suffered.[g]

[f]Ambivalence about peer ratings was chronic. Annapolis had eliminated them in 1975; West Point was to do so after the honor code scandal of 1976. The Air Force Academy continued to use them for purposes of counseling but eliminated them from the MOM score in spring 1978.

[g]Nevertheless, the numbers would not show that they had done "as well as," and it was not clear that the circumstances affecting their low ratings would change.

Cadet attitudes toward the "Dollys" or "Doilies" showed little change as a result of their exposure to the women during BCT. In the early stages of speculation about the coming of women, there had been some debate about the wisdom, correctness, and justness of women's coming to the academy. As the day approached, however, the officially correct response was made clear, and among cadets an unofficial response also developed. Within the wing, cadets stopped arguing on behalf of women; peer pressure simply did not permit active support for or defense of them.[h] Moreover, fourth class cadets began to think more like upper class cadets. At least for a while women's advocacy became nearly extinct.

The existence of an approving or at least not disapproving audience (a third party) gives legitimacy to actors. In this case neither punishment nor disdain was felt by cadets who displayed opposition to women cadets. Verbal abuse continued. Jokes proliferated. Rumors started. Fantasy flourished. Women were said to be sleeping, not just rooming, together. A woman referee at a women's basketball game was told to "go back to being a housewife." When another member of the audience looked at the cadet quizzically, he shouted more loudly, "I mean go back to being a househusband." Male cadets chalked up a "hit" each time they could make a doolie cry. Notes were left for women to "meet me in the parking lot. I love to rape cadets." Women's official recourse was the (male) cadet chain of command, but cadet practice did not permit doolies to report an upperclassman. Partly it was felt that doolies have to be able to take it. To others it was simply "the burden of the token" that women must expect and bear. By the second semester, at least one male cadet was "buried" (punished) for addressing a woman officer as "you bitch," another must have wished he could bury himself after he mistakenly hallooed a woman officer as a "fucking mamacita." One Commandant's Disciplinary Board incident occurred in which an upper class cadet with a good record spit on a woman standing in formation. Whether his action represented an attack or an uncontrolled outburst, or whether "the wind took it," the cadet himself may not have known. The important point is that the incident finally did define a boundary that could not be passed: it resulted in formal charges, and, perhaps more important, peer opinion seemed to be against the male cadet.[i]

[h] And peer pressure could be directly exerted in the form of peer ratings.

[i] That same year a first class man was called before the Commandant's Disciplinary Board for saying, "Smile, so I can see you" to a black cadet. In this case, peer opinion was at least partially with the "firstie."

Two procedures made control of anti-female language and behavior difficult.[j] One, demerits could not be given for it—the only remedy was a Commandant's Disciplinary Board (CDB)—and, two, the charges had to be grave ("conduct unbecoming" or "harassment"). Thus there was no graduated deterrence—a cadet was either immune or "nuked." The second difficulty involved "freedom of speech" and the need to let cadets make mistakes in judgment and learn from them.[k] A group of cadets explained it as follows: First, this is an educational institution; disagreement and inquiry are essential. Second, our life here is a whole; we have no separate living and job locations, so it is difficult to make an "on-" and "off-duty" distinction. Third, every detail cannot be policed.[l] Fourth, "The few rights we have we hang on to—and free speech is one of them."

Stereotypical behavior on the part of individuals was not eliminated, nor did policy absolutely dictate its elimination. In one squadron a woman tried to relate to her fellows by regularly baking cookies for them. In that same squadron a cake sale was held as a fund raiser, but the cakes were baked *not* by the cadets but by the wives of officers associated with the squadron. The woman officer associated with the unit *also* baked for the sale. Thus she chose to be "a woman" and different from the other officers.[m] The squadron also held a pie-throwing contest, which nicely demonstrated that its women were beginning to be included as full members. After astronomical bids had been made to honor the cadet commander and the deputy commandant of the academy with pie in the face, and after doolies had pooled their resources to get a squadron officer, one of the women began bidding for the chance to get a particular upperclassman. Her action was clearly revenge-motivated, and before the bid went out of bounds, cries went out to "let her have it, let her have it." She got it and dished it out, but then came a final proof of her "inclusion." Her adversary began bidding on the last pie—with her as the intended victim. The price was high, but ultimately she,

[j] Both have obvious parallels in civilian settings.

[k] Thus on Halloween, when cadets attended dinner in costume, no one penalized the cadets dressed as members of the Ku Klux Klan, but the disapproval of certain other cadets was made known.

[l] One officer summed it up nicely. "You can make one cadet do anything; you have to work a lot harder but you may be able to control two. With a group (or the wing) you'd better listen to them!"

[m] Having to choose between their gender and professional role is common for women officers. For men the roles seem nearly congruent.

too, ended up with lemon cream dripping down her face and splat-
tered through her hair.

Strong cadet feelings of disapproval of the academy's management of news about women surfaced on two occasions in the first
semester. The first involved *Air Force Now*, an information film
distributed monthly through the Air Force. The October 1976 film
included sequences on the Kennedy Space Center, the Outstanding
Airmen of 1976 (one of whom was a woman), and women cadets
undergoing BCT at the academy. One cut showed the superintendent
saying "The women are undergoing the same training program that
the men are undergoing . . . with insignificant changes." Another
showed the cadet commander: "We just didn't think the women
could do it . . . My experience in the last two weeks has shown me
women are able to keep up with the men in most cases. . . . In
some cases they're able to do better than some of the men did." To
an outsider, even to Air Force personnel outside the academy, these
phrases did not seem portentous. But the wing (which saw the film
by class) was angered. Equal-effort theories cut no ice. The cadets
did not understand that the women had done "as well as" the men.
The program's physical emphasis and the differences in women's
and men's absolute achievements in that area were too large. To
some their commander's statement was just a lie. A discussion period followed the film, and even some of the AOCs admitted that
the cadet response was completely unanticipated.

This flap had only just cooled (people were tired of it, not recon-
ciled) when the superintendent was quoted in a Denver newspaper
as having said, "The only problem we've had is finding that there's
no way to hold the women back to equal effort. . . . They've been
working harder than the men all summer." The dormant issue rose
again.[n] This time there was such disquiet that a formal explanation
was offered by the administration. The root of the problem was the
administration's conventional need to use language in discussion
with members of its organization different from that which it used
with the public. Moreover, it may be that physicalness and manliness are so fundamental to the male cadet's motivation structure that
"women" *cannot be* collectively accepted as equals even though
physical strength does not ordinarily limit a man's Air Force career.
Finally, perceptions about what was and was not "serious" were not

[n]The degree to which opinions lie dormant, or to which views are "suspended" rather than
altered, is of importance to understanding women's acceptance in male institutions.

the same. Male officers were grave about vulgar insults such as ("whore" or "bitch"), while the women saw such language as degrading to the speaker and not very imaginative. On the other hand, women were upset by assertions that they were trying to get by "by batting their eyelashes" or that they were selected for something (only) "because they were women." Perhaps they were especially upset because there was no way to disprove such comments.

Soon after the second "information" incident, a major policy decision was made to reduce the dormitory isolation of the women and to end the total isolation of third and fourth group from the women.[o] This decision was to be implemented by establishing a second women's area on the opposite side of the quad, and by administratively placing women in all forty squadrons.

There had been strong support for more integrated billeting from the beginning. The apparent precipitant was a single cadet's inquiry of the superintendent during a routine class meeting. In fact, however, the climate was ripe. Believing that increased contact would create better relationships, both officers and cadets (men and women) had been expressing a desire for more integration. Indeed, virtually everything that was less than perfect was attributed (by one person or another) to the segregated billeting for women. The fact is that separate billeting probably served as a marvelous scapegoat. Everything could be blamed on physical separation; the social separation could go overlooked.[p]

Since both survey and savvy showed that the all-male third and fourth groups were more hostile to women than first and second groups, the obvious answer was to assign women there too. To do so meant, however, that the number of women per squadron would be reduced from seven or eight to three or four. Thus all men would be in contact with women, but women would have less contact with each other. The decision to move the women was made the day before first semester finals and was completely unexpected. Even

---

[o]The disruption caused by the public relations incidents also prompted a closer consideration of new materials being developed by various academy offices. One issue concerned recruitment material. The question was asked, "What is the right proportion of shots of and discussion about women? Should 50 percent of photos include women? Or 2.5 percent? Or 10 percent? Or should one abandon consciousness and shoot academy activities randomly, letting the chips fall where they may?"

[p]By June it was decided that in 1977–78 women would be further distributed into seventeen clusters placed at the intersections of the living quarters of two squadrons. Since there would be twice as many women in the second year, each cluster would include about sixteen women, who would be living "with" but at the margin of their squadron, and each squadron would include about seven or eight women (over 5 but under 10 percent).

women who had argued for integration were stunned by the immediacy and disruptiveness of the decision. They did not respond with unanimity, but many did not want to have to re-establish themselves in a new (and supposedly hostile) environment. Men wanted to know why "they" were moving "our" women. But it was explained that these were "orders." During the semester break, a human chain was formed from one side of the quad to the other, and the belongings of half the women were handed across to their new quarters.[q]

The decision as to who moved rested with the AOCs. Fairness dictated that an officer not send his four "worst" women, but for some women a shift could mean the kind of fresh start the academy regularly gives cadets by redistributing them through the squadrons after their first year. Still, it also meant that women who had established a place for themselves in one squadron would have to learn the ways of a new unit—and do so with much less support (two or three other women) and among men who had, until then, had an all-male unit.[r]

The social life of the women cadets was a worry. While administrators wanted to keep them "safe," they also worried that the women cadets would not have an active social calendar since they tended to be rather untraditional women surrounded by very traditional men. The important point, of course, is that they *were* surrounded. Even among the doolies (whom they *were* permitted to date), the ratio was ten to one. Perhaps the formal balls sum up the variety of experiences the young women had.

The first ball was held during the first semester, and at least some of the ATOs let the women know that attendance was appropriate. However, cadets attend such events in uniform and the women's mess dress had not yet arrived. Thus the women cadets who did go were in short-skirted uniforms unlike the officers' wives and cadet "escorts," who were in splendid gowns. Some men cadets did come without dates (as did many of the women), but upperclassmen had not been told whether they could dance with the women or not. Most did not, and most women attended only as a social obligation.

[q]Some upperclassmen grumbled that if they had been men they would have moved themselves. More cadets found it an appropriate welcoming gesture for people who were being uprooted.

[r]The AOCs of receiving squadrons briefed their unit according to their own style. One was tough: "We don't care about your philosophy, logic, or attitudes; you behave correctly; do not screw up just because a few cadets have a new address." Another noted that while three new doolies would be coming in, they were *not* "to repeat the doolie experience. They are in their second semester and *not* new cadets." Another was casual: "A few new cadets shouldn't change the way a good squadron operates."

The Commandant's Ball came after the mess dress became available; indeed, it presented the first opportunity to wear that uniform, and the women cadets who went *chose* to go, for they realized that women doolies were not required to attend a ball planned for one thousand when there was a potential attendance of nine or ten thousand.[s] Those who went seemed to have had a better time than at the first ball.

But most interesting was the Ring Dance, held during the graduation festivities of June Week. "Recognition" of the fourth class occurred just before the dance. "Recognition" is the acceptance of the doolies as full cadets; at the end of the ceremony, upperclassmen remove their "prop and wings" insignia and pin them on the ex-doolies.[t] A crucial question arose. Were fraternization regulations no longer applicable? Recognition *had* occurred; nonetheless, the school year was not yet over. The AOCs were polarized on the issue. Ultimately, it was decided that recognition *did* mean fraternization barriers were removed, and at the Ring Dance upperclassmen appeared with a number of cadet dates—that is, with women with whom they were not supposed to have had previous personal contact![u] At least one woman cadet who was on the Commandant's List quit to marry a graduating cadet. Officer response varied from amusement to disappointment, from "It's natural" to "It's outrageous," and from "He's being taken" to "She's being taken."

Interestingly enough, some of the very officers who most opposed women cadets were also the ones most vigorous in protecting their career potential. Their thought process seemed to be: they do not belong here, but since they are here, they do belong and nobody better do anything to hurt their chances! As one officer put it, "My advice to young women is to fly—to get their wings." When asked if he opposed women as pilots, he replied, "Yes." When asked if the two views were not contradictory, his answer was, "Hell, no! The most important thing those women have to do is beat guys like me."

[s]In fact, eighteen hundred attended the Commandant's Ball that April, almost overtaxing the resources of the ballroom and its manager. Announcements had indicated that the appropriate dress for dates (who were obviously assumed to be female) was a "long formal gown." "Color is optional."

[t]One young woman received eight pins. Another multi-pinned woman cadet was said to have reversed her decision to resign as a result of that ceremony.

[u]Fraternization occurred frequently. Seven percent of the Commandant's Disciplinary Boards (CDBs) were for fraternization. Over the course of the year, ninety-two cadets were put on conduct probation, and seventeen of those were for "frat." Like the hair regulation, "frat" seemed to be a "take your chances" proposition. Cadets did. Even walkie-talkies were pressed into service by ingenious cadets.

Women's Responses

In assessing the end of the first year, the superintendent noted that he had been warning Air Force Personnel (a Pentagon office) that it had better be thinking about how to use these women three years hence, because he was producing a whole crew of "Jeanne Holms."[v] He added with some pride, "And there's not a woman's libber in the lot."

Here again perceptions by sex seemed dramatically different. Male officers tended to agree with the superintendent's assertion about libbers, or, after consideration, to think that perhaps the term should be defined. Most women officers did not credit the remark at all, although the dignity of their responses varied from a hooted "bullshit!" to a rueful "sooo wrong!" Some, of course, said that a woman had demonstrated she was liberated simply by enrolling at the academy, whether she was conscious of having done so or not, and even if she did not identify herself as a libber. The point is that male officials apparently saw no "libbers" among the cadets, but women officers did. One of the latter noted, "They're not dumb. They know when, where, why, and to whom they can speak their mind."

The women also learned how to cope with the academy system quickly. In fact, the women were probably quicker to catch on (to get feedback and to modify their behavior in the interests of survival) than were the men in the fourth class. Men lived with their squadrons and tended to think the academy was like their squadron, their fellow cadets, and their element leaders. Administrators clearly understood that different squadrons have different styles, accomplishments, capacities, and attitudes.[w] Because the women participated in twenty different squadrons the first semester but lived together in the dormitory, they quickly learned the various approaches to "being military" and the nonessentiality of certain requirements. Thus the breadth of their shared vision gave them a perspective rarely afforded to fourth class men.

Women did have some special camaraderie with women officers too. One woman officer (not an ATO) told of stopping an activity because a frustrated woman had said, "Oh, fuck." She cornered her

[v]The first woman officer to receive two stars, she was at that time an adviser to President Gerald Ford.

[w]Sometimes a complete rehabilitation is done on a squadron that has fallen on hard times. New (and extra) leadership is assigned, morale building activities are encouraged, and sometimes even a new identity and squadron patch are created.

and chewed her out. Then the cadet said, "M'am, you should just see the faces on those guys! They're feeling sorry for me." The officer replied, "Oh, yeah? Let's give them a really good show. Let those boys think we women are *really* mean!" The officer crescendoed, the cadet sobbed, and the "guys" saw a woman doolie apparently devastated by a tough woman officer.

Women also learned the standard fourth class techniques of hiding, playing dumb, stone-facing, nicknaming, and planning delicious revenge. However, smiling and singing were new techniques of passive aggression developed by the women; so was the superbrace in which chests were thrown forward to challenge and sometimes embarrass the trainer.

The last event of the first twelve months for one-third of the women (the others would rotate through it later) was SERE (Survival, Evasion, Resistance, Escape), a strenuous program culminating in a three-day "trek." The most anxiety-producing portion of SERE was the mock POW compound, a part of the exercise designed to produce substantial psychological stress through deprivation and interrogation. The administration worried about how women would react and decided there was a need to have women monitors. As happened for most of the other events of the first year, the officer who had anxiously supervised the women being "first" ended by saying: "They really did well in SERE, even in the POW compound." The young woman officer to whom the comment was made responded, "Of course they did well in the POW compound; where do you think the women have been all year?"

CHAPTER

10

Wives, Military Women,
and Warriors

Wives: the Military Is a Family Affair

"Being an Air Force wife is a truly demanding profession. If there was ever a classified ad for the position of an Air Force wife it would read something like this: Wanted, mature woman to take care of children, home, pets. Must be able to cope with transient husband and be qualified in plumbing, auto and bicycle repair, yard care. Experience in packing and unpacking entire household helpful but not mandatory." This is the message given cadets by *Talon* as it congratulated seniors "soon to be married and their wives to be."[1]

"The Air Force performs a vital function in keeping the peace . . . and we sincerely believe that as an Air Force wife, *your* mission is equally vital. Thanks for standing beside your man, while he stands behind his country. . . . We hope you'll *both* be with us for many years to come!" This is the message addressed to wives by the U.S. Air Force Recruiting Service in one of its brochures.

And how do the wives see themselves? Not long ago the Army Officers Wives Club of Washington, D.C., adopted a seal incorporating their understanding of their many roles. In describing the seal, the designer said:

The eagle at the top of the circle represents the Army wife, who in protecting her nest also protects the flag and the future it represents. Alert and poised, she is ready to defend either when the need arises.

As the ultimate goal of her husband's profession is peace, so is it hers. The olive branch held by the eagle represents this peace, her hope for an end to wars for her husband and her children.

The lyre, symbol of harmony, gentility and romance, surrounds the four phases of her life that she holds dear.

The cradle represents her children, her mother—her own motherhood.

The sheaf of wheat represents the staples and stability she provides for her family—her duty.

The grapes represent the social life, the wine, the fun, sense of humor—her lighter side.

The open book represents her individuality and personal self-fulfillment through knowledge and wisdom. The person she is and becomes—her personal self.

The double circle enclosing all is her wedding band, symbol of eternity and never-ending love. This circle is broken only by the eagle, here a symbol of her duty to country. For the Army wife, the break in the circle represents the many separations and the possible ultimate sacrifice.

Taken alone this explanation seems sentimental and overblown, but it is not trivial. It is an expression of a serious partnership in which two persons jointly pursue a single career while raising a family. It expresses the importance (to both partners) of the private and unsalaried aspect of the military profession. The "two-person career" has been described elsewhere.[2] Professionals of all kinds engage in it, but it has a special significance to the military because the family is more than the economic beneficiary of the husband's labors. The family's existence also justifies his work, which is unique in that it involves preparing for the possibility of killing or of being killed for his country. As more than one officer has said, "My wife and children represent my country for me. They are the concrete answer to the question 'why.'"

Families are specially valued on military bases. They loom large in conversation; formal entertaining and female nurturing, which have disappeared in other contexts, are still practiced (especially by the wives of officers); wives attend classes in gourmet cooking and flower arranging; they hold luncheons with speakers; they welcome and help orient new arrivals. The academy newspaper announces programs for children and prescribes when and where things like trick-or-treating "will" occur. Indeed, single officers are probably hampered in the development of their career.[a]

Even though sex-roles may be well defined in military families, female-dependency and male-centeredness are not adequate descriptions of the family's organization. Officers' wives move their families often. Their husbands go on remote assignments for months. For certain periods a wife must manage, decide, and act—either alone or within an all-female, military-wives support network. Many wives articulate beautifully and with some humor the transition they must make between auxiliary and central status as their husbands come and go. Most of them see themselves as operating

---

[a]Before World War II, singleness was very much the military way. After the war, it became the norm for officers to have families, and policies began to reflect this change. More recently the military has had to assume that enlisted personnel, too, would have dependents. Whereas women in the military are less likely to have dependents than men, and therefore represent a substantial saving over male personnel, this pattern is unlikely to continue because women must now be given dependency allowances on the same basis as men (a Supreme Court decision) and they are not automatically discharged for becoming pregnant (an administrative decision). Thus their "cost per unit" should begin to climb.

Military families have not been insulated from the divorces and distress of civilian society. Divorces occur and no longer seem to blight a career; however, remarriage seems unofficially preferable to staying single.

as a team with their husbands and appreciate their own worth. Some officers' wives describe with disdain the dominating roles they observe in young male cadets who appear to value ornamental but dependent women, believing that both the cadets and their "girls" fail to anticipate the strength, competence, and versatility that will be required of an officer's wife.

·In informal discussion few academy wives voiced support for the admission of women to the academy. Some regretted the changes that would come to the choral music (then arranged for all-male voices); others' eyes were offended by the mix of hosieried and trousered legs on the terrazzo. In one family, a retired senior officer, his wife, and college-age daughter agreed that women did not belong at the academy. His arguments were based on cost effectiveness. His wife's were rooted in tradition: "They'll just mess it up. When they parade, it's such a thrill—and at the same time one feels such a chill, because you know many of them may be called upon to sacrifice their lives." The daughter's view was that no one in her right mind would put up with the childish treatment accorded cadets: "They take everything away, then give it back to you—one thing at a time—and you're supposed to be grateful!"

None of the wives expressed a sense of threat, although some women officers believed that wives of their male colleagues felt threatened. Perhaps the cadet women's youth and doolie status minimized the potential for emotional involvement between officers and cadets, but the involvement of some ATOs with male cadets, including one marriage, and the involvement of male and female officers who were married to others suggest that *that* kind of problem will be exacerbated by integration-created temptation. Or at least those kinds of problems will not be as easy to overlook when both partners are military.[b]

The military does do research on the family. At present much of it focuses on personnel costs and the effects of the POW families' experience. In addition to receiving a straight salary on the basis of rank, military personnel receive benefits associated with the number of their dependents. (Since 1960 there have been more military dependents than military personnel.) Because dependents are civilians and usually prefer to live as civilians, because families are young, have children, and tend to have nonworking spouses, the trend seems to be toward ever-increasing personnel costs. If there is a

[b]Officers are expected to meet certain standards whether on or off duty. Thus an aggrieved spouse can anticipate some redress by going to a mate's commanding officer, and a commanding officer can threaten a court martial with some credibility.

desire to retain top personnel with families, it might be wise to extend military research beyond a cost analysis into areas dealing more directly with the quality of military life, such as the effect of numerous forced moves, the effect of a father's absence, and the prospects and need for maintaining traditional families within the military—even in the face of increased recruitment of women and increased variegation of civilian family patterns.

Military Women

Military women include both officers and enlisted women, but, because the academy is a training ground for future officers, the roles available to women officers are of special concern there. Cadets, after all, make decisions based upon what they see around them. They must decide whether the private and professional lives of women officers are what they want for themselves.

From 1966 through 1976, the *Air Force Times* reported one military first after another: 1967, first woman M.D.; 1968, first woman in the Air National Guard; 1969, first woman at Air War College; 1970, first women generals (Army); 1971, first woman Air Force general; 1972, first women pilots (Navy); 1973, first black woman AFROTC graduate; 1974, Military Wife-of-the-Year Program expanded;[c] 1975, Congress orders admission of women to the academies; 1976, WAF ends. The rush into the future sometimes seemed shocking; at the same time, a look into the past sometimes made what was referred to as "new" seem old.

After all, women have always participated in this country's wars, even if in an "irregular" and temporary status, Margaret Corbin (not Molly Pitcher) for example, or as nurses in the Civil War (still irregularly). In World War I, our first "total" and major foreign war, women served under contract (even overseas) for the Army and as active duty "yeomenettes" in the Naval Reserve.[d]

World War II saw women become officers for the first time. They became reserve officers in the Navy but, at first, were only auxiliary members of the Army. WASP (Women Airforce Service Pilots) was

[c]The first Air Force women assigned to the security police were not given any publicity, but that happend in 1973, too. Trends are rarely unidirectional. A thrust in one direction (generalship) often provokes a counterthrust (Wife of the Year).

[d]At that time the law permitted the Army to enlist only men. However, the legislation controlling Navy enlistments referred to "persons," and the Navy enrolled some twelve thousand (women) yeomen.

a civilian organization, although it was subject to a number of military procedures. Following the war, women were the first demobilized, but in 1948 they achieved regular status for the first time. However, a ceiling of 2 percent was established for women, and a ceiling was also placed on the rank they could hold.[e] Further, only certain jobs were available to them.

In 1967 rank restrictions were removed by Congress, but the combat restriction was not. From 1967 to 1976, the military consistently increased the number of women service members and the kinds of positions open to them. ROTC was integrated and so was Officer Candidate School.[f]

With this record the military came to perceive itself as consistently moving toward more and more equality. Indeed, many officers began to feel that equality may have gone further than was wise, and most still believe that there are limits to what women can and should do.

A feminist perspective counters that, while there has been variation in women's participation, there has not been steady progress; and because decisions have not and are not being based on women's rights and responsibilities but on needs as determined by men, women's role remains, in essence, auxiliary. Women are used primarily when there are not enough men available, they are asked to do only certain specified tasks that are marginal to the mission, and there is no expectation that they will enter the mainstream; that is, become chiefs of staff or even stay in service once the personnel shortage is over or once they marry and have children.

The Air Force has gone farther than the other services in utilizing womanpower. Following the 1967 legislation, it doubled its number of military women by 1972 and planned to almost triple it by 1978. It opened new fields, set numerical "goals" for nontraditional fields, and sought to make overseas slots as available to women as to men.[g]

But this Air Force boldness was not always successful. The drive to place women in nontraditional fields resulted in too many misplacements, namely, in small women assigned to tasks involving physical strength. As a result, strength qualifications had to be developed for a number of jobs. The 15 percent goal for each specialty also misfired. There was already a much larger percentage of women in the traditional fields—so no new women could be re-

[e]The 2 percent quota was never filled.

[f]By 1976–77, 22 percent of Army ROTC were female, although West Point accepted less than 10 percent women.

[g]The Air Force goal was to have 15 percent women in all nonrated (nonflying) jobs.

cruited for assignment to them—and there were so few women with degrees in math, science, and engineering that 15 percent was an almost impossible objective for recruiters. In fact, on further consideration, Air Force planners decided to aim for only a 7.5 percent goal in nontraditional fields and to permit a higher percentage of women in traditional fields. Still, by 1976 women's recruitment was stable rather than increasing. Both the Air Force and women seemed to be rethinking the decade of change.

It is true that the excesses experienced by some women during World War II were gone. Women were no longer subjected to monthly pelvics for venereal disease, they were not denied birth control devices, their compounds were not surrounded by barbed wire to "protect" them from their military colleagues and peers, nor were they required to enter the hospital if incapacitated by menstrual cramps. Nevertheless, women officers were still experiencing limitations and aggravations, and they were not new; they had all been recorded in Treadwell's history of women in World War II. Even that many of the women thought of their problems as new (because they knew nothing of women's history) was not new!

One particular complaint women officers have (and have had) is that they are continually being asked to "prove" something to someone. Apparently because the number of women who accomplish particular feats is always quite small, men seem to be able to accept a single good performance as real, but they do not seem able (or willing) to generalize from it. Instead, they regard whatever they have witnessed as exceptional. Thus even when proof of competence is explicitly asked for and received, it may not be accepted. For example, in 1976 a small group of women entered pilot training as an "experiment." All but one successfully completed the training. Another group of women was then accepted—but still on a trial basis. Even after the second group had graduated, the Air Force did not officially decide whether the women's training had been successful. Because there was no research design or criteria established to define "success," women were unable to insist that their success be recognized. Indeed, some senior women came to believe that test programs were no more than a dilatory device—that they were designed to let administrators mark time until they could determine whether they would be forced to carry out a prescribed change. In contrast, at least one senior male officer also expressed disbelief about the legitimacy of "tests," but for quite a different reason. He believed that the women would get "inevitably prejudiced treatment" and that "all would have to be gotten through." Persuaded as

[margin handwritten note: a change or never define goals of success thus ensuring non-success]

he was of a rigged outcome, no conventional "proof" could have
→ proved anything to him. What all this may mean is that a "critical
mass" is required not only to give women a sense of identity and a
source of protection but also to give their efforts legitimacy with
men. Perhaps there must be regular activity by a certain size group
before a generalization (as opposed to a particular observation) can
emerge as an assessment of performance.

Women still found themselves in absurd positions; for example,
in early planning one woman was asked to assist in planning
women's billeting but she was forbidden to see the billets.[h] Similarly, one woman was asked to attend a meeting at which the agenda
item was how to block the "forced increase" of women personnel.[i]

Another frustration was the military's habit of referring to a promising future for women entering the profession and looking right
past the women already there and eager for promotion. It has already been noted that women "role models" were needed not just
for women to imitate but for men to see and to learn from—especially for men to learn how to accept women in command. Unfortunately, the "new" (1976) acceptance of women in the military
came at a time when the officer pipeline was virtually empty of
women. Few had been promoted in the past decade, and no lateral
entry is permitted to the services. So it was considered just an "accident of history" that on December 31, 1976, women line officers
in the entire Air Force included only one general, four colonels,
thirty-six lieutenant colonels, and eighty-two majors. (Down substantially from previous years.) Moreover, women worried that such
an "accident" could be compounded because most of the women
from major up had worked their way up "the petticoat chain of command." As a result they lacked male connections and their experience as commanders (of women only) might be discounted. Again,
some who "looked to the future," to "the new generation," quite
overlooked the older women officers who had once been "new" and
"firsts" too. They overlooked the fact that writing off the generation
of women officers already in place as out-of-touch could also be
construed as a refusal to accept mature women—a refusal to accept
women as peers for themselves while advocating them as peers for
junior officers. To pin military hopes on the youngest women (the

[h]This happened at the Air Force Academy, where the "privacy" of male cadets at first
precluded inspection by women officers.

[i]Air Force policy at that time asked each base to take a percentage of women approximately equal to the percentage of women in the Air Force. Before 1975 the academy was
substantially below its "share," and some did not wish to come up to it.

cadets) was to discount the women already trying hard to succeed in an integrated military. Those women, the ATOs, for instance, were not finding it easy; even the (more senior) women captains at the academy during the first year of integration found the going rugged. Denied ratings (to fly), they found themselves competing against rated officers. And their evaluations were disappointing. Apparently not one woman captain received the top score, a "one," on her efficiency report, although the forced distribution permitted 22 percent "ones." Why, the women asked, should we expect the future to be different? If several successive generations of women officers have done poorly, why should this (or the next) generation expect to do better?[j]

Things had progressed since the days of World War II, when women officers were alleged to be either whores or lesbians. Nevertheless, women officers did seem to feel a need to defend their morality, even though morality is not easy to defend. They were determined not to be perceived as "husband snatchers," although they reacted to the possibility of such a charge in a variety of ways— some by completely separating their social and professional lives, some by developing direct ties to their colleagues' wives, some by following their own inclinations but doing so with discretion. The independence of women entering military service may lead to perceptions of "looseness" (as compared to military wives), but if their behavior is compared to that of male officers, it is hard to imagine that the conduct of women officers could be judged negatively.

Proven lesbianism is currently grounds for dismissal. The term is also a "cheap shot" (like "menopausal") sometimes muttered about a woman who fails to exhibit conventionally deferential behavior. Like an accusation of "frigidity," it denies a woman the right to be hostile toward or to reject an individual man or group of men by accusing her of rejecting the species. Thus she receives the blame and male self-esteem endures. Of course, casual slurs about one woman officer or a group of officers are not necessarily meant seri-

---

[j]One answer might be that the rules no longer preclude marriage and motherhood for women officers. Thus women will not be required to make the either/or choice so rarely required of men. (Priests are an exception.) This is a new policy, however, and the Army is now reconsidering its policy permitting motherhood. Also, a woman Air Force general has recommended reconsideration: "Women with children don't belong in service." Generally, the women officers at the academy in 1976–77 worked at their problems individually. Most believed that the academy would consider it "unprofessional" to organize, either formally or informally. The women had little solidarity, and some feared repercussions if they tried to build it.

ously or literally, but their effect on women's morale can still be of import.

The women officers at the academy managed their personal relationships in a variety of ways. The ATOs were chosen because they were single.[k] Three other women lieutenants were single, and two were married. Both of the married lieutenants were married to military officers, and both of them joined the military *after* their marriage to maintain their "employment" when their husbands (and usually they) were transferred. Just half of the sixteen women captains were married. Some were married to officers (both junior and senior to them), and some were married to civilians (some of whom were retired military). No women majors were on base; the lieutenant colonel was single (divorced). *None* of the women officers had taken advantage of the new regulations that permitted officers to have children, although one soon did.

The older officers had been WAFs. They had trained with and been commanded by women, and appeared to share a consciousness of being "women" officers. The younger women had come through integrated training programs and sought identification as simply "good" officers. Ironically, which was the better strategy (to think of oneself as a woman officer, or to think of oneself only as *an* officer) really depended not on the women but on their male superiors. Academy policy clearly dictated that each individual should be assessed only as an "officer" or as a "cadet." Nevertheless, the women often found themselves most appreciated when they filled women's roles: for cadets, as members of women's winning athletic teams; for officers, as go-betweens who bailed out commanding officers stuck with an embarrassing situation (e.g., confronted with a brand-new cadet mother), and as ratifiers who gave their "consent" to a male's decisions concerning women cadets.

Warriors

Within the military, special honor goes to the warrior, the combatant.[l] At present women are not permitted to become warriors. In the past minorities were not. Even if an individual does not want to go into combat, he or she may feel compelled to do so to prove that persons like him (or her) are good enough to do so.

[k]One was married; her husband was serving in Greece.

[l]Men who have seen combat have always held men who have not in a certain contempt, and described them as "titless WACS," "cherries," and "virgins."

In other areas of social change the civil rights and women's rights movements have been uneasy allies for 150 years. Also, analogies between the status of minorities (especially blacks) and women are common. Some analyses suggest that the two groups should work together; occasionally they do. More often they work in parallel, with black and white women claiming their rights somewhat after black men have won theirs.

Only in the 1970s have more than five or ten black cadets graduated from the Air Force Academy in a single year. Special recruitment programs have found minority cadets, but keeping them at the academy has been a problem. In December 1975 (while the planning for women was proceeding), one-fourth of the black students left or were lost in a single semester. When women entered the academy in 1976, in fact, there were about as many women in one class as there were blacks in four classes.[m] Too easily the minority question becomes one of numbers—of representation, or, more specifically, of under-representation among officers and of over-representation in the ground combat arms.[n] The point is that the arguments over minority representation are based on the percentage of the population they encompass. Such a position is rarely taken with women. Even in the civilian sector, discussions of representation are based not on population but, at best, on the pool of "already qualified and available women."

While some women believe representativeness by percentage of population is relevant to the armed forces, most military personnel do not. They do not because the rule is that *no* women can be warriors. This is an important difference between the roles of women and minorities in the military. *No* representation of women is thought to be the correct representation for the role of warrior.

The belief that women cannot and should not fight is reinforced by the perception that they do not. In contrast, it is known that minorities do and that certain words can almost guarantee it. When angry blacks get together, an aura of threat exists. In the case of women, however, much of the pressure for change has come from male courts and legislatures acting chivalrously, rather than from women themselves. In fact, when angry women get together, they

[m]The academies did not slip back in minority enrollments as other institutions were doing by the mid-1970s. In June 1978 a record number of minorities graduated (66) and a record number entered (227). (The academy counts Asians as a minority. They represented 13 and 40 of the respective groups.)

[n]The representativeness debate can be followed in *Armed Forces and Society*—winter 78, spring 76, fall 1974.

often provoke amusement, ridicule, or even "constructive criticism." Women just seem to have no credibility when it comes to the use of violence. If they desire the best opportunities as officers, women will have to follow the lead of the minorities and insist upon becoming warriors too.

Another point is crucial here: many white males officers are *de facto* noncombat officers. At a minimum women should have full parity with them. That is, the question should not be "How many women can the military use?" but "How many noncombat officers (male or female) can the military use?"[o]

Women's admission to the academies almost necessarily called attention to the number of military men who were not, in fact, warriors. In the Air Force the distinction between rated and nonrated is associated with the combat-noncombat distinction. However, pilots (and navigators) are not "different" only because their jobs are risky. They are also a minority rather than a majority in their service, and they are a very invested-in minority.

Undergraduate pilot training is estimated to cost $150,000 per individual and a combat-ready jet pilot represents an investment of $500,000 to $800,000. These expensive officers also have attractive nonmilitary career opportunities. This means that, on the one hand, they are the "heart" of the Air Force and they appropriately occupy most of the important command positions; on the other hand, they are like expensive machinery or thoroughbred horses—really too valuable to be used for anything but their specialty and constantly tempted to leave the military for civilian opportunities.[p]

Certain military exemptions have always existed under the draft. Both married men and fathers have had deferments. However, once drafted (or volunteered) they have shared the risk with all military men; they have not been separated into noncombat units. Why has the same not been true for women? Once in, why are they restricted in function? Is it possible that "warriorship" somehow requires female exclusion? Are women essential as an audience? as a justification? Why did women's entrance into an academy already training numerous nonrated officers generate these comments by officers:

"Since the Air Force Academy is as it is, women should be here.

---

[o]This would require redesignating and would be strongly resisted by men who do not want the "noncombat" designation, who would claim that they, at least, are potential combatants.

[p]Air Force pilots are becoming more and more specialized and less numerous. In fact, the Army now has more planes than the Air Force, including 90 percent of the helicopters. Missiles and their operators are also taking over functions that once belonged to pilots.

But if the Air Force Academy were as it should be. . . ." "*No* non-rateds should be here; we need to *re*blue the academy."[q] "It's a problem in misdirection—cadets are looking at the academy as a place to prepare them for civilian careers!" "Women's admission didn't cause the weakness, they just made it visible." "This should be an inner sanctum, a man's world; it's the place where we do the uglies."

A Recapitulation

1976–77 was a special year. It was the first year. It was a well-scrutinized year. Women were only doolies and fewer in number than they would be at any time in the future. They were only in one class of four, in two of four groups (until the second semester), and in less than a quarter of the academic classes. It was very easy for hostile cadets to avoid them altogether. The women were also more separate than they would be in the future, notably in housing arrangements and in physical education courses.

The conditions of women's entrance were set by federal legislation that mandated women's admission, based upon the principle of equal access to educational and employment opportunities. In addition, the Equal Rights Amendment had not yet begun to falter; and, because of the all-volunteer force, the services were having difficulty attracting enough first-rate men.[r] The academies were enjoined to admit as many women as they could use and to make only minimum program changes (those required by "physiological differences"). Because Congress did not remove restrictions against the use of women on combat ships and in combat aircraft, the women would be receiving training only "as if" they were to become members of the military elite. But because they would not be allowed to use the combat training they received, it was unrealistic to think that they would ultimately succeed in the same way as their male peers.

During the first year, the usual experience for academy women was to participate in activities in which they were far outnumbered by men. Few men can imagine a reverse but comparable environment, and even fewer have tested it.[s] Thus the fundamental experi-

[q] In its early years all cadets were eligible to fly.

[r] Women recruits have always had to meet higher standards than men: first, by law, and, later, because of competition with other women for a limited number of slots.

[s] One example might be the male students who enrolled at Vassar.

ence of the women and men cadets was different even when they followed precisely the same program.

New staff and fourth class cadets had no sense of how the academy had "changed." Old hands often see change as degeneration, but new and old would have had to agree that there were at least two ways women's entrance affected the academy primeval. First, it increased cadet heterogeneity and, second, it created a great deal of self-consciousness about situations that had previously been "unconscious." The question that continually emerged from that self-consciousness was "Is this so because it is male or because it is military?"

The planning of women's admission, then, was undertaken with self-consciousness. Planners described themselves as being in a fishbowl. The external audience ranged from the Board of Visitors, Congress, and the GAO, to DACOWITS and the National Organization for Women (NOW); the academy also had a highly critical internal audience of cadets, faculty, and staff. In planning, *anticipation* was the watchword: anticipation of every problem that might arise and anticipation of the responses of the different watchers to decisions and policies. Ironically, the Air Force Academy had more difficulty with its internal audience (e.g., the cadet response to the *Air Force Now* film) than with its external audience. Ironically, too, its early planning (beginning in 1972) led it to policies that were different from (and probably more conservative than) what would have been developed if all planning had been deferred until just before the women came.

In their planning, Air Force officials made several decisions that differed from those of West Point and Annapolis. Well buttressed with social science theories about role models and the need for a critical mass, it decided to billet the women separately, to use ATOs (modeled after a similar position that existed when the academy was founded), and to admit some 150 women. These decisions (conceived as early as 1972) tacitly assumed separate training for the women. By June 1976, however, integrated training had been decided upon. Yet the effect of that decision on earlier administrative decisions was not fully appreciated, which meant that the ATOs were left in a somewhat ambiguous role.

Athletic department personnel (not medical staff) were assigned the assessment of physiological differences. They found that academy women were a select group. They were much stronger and faster than either national norms or norms of other groups of military women had led officials to expect. Still, physiological differences between women and men (especially in upper body strength) meant that women had to be scored differently if the goal was to require equal effort from women and men cadets.[t] This concept never really was accepted by the male cadets: "for a woman" standards meant an inferior standard to them. The absolute time or distance had been the athletic goal for so long that the concept of an 84 percent, 89 percent, 93 percent, 100 percent, or 105 percent effort sounded like rationalizing to them. Because absolute results could differ under the equal-effort principle, it sounded like a double standard—even though officials again and again insisted that there was a single program based on a single standard—equal effort.

The differences issue also emerged in the great fat debate of the second semester. Men saw the women cadets as fat. Yet none really wanted the women to look like men or to be held to the same percentage of body fat as men.[u] Researchers in the athletic department were able to demonstrate that even though the women were gaining weight, they were not necessarily adding body fat. They were adding muscle, and, although their legs might be getting sturdier, the ratios between chest, waist, and abdomen measures were holding or "improving."

Thirty-six of the commandant's AOCs were rated, and the four who were not had had combat assignments; several were minorities, others had been POWs. The military side was explicit about teaching leadership through role models. Yet it provided women no role models above the rank of captain, and none were in a command or leadership position. During the first year, men did learn to command women.[v] They did *not* learn that women could command men. In fact, they did not even let a woman try.

Men in the commandant's shop were especially cross-pressured. There is no doubt about their commitment to making integration work.[w] There is also little doubt that many had personal reservations

[t]There was nothing absolute about the PFT standards even for men. They were annually adjusted by administrators who tried to elicit the best possible performance from cadets.

[u]Different body composition, then, was fine. The acceptability of different scores, which might be related to that composition, was not fine.

[v]At first, some doubted they could overcome their chivalrous instincts.

[w]At the Air Force Academy the professionally ambitious knew the success of integration was required. Some thought one colonel would win his star for his role in integration, and the superintendent actually received two stars during his three years at the academy. In interviews most officers were happy to fully describe their involvement and to take credit for anything they had done. They were not disassociating in 1976–77.

and little grasp of feminist thinking. One general said, "My wife and I agree that every family requires a head; . . . the children must come first, perhaps we'll have to let women officers out for five years to raise their children. . . ."[x] I'm really just not ready for one on my wing. . . ."[y] These, then, were the kinds of feelings expressed by the officers most responsible for policies affecting cadet life.

Because the cadet wing is responsible for much administration and training, it was imperative that it "accept" the women. Ordering it to do so was complicated because the administration had just embarked on a policy of positive motivation and therefore had to be positive instead of punitive, even about the acceptance of women. But the positive policy was not popular, and the staff had to use up the good will on it that it might otherwise have used on behalf of integration.[z]

To win acceptance, the command followed a well-accepted principle: make the new seem old.[a] It tried to do so by insisting that there would be "no changes" and by insisting on consistency (over time and between issues) in decision making. Perhaps officials oversold, for when changes did occur or when an inconsistency cropped up cadets were quick to complain. Or perhaps cadet complaints really stemmed from their belief that the academy administration was "on the women's side." At West Point the administration was perceived as grudgingly doing only what it must, and at Annapolis the middies knew the women would never "really" belong.

The commandant worked with academy social scientists in planning and also in documenting women's integration: the terrazzo gap shrank a bit that year. Yet while some academics were participants in integration, and a number had had training at the Race Relations Institute, others were as resistant as any of the military trainers. Part of the resistance was manifested in a refusal to change; faculty members expressed intentions to use the language they had always

[x] It is unusual to leave and reenter at the officer level, but provisions are made for pilots to do so. However, it would be very difficult to establish such a policy for women without being charged with reverse discrimination.

[y] Assignment of the first group of women pilots required some arm-twisting. Apparently many officers were not ready for a woman in their wing.

[z] The staff had decided on the new discipline system because it was trying hard to reduce attrition.

[a] It also tried to get cadets to "buy into" the program by having them assist in implementing it.

used and to appeal to cadet "machoism" as they had always done.[b] Some language was unconscious: "I have twenty students and one girl."

After June 28, 1976, no one had special responsibilities for implementing and adjusting policies concerning women. However, when worst came to worst, brave men were delighted to have a woman officer deal with the cadet mother and her mother. Still, implementation proceeded as part of the normal routine—but on two levels. On one level fine-tuning occurred. This tuning was difficult to capture for the record because it was so "natural" (e.g., women's skirts were gored and lengthened). On another level the administration changed major policies (ATO functions and billeting) in a way that demonstrated flexibility. In fact, the administration went beyond its own instincts when the various forms of feedback told it to do so. In making the changes the administration could say it was doing so because things were going "so much better, so much faster" than expected. This was not just whistling in the dark. The "so much better than expected" was generally confirmed: in one instance by an AOC (academy alumnus) who was originally pessimistic about women's capacity, and in another by a woman staff member fresh from the Pentagon and also originally dubious—in her case about men's good faith.[c]

By June 1977 many staff believed that the academy's promise that "we will do better than any other institution if we are directed to take women cadets" had been kept. Their academy had taken more women, and it had kept most of them. They recalled their apprehensions with amusement and described their past concerns as foolish. They especially credited their success to meticulous preparation, although in retrospect they believed they had, perhaps, been overly cautious and overly anticipatory. Most assumed continued success and believed that special arrangements were no longer necessary. A few believed, however, the second year would be less successful. They turned out to be correct. By the end of the second year, 33.5 percent of the women in the class of 1980 and 32.5 percent of the women from the class of 1981 had left. More embarrass-

---

[b]Mostly faculty had no women in their classes the first year, and there is reason to suppose that they might, in fact, change their language and teaching methods when women were actually in their classrooms.

[c]Both believed a "lack of negative behavior" had been achieved by the end of the first year, even if "acceptance" had not yet been accomplished.

ingly, West Point's attrition for the women of 1981 was only 21.9 percent and the Naval Academy's 14.4 percent.

Conclusions

The Air Force Academy tried hard and intelligently to carry out the integration mandate. At the end of the first year, 84 percent of the women remained. Optimism seemed justified, but those who were most confident success would continue were those who focused on how much their own attitudes had changed. For most that change was from apprehension to confidence. In particular male officers gained confidence in themselves and believed they (and male officers, generally) could manage without women's assistance and monitoring. They were relieved that no sex scandals had occurred, they believed that they had learned to deal with their chivalrous instincts, and they had overcome their fear of being manipulated. However, they had not considered the effect of rapid rotation, which meant that almost as quickly as officers learned to cope they moved on—to be replaced by new and naive personnel who would have to learn the same lessons. (By the end of the second year most of the commandant's staff had been replaced.) Nor had they considered how the women would feel as they came to realize that their status was one of being a member of a permanent and marginal minority. Women could not become rated routinely, and their number was severely limited. They were not and would not become central to the mission of the Air Force. Thus to predict continued success, one had to assume that women's morale would remain high, that their motivation would be unchanged, even in the face of such a realization.

Officials had continually expressed concern that once the women's "pioneering" spirit had diminished, they would begin to leave. Usually, they implied that pioneer women had insufficient or poor motivation. This sentiment did not quite "blame the victim," but for a woman to enroll in and survive a year at the academy, she had to be independent, individualistic, and perhaps somewhat insensitive. Her motivation might even be described as a negative: "I'll show them!"[d] If anyone (male or female) is to achieve real success, how-

[d]Women who are serious about achievement probably need these qualities to conquer any nontraditional field.

ever, a shift must eventually occur. "They" must *be* shown, and the individual must be integrated into the institution's multiple networks. She (or he) must acquire mentors, peers, and apprentices. She or he must become *inter*dependent, cooperative, and sensitive. She or he must be rewarded or anticipate being rewarded. Motivation must shift; it must acquire a positive meaning. Let me be clear: this shift is not under the individual's control; incorporation must come from the institution.[e] The question administrators had not considered, then, was whether this shift would or could be made to occur in year-two. They did not ask themselves whether they had provided sufficient positive motivation to the women, or whether they had communicated to the women that they had succeeded and could expect to continue to succeed.

"What is the women's biggest complaint?" "What changes do you think they may ask for as members of the third class?" To answer such questions requires some empathy, some attentiveness; yet very few academy officials had answers.[f] In the same way virtually no officers had answers to the question "What benefit do you see in having women at the academy?"[g] Nor could they answer the question "What are the women better at?" The point is: no one was trying to think as the women were thinking. The men were feeling comfortable and the women were still there; thus no need was seen to try to "think like a woman."[h]

However, the contrasting perceptions of cadets and administrators and of women and men should have signaled trouble to come. There is little question about the existence of contradictory understandings. They surfaced in luncheon conversation and in survey data. Where one saw discrimination, another saw reverse discrimination. Where one saw a pragmatic adjustment, another saw the violation of a promise. Where one saw achievement, another saw deficiency.

[e]In fact, academy women seemed to do their part. Women cadets seemed to internalize Academy values more fully and commit themselves to the institution more fully than men. Many of the problems of the captain first involved in planning for women derived from the intensity and literalness of her commitment.

[f]The women might not have answered very coherently themselves, and the survey data, too, might have been inconclusive. For instance, that data showed both men and women were "motivated" by jet fighter rides—but could that motivation be the same for women (who could only anticipate watching a jet fly overhead) as that experienced by men (who could anticipate *becoming* a jet fighter pilot)?

[g]One cadet observed that it made shaving in the morning worthwhile.

[h]In this mandated change, the opponents of change rather than its advocates, its beneficiaries, or neutral parties were put in charge of the change, so this attitude is not surprising.

Where women sought to demonstrate equality, men felt compelled to prove superiority.[i]

The compulsion to be superior, of course, provided men another reason for not wanting women around. If men must always be better, if they cannot be comfortable being second, or even equal, then women's presence will increase the pressure on men to perform. Indeed, the prospect of competition with women may be most unbearable for men between the ages of seventeen and twenty-two. At this age, men typically cast off the last vestiges of female authority and commit themselves to assuming responsibility and risks *for* women.

The timing of women's entrance may have exacerbated the situation in yet another way. This is probably the first generation of young white men that believes it must compete with minorities and women for career opportunities. Even if they remain advantaged, these men perceive themselves as "relatively deprived." They do so because they look to their fathers and older brothers as their models—fathers and older brothers who were mostly spared the full competition of today. Thus the men of the 1970s can feel deprived even when they remain privileged!

In Chapter 4 ("The Fishbowl") it was noted that cadets and academy personnel were used to having an audience. Much of that audience was female. Thus when women were integrated into the academy, the audience for men's performance declined.[j] Some of the ex-audience joined the performers. When this occurs previously private behavior becomes known and action becomes self-conscious. Indeed, a woman's presence has the effect of making men scrutinize their own behavior. Just as "The Emperor's New Clothes" revealed the foolishness of relying on elites and "All That Glitters" (a 1976–77 television series) revealed the absurdity of sex-stereotyped behavior by reversing male-female roles (so that a gentle, fat, male househusband was deceived and abandoned, and trim young male secretaries had their bottoms patted), so women's presence forced male cadets and officers to admit to themselves that some of their private ways were by any measure juvenile and silly. The

---

[i]An incapacity to accept being beaten by someone reveals a deep prejudice. So does an unwillingness to be represented or directed by a certain category of people.

[j]An audience gives permission and sometimes applause. When there is no audience, actors must question themselves; they require a self-justification they had not needed before. Or their performance must be so good that other actors relinquish their own presentation to watch. Thus when women enter as equals, not only is the competition doubled but the work must also be superb enough to gain an audience of fellow-workers, not of naive dependents.

women did not "dampen" men's behavior. Their presence, however, did lead men to squelch (stifle) themselves.[k]

Making women official peers raised the question whether they could become equal peers. A first-year analysis showed that, in assigning ratings, (1) peers favored their own sex and (2) doolie women received their poorest ratings from doolie men. But doolie men were supposed to be least opposed to women (general principle), no matter that they were directly competing with them (particular rivalry). In thinking about what this means, one should remember that in an environment where fierce competition is the norm, even a small amount of prejudice or discrimination can go a long way. Small but systematic bias can have a substantial impact.[l] If collective opinion is poorly disposed toward women, furthermore, women's supporters may be led to conceal their positive feelings about them. This concealment would lead to the impression that things are worse than they, in fact, are. At least one study has shown that both men and women attribute more prejudice to others than to themselves.[3] Either they are deluding themselves *or* a reservoir of good will lies untapped. Perhaps policy makers will find that they *can* go as far as their instincts allow, that they should not assume that others are more conservative than they.

Peer acceptance (or lack of it) may have another interesting effect. As noted before, at least one study has shown that as men are promoted within the military they become happier and happier with their peer support. As women are promoted, they seem to become more and more unhappy.[4] One explanation of this phenomenon is that with promotion women lose peers, while men gain new and "better" ones. As women rise, then, any benefits they have derived from "sisterhood" decrease. It seems women in the military are just too few, too marginal, and too much on trial to routinely enjoy any success they may have.[m] Even the most admired women have an

[k]In *Thinking About Women* (p. 190) Mary Ellman points out that no group "steadily scrutinized by another can afford to be open." Until recently men have been open because they have not felt themselves scrutinized by another group. As women entered the men's group, women still remained "outsiders" in one sense, but in another they became close enough to scrutinize, and men may have begun to be less open.

[l]For instance, even if women are treated objectively, how can they compete in an environment if it is "pro-men"? The point is that even if "anti-women" behavior ceases, women cannot compete if positive behavior (i.e., "sponsorship," "patronage," "adoption") favors men. Even if women are guilty of the equally prejudiced favoring of women, its effect is fully cancelled because women represent such a small part of the military population.

[m]In fact, in the absence of women peers, some women become suspicious of or anti-women. They identify with men's views and spend most of their time in men's company,

existence different from that of their male peers. In numerous ways they pay a higher price for their success and receive a smaller reward.

At the academy, women cadets were probably pushed closer to their physical limit and subjected to more individual harassment than were men cadets. And as they looked into the future, they saw no women in the air, few in command, and none who were mothers. Even the "superwomen" seemed to be failing relative to their peers. For example, one of the first woman (Navy) pilots rated a photo and a headline story when she resigned after fewer than four years of flying. The article pointed out that although 60 percent of all service women who become pregnant continue to serve, "this kind" of resignation raised questions about increasing the number of women, investing in them, and widening their opportunities. Some time later, in a one-paragraph, nonheadlined item, the same newspaper carried a second story in which the woman officer explained her decision. It was based, she said, on her *limited* career opportunities. As she had "succeeded" during the previous three-and-one-half years, she found herself falling behind her male peers. While they had logged some fifteen to sixteen hundred hours of flying time, she had been able to put in only eleven to twelve hundred because of Navy restrictions. Her costs and benefits clearly differed from theirs.

But men felt special constraints too. They expected not just to be independent but to have dependents. In their estimation women always had the choice between being independent and *being* dependent and not *having* dependents. Men found it hard to believe that a pregnant woman would not find some way of escaping an incurred military obligation. Also, young men who are susceptible to the appeal to masculinity used in recruitment brochures may later find that they have been gradually entrapped in a career they did not fully comprehend at the time they began it. The decorum taught to cadets until 1976 included treating "the fairer sex with special consideration." "Historically, the term 'lady' was used by a person of inferior social station; . . . it is . . . a sign of the special courtesies due them."[n] This training left no room for women as peers or superiors. What one learned from mothers, big sisters, little sisters, or dates

---

and thereby avoid isolation. They do not necessarily gain acceptance, and some pay the price of self-hatred.

[n]"Lady" conveys superiority no longer. According to one woman cadet, both ladies and gentlemen are "half" people. Their being depends on each other, and the words are mostly used together. She claimed that, in contrast, women and men refer to whole human beings.

did not apply either. Adult men had just never considered following a woman, and they had probably not tried to lead them in instrumental activities either.

The upshot seems to be that for the Air Force Academy "success" lay more in maintaining than in changing. In a required behavioral science course, cadets were taught that change (whether by Chinese communists, Roman Catholic sisters, or U.S. fraternity men) comes about by (1) unfreezing, (2) identifying/internalizing, and (3) refreezing. However, the academy's policies toward change seemed to rely *only* on contact as a strategy. Accordingly, during the first year any less-than-optimum results were attributed to either the need to let the four-year cycle run its course so no one with memories of other years would be around, or women's separate billeting. Some officials were concerned about male-female competition for the same positions, but for the most part, role and number restrictions for women were assumed rather than questioned; for the most part, a male cadet enhanced peer-esteem (and maybe self-esteem) by opposing women instead of by aligning with them.

Interdependence was not created. Women doolies had no rewards to give in return for acceptance, and they had few allies or sponsors. No one could quite imagine them "grown-up." Instead, the women seemed to be judged for what they were or had been, while the men seemed to be valued for their "promise," for what they would become. It was understood that the young men had much to do and learn before they were complete. With the women it was different. It was almost as though the double standard of aging led young women to deny rather than plan for their middle years, and led men to think of them chivalrously, as they presently were rather than as they would be.°

By June 1977, men at the academy understood that *they* had come a long way. Women realized there was a long way yet to go. The Air Force officer who said "This is history!" and the West Point documents that called 1976–77 "revolutionary" may have struck the right tone. However, history is never complete, and the revolution has not yet come to pass.

°Aging is said to cost women more.

Reflections on
Women and Combat

In 1976–77 public attention was drawn to the Air Force Academy's efforts to comply with a Congressionally mandated change— women's integration. Those efforts were not entirely successful, probably because of the change Congress did *not* mandate. Equal opportunity, treatment, and experience cannot be achieved when the participation of one group (in this case women) is numerically restricted (in this case to approximately 10 percent), and when that same group is denied routine access to the organization's most valued role (in the Air Force, that of pilot). Both of these restrictions followed from Congress's failure to change a legislative prohibition against the use of women in combat aircraft. And that failure derived from Congress's desire to avoid addressing the question "Should women serve in combat?"[a]

Indeed, few Americans seem to be interested in reasoning about this issue, even those who sometimes must do so. Those who ordinarily oppose all female exclusion often beg off by saying no one, male or female, should have to engage in combat. Others wonder

[a]Sometimes questions are more interesting than their answers. F.M.H. Bradley begins his *Ethical Studies* by asking "Why should I be moral?" Then, instead of pursuing an answer, he probes the meaning of the question itself, concluding that it is an inherently immoral question.

that there can be serious debate about legislating women's presence in or absence from combat when circumstances, not lawmakers, so often determine who participates in that regularly occurring activity, war. Mostly, the question is asked rhetorically by those who believe that "the battlefield is no place for a woman" or that women's participation "just isn't right." Their conviction is strong. Indeed, it is so strong they often find it hard to amplify their argument, so persuaded are they of the absurdity of an affirmative answer. Yet they are forced to ask the question by pressures arising from (1) women's demands for legal equality, (2) recruiting difficulties associated with the all-volunteer force, and (3) the continuing civilianization of a peacetime, technology-based military.[b]

Instead of seeking an answer to the question, then, let us explore why it is asked, why so many find it absurd, and why a few find a men-only combat policy equally absurd.

Why Does the Question Arise?

The most obvious, but not necessarily the most important, question posing is done by feminist groups committed to the desanctification of male sanctuaries. One aspect of feminism includes refusing to be excluded. If it is not "natural" for women to do certain things, it is argued, no laws are required to prohibit women from doing them.[1] Or without actually advocating an androgynous world, feminists may grasp Rousseau's understanding that freedom is experienced only through participation in the General Will; or they may sense that Kant's pursuit of the categorical and Hegel's pursuit of unity demonstrate the inequity, unhappiness, and alienation inherent in separateness. On the other hand, being human, feminists have not always understood (and if they have understood, have not always accepted) all the implications of the equal and similar treatment they seek.

A second reason the combat question arises is that the abolition of the draft in July 1973 made military recruitment difficult. The Volunteer Army, produced by an alliance of libertarians, liberals unsympathetic to the military, and others pragmatic about the consequences of drafting too many young men opposed to the war, has

---

[b]While interrogative in form, the question is more like a plaint thrown up (like a pressure-induced crack on a lake's frozen surface) as strong forces move in opposition.

relied upon recruiting techniques that emphasize career, vocation, or both. The military has always provided some recruits with an upward mobility and others with a security they would not otherwise have known. Education and employment are military benefits, but they are also opportunities—the kind of opportunities to which women in this country now lay full claim. In the early 1970s, women's claims coincided with a lack of interest in the military on the part of men. Even though the military improved the economic inducements associated with service, male recruits were in short supply and had scored lower on aptitude tests than the military thought desirable.

When an opportunity is opened to women, the recruitment pool is (at least theoretically) doubled; also, its new members are likely to have comparatively modest economic expectations. Women's entrance into a labor market, then, changes that market for the men already there. In the case of the military, however, new opportunity was made only partially available. Because federal law and/or policy still prohibits women's use in combat, they are kept out of certain units and career patterns. Indeed, present plans are to keep the military about 89 percent male.[2] Women's "opportunity," then, will be to compete for 11 percent of the jobs. Also, by definition women cannot obtain the experience that is the essence of their organization's purpose. Therefore, even though the armed services are "integrated," women's opportunities for advancement and command remain limited; conversely, men's chances of entering combat are increased in proportion to the extent that women take over the non-combat slots. To the ambitious male professional, both results might be welcome. To those who wish to be in the military but prefer long odds against actually seeing combat, women's entrance has a less welcome effect. This phenomenon was made evident when World War II women's recruitment posters that used the "replace a man" slogan were withdrawn. Men did not want to be released to combat, and women felt guilty releasing them.[3]

The prohibition against assigning Navy women to combat ships (not combat) has been tested in the courts by women who argued that the combat ship restriction limited their career development.[4] Also, men in the military (like their civilian counterparts) are beginning to express concern about "reverse discrimination." None has yet resorted to litigation to force those who share rank and salary to share risk as well, but such action will undoubtedly occur; and since the President and the Congress have been reluctant to decide the combat issue, the Supreme Court may be the institution ultimately forced to give the military its marching orders. Congress did not provide a military exemption for women in the Equal Rights Amendment, but it also did *not* provide for women's use in combat when it admitted them to the military academies. The White House asked that women be eligible for honor guard duty there, but it left standing a nearly prohibitive height requirement. No one seems willing to answer the question of women's suitability for combat; still, questions continue to arise.

Finally, the increasingly constabulary nature of the military, as well as its "civilianization," makes women in uniform more acceptable today than they were to a military symbolized by the traditional hero of World War II, who won ground victories overseas and returned to Washington, D.C., for a homecoming parade celebrated with a giant fireworks display at the foot of the Washington Monument.[5] The military role and image have become quite different in the 1970s.

"It Just Isn't Right"

The view that the combat question has only one possible answer is widely and strongly held; it must be taken seriously. It must be fully examined, even if doing so requires teasing out sensible arguments from seemingly impenetrable bombast.[6]

The principal theme of those opposing women in combat is that women should not be subjected to the sufferings of war. Because Americans have not fought a war on U.S. soil for over one hundred years, we are peculiarly susceptible to this argument. Our experience has been that men pack their bags and travel long distances in order to "go to war." Women stay home. They are exempt from war's horrors. Thus command personnel are serious when they argue against the use of women because "they should not suffer," and "they especially should not suffer the ordeal of being a Prisoner of War [POW]." An extension of the POW argument offered by some commanders is that they not only wish to avoid the ravishing of women but that they also worry about how such ravishment would affect the judgment of military commanders. Further, some worry that the likelihood of public anguish, were women made POWs, is good and sufficient cause for keeping them out of combat altogether.

But is women's suffering so special and does it affect men so much? Or is it possible that women actually find female distress more distressing than do men, if only for empathic reasons? Is it not possible, moreover, that men's aversion to women's suffering is based on their feeling that a suffering woman implies men's failure to be protective? Thus the pain men feel may derive not from sympathy but from a feeling of failure.

The fact, of course, is that in war men on both sides terribly and regularly hurt women on the other side. Half the victims in any war are "noncombatants"—largely women, children, and the elderly. Quite obviously, a desire to avoid hurting women does not control men's behavior. At best, men do not want "their" women hurt. In fact, men do not object to having women in combat so much as they object to having women on *their* side. This is important. It means that even if some women are physically able and are so moved by logic or by their sense of justice as to insist upon sharing war's risk, their offer will probably be refused. Men do not want women's assistance in the waging of war.

But chivalry is not the only reason men are reluctant to have women fighting by their side. In extremis they do not want to depend on individuals whom they perceive as small and weak. Probably everyone in combat would be comforted by compatriots larger and stronger than they, and men's chances of having a (physically) bigger "buddy" do increase if women are eliminated as combatants. Nevertheless, physical size is not required for combat effectiveness.

We have been taught this fact by the biblical story of David and Goliath and by the small enemies of our past (the Japanese and Vietnamese for example); this we know, too, from the technological nature of our warfare. At present, women may be less competent than men to handle some military equipment, mainly because it is now built for a male "standard." A redesigning of military equipment, then, might greatly enhance women's performance.

More important to victory than size is organization, cooperation, pooled effort.[7] Relatively small and weak but well-motivated men have always fought effectively. One might think that women, too, if properly equipped and integrated into military units, could be effective as combatants. However, some argue strongly that mixed-sex units *by definition* cannot achieve cohesiveness.[8] On the one hand, the presence of women is said to produce rivalry and jealousy between male group members; on the other hand, it is argued that men *can* maintain their unity, but to do so they must isolate the women.[9] It is argued, further, that women necessarily provoke chivalrous behavior, which cannot be tolerated in combat for reasons of safety and morale (the latter eroding with the application of any double standard). The crux of these arguments is that women should not be in combat because their presence will adversely affect men. The problem, then, would seem to lie either with the men, or with their leader's inability to fuse a heterogeneous group of individuals into an effective, purposeful unit.

There is, I suspect, another motive underpinning these arguments against the use of women in combat. Think for one moment of a male versus female tennis match.[10] The male usually wins. Often women are thought to hold back, to deliberately fail to win (even if only subconsciously). A less investigated but surely operative tension is the male's strong need not to be beaten by a woman. Almost certainly this need stimulates him to at least try to demonstrate his superiority. Now if one competitor's goal is to demonstrate competence or equality, while the other's is to demonstrate superiority, the former will probably be disadvantaged in the competition. The fact is that the two are not playing the same game at all. How might this difference affect their combat performance? If men feel a special pressure to beat women opponents, an all-male force facing an all-female or mixed-sex unit might outdo itself. To the motives felt equally by both sides would be added the negative motive of not wanting to be beaten by women. This new motive could lead men to accept excessive losses. It is easy to see that soldiers might wish to avoid giving such an incentive to their enemies. After all, they would not want to encourage their foes to an "unnatural" effort; clearly all soldiers prefer an enemy who has the option of surrendering to one who prefers death. All this means that *both* sides would wish to prevent women's serving with them.[11]

Arguments with a larger frame of reference are sometimes made against women's serving in combat. In discussing the volunteer Army, Margaret Mead has said there is no society that places women in offensive warfare. She argues that women may be too vicious and too violent for combat because they have traditionally wielded weapons only in immediate defense of the home.[12] There, a last-ditch, no-holds-barred behavior may be appropriate, but it is completely inappropriate to the ritualized form of warfare that must be practiced if the human race is to survive. Men, Mead insists, are schooled, disciplined, and trained to obey certain rules of the game—rules that check unrestrained destruction. Men do not fight to the finish; they fight to establish hierarchy and to create order.

Therefore, they can be trusted to use violence, because they will
also stop using it at an appropriate time.

George H. Quester, who begins his recent study with the same
observation—that women have always been associated with defensive warfare—has explored the propaganda effect of using women
in combat. He argues that this effect is associated not only with
being the underdog but also with a fierce commitment to the justness
of one's cause. Thus to put women into combat roles could be to
signal the defensive nature of one's activity.[13] (Others concerned
with images might argue that while this action signals determination, it also signals desperation.) The point is: the use of women
may convey a significant message. However, if women are deployed randomly, in combat and support roles, their use will no
longer signal an intensity of commitment. If there is no differentia-
tion in their use, an enemy will have to find another way to determine an adversary's tactics. To the degree that the enemy must infer
an adversary's intent, the capacity for tacit communication and con-
comitant tacit bargaining may be reduced.[14]

A different argument against assigning women to combat was
made in the Hoover Commission's report following World War II.
There the position was taken that women might, indeed, be trained
to think and act as men but that to so train them might seriously alter
society's equilibrium, which depends upon a male-female or rather
a military-nonmilitary balance.[15] This view accords well with a conception of a healthy whole as composed of opposites. It also
launches us into that slippery area of discussion that concerns "masculinity" and "femininity."

Experts state that an individual's gender identification is deep and
stable.[16] Still, there is also a fear lest women "lose their femininity"
by participating with men in men's activities. But this fear is not
expressed by the women involved, their identification is secure, and
they do not feel they lose it by doing something new; nevertheless,
they are perceived as losing something by others. By whom, and
why does it matter? It seems to matter principally to male observers,
perhaps because their own sense of identity, which is partially defined by being opposite, is affected. They are thrown into disarray
when what is supposed to be opposite becomes like. Part of the
answer must be, then, that men feel they lose their masculinity when
women do what they do.[c] In fact, they are not just worried about

---

[c]In the case of women and men, imitation is *not* thought to be the highest form of flattery.
In fact, when women act like men they are not called "manly" but castrating—man-destroy-

women and their "femininity"; they are worried about themselves and their "masculinity."

There is a curious difference between what is labeled "masculine" and "feminine" behavior. Women are their most passive, dependent, ornamental, in short, "feminine," in the presence of men. Women mostly make decisions, work, and study in men's absence. Thus when women behave competently in a mixed-sex milieu (as they do when supervising a home remodeling job or a junior high ski trip, for instance), they can understand themselves as acting "naturally." Because women often act this way (although usually not in a man's presence), they experience no sense of "loss of femininity." However, men who usually see women only socially (e.g., when they are being their most "feminine") often do not understand that women can be quite comfortable in effective roles, even if those roles make men uncomfortable.

With men the situation seems to be reversed. While they are gentlemanly in the presence of women, men are more likely to consider themselves *really* men in all-male groups. There they demonstrate their relative strength, take risks, brag, and too often behave as if out of control. Since men's horseplay, foul language, and overindulgence diminish in the presence of women, men regard sex integration as inhibiting and even emasculating. Thus if men feel they "lose their masculinity" in mixed-sex groups, it may be natural for them to attribute (erroneously) a comparable feeling to women.[d]

How might these phenomena affect the capacity of men and women to serve in combat? Women's effectiveness is apparently increased when they behave as they would in an all-female group. If resources, supplies, respect, challenge, and all other items were equal, women might conceivably perform better in an all-female unit. For them, the advantage of the mixed-sex unit would be that "all other items" would more likely be equal. For men, some argue, the effect would be different. They aver that men are more realistic and effective in a mixed group that tempers machoism and braggadocio with responsibility. However, in combat the irrational, sacrificial, non-face-losing emotional drive to show oneself "a man among men" can produce acts of outrageous valor that might be lost

---

ing. There seems to be no equivalent for "castrating" as applied by women to men who fill women's roles. Women's identity does not seem to depend on men's; women may scorn men who behave as they do, but they do not feel themselves mutilated.

[d]Women may also feel increased inhibitions in a mixed-sex group, but the direction of change is toward enhanced femininity. The key may be that both men and women feel compelled to be their "distinctive" selves before the more-valued male audience.

in a mixed group.[17] Thus if the antics of a hero often look foolish, even childish, to the practical-minded, men might be less heroic (masculine) in the presence of women. They might reduce their flamboyant and sacrificial behavior and thus end the noble acts that cost the individual too much but that drive combat forward. While integrated combat might enhance women's performance by offering equal circumstances, it might at the same time diminish the hyper-military performance of men.

Let us examine some possible reasons for this phenomenon by first supposing that men need to feel masculine and women feminine. If a women's femininity, her uniqueness, lies in her capacity to bear children, she needs to demonstrate that capacity only once. That demonstration will be absolutely definitive: good for all time and for all audiences.[e] Because proof of fatherhood is unsure, proof of manhood is more difficult. The only unique role men have had in society is a social one—that of warrior—a role that is risky, unpleasant, and often short in duration. During peacetime modern men lack a specific way of proving that they are men. There is no initiative feat, no lion to kill and pelt to wear that proves them. Instead, they must continually show (in inconclusive ways) both that they are adult and that they are not women. Women's singularity is clear; men's, problematical. In fact, because evidence of masculinity is ephemeral and fragile, men may depend on women's not being the same as they. Indeed, it may be that women are clearly defined and men are the other, the second sex. Perhaps to "find themselves," men require women's "otherness."

Were women to enter combat, men would lose a crucial identity—warrior. This is the only role now exclusively theirs, the one that is as male-defining as child-bearing is female-defining. In fact, as noted in the Introduction, if the role of warrior no longer defined "a man," its undesirability might become so apparent that men would no longer accept it!

Because we have recently fought our wars on others' territory, we have tended to forget a final and practical reason for not sending women into combat, a reason related to the sexes' separate functions. Many lives are lost in a war. New lives can, of course, be created, but one woman can seldom bear more than one new child each year, while one male can father five, ten, twenty, even fifty

---

[e]Even if a woman chooses not to have children, her assumed potential for doing so distinguishes her from all men.

children a year. As any herder knows, many females are required to replenish a population; only a few males are needed. Women, then, may simply be too valuable to society to risk their being squandered in combat.[18]

Implications of a Men-Only Combat Policy

Many of the arguments against letting women participate in combat seem, at first, silly, sexist, and advantageous to women. However, if women insist upon sharing in the military, they must remember that they are asking for a radical change, change that, among other things, will disorient men and deprive them of their only unique role. Nevertheless, the most radical aspect of the change may not be women's participation in combat but their final, long-delayed acceptance as full citizens.[19]

Even though U.S. women received the vote some fifty years ago, they have not participated much in governing. One explanation might be that the government pleases them as it is. A second could be that voting is not a very important part of the political process and does not lead to participation in governance. A third could be that governmental participation comes only after participation (or at least eligibility or liability for participation) in the state's unique function, the exercise of society's legitimate force.[20]

Citizenship has never been defined as simply being subject to a state's jurisdiction. Historically, citizenship has been based on what one contributes to the state. The two principal contributions have been the payment of taxes and service in the military. Owning property was long a basis for the right to vote, in spite of Benjamin Franklin's questioning who it was that *had* the vote if a man could lose his suffrage upon the death of his valuable mule.

Voting has also been closely associated with military service. During the Civil War, male slaves joined northern military forces and used that contribution as an important part of their pressure to gain both their freedom and the vote. Women's claims to legal rights have also been most successful after war service. In both the U.S. and the U.K., women's suffrage followed World War I; in France, World War II marked an important shift in the direction of equality for women. In developing countries like Algeria, rights have sometimes been bestowed on women in a postwar era of gratitude, even though the culture was not, in fact, ready for the change.[21] Even today many aliens find that the easiest way to obtain American citizenship is to join the U.S. military. Conversely, a quick way to lose one's citizenship is to serve in the military of another country.

The close link between formal citizenship and military participation becomes more obvious if one remembers that the exercise of legitimate (approved) force is the unique function of the state, and that for two reasons, democracy of some kind has almost become the only manageable form of government. First, complex, interdependent technological states require at least the passive cooperation of all citizens. A small percentage of resisting citizens can easily paralyze an industrial nation. Any organization, in fact, depends on the consent of its members and works to encourage as much of their support as possible. Even so, few large organizations enjoy an active membership as large as 10 percent, and any one of them would collapse or at least change drastically if as much as 10 percent of its membership actively opposed its policies.

The special problem that confronts a government is that few citizens can quit or conveniently leave. Room must be found within the system for all, including opponents. Now, democracy has never been adopted simply because it is a "good" system of governing, nor has it ever been adopted whole. Instead, it has been built piece by piece to accommodate new power not incorporated in previous governmental mechanisms. Churchill's assertion that democracy was to be valued if only because it works better than anything else suggests democracy's crucial function—it establishes mechanisms (e.g., voting) that serve as ritual tests, as trials by ordeal, as ways of choosing sides and estimating relative strength both as to numbers and as to intensity of purpose.[22]

Intensity of purpose does count. It can be demonstrated by money, time, self-sacrifice, or by a potential for violent action. The last element is important, and women who are seldom collectively and legally violent may not realize the politically limiting consequences of their inaction: women have no credibility with regard to the use of force. They are believed to have no capacity for forceful insistence *or* retaliation. Because they are *de facto* pacifists, they wholly lack a crucial political weapon. To illustrate, on a U.S. Marine base a Ku Klux Klan chapter must expect attack.[23] But would any male group consciously or subconsciously organized to promote male supremacy ever dream of having to defend itself physically? Such groups find little need to defend themselves even verbally. Few politicians worry that membership in prestigious clubs that discriminate against women will hurt their careers. Indeed, women can be and are ignored regularly and with impunity. Moreover, men who ally themselves with women are often ridiculed and sometimes punished for doing so.[24]

This discrimination does not "just happen." Women have been deliberately and legally excluded from society's legitimate, organized, planned, rewarded, technological use of force, that is, the force applied by the police and the military. Sometimes it is suggested that women will not use force. Yet in 1977 more women are said to have killed their husbands than vice versa, and the Symbionese Liberation Army women dominated the F.B.I.'s "Ten Most Wanted" list for some time. Individually and illegally, then, women do use force. But society clearly does not want them to use *its* force. Perhaps this seeming contradiction does represent the collective oppression of one sex by the other, just as rape is said to be a "conscious process of intimidation by which all men keep all women in a state of fear."[25] The placing of all weaponry in the hands of men may be an equally intimidating policy. When women are "protected" by a group of men with weapons but are not permitted to have weapons themselves, the result does begin to sound like a protection racket. Charlotte Perkins Gilman vividly describes the dilemma for women:

> A stalwart man once sharply contested my claim to this
> [my] freedom to go alone. "Any true man," he said with
> fervor, "is always ready to go with a woman at night.
> He is her natural protector." "Against what?" I inquired.
> As a matter of fact, the thing a woman is most afraid to
> meet on a dark street is her natural protector.[26]

In this country the civilian government and the military have long worked in harmony. The armed services take direction from civilians appointed by an elected official. In the abstract this relationship may seem unusual; in the concrete it *is* unusual, for in many countries the military *is* the government. If women are barred from the military, they are barred from government as well. This holds true in revolutionary governments (Algeria) as well as in reactionary ones (Franco's Spain.)[27] After all, just what is the position of the unarmed in an armed society? How many and what kind of people voluntarily choose such a position? What are the chances of rejecting that status when it is imposed on one?

If one rejects the possibility that men keep women unarmed in men's own interest, one might want to ask if the taboo is related to women's role as primary child-rearer. Is it possible that society attempts to inhibit all use of force by those who raise defenseless infants and young children just as it encourages chivalry in armed men? Or is force the ultimate sanction even in this most intimate and apparently protecting relationship? After all, even the gentlest parent is *able* to physically control a child, and even God's omnipotence is as crucial to His definition as His omniscience. Perhaps the issue centers on mothering, but in a different way. That both women and men are raised almost exclusively by women may lead to a shared understanding that one is grown up, one becomes an adult, when one no longer submits to female authority. Thus women are not given command over grownups, nor are they given the weapons that would enable them to command.[28]

Or does men's use of force *depend* on women's not using it? Women die in war whether in Holocaust or Hiroshima.[29] Is it possible that their "innocent" victimization justifies men's military action? Does offering protection justify more aggressive behavior than self-interest would permit? Did the ancient holding of hostages make war's cost more concrete for policy makers than they are for our policy makers now? Do civilians, and particularly women, give both justification and "permission" to defense and foreign-policy planners? Do they give informed consent? Or does their consent, in fact, depend on their profound ignorance—on their *not* being well informed about the costs of war and the military's inability to guarantee protection?

Further, is it not ironic that women are more excluded in peace than in war? Yet it is peacetime service that would enable them to (1) defend themselves, (2) accept responsibility and command should war develop, and (3) enjoy a satisfying career even if no war were to occur.

Accepting liability to participate in the legitimate use of violence may be required of all who wish to be full-fledged citizens—those who not only ratify decisions by voting but also those who stand for (represent) others. If one is to represent, one must advocate and do so effectively; one's electors (or appointer) must have confidence. But to win this confidence, must women become like men? Not necessarily. First, there have always been small groups (e.g., Quakers) that have deliberately refused to participate in any violent activity, individual or collective, legal or illegal. Because of the strength and longevity of their commitment, they have won respect; they seem not to have been excessively exploited, and they can and do exercise moral and political leadership. But their resistance to violence has been active, not passive. Their social concern and their participation have been consistent and strong. They have not abandoned the use of power; rather, they employ a different kind of power.[30] Women, too, might choose to exercise nonviolent power, but they are unlikely to do so unless they also assume positions that require them to be responsible and effective. Only when they *can* exercise power will women fully evaluate how they wish to do so.

Perhaps more important, when women become eligible to be warriors, when they take on this male-only role, men will no longer be able to use it to define themselves. They may then drop that role. Possibly a new "unique" role will then emerge for men, or men may usurp roles hitherto considered feminine, such as infant nurturing. Whichever, when the role of the warrior is no longer exclusively masculine, much of its luster will be lost. Then its social function can be better evaluated. Perhaps "warrior" will become an age role, one that marks the entrance to adulthood for both males and females. Or possibly the value of communication and cooperation will continue to be enhanced, and the old "male" violence will be redefined as "plain" violence and be gradually disapproved. Indeed, it may be that the real root of the opposition to women in combat stems from men's subconscious belief that women's presence would ultimately lead to the abolition of arms as a profession.

Appendix I

Air Force Ranks, Insignia, and Career Progression

General of the Air Force: five silver stars
General: four silver stars
Lieutenant General: three silver stars
Major General: two silver stars
Brigadier General: one silver star
Colonel: silver eagle
Lieutenant Colonel: silver oak leaf
Major: gold oak leaf
Captain: two silver bars
First Lieutenant: silver bar
Second Lieutenant: gold bar

Although retired by 1976, Jeanne Holm was the first Air Force woman to reach the rank of major general. In December of that year women line officers included one general, 4 colonels, 36 lieutenant colonels, 82 majors, 558 captains, 560 first lieutenants, and 467 second lieutenants. To put these numbers in perspective, on the Air Force Academy's academic faculty and staff alone there were between 15 and 20 men who were colonels, 40 to 50 lieutenant colonels, and 175 to 200 majors.

Advancement from second to first lieutenant and from first lieutenant to captain requires two two-year periods.[a] The first rigorous screening occurs after approximately eleven years of service, when an individual is considered for promotion to major. Some 70 percent

[a]The changing needs of the Air Force affect both the time-in-grade before an officer becomes eligible for promotion and the percentages of officers selected for promotion.

are promoted the first time they are eligible, while 5 percent receive an early promotion. Promotion to lieutenant colonel occurs after approximately sixteen years of service. About 60 percent of the first-time eligible officers are promoted. Five years later the selection to colonel is made; about 35 percent are successful. Promotion to brigadier general can occur soon thereafter. However, only 1 percent of the eligible colonels become generals each year.

While approximately one-third of Air Force officers are pilots, 90 percent of generals are pilots. In addition, most generals have served in a combat theater during active hostilities and have held command positions.[b]

[b]For further discussion see Franklin D. Margiotta, "Making it in the Air Force: Officer Perceptions of Career Progression." Note also that 80 percent of the officers sampled by Margiotta believed that brigadier general selectees enjoyed "sponsorship," i.e., that one or more senior officers assisted them by having them assigned to appropriate and responsible positions.

Appendix II
West Point Training in Preparation for Women's Entrance

October 1975	Lecture to class of 1977, "Management of Army Women."
October 1975-February 1976	Briefings at company, battalion, and regimental levels by women staff officers.
November and December 1975	Superintendent, commandant and dean's combined briefings, classes of 1976, 1977, 1978, 1979.
December 1975	Information packet with superintendent's and commandant's letters to each cadet.
January 1976-March 1976	Upper class participation in and observation of Project 60.
March 1976-April 1976	Upper class participation in Project 60A.
March 1976	Class of 1977 briefing on Project 60 and CBT (Cadet Basic Training).
March 1976	Class of 1977 human relations training.
March 1976	Thirty-six class of 1977 cadets observe Army women in basic training.
March 1976	Human Relations Training.
April 1976	Project 60 findings and CBT planning update—class of 1977—by regiment.

May 1976	Briefing to CBT cadet detail on plans and philosophy by Colonel West.
May 1976	Lecture to classes of 1977 and 1979 on "Human Sexuality Relating to Women at West Point" by Dr. Evalyn Gendel.
June 1976	Eight hours of human relations training—CBT detail by small groups led by one man officer, and one woman officer and one trained cadet counselor for each of the eight groups training at one time.
June 1976	Two-hour presentation to CBT detail— "Female Physiology and Reproduction/Menstruation—Fact and Fantasy/Common Gynecological concerns"—Dr. Pettit (MEDDAC).
June and July 1976	Two hours on stress and the psychology of the adolescent, five hours on counseling and communications skills, and two hours on counseling programs for CBT during cadet preparation training for CBT.
June 1976	Twelve cadets volunteered to spend two weeks at Fort McClellan, Alabama, to work with units training women.
July 1976	One-hour presentation to class of 1980 (new cadets) on stress and counseling in CBT by Major Prince and class of 1977 cadet counselors.
July 1976	Orientation to sick call, physiology, sex hygiene, and common reproductive systems concerns —to class of 1980 by Dr. Servis and Dr. Pettit.
July 1976	Two-hour briefing/discussion, class of 1980 on "Stress and the Detail Change" by officers and class of 1977 cadet counselors.

August 1976	Presentation to class of 1979 at Camp Buckner on CBT—"Rumor Control" and the CBT experience of the new cadet—by class of 1977 Basic Cadet Training cadet detail staff and Colonel West, CBT commander.
August 1976	Four hours of seminars on group progress and adjustment to regular letter company to class of 1980 by officers and cadet counselors.
August and September 1976	Report on class of 1980 and academic year plans to upperclassmen in newly reorganized companies—given by cadet commanders and officer regimental commanders.
July-August 1976	Five enlisted women trained and completed Cadet Field Training at Camp Buckner with 5th Company. All were volunteers who had just completed Basic Training at Fort Jackson.

Based on Alan G. Vitters and Nora Scott Kinzer, *Report of the Admission of Women to the United States Military Academy* (West Point, N.Y.: USMA, Department of Behavioral Science and Leadership, 2 September 1977, Inclosure 3, pp. 4–7).

Appendix III

A Partial Air Force Academy Organization Chart

Focusing on Units and Personnel Relating to the Admission of Women, 1976–77

SUPERINTENDENT
Lt. Gen. James R. Allen

Staff

Directorate of Information
Lt. Col. John Price

Directorate of Plans & Programs
Lt. Col. Robert Hess

Inspector General
Col. L. G. Jackson

Directorate of Protocol
Maj. D. Caffrey

Cadet Clinic
Col. L. J. Kirschner

Command Chaplain
Col. J. E. Townsend

Directorate of Historical Studies
Mr. Henry S. Fellerman

Judge Advocate
Lt. Col. M. H. Knutson

Faculty

Dean of the Faculty
Brig. Gen. William T. Woodyard

Vice Dean
Lt. Col. Diane Ordez

Counseling and Scheduling
Lt. Col. Warren Simmons

Academic Departments
Behavioral Sciences and Leadership
Col. John Williams, Chair
Dr. Lois De Fleur, Distinguished
Visiting Professor

USAF Academy Prep School
Commander
Col. Ben Pollard

Office of Admissions and Registrar
Director
Lt. Col. Warren Simmons

Director of Evaluation
Mr. R. J. Westen

Directorate of Cadet Counseling
Maj. L. E. Taber

Cadets

Commandant of Cadets
Brig. Gen. Stanley C. Beck

Vice-Commandant
Col. James P. McCarthy

Deputy Commandant for Military
Instruction
Col. W. J. Breckner

Deputy Commandant for the Cadet
Wing
Col. S. R. Musser

Staff Management
Maj. Ken Redding
Capt. Judy Galloway
(Capt. Helen Minor)

Air Officers Commanding
Groups 1–4 with ten squadrons
each

Air Training Officers

Cadet Wing Media
Maj. Dennis Weedle

Athletics

Director of Athletics
Col. John C. Clune

Physical Education
Col. Robert Strickland, Head
Deputy Head
Lt. Col. P. F. Arata
Instruction
Maj. Gene Miranda
Capt. Maxine King
Intramurals
Capt. P. K. Maruyama
Evaluation
Maj. R. W. Baughman
Research
Col. James Thomas

Appendix IV
Organization of Service Academies'
Student Bodies

United States Air Force Academy

Element	$= \sim 6$ people
Flight	$= 4$ elements
Squadron	$= 4$ flights
Group	$= 10$ squadrons
Cadet Wing	$= 4$ groups

United States Military Academy

Squad	$= \sim 8{-}10$ people
Platoon	$= 3$ squads
Company	$= 3$ platoons
Battalion	$= 3$ companies
Regiment	$= 3$ battalions
Corps of Cadets	$= 4$ regiments

United States Naval Academy

Squad	$= \sim 10$ people
Platoon	$= 3$ squads
Company	$= 3{-}4$ platoons
	(~ 125 people)
Battalion	$= 6$ companies
Regiment	$= 3$ battalions
Cadet Brigade	$= 2$ regiments

Notes

Introduction

1. As quoted by Pete Hamil in "The Cult of Amelia Earhart," *Ms.*, 3:3 (September 1976):90.

Chapter 1

1. Title VIII, *Department of Defense Appropriation Authorization Act.*, sect. 803 (a) and (c) (89 *Stat.* 537), *Pub. L.* 94–106 (H.R. 6674), 7 October 1975. Reference is to 10 *USC* 4342.
2. U.S. Congress, Senate, Concurrent Resolution Relating to the Denial of Admission of Women to Service Academies, S. Con. R. 71, 118 *Cong. Rec.* 10425, 28 March 1972.
3. U.S. Congress, House, Statement of Secretary of the Army, Howard H. Callaway, *Hearings on H.R. 9832, et al. before Subcommittee No. 2 of the House Committee on Armed Services*, 93rd Cong., 2nd sess., 1974, p. 165.
4. Ibid., p. 174.
5. Ibid.
6. Testimony of Army Vice Chief of Staff, Gen. Fred C. Weyand, *Hearings on H.R. 9832*, p. 177.
7. Callaway, p. 201.
8. Weyand, p. 177.
9. Callaway, pp. 197–98.
10. Weyand, p. 205.
11. Statement of U.S. Air Force Academy Superintendent, Lt. Gen. A. P. Clark, *Hearings on H.R. 9832*, p. 136.
12. Ibid., p. 137.
13. As reported by Gen. Jeanne Holm, November 18, 1980.
14. Background study, *Use of Women in the Military*, 2nd. ed., September 1978, Office of the Assistant Secretary of Defense, p. iii.
15. Clark, *Hearings on H.R. 9832*, p. 138.
16. Testimony of U.S. Naval Academy Superintendent, Vice Adm. William P. Mack, *Hearings on H.R. 9832*, pp. 96, 97.

311

17. U.S. Department of the Navy, *An Appraisal of the Impact of Integrating Women into the U.S. Naval Academy and Aboard Ship, Hearings on H.R. 9832*, pp. 120, 121.

18. Testimony of Rep. Patricia Schroeder, *Hearings on H.R. 9832*, pp. 23, 25, 28.

19. Statement of Rep. Samuel S. Stratton, *Hearings on H.R. 9832*, p. 35.

20. Ibid., pp. 36–37, 39.

21. Statement of Rep. Pierre DuPont, *Hearings on H.R. 9832*, p. 55.

22. Testimony of Rep. Bill Frenzel, *Hearings on H.R. 9832*, p. 63.

23. Exchange between Rep. Charles Wilson and Vice Chief of Naval Operations, Vice Adm. Worth Bagley, *Hearings on H.R. 9832*, p. 110.

24. Statement of Lt. Col. Grace M. King, *Hearings on H.R. 9832*, p. 228.

25. *Congressional Record*, House, 121: H4438, May 20, 1975.

26. *Edwards, et al.* v. *Schlesinger, et al.*, and *Waldie, et al.*, v. *Schlesinger, et al.*, Civil Action No. 1825–73 and 1826–73, U.S.D.C., 377 F. Supp. 1091, 1974.

27. Shirley Bach and Martin Binkin provide the fullest account of women's contemporary role in the military in *Women in the Military* (Washington, D.C.: The Brookings Institution, 1977).

28. *American Education*, 9 November 1976, back cover. By 1978 the number of women in college would exceed that of men for the first time.

Chapter 2

1. Stephen Ambrose, *Duty, Honor, Country* (Baltimore: Johns Hopkins Press, 1966).

2. J. Arthur Heise, *The Brass Factories* (Washington, D.C.: Public Affairs Press, 1969).

3. K. Bruce Galloway and Robert Bowie Johnson, Jr., *West Point: America's Power Fraternity* (New York: Simon and Schuster, 1973).

4. Richard C. U'ren, *The Ivory Fortress* (Indianapolis: Bobbs-Merrill, 1974).

5. Joseph Ellis and Robert Moore, *School for Soldiers* (New York: Oxford University Press, 1974).

6. Gary L. Wamsley, "Contrasting Institutions of Air Force Socialization: Happenstance or Bellwether," *American Journal of Sociology* 78 (1972): 399–417.

7. See "The Making of the Infantryman," *American Journal of Sociology* 51 (1946): 376–79; and John H. Faris, "The Impact of Basic Combat Training: The Role of the Drill Sergeant," in *The Social Psychology of Military Service*, eds. Nancy L. Goldman and David R. Segal, Sage Research Progress series on War, Revolution, and Peacekeeping (Beverly Hills, Calif.: Sage Publications, 1976), vol. 6.

8. See Sissela Bok, *Lying: Moral Choice in Public and Private Life* (New York: Pantheon Books, 1978); and Jerald M. Jellison, *I'm sorry, I Didn't*

Mean to and Other Lies We Love to Tell (New York: Chatham Square
Press, 1977).
9.   Mary Wollstonecraft, *A Vindication of the Rights of Women* (London:
Source Book Press, 1971), p. 179.

Chapter 3

1.   In general, visibility creates a pressure to perform. In "Some Effects of
Proportions on Group Life: Skewed Sex Ratios and Responses to Token
Women," *American Journal of Sociology* 82 (1977): 965–90, Rosabeth
Kanter elegantly describes the pressure to perform experienced by "token"
members of a group. Her description agrees so well with military expres-
sions of their role, *vis-à-vis* the public, that one comes to understand that
within U.S. society, professional military officers sometimes experience
the kinds of feelings women and minorities feel in institutions composed
mainly of white males.
2.   U.S. Comptroller General, *Student Attrition at the Five Federal Service
Academies*, Report to the Congress, FPCD 76–12, 5 March 1976, p. 47.

Chapter 4

1.   Patricia J. Thomas, "Enlisted Women in the Military," *Defense Manpower
Policy: Presentations from the 1976 Rand Conference on Defense Manpower*, ed. Richard V. L. Cooper, R-2396-ARPA (Santa Monica, Calif.:
Rand Corporation, 1979), p. 309.
2.   "History of the Women in the Air Force, 1 July 1974–31 December 1974,"
p. 10, prepared by the Staff of the Directorate, Women in the Air Force.

Chapter 5

1.   U.S., Department of the Army, *Final Report of the West Point Study
Group*, 27 July 1977, p. 2.
2.   Robert F. Priest, "Cadet Attitudes toward Women—1975," Report No.
76–015 (West Point, N.Y.: United States Military Academy [USMA], Office of the Director of Institutional Research, May 1976), p. 27.
3.   Ibid., p. 7.
4.   Priest, "A Comparison of Faculty and Cadet Attitudes toward Women,"
Report No. 76–017, USMA, Office of the Director of Institutional Research, May 1976, pp. 3–4. See also Priest, "Changes in Cadet Attitudes
toward the Admission of Women to West Point," also entitled, "Cadets'
Attitudes toward the Admission of Women to West Point," Report No.

76–018, USMA, Office of the Director of Institutional Research, June 1976.

5. Robert F. Priest and John W. Houston, "Analysis of Spontaneous Cadet Comments on the Admission of Women," Report No. 76–014 (West Point, N.Y.: USMA, Office of the Director of Institutional Research, May 1976), pp. 1–2.

6. Ibid., pp. 129–31.

7. Kathleen P. Durning, "Women at the Naval Academy: The First Year of Integration," Report No. TR 78–12 (San Diego, Calif.: Naval Personnel Research and Development Center [NPRDC], February 1978), pp. 3–4.

8. The literature on sex differences in achievement motivation, self-evaluation, and performance evaluation is reviewed in Kay Deaux, *The Behavior of Women and Men* (Belmont, Calif.: Brooks/Cole, 1976).

9. Durning, "Assimilation of Women into the Naval Academy," Table 8.

10. Ibid., Table 10.

11. Ibid., Table 11.

12. Beth F. Coye, "The Restricted Unrestricted Line Officer: The Status of the Navy's Woman Line Officer," *Naval War College Review* 24, (March 1972): 53–64.

13. Beth F. Coye, Sara P. Denby, C. Cort Hooper, and Kathleen A. Mullen, "Is There Room for Women in Navy Management: An Attitudinal Survey," *Naval War College Review* 25 (January-February 1973): 69–87.

14. Constantina Safilios-Rothschild, Ronald A. Wells, and Marcellinus Dijkers, "Women in a Male Domain: Attitudes and Reactions at the Coast Guard Academy," paper presented at the National Biennial Conference of the Inter-University Seminar on Armed Forces and Society (Chicago: 20–22 October 1977).

15. Robert W. Shomer and Richard Centers, "Differences in Attitudinal Responses Under Conditions of Implicitly Manipulated Group Salience," *Journal of Personality and Social Psychology* 15 (June 1970): 125–32.

Chapter 6

1. James A. Michener, *Sports in America* (New York: Random House, 1976), p. 15.

2. Harry Edwards, *Sociology of Sport* (Homewood, Ill.: Dorsey Press, 1973), p. 102.

3. U.S. Air Force Academy, "Admission of Women into the Cadet Wing," *Operations Plan* 76–75, 7 October 1975, pp. D–V–1, D–VI–1.

4. See Susan Brownmiller's widely acclaimed *Against Our Will: Men, Women, and Rape* (New York: Simon and Schuster, 1975).

5. United States Air Force Academy, Department of Physical Education, Integration of Women, Historical Report, 12 January 1976, p. 1.

6. Memo from James C. Thomas, Phase 3 briefing on integration of women cadets: physical fitness testing, 15 November 1976.

7. Interview with Robert Strickland, Director of Physical Education, U.S. Air Force Academy, June 1977.
8. Thomas H. Allen, "Measurement of Body Fat: A Quantitative Method Suited for Use by Aviation Medical Officers," *Aerospace Medicine* 34, October 1963, 300.

Chapter 7

1. Kay Deaux and Janet Taynor, "Evaluation of Male and Female Ability: Bias Works Two Ways," *Psychological Reports* 32 (1973): 261–62.
2. Janet Taynor and Kay Deaux, "When Women Are More Deserving than Men," *Journal of Personality and Social Psychology* 28 (1973): 360–67.

Chapter 8

1. William Joseph Wallisch, Jr., "The Admission and Integration of Women into the United States Air Force Academy" (unpublished Ph.D. dissertation, University of Southern California, 1977).
2. Kathleen P. Durning and Sandra J. Munnford, "Attitudes toward the Navy of Enlisted Men and Women," *Symposium Proceedings of the 5th Symposium on Psychology in the Air Force*, United States Air Force Academy, Department of Behavioral Sciences and Leadership (8–10 April 1976), pp. 83–86.
3. Marcelite C. Jordan, "Utilization of Women in Air Force Industrial Career Fields," *Symposium Proceedings*, pp. 91–94.

Chapter 10

1. SSgt. Rick Racquer, "What Makes an Air Force Wife," *Talon*, June 1978, p. 18.
2. Hannah Papanek, "Reflections on the Two-Person Career," *American Journal of Sociology* 7 (January 1973): 352–72.
3. Patricia J. Thomas, "Enlisted Women in the Military," *Defense Manpower Policy: Presentations from the 1976 Rand Conference on Defense Manpower*, ed. Richard V. L. Cooper, R-2396-ARPA, (Santa Monica, Calif.: Rand Corporation, 1979), p. 313.
4. Kathleen P. Durning and Sandra J. Munford, "Attitudes toward the Navy of Enlisted Men and Women," *Symposium Proceedings of the 5th Symposium on Psychology in the Air Force*, United States Air Force Academy, Department of Behavioral Sciences and Leadership (8–10 April 1976), pp. 83–86.

Postscript

1. John Stuart Mill and Harriet Taylor Mill, *Essays on Sex Equality*, ed. Alice Rossi (Chicago: University of Chicago Press, 1970), p. 154.

2. Martin Binkin and Shirley J. Bach, *Women and the Military* (Washington, D.C.: The Brookings Institution, 1977), p. 19.

3. Mattie Treadwell, *U.S. Army in World War II: Special Studies–The Women's Army Corps* (Washington, D.C.: Department of the Army, 1954), p. 184. See also Michele J. Shover, "Roles and Images of Women in World War I Propaganda," *Politics and Society* 5 (1975): 469–86.

4. *Owens v. Brown*, 17 FEP 1292, 1978.

5. Morris Janowitz develops the theme of civilianization in "Volunteer Armed Forces and Military Purpose," *Foreign Affairs* 50 (April 1972): 427–43.

6. For example, see William F. Buckley, Jr., "Women's Place: In the Fox-hole," *Los Angeles Times*, March 20, 1978.

7. Hannah Arendt discusses this eloquently in *On Violence* (New York: Harcourt, Brace, and World, 1970).

8. George Gilder, "The Case against Women in Combat," *New York Times Magazine* (January 28, 1979), pp. 29–30. Similar arguments were once made concerning mixed-race units. Interestingly enough, in this case, some officers favored integration more than the troops because they believed black soldiers were most effective when well dispersed. For discussion see *Social Research and the Desegregation of the U.S. Army*, ed. Leo Bogart (Chicago: Markham, 1969).

9. For an interesting analysis of sex integration in small groups, see Carol Wolman and Hal Frank, "The Solo Woman in a Professional Peer Group," *American Journal of Orthopsychiatry* 45 (January 1975): 165–67; and Rosabeth Moss Kanter, "Some Effects of Proportions on Group Life: Skewed Sex Ratios and Responses to Token Women." *American Journal of Sociology* 82 (March 1977): 965–90.

10. The King-Riggs tennis match of 1973 provoked a complex public response that has never been adequately examined.

11. One reason why Israelis have not put their women into combat since 1967 is said to be their fear that Arab men might never surrender to a woman. See Michener, *Sports in America*, p. 128.

12. Margaret Mead, "National Service as a Solution to National Problems," *The Draft*, ed. Sol Tax (Chicago: University of Chicago Press, 1967), pp. 107–8.

13. George Quester, "Women in Combat," *International Security* 4 (Spring 1977), p. 91.

14. One place where the human dimensions of rational calculation are discussed is in Thomas Schelling, *The Strategy of Conflict* (Cambridge, Mass.: Harvard University Press, 1960).

15. Treadwell, *Women's Army Corps*, pp. 762–63.

16. The best-known authority on this subject may be John Money. See John

Money and Anke A. Erhardt, *Man and Woman, Boy and Girl* (Baltimore: Johns Hopkins Press, 1972), p. 4.

17. Vietnam War fighter pilots cited the "craziness" generated in male barroom bragging as an important part of the willingness to undertake hazardous missions. Glenn Gray also discusses the communal experience as an appeal of battle. See J. Glenn Gray, *The Warriors* (New York: Harper and Row, 1959).

18. This is another reason Israel may not send its women into combat. Quester calls it a "primeval calculation."

19. Nora Scott Kinzer, David Segal, and John C. Woelfel argue that the principal reason for women's combat service is to permit them to be full citizens in "The Concept of Citizenship and Attitudes Toward Women in Combat," *Sex Roles* 3 (1977) 469–77.

20. Max Weber, "Politics as a Vocation," *From Max Weber* (New York: Oxford University Press, 1958), pp. 77–78.

21. Judith Stiehm, "Algerian Women: Honor, Survival, and Islamic Socialism," *Women in the World*, eds. Lynn Iglitzin and Ruth Ross (Santa Barbara, Calif.: Clio Books, 1976), pp. 229–43.

22. For a thorough discussion see Harold Nieburg, *Political Violence* (New York: St. Martin's Press, 1969).

23. See, for example, the late 1976 attack by black marines on a suspected KKK meeting at Camp Pendleton, California.

24. Wolman, "Solo Woman," p. 167.

25. Susan Brownmiller, *Against Our Will*, p. 5.

26. Charlotte Perkins Gilman, *The Living of Charlotte Perkins Gilman* (New York: Harper Colophon Books, 1975), p. 72.

27. The only author to make this connection is Ali Mazuri, a keen observer of African politics. See his "Military Technology and the Masculinity of War: An African Perspective," *Impact of Science on Society* 26: 1/2 (1976): 71–75. Mazuri also points out that the growing power of Muslim OPEC nations bodes ill for the participation of women in government. Note the deferential posture of Mrs. Rosalyn Carter during her visit to Saudi Arabia and the treatment of women in contemporary Iran.

28. For a full discussion of the effects of family socialization on women and men see Nancy Chodorow, "Being and Doing: A Cross-Cultural Examination of the Socialization of Males and Females," in Vivian Gornick and Barbara K. Moran, *Women in Sexist Society* (New York: New American Library, 1971), pp. 259–91; and Dorothy Dinnerstein, *The Mermaid and the Minotaur* (New York: Harper Colophon Books, 1977).

29. As Mary Ellman notes, Vietnamese women were not feminists who "preferred napalm to a double standard"; they simply had no one who could provide protection for them. See her *Thinking About Women* (New York: Harcourt and Brace, 1968), p. 73.

30. Judith Stiehm, *Nonviolent Power* (Lexington, Mass.: D.C. Heath, 1972).

Glossary

Air Officer Commanding (AOC). Military officer in charge of a cadet squadron at the U.S. Air Force Academy.

Air Staff. Personnel working for the Chief of Staff of the United States Air Force (often) at the Pentagon.

Air Training Officer (ATO). Junior woman officer brought to the Air Force Academy 1976–77 to assist in the integration of women and to serve as a role model for the women cadets.

Basic Cadet Training (BCT). Rigorous summer program undertaken by cadets before beginning their first academic year at the Air Force Academy.

Commandant. Officer in charge of the cadet wing and of its military training.

CQ. Duty that consists of being "in charge of quarters" for a specified time.

DACOWITS. Defense Advisory Committee on Women in the Services. A committee appointed by the Secretary of Defense.

DFBL. Department of Behavioral Science and Leadership.

Doolie. A cadet in the entry (first) year at the Air Force Academy.

Firstie. A first class cadet, one who is in the final (fourth) year at the academy.

GAO. General Accounting Office.

Line Officer. A naval officer not restricted to specialized duties. Holding command and going to sea are essential to his or her career.

MOM. Military Order of Merit.

OTS. Officer Training School (for college graduates).

PAE. Physical Aptitude Exam given all candidates for admission to Department of Defense academies.

PFT. Physical Fitness Test given cadets regularly at the Air Force Academy to determine fitness.

POW. Prisoner of war.

Pugil stick. Padded stick similar to a kayak paddle used in competition during BCT.

Rated officer. Air Force officer eligible to fly.

ROTC. Reserve Officers' Training Corps. Program to prepare college students for military service as officers upon graduation.

SERE. Survival, Evasion, Resistance, Escape. Summer program given all cadets following their doolie year.

Shower formation. Exercise session once required of doolies, supposed to continue until they sweat through their bathrobes.

Spirit mission. Prank played by cadets, usually at night, sometimes considered a morale booster.

Squadron. The basic cadet organizational unit at the Air Force Academy. Composed of about one hundred cadets from all four classes.

Terrazzo gap. The difference in views attributed to the faculty's and commandant's staffs, whose offices are located at opposite ends of the terrazzo at the Air Force Academy.

Tour. A specified amount of marching assigned as a punishment.

WAC. Women's Army Corps.

WAF. Women in the Air Force.

WASP. Women Airforce Service Pilots. Civilian pilots who served during World War II.

Wing. The Air Force Academy's student body.

Bibliography

Books

Abrahamsson, Bengt. *Military Professionalization and Political Power*. Beverly Hills: Sage Publications, 1972.

Ambrose, Stephen E. *Duty, Honor, Country*. Baltimore: Johns Hopkins Press, 1966.

Ambrose, Stephen E., and Barber, James Alden, Jr., eds. *The Military and American Society*. New York: Free Press, 1972.

Arendt, Hannah. *On Violence*. New York: Harcourt, Brace and World, 1970.

Bach, Shirley, and Binkin, Martin. *Women in the Military*. Washington, D.C.: The Brookings Institute, 1977.

Bettelheim, Bruno, and Janowitz, Morris. *Social Change and Prejudice*. London: The Free Press of Glencoe, 1963.

Bogart, Leo, ed. *Social Research and the Desegregation of the U.S. Army: Two Original 1951 Field Reports*. Markham Series in Public Policy Analysis. Chicago: Markham Publishing Company, 1969.

Bok, Sissela. *Lying: Moral Choice in Public and Private Life*. New York: Pantheon Books, 1978.

Brownmiller, Susan. *Against Our Will: Men, Women, and Rape*. New York: Simon and Schuster, 1975.

Chodorow, Nancy. *The Reproduction of Mothering*. Berkeley: University of California Press, 1978.

Deaux, Kay. *The Behavior of Women and Men*. Monterey, Calif.: Brooks/Cole, 1976.

Dinnerstein, Dorothy. *The Mermaid and the Minotaur*. New York: Harper Colophon Books, 1977.

Edwards, Harry. *Sociology of Sport*. Homewood, Ill.: The Dorsey Press, 1973.

Ellis, Joseph, and Moore, Robert. *Schools for Soldiers*. New York: Oxford University Press, 1974.

Ellman, Mary. *Thinking About Women*. New York: Harcourt Brace Jovanovich, 1968.

Ewing, Elizabeth. *Women in Uniform*. Rowman and Littlefield. Totowa, N.J., 1975.

Galloway, K. Bruce, and Johnson, Robert Bowie, Jr. *West Point*. New York: Simon and Schuster, 1973.

Ginzberg, Eli. *The Lost Divisions*. New York: Columbia University Press, 1959.

Goldman, Nancy L., and Segal, David R., eds. *The Social Psychology of Military Service*. Sage Research Progress Series on War, Revolution, and Peacekeeping. Vol. VI. Beverly Hills: Sage Publications, 1976.

Gilman, Charlotte Perkins. *The Living of Charlotte Perkins Gilman*. New York: Harper Colophon Books, 1975.

Gornick, Vivian, and Moran, Barbara K., eds. *Women in Sexist Society: Studies in Power and Powerlessness*. New York: New American Library, 1971.

Gray, J. Glenn. *The Warriors*. New York: Harper and Row Publishers, 1959.

Grundy, Kenneth, ed. *Armed Forces and Society* 2 (Winter, 1976). Special issue on "Racial and Ethnic Relations in the Armed Forces."

Habenstein, Robert W., ed. *Pathways to Data*. Chicago: Aldine Publishing Co. 1970.

Heise, J. Arthur. *The Brass Factories*. Washington, D.C.: Public Affairs Press, 1969.

Hoiberg, Anne, ed. *Armed Forces and Society* 4 (Summer, 1978). Special issue on Women as "New Manpower."

Hunter, Edna J., and Nice, D. Stephen. *Children of Military Families: A Part and Yet Apart*. Washington, D.C.: U.S. Government Printing Office, 1978.

Huntington, Samuel P. *The Soldier and the State*. New York: Vintage Books, 1957.

Iglitzin, Lynn, and Ross, Ruth, eds. *Women in the World*. Santa Barbara, Calif.: Clio Books, 1976.

Janowitz, Morris. *The Professional Soldier*. New York: Free Press, 1960.

————. *The U.S. Forces and the Zero Draft*. Adelphi Papers, No. 94. International Institute for Strategic Studies, 1973.

————, ed. *The New Military*. New York: W.W. Norton, 1969.

Janowitz, Morris, with Little, Roger W. *Sociology and the Military Establishment*, 3rd ed. Beverly Hills: Sage Publications, 1974.

Jellison, Jerald. *I'm Sorry, I Didn't Mean to and Other Lies We Love to Tell*. New York: Chatham Square Press, 1977.

Kanter, Rosabeth. *Men and Women of the Corporation*. New York: Basic Books, 1977.

Lang, Kurt. *Military Institutions and the Sociology of War*. Sage Series on Armed Forces and Society. Beverly Hills: Sage Publications, 1972.

Lever, Janet, and Schwartz, Pepper. *Women at Yale*. Indianapolis: Bobbs-Merrill, 1971.

Lovell, John. *Neither Athens Nor Sparta?* Bloomington, Ind.: Indiana University Press, 1979.

Mandelbaum, David G. *Soldier Groups and Negro Soldiers*. Berkeley: University of California Press, 1952.

Margiotta, Franklin D., ed. *The Changing World of the American Military*. Boulder, Colo.: Westview Press, 1979.

Marshall, S. L. A. *Men Against Fire*. New York: William Morrow Co., 1947.

Mazrui, Ali A. *Soldiers and Kinsmen in Uganda*. Beverly Hills: Sage Publications, 1975.

McCubbin, Hamilton I.; Dahl, Barbara B.; and Hunter, Edna J., eds. *Families in the Military System*. Sage Series on Armed Forces and Society. Vol. IX. Beverly Hills: Sage Publications, 1976.

Mehrabian, Albert. *Tactics of Social Influence*. Englewood Cliffs, N.J.: Prentice-Hall, 1970.

Michener, James A. *Sports in America*. New York: Random House, 1976.

Milgram, Stanley. *Obedience to Authority*. New York: Harper and Row, 1974.

Mill, John Stuart, and Mill, Harriet Taylor. *Essays on Sex Equality*. Chicago: University of Chicago Press, 1970.

Millman, Marcia, and Kanter, Rosabeth Moss, eds. *Another Voice*. New York: Anchor Books, 1975.

Money, John, and Erhardt, Anke. *Man and Woman, Boy and Girl*. Baltimore: Johns Hopkins Press, 1972.

Moore, Robin. *The Green Berets*. New York: Avon Books, 1965.

Moskos, Charles C., Jr. *The American Enlisted Man*. New York: Russell Sage Foundation, 1970.

————, ed. *Public Opinion and the Military Establishment*. Sage Research Progress Series on War, Revolution and Peacekeeping. Vol. I. Beverly Hills: Sage Publications, 1971.

Nieburg, Harold. *Political Violence*. New York: St. Martin's Press, 1969.

Olson, Mancur. *The Logic of Collective Action*. Cambridge, Mass.: Harvard University Press, 1971.

Oppenheimer, Martin, ed. *The American Military*. Chicago: Aldine Publishing Co., 1971.

Osborn, Frederick, et al., gen. eds. *Studies in Social Psychology in World War II*. 4 vols. Princeton: Princeton University Press, 1949. Vol. 1: *The American Soldier: Adjustment During Army Life*, by Samuel A. Stouffer, et al.

Rich, Adrienne. *Of Woman Born: Motherhood as Experience and Institution*. New York: W. W. Norton, 1976; Bantam, 1976.

Rodberg, Leonard S., and Shearer, Derek, eds. *The Pentagon Watchers*. Garden City, N.Y.: Doubleday and Company, 1970.

Sarkesian, Sam C. *The Professional Army Officer in a Changing Society*. Chicago: Nelson-Hall Publishers, 1975.

Schelling, Thomas. *The Strategy of Conflict*. Cambridge, Mass.: Harvard University Press, 1960.

Stiehm, Judith. *Nonviolent Power*. Lexington, Mass.: Heath and Company, 1972.

Stoessinger, John G. *Why Nations Go To War*. New York: St. Martin's Press, 1974.

Stogdill, Ralph M. *Handbook of Leadership*. New York: Free Press, 1974.

Stone, Gregory P., ed. *Games, Sport and Power*. New Brunswick, N.J.: E. P. Dutton and Company, 1972.

Tax, Sol. *The Draft: A Handbook of Facts and Alternatives*. Chicago: University of Chicago Press, 1967.

Teitelbaum, Michael S., ed. *Sex Differences: Social and Biological Perspectives*.

Garden City: Anchor Press/Doubleday, 1976.

Tiger, Lionel, and Shepher, Joseph. *Women in the Kibbutz*. New York: Harcourt Brace Jovanovich, 1975.

Treadwell, Mattie. *U.S. Army in World War II: Special Studies–The Women's Army Corps*. Washington, D.C.: Dept. of the Army, 1954.

U'Ren, Richard C., M.D. *Ivory Fortress*. Indianapolis: Bobbs-Merrill, 1974.

USAFA Library. *Women in the Military*, Special Bibliography Series, No. 51. Nov. 1975.

Van Doorn, Jacques, ed. *Armed Forces and Society Sociological Essays*. The Hague: Mouton, 1968.

Waltz, Kenneth N. *Man, the State and War*. New York: Columbia University Press, 1959.

Weber, Max. *From Max Weber*. New York: Oxford University Press, 1958.

Wolfe, J. N., and Erickson, John, eds. *The Armed Services and Society*. Edinburgh: Edinburgh University Press, 1969.

Wollstonecraft, Mary. *A Vindication of the Rights of Women*. London: Source Book Press, 1971.

Woolf, Virginia. *Three Guineas*. New York: Harcourt, Brace and World, Inc. 1966.

Yarmolinsky, Adam. *The Military Establishment*. New York: Harper and Row, 1971.

ARTICLES AND PAPERS

Allen, Thomas H. "Measurement of Human Body Fat: A Quantitative Method Suited for Use by Aviation Medical Officers." *Aerospace Medicine* 34, 10 (1963): 296–300.

Bay, Christian. "Gentleness and Politics: The Case for Motherhood Reconsidered." *Politics* 10 (November 1975): 125–38.

Bey, Douglas R. M.D. and Tange, Jean. "Waiting Wives: Women Under Stress." *American Journal of Psychiatry* 131 (March 1974): 283–86.

Bidwell, Charles E. "The Young Professional In the Army: A Study of Occupational Identity." *American Sociological Review* 26 (June 1961): 360–72.

Braty, Howard, and Wilson, Everett. "Characteristics of Military Society." *American Journal of Sociology* 51 (March 1946): 371–75.

Buckley, William F., Jr. "Women's Place: In the Foxhole." *Los Angeles Times* March 20, 1978.

Clark, Robert A., M.D. "Aggressive and Military Training." *American Journal of Sociology* 51 (March 1946): 423–32.

Coté, Richard W., et al. "Maximal Aerobic Power in Women Cadets at the U.S. Air Forces Academy." *Aviation, Space and Environmental Medicine* 48, 2 (1977): 154–55.

DeFleur, Lois B., and Gillman, David C. "Beginning Months of Co-Education at
the U.S. Air Force Academy." Paper presented at the American
Sociological Association Meeting. September 1977.
———. "Cadet Beliefs, Attitudes and Interactions During the Early Phases of
Sex-Integration." *Youth and Society*. In Press.
———. "Sex Integration of the U.S. Air Force Academy: Changing Roles for
Women." *Armed Forces and Society*, 4:4 (August 1978): 607–22.
———, and Marshak, William P. "The Development of Military Professionalism
Among Male and Female Air Force Academy Cadets." Paper presented at
the Inter-University Seminar on Armed Forces and Society. October 1977.
———. "Sex Integration at the U.S. Air Force Academy—Changing Roles for
Women." Paper presented at the Pacific Sociological Association Meeting.
April 1977.
DeFleur, Lois B., and Marshak, William P. "Changing Attitudes Toward
Women's Roles and Women in the Military at the U.S. Air Force
Academy." Paper presented at the Inter-Service Conference on the Military
Family. May 1977.
Deaux, Kay, and Taynor, Janet. "Evaluation of Male and Female Ability: Bias
Works Both ways." *Psychological Reports* 32 (1973): 261–62.
Durning, Kathleen P. "Assimilation of Women Into the Naval Academy: An
Attitude Survey." Paper presented at the National Biennial Conference of
the Inter-University Seminar on Armed Forces and Society. Chicago:
October 20–22, 1977.
DuPont, Nicholas. "The Military Husband." *The Times Magazine* (November 1,
1976): 16, 32.
Edelman, Murray. "Language and Social Problems." Presented as a part of the
symposium dedicating the new Foreign Languages Bldg., University of
Illinois at Champaign-Urbana. April 5, 1974.
Elkin, Henry. "Aggressive and Erotic Tendencies In Army Life." *American
Journal of Sociology* 51 (March 1946): 408–22.
Galluscio, Eugene H. "The Effect of Combat Oriented Training on the Perception
of Femininity of Women Cadets." *Journal of the Colorado-Wyoming
Academy of Sciences* (April 1977).
Gault, William Barry., M.D. "Some Remarks on Slaughter." *American Journal of
Psychiatry* 128 (October 1971): 450–54.
George, Margaret. "The 'World Historical Defeat' of the *Republicaines-
Revolutionnaires*." *Science and Society*, 4:4 (Winter 1976–1977): 410–37.
Gilder, George. "The Case Against Women in Combat." *New York Times
Magazine* (January 28, 1979): pp. 29–30.
Gillman, David C. "Patterns of Accommodation for Female Cadets of the U.S.
Air Force Academy." *Journal of the Colorado-Wyoming Academy of
Sciences* (April 1977).
Goldman, Nancy. "The Utilization of Women In The Armed Forces of
Industrialized Nations." *Sociological Symposium* (Spring 1977): 12–24.
Gunderson, E. K. Eric. "Body Size, Self-Evaluation, and Military

Effectiveness." *Journal of Personality & Social Psychology* 2 (1965): 902–6.

Hall, Richard C. W., and Simmons, William C. "The POW Wife." *Archives of General Psychiatry* 29 (November 1973): 690–94.

Hamil, Pete. "The Cult of Amelia Earhart," *Ms.*, 3:3 (September 1976).

Hanushek, Eric Alan. "The Volunteer Military and the Rest of the Iceberg." *Policy Studies* 8:3 (1977): 343–61.

Hartinagel, Timothy F. "Absent Without Leave: A Study of the Military Offender." *Journal of Political and Military Sociology* 2 (Fall 1974): 205–20.

Hein, Hilde. "On Reaction and the Women's Movement." In *Women and Philosophy*, pp. 248–70. Edited by Carol C. Gould and Marx W. Wartofsky. New York: G. P. Putnam's Sons, 1976.

Heyder, D. W., M.D., and Wombach, Helen S., M.A. "Sexuality and Affect in Frogmen." *Archives of General Psychiatry* 11 (September 1964): 286–89.

Hillinger, Charles. "In the Military, War of Sexes Is All But Won." *Los Angeles Times* (December 18, 1978). Part one.

Hollingshead, August B. "Adjustment to Military Life." *American Journal of Sociology* 51 (March 1946): 439–47.

Horton, Mildred McAfee. "Women in the United States Navy." *American Journal of Sociology* 51 (March 1946): 448–50.

Jackson, Elton F. "Status Consistency and Symptoms of Stress." *American Sociological Review* 27 (August 1962): 469–80.

Janowitz, Morris. "Volunteer Armed Forces And Military Purpose." *Foreign Affairs* 50 (April 1972): 427–43.

Kanter, Rosabeth Moss. "Some Effects of Proportions on Group Life: Skewed Sex Ratios and Responses to Token Women." *American Journal of Sociology* 82 (March 1977): 965–90.

Kershaw, Joseph A., chairman. *Report of the Committee on College Expansion*. Williams College, Williamstown, Mass., July 1975.

Komisar, Lucy. "Violence and the Masculine Mystique." KNOW. P.O. Box 86031 Pittsburgh (n.d.).

Levine, Adeline, and Crumrine, Janice. "Women and the Fear of Success: A Problem in Replication." *American Journal of Sociology* 80 (1975): 964–74.

Lichtenstein, Grace. "Kill, hate—mutilate!" *The New York Times Magazine* (September 5, 1976).

Lipman-Blumen, Jean. "Vicarious Achievement Roles for Women: A Serious Challenge to Guidance Counselors." *Personnel and Guidance Journal* 53 (May 1975): 650.

Lovell, John P. "Growth and Change at the Service Academies: Some Organizational Consequences." Prepared for delivery at the 1976 Regional Meeting of the Inter-University Seminar on Armed Forces and Society, Air Command and Staff College, Maxwell AFB, Alabama. October 22–23, 1976.

————. "Professionalism and the Service Academies." *American Behavioral Scientist* 19 (May/June 1976): 605–25.

Marsden, Martha A. "The Military Family and the Changing Military Profession." Paper presented at the 1976 Regional Meeting of the Inter-University Seminar on Armed Forces and Society, Air Command and Staff College, Maxwell AFB, Alabama. October 22–23, 1976.

Marshak, William P. "Correlates of Attitudes Toward Women as a Function of Personality Factors." *Journal of the Colorado-Wyoming Academy of Sciences* (April 1977).

Marshak, William P.; Gillman, David C.; and DeFleur, Lois B. "Cadet Attitudes During the Admission of Women to the U.S. Air Force Academy." Paper presented at the American Psychological Association Meeting. August 1977.

Mazrui, Ali A. "Military Technology and the Masculinity of War: An African Perspective," *Impact of Science on Society* 26/1/2 (1976): 71–75.

McKain, Jerry Lavin. "Relocation in the Military: Alienation and Family Problems." *Journal of Marriage and the Family* 35 (May 1973): 205–9.

Metres, Phillip J., Jr.; Robertson, Marilyn L.; and Lester, Gary R. "The Change in Returned Prisoner of War Family Adjustment During Two Successive Years Following Reunion." Paper presented at the Inter-University Seminar of the Armed Forces and Society, Regional Meeting, Arizona State University, Arizona. February 27, 1976.

Nottingham, Elizabeth K. "Toward an Analysis of the Effects of Two World Wars on the Role and Status of Middle-Class Women in the English Speaking World." *American Sociological Review* 12 (December 1947): 666–75.

Papanek, Hannah. "Reflections on the Two-Person Career." *American Journal of Sociology* 7 (1973): 352–72.

Quester, George. "Women in Combat," *International Security* 4 (Spring 1977): 80–91.

Rogin, Michael. "Andrew Jackson: The Sublimation of Death Into Authority." Prepared for delivery at the Annual Meeting, Western Political Science Association, Colorado. April 4–6, 1974.

Rose, Arnold. "The Social Structure of the Army." *American Journal of Sociology* 51 (March 1946): 361–64.

Safilios-Rothschild, Constantina; Wells, Ronald A.; and Dijkens, Marcelliuus. "Women in a Male Domain: Attitudes and Reactions at the Coast Guard Academy." Paper presented at the Inter-University Seminar on Armed Forces and Society. Chicago: October 1977.

Sarkesian, Sam C. "An Empirical Re-Assessment of Military Professionalism." Prepared for delivery at the 1976 Regional Meeting of the Inter-University Seminar on Armed Forces and Society, Air Command and Staff College, Maxwell AFB, Alabama. October 22–23, 1976.

Sattin, Dana B., M.A. (Spec. 5), and Miller, John K., M.S.W. (Lt. Col.). "The Ecology of Child Abuse Within a Military Community." *American Journal of Orthopsychiatry* 41 (July 1971): 675–78.

Schloemer, Maj. Ronald F., and Myers, Maj. Gus. E. "Making it at the Air
Force Academy: Who Stays? Who Succeeds?" Prepared for delivery at the
1976 Regional Meeting of the Inter-University Seminar on Armed Forces
and Society, Air Command and Staff College, Maxwell AFB, Alabama.
October 22–23, 1976.

Segal, David R.; Kinzer, Nora Scott; and Woelfel, John C. "The Concept of
Citizenship and Attitudes Towards Women in Combat." *Sex Roles*, 3:5
(1977): 469–77.

Sherman, Julia A., Ph.D. "The Coatlicae Complex: A Source of Irrational
Reactions Against Women," *Transactional Analysis Journal* Sec. III, 5
(April 1975): 188–92.

Shomer, Robert W., and Centers, Richard C. "Differences in Attitudinal
Responses Under Conditions of Implicitly Manipulated Group Salience,"
Journal of Personality and Social Psychology 15 (1970): 125–32.

Shover, Michele J. "Roles and Images of Women in World War I Propaganda,"
Politics and Society (1975): 469–86.

Student Committee on Human Sexuality. *Sex and the Yale Student*. New Haven:
By the Committee, 1970.

Taynor, Janet, and Deaux, Kay. "When Women Are More Deserving than Men:
Equity, Attribution, and Perceived Sex Differences." *Journal of
Personality and Social Psychology* 28 (1973): 360–67.

Toman, A. Anthony, and Reed, Larry W. "The Military and Higher Education:
An Analysis of Factors Affecting the Future of ROTC." Prepared for
delivery at the 1976 Regional Meeting of the Inter-University Seminar on
Armed Forces and Society, Air Command and Staff College, Maxwell
AFB, Alabama. October 22–23, 1976.

Wachtel, Sidney B., and Fay, Leo C. "Allocation of Grades In the Army Air
Forces." *American Journal of Sociology* 51 (March 1946): 395–403.

Wallisch, William Joseph, Jr. "The Admission & Integration of Women into the
United States Air Force Academy." Ph.D. dissertation (1977), University
of Southern California.

Wamsley, Gary L. "Contrasting Institutions of Air Force Socialization:
Happenstance or Bellwether? *American Journal of Sociology* 78
(September 1972): 399–417.

Weinberg, Kirkson. "The Combat Neuroses." *American Journal of Sociology* 51
(March 1946): 465–78.

Wilson, Dean H., and Gillman, David C. "The Effects of Integrating Females
into a Previously All-Male Initiation Rite—A Case Study of the USAF
Academy." Paper presented at the Western Social Science Symposium.
April 1978.

Wolman, Carol, and Frank, Hal. "The Solo Woman in a Professional Peer
Group," *American Journal of Orthopsychiatry* 45 (1975): 164–71.

Wood, Marion M., and Greenfield, Susan T. "Women Managers and Fear of
Success: A Study in the Field." *Sex Roles* 2 (1976): 375–87.

Zacchino, Narda. "Fitting the Uniform Isn't an Easy Fight." *Los Angeles Times*
(June 13, 1977).

GOVERNMENT AND MILITARY SOURCES

Bettle, Maj. G. R. "Use of Women as Warriors Threatens Our Society." *Marine Corps Gazette*. September 1978.

Carr, Thomas W. "Women in ROTC," *Commanders Digest*. September 18, 1975: 2–16.

Cooper, Richard. *Military Manpower and the All-Volunteer Force*. Report prepared for the Defense Advanced Research Projects Agency. Santa Monica, California. Rand Corporation: R-1450-ARPA. 1977.

——, ed. *Defense Manpower Policy: Presentations from the 1976 Rand Conference on Defense Manpower*. Prepared for the Defense Advanced Research Projects Agency. Santa Monica, California. Rand Corporation: R-2396-ARPA. 1978.

Coye, Beth F. "The Restricted Unrestricted Line Officer: The Status of the Navy's Woman Line Officer," *Naval War College Review*. 24, 7 (March 1972): 53–64.

Coye, Beth F., et al. "Is There Room for Women in Navy Management: An Attitudinal Survey," *Naval War College Review*. 25, 3 (January-February 1973): 69–87.

Defense Manpower Commission. *Defense Manpower: The Keystone of National Security*. Washington, D.C.: U.S. Government Printing Office. April 1976.

Fellerman, H. S. *History of the United States Air Force Academy*. Special Collection at the USAFA.

Galloway, Capt. Judith M. "The Impact of the Admission of Women to the Service Academies On the Role of the Woman Line Officer." Prepared for the 10th Annual Inter-University Seminar on Armed Forces and Society. October 17, 1975.

History of the Women in the Air Force. Prepared by the Staff of the WAF Directorate.

Jordan, Marcelite C. "Utilization of Women in Air Force Industrial Career Fields." Paper presented at the 5th Annual Symposium, Psychology in the Air Force. Department of Behavioral Sciences and Leadership. United States AF Academy. April 8–10, 1976.

McNitt, Robert W. "Naval Academy Admissions." Reprint from *Shipmate*. September 1975.

Margiotta, Lt. Col. Franklin D. "Making It in the Air Force: Officer Perceptions of Career Progression." Prepared for the 1975 Annual Meeting of the Inter-University Seminar on Armed Forces and Society, Chicago, Illinois. October 16–18, 1975.

Martin, James Ingram, Ph.D. "Habitability Aspects of Women Aboard Ship." Presented to the 5th Annual Symposium, Psychology in the Air Force, Department of Behavioral Sciences and Leadership. United States AF Academy. April 8–10, 1976.

"Navy Women," *All Hands*. 703 (August 1975): 70–73.

U.S., Controller General. *Report to the Congress: Academic and Military*

Programs of the Five Service Academies, Report No. FPCD 76–8. October 1975.

———. *Report to the Congress: Financial Operations of the Five Service Academies*. Report No. FPCD 75–117. February 1975.

———. *Report to the Congress—Job Opportunities for Women in the Military: Progress and Problems*. May 1976.

———. *Report to the Congress: Student Attrition at the Five Federal Service Academies*, Report No. FPCD 76–12. March 1976.

U.S., Congress, House. Committee on Armed Services. *Hearing before a subcommittee of the Committee on Armed Services on H.R. 9832, H.R. 10705, H.R. 11267, H.R. 11268, H.R. 11711, and H.R. 13729*, 93rd Cong., 2nd Session. 1974.

———. Committee on Armed Services. *Hearing on United States Military Academy Honor Code* before a subcommittee of the Committee on Armed Services, 94th Cong., 2nd Sess. 1976.

U.S., Defense Manpower Commission. *Report to the President and the Congress: Defense Manpower: The Keystone of National Security*. April 1976.

U.S., Department of the Army. *Final Report of the West Point Study Group* by Hillman Dickinson, Jack V. Mackmill, and Jack N. Merritt. July 27, 1977.

U.S., Department of Defense. *Use of Women in the Military: A Background Study*. May 1977.

U.S., United States Air Force Academy. *Admission of Women into the Cadet Wing*, Operations Plan Number 76–75. October 7, 1975.

———. *Curriculum Handbook 1976–77*. n. d.

———. *Final Progress Report Class of 1980*. May 1977.

———. *Instructional Booklet on Sex Differences in Response to Physical Activity*. n.d.

———. *Integration of Females into the Cadet Wing*, Contingency Plan Number 36–72. September 15, 1972.

———. *Integration of Females into the Cadet Wing*, Operations Plan Number 7–75. July 1, 1974.

———. *Proceedings of the 5th Annual Symposium on Psychology in the Air Force*. April 1976.

———. *Women's Integration Research Project: Project "Blue Eyes"—Phase I*, by James C. Thomas, et al. December 1976.

———. *Women's Integration Research Project: Project "Blue Eyes"—Phase II*, by James C. Thomas, et al. April 1977.

———. *Women's Integration Research Project—Phase III* by James C. Thomas, et al. April 1978.

U.S., United States Military Academy, *Comparison of USMA Men and Women on Selected Physical Performance Measures . . . "Project Summertime"* by Robert Stauffer. October 1976.

———. *Summary Report Project 60: A Comparison of Two Types of Physical Training Programs on the Performance of 16–18 Year-Old Women* by James A. Peterson, et al. May 3, 1976.

————. Department of Behavioral Sciences and Leadership. *Report of the Admission of Women to the U.S. Military Academy* (Project Athena) by Alan G. Vitters and Nora Scott Kinzer. September 2, 1977.

————. Office of Institutional Research. *Admission Scores on the USMA Class of 1979* by John W. Houston. November 1975. No. 76–005.

————. Office of Institutional Research. *Analysis of Spontaneous Cadet Comments on the Admission of Women* by Robert F. Priest and John W. Houston. May 1976. No. 76–014.

————. Office of Institutional Research. *Cadet Attitudes to a One Semester Visit at a Second Service Academy,* by Robert F. Priest. April 1976. No. 76–013.

————. Office of Institutional Research. *Cadet Attitudes Toward the Admission of Women to West Point* by Robert F. Priest. June 1976. No. 76–018.

————. Office of Institutional Research. *Cadet Attitudes Toward Women—1975* by Robert F. Priest. May 1976. No. 76–015.

————. Office of Institutional Research. *A Comparison of Faculty and Cadet Attitudes toward Women* by Robert F. Priest. May 1976. No. 76–017.

U.S., United States Navy Personnel Research and Development Center. "Differential Perceptions of Organizational Climate Held by Navy Enlisted Women and Men" by Kathleen P. Durning and Sandra J. Munford. Report No. NPRDC TR 76TQ-43. August 1976.

————. "Utilization of Enlisted Women in the Military" by Patricia J. Thomas. NPRDC. February 1976.

"Why Women Enlist: The Navy as an Occupational Choice" by Patricia J. Thomas, Report No. NPRDC TR 77–20. March 1977.

————. "Women at the Naval Academy: The First Year of Integration" by Kathleen P. Durning. Report No. NPRDC TR 78–12. February 1978.

JOURNALS

Air Force Times
Airman
Armed Forces and Society
The Association of Graduates Magazine USAF Academy
Commanders Digest
Falconnews Mail
The Journal of Political & Military Sociology
Minutes, Defense Advisory Committee on Women in the Services (DACOWITS)
Talon: Cadet Magazine of the USAF Academy.

Index

333

Designer: Richard Hendel
Compositor: Graphic Composition, Inc.
Printer: Vail-Ballou Press
Binder: Vail-Ballou Press
Text: Linotron 202 Times Roman
Paper: 50 lb. Cream Smooth

DATE DUE

~~APR 1997~~			
~~OCT 19 1998~~			
~~APR 26 2000~~			
~~MAY 02 2001~~			